FRANKLIN

Books by David Freeman Hawke

In the Midst of Revolution (1961)

American Colloquy (co-editor, with Leonard Lief, 1963)

A Transaction of Free Men (1964)

The Colonial Experience (1966)

U.S. Colonial History: Readings and Documents (editor, 1966)

Benjamin Rush: Revolutionary Gadfly (1971)

Paine (1974)

Honorable Treason: The Declaration and the Men Who Signed It (1976)

Franklin (1976)

FRANKLIN

by David Freeman Hawke

HARPER & ROW, PUBLISHERS
New York, Hagerstown, San Francisco, London

1817

FIRST EDITION

Library of Congress Cataloging in Publication Data

Hawke, David Freeman.
  Franklin.

  Bibliography: p.
  Includes index.
  1. Franklin, Benjamin, 1706–1790.   I. Title.
E302.6.F8H38   973.3′092′4 [B]   75–23886
ISBN 0–06–011779–6

76 77 78 79 10 9 8 7 6 5 4 3 2 1

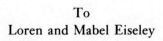

To
Loren and Mabel Eiseley

CONTENTS

AUTHOR'S NOTE

The working title for this volume was "Benjamin Franklin—What Manner of Man?" I liked it because it suggested what I wanted the book to be—a study that focused on Franklin's character. But a friend complained that it sounded too much like the title of a Sunday sermon. Others agreed with him, and I, too, became convinced upon noticing an announcement of the upcoming sermon in a neighborhood church: "Job—Man or Mouse?" And so the title was stripped to its present lean form. Its terseness is appealing but also ambiguous, and that calls for an explanation. This is not a full-scale biography of Franklin. It ends in 1776 with the signing of the Declaration of Independence.

Originally I planned to carry the story down to Franklin's death in 1790, but a few months after wading into the documents covering those last fourteen years I found myself overwhelmed by the sea of paper. When the editor of the new edition of Franklin's papers remarked that the first fifteen published volumes covered little more than one-sixth of the accumulated material waiting to be edited, I knew I was in over my head. Also, the attempt by one with slight expertise in the area to unravel and make sense of the intricate diplomacy carried on during Franklin's eight years in France gave further reason to pause. It soon became clear it would take several years more of research before there was even a chance to improve upon the accounts of Franklin's years abroad given by such previous biographers as Thomas Fleming, Richard B. Morris, James Parton, and Carl Van Doren. At that point it seemed sensible to end the book on the epochal day that Franklin signed the Declaration. By then, I assured myself, the reader had been carried through seventy years of Franklin's life and seen enough to pass judgment on the man.

CHAPTER

1

"A SHORT, FAT, TRUNCHED
OLD MAN"

PHILADELPHIA STILL TALKED ABOUT the news from Lexington and Concord when Benjamin Franklin returned from England on 6 May 1775. His arrival was "announced by ringing of bells, to the great joy of the city," and the provincial Assembly, then in session, immediately added his name to the Pennsylvania delegation chosen for the Second Continental Congress. Franklin was in his seat when the Congress convened four days later. For over two decades delegates had heard about the "prodigious genius" of Doctor Franklin. His "iron points" dotted rooftops in every village. He had lived in England some sixteen years and come home a man of world renown, the single American whose name was familiar in every household the length of the land. Now here he sat, "a short, fat, trunched old man in plain dress, bald pate, and short white locks." And he sat saying nothing, in *"expressive silence."*

So great was his reputation that men hardly dared to consider the effect if Franklin had announced for or against independence within a few days of his return. But to do so would have required him to act against his nature. He had never been a man to hurry a decision and now, nearly seventy, he was even less prone to haste—or eager to find himself on the losing side of a cause. "Didst thee ever know Dr. Franklin to be in a minority?" a Quaker once asked rhetorically. Franklin held his peace.

The first month and a half he kept to his house and went abroad only on public business. Those for reconciliation hoped he would use his influence to make Congress act with moderation. Rumors circulated that he planned soon to sail back to London on a peace mission, and then his long silence evoked gossip of another sort. It was whispered about the

I

city that the delegates in Congress "begin to entertain a great suspicion that Dr. Franklin came rather as a spy than as a friend, and that he means to discover our weak side to make his peace with the ministers by discovering information with regard to affairs at home, but hitherto he has been silent on that head and in every respect behaved more like a spectator than a member." A British agent in Philadelphia knew Franklin was no spy, but he knew little else. "By every intelligence I can get," he reported home later that month, "Dr. Franklin keeps much on the reserve, and has not hitherto opined in the manner that was expected; if he is not blinded by faction, he can be of more use to Great Britain and America than any man in this country." The next month the spy reported that Franklin remained "among those who are for moderation, and bringing about reconciliatory measures, but," he added, "as he is a deep, designing man, it is not easy coming at his real intentions. . . ."

Franklin's reticence "highly offended" the volatile Richard Henry Lee of Virginia, but Lee's New England counterpart, John Adams of Massachusetts, remarked only that "Dr. Franklin has been very constant in his attendance." Adams charted Franklin's curious course during these weeks with precision. "He has not assumed anything, nor affected to take the lead; but has seemed to choose that the Congress should pursue their own principles and sentiments and adopt their own plans."

Though Franklin had been reared in Boston, he resembled no man ever met there by Adams. "More of a philosopher than a politician," he said of him. Adams thought politics to be a noble profession and a politician one who took a firm stand on an issue, then fought for it. Franklin had a different view. When he saw others headed in the direction he was going, he husbanded his energy, satisfied "to cooperate and assist" while companions fought the battles. As long as possible he avoided taking a flat-footed stand on an issue. He did not appear to be a man of vision. The question for him seemed not to be who was right or who was wrong but what could be achieved under the prevailing circumstances.

Adams in time would rage at Franklin's "passion for reputation and fame," which even friends admitted to be one of the old man's weaknesses, but he failed to see that Franklin used that fame deftly for ends beyond the reach of lesser mortals. James Wilson, a Pennsylvania colleague, had a story to prove it. A citizen once proposed to divert the waters of a creek north of Philadelphia into the city for public use. His family carried the man into court "to prove him insane." Later Franklin donated one thousand pounds to get the project under way, "and obtained for his legacy the character of a wise and benevolent man."

On committees Franklin was always "punctual and indefatigable," but in Congress he spent "a great part of the time fast asleep in his chair," to John Adams's dismay. His indolence "will prevent any thorough reformation of anything and his"—"cunning" was the word Adams wanted and wrote but hardly dared use; he crossed it out—"and his silence and reserve render it very difficult to do anything with him." Occasionally, though, when politics was not involved, Franklin could be garrulous, as Adams knew from a night when the two shared a bed in a small tavern. Before blowing out the candle Adams closed the bedroom window.

"Oh!" said Franklin, "don't shut the window. We shall be suffocated."

Adams said he feared "the evening air."

"The air within this chamber will soon be, and indeed is now worse than that without doors," Franklin said. "Come! Open the window and come to bed, and I will convince you. I believe you are not acquainted with my theory of colds."

Adams opened the window and leaped into bed, saying he "had so much curiosity to hear his reasons that I would run the risk of a cold." Thereupon, Franklin "began an harangue upon air and cold and respiration and perspiration, with which I was so much amused that I soon fell asleep and left him and his philosophy together."

Not all of Adams's tales about Franklin were so genial. As a rule members of Congress took care to protect one another's reputations out of doors, seldom committing to paper anything that might harm a colleague's public image. But John Adams in old age wearied of the laurels heaped upon Franklin and twice broke with discretion, hoping to cut the sage down to size in the eyes of posterity. "Was not the Grand Franklin ridiculed?" he asked, launching into a tale that centered on Louis XVI and a lady of his court who babbled incessantly about Franklin's virtues. "The king sometimes smiled, sometimes snickered, but said very little," Adams recalled. "After sometime upon a visit to the royal manufactory of porcelain . . . he gave secret orders to have a chamber pot made of the finest materials and most exquisite workmanship with the most exact portrait of the Grand Franklin painted on the bottom of it on the inside; and this most elegant piece of furniture for a lady's bedchamber the king presented to the duchess with his own hand, that she might have the satisfaction of contemplating the image of her great philosopher and politician whenever she had occasion to look at it."

Another time, at a banquet he and Franklin attended in Paris, Adams "observed something circulating from hand to hand round the table, and very shrewd looks, shrugs, and gesticulations with some half-suppressed tittering. . . . It was carefully concealed from me. But after the company rose from table, two abbés of my acquaintance came to me . . . and showed me the picture. . . . With all the skill of the finest artists in Paris, America was represented as a virgin, naked and as beautiful . . . as the Venus of Medicis; and the Grand Franklin, with his bald head, with his few long scattering, straight hairs, in the act of debauching her behind her back." One cannot imagine any ridicule more exquisite than this, both upon America and Franklin.

What manner of man was this gentleman Adams grew to hate?

A genius? "His understanding is good enough for common uses, but not good enough for uncommon ones," said Thomas Jefferson, who liked and admired him. "He has very moderate abilities. He knows nothing of philosophy, but his few experiments in electricity," said John Adams.

Dispassionate? "I always knew him to be a very factious man," said the philosopher David Hume, a friend. "I am afraid that B. F., whose face at times turns white as the driven snow, with the extremes of wrath, may assert facts not true," said Richard Peters, first a friend, later an enemy.

Virtuous? The most "hypocritical old rascal that ever existed—a man who, if ever one goes to hell, he will," said Lord Hillsborough, an enemy who had known him well in England. "I have a very high opinion of B. F.'s virtue and uncorrupted honesty," said Peters, "but party zeal throws down all the poles of truth and candor and lays all the soul waste to temptation without knowing or suspecting it."

Beloved? "I never really was much of an admirer of the doctor," remarked a citizen of Pennsylvania after listening to companions tear apart Franklin's character, "but I could hardly find it in my heart to paint the devil so bad." William Allen, one of the richest, most powerful men in Philadelphia, and once a close friend, called him "a very artful, insinuating fellow, and very ready at expedients." John Dickinson, who headed the Pennsylvania delegation in Congress, hated him so much he refused to have a lightning rod on his city mansion, an obstinacy later paid for when lightning struck the house.

What manner of man was he? Franklin had his own answer to the question in the motto embedded in his coat of arms—*Exemplum adest ipse homo,* "The example presents the man himself."

Each of the delegates in Congress arrived at his own judgment as he watched the old man sit day after day in *"expressive silence,"* but all would have agreed with the British spy's remark—"It is not easy coming at his real intentions."

CHAPTER

2

GROWING UP IN BOSTON

His FATHER JOSIAH was forty-nine and his mother Abiah thirty-nine when Benjamin Franklin was born on 7 January 1706. He was the youngest son of seventeen children, thirteen of whom "lived to grow up and settle in the world." The children in 1706 ranged from Elizabeth, aged twenty-eight, to Sarah, aged seven. The nearest brother, James, was nine, too old to share a childhood with.

The family regarded the male babe of the brood with bemused affection. When seven years old he bought a whistle with the coppers given him to celebrate a holiday. He paid four times the whistle's worth, and the family "laughed at me so much for my folly that I cried with vexation"—one of the few times recorded that anyone laughed at, not with, Benjamin Franklin. He never forgot the incident. Years afterward he drew a moral from it—"*don't give too much for the whistle.*" A sharper lesson driven home goes unmentioned—don't let anyone know how much you gave for the whistle. Throughout a long life Franklin seldom revealed more of himself than the moment called for. Few boasted, and none with reason, that they knew the whole man. "Tho' I flatter myself with having as much of his confidence as he gives anybody, I can neither learn nor conjecture what he means," an intimate once remarked. His enemies, and they were many, called him devious. His friends preferred to judge him "rather deliberate in communicating the treasures of his mind."

If the family's laugh over the whistle taught Franklin to be wary with words, enough affection lay behind the laugh to nourish the congenial side of his nature. It was, as large families go, unusually free of strife. They all lived in "a lowly building," one recalled, "but we were fed plentifully, made comfortable with fire and clothing, had seldom any contention among us, but all was harmony—especially between the heads; and they were universally respected, the most of the family in good reputation." Harmony, however, did not breed intimacy. Franklin was close only to John, sixteen years his senior; they shared a love for books. When Franklin years later verged on world fame, he looked to John for approbation: "You have never mentioned anything to me of my electrical papers nor of that on the peopling of countries, nor that on meteorology, which have passed through your hands; so I conjecture you have either not had time to read them, or do not like them."

His recollections were few but mainly pleasant of life in the small frame house on Milk Street. "I feel some affection for that old-fashioned clock," he wrote when the furnishings of the house were being dispersed after his father's death in 1745. "It had I remember a sweet bell." Another time, after two years had passed without "a line from any relation, my father and mother only excepted," he confessed he would be "mighty glad" to hear from Sister Mecom and Sister Homes, meaning Jane and Mary. (Married sisters were called by their married names.) Later, the brothers and sisters would share in his prosperity. He would set Peter up in business in Philadelphia, appoint John postmaster of Boston, buy up the mortgage of Sister Douse's house, rear James's son in his own home and train him to the printing trade, spend a small fortune on his namesake, Sister Mecom's unstable son Benny. But affection and familial obligations had limits. He always kept the family at a distance. After leaving Boston he returned only occasionally over the next sixty-odd years. "Our father, who was a very wise man," he once remarked, "used to say nothing was more common than for those who loved one another at a distance, to find many causes of dislike when they came together; and therefore he did not approve of visits to relations in distant places, which could not well be short enough for them to part good friends." (As Poor Richard, he modified that view into a blunt aphorism: "Fish and visitors stink in three days.")

The judgment of his father as "a very wise man" came early, or so Franklin said in old age. When Josiah Franklin ridiculed some ballads the boy wrote, "telling me verse makers were generally beggars," he listened, and so "escaped being a poet, most probably a very bad one." When the father criticized an early essay of Franklin's, saying he "fell far short in elegance of expression, in method and in perspicuity," the boy "saw the justice of his remarks, and thence grew more attentive to the *manner* in writing and determined to endeavor at improvement." Franklin continued all his life to admire his father's "sound understanding and solid judgment in prudential matters, both in private and public affairs."

Josiah Franklin ran the family with a firm hand. His son Benjamin when nearly forty still addressed him in letters as "Honored Father." When arguments flared among the boys, the father's judgment of the issue came down as law. The books on his shelves ran mostly to religion, and though a devout member of the Congregational Church he left room for humor in life. Once when salting down a barrel of herring Benjamin dared to remark without fear of a hand across the face, "I think, father, if you were to say grace over the whole cask, once for all, it would be a vast saving of time." The father was handy with tools, and it satisfied him to do well the tasks God had assigned him. *"Seest thou a man diligent in his calling,"* he often told his sons, quoting a proverb from Solomon, *"he shall stand before kings, he shall not stand before mean men."* He enjoyed good talk, and "at his table he liked to have, as often as he could, some sensible friend or neighbor, to converse with, and always took care to start some ingenious or useful topic for discourse, which might tend to improve the minds of his children." He had an even temper and "a clear pleasing voice, so that when he played Psalm tunes on his violin and sung withal as he sometimes did in an evening after the business of the day was over, it was extremely agreeable to hear." The only unpleasantness Franklin could remember was the "disgusts" between his father and his godfather, Uncle Benjamin, who had come from England in his old age and lived four years in his brother's house.

Reminiscences between the brothers sparked Franklin's later inordinate interest in the family's history. (Eagerness to see how far he had risen above previous Franklins also spurred his curiosity.) From them he learned that the Franklins had lived in the village of Ecton, some fifty miles from London, for over two hundred years and in that time every eldest son had been trained as a blacksmith. Concern for the well-being of his stomach had carried the patriarch of the family, Benjamin's great-great grandfather, into the trade. "In his travels he went upon liking to a tailor," Josiah recalled, but the tailor "kept such a stingy house, that he left him and traveled further." Next he visited a blacksmith's house, and there for breakfast "came a good toast and good beer, and he found good housekeeping there; he served and learned the trade of blacksmith." Josiah's father in 1598 married a girl from Banbury, a nearby village, and "there was nine children of us who were happy in our parents, who took great care by their instructions and pious example to breed us up in a religious way." The walls of the parlor of the small stone house were decorated with verses from the Bible, one of which read: "For God sent not his son into this world to condemn the world but that the world through him might be saved."

Josiah's eldest brother, Thomas, inherited the blacksmith shop and the family homestead in Ecton. Brother John, next in line, moved to Banbury and there in a house by the millstream set up as a dyer. The younger brothers, Benjamin and Josiah, moved to Banbury and apprenticed themselves to John. Even as a young man Josiah faced life on his own terms. In Banbury he broke with the Church of England, in which the family had worshiped for over a century, and joined with those called Puritans. He dared to marry when barely twenty. In 1683, when twenty-five, he took a bolder leap into the dark by carrying his wife and three children to Boston. There he found no call for the dyer's trade and learned to make soap and candles, which he did for the rest of his life. His wife died in 1689 giving birth to a seventh child. Less than four months later he married a girl of twenty-two from Nantucket named Abiah Folger. She gave Josiah Franklin ten more children, the seventh being Benjamin.

Through his mother Franklin could trace his roots in America back to the early settlement of Massachusetts Bay. Abiah's father, Peter Folger, came to the Bay colony in 1635, and after several moves ended up on the island of Nantucket, where he reared nine children, of whom Abiah was the last. The Folgers of Franklin's generation lived mainly on the sea, but he did his best to keep them in sight all his life. "By the way, is our relationship with Nantucket quite wore out?" he asked Sister Mecom a year before he died. "They are wonderfully shy. But I admire their honest plainness of speech. About a year ago I invited two of them to dine with me. Their answer was, that they would, if they could not do better. I suppose they did better, for I never saw them afterwards, and so had no opportunity of showing my miff, if I had one."

Franklin acquired longevity and a strong constitution from both parents, but tradition has it that physically he took after the Folgers. He had the large Folger head, the square, homely face, the heavy chest and shoulders, the same hazel eyes. His hair was brown, his mouth wide, and he stood tall for the times, about five feet ten inches. Franklin rarely spoke of his mother, but in a day when it satisfied men to forgo middle names and call their sons George Washington, Thomas Jefferson, or John Adams, Benjamin Franklin honored his mother in a remarkable way—by naming his first legitimate son Francis Folger Franklin. As an old man he recalled how much he owed to her judgment and common sense. He remembered announcing to her one day that he would hereafter eat only vegetables. She received the news without a remark. Later a neighbor asked who had converted the boy to this wild diet. "A mad philosopher," said Abiah Franklin, but "there is no great harm—this will give him the habit of self-control; he will learn that everything is possible with a strong will."

2

When touring New England on business in his fiftieth year, Franklin came upon a strange native beast *"called a woodchuck."* Later he described it to a knowledgeable friend in Philadelphia, who, perhaps with a smile, said "it is what we here call a *groundhog,*" an animal common as a rabbit. Though he talked often of the glories of agriculture and urged both son and grandson to become farmers, few men reared in America at the turn of the eighteenth century knew less about country life than Franklin. He was a city man. He prospered in Philadelphia, gained fame in London and Paris. He had the luck to be shaped by Boston.

Boston had a population of six thousand at Franklin's birth, which made it the largest town in America. It was a fine place for an inquisitive boy to grow up in—too small to overwhelm, yet large enough to escape the oppressive intimacy of village life. The twisting streets that stretched back from the waterfront were crammed with carts and dogs and romping youngsters and never silent from dawn to dark. A boy could be middling poor, as Franklin was, yet not be afraid to approach one of the leading lights like the renowned clergyman Cotton Mather. The rich resided in elegant brick houses in the North End and rode in resplendent coaches tended by Negro footmen; they gave a lad who lived in a small frame house and had only his feet to carry him about something to aspire to.

Outwardly Boston resembled an English provincial seaport. Over fifty wharves piled with goods from all parts of the empire jutted into the bay. Long Wharf, the town's pride, could accommodate some thirty vessels "at the same time with great conveniency." Sailors on shore leave rolled through the town after dark in search of the sort of females who, the fascinated young Franklin remarked, "by throwing their heads to the right and left, at everyone who passed by them, I concluded came out with no other design than to revive the spirit of love in disappointed bachelors, and expose themselves to the sale to the first bidder." Though three thousand miles from the mother country, Bostonians refused to be outlanders. "In the concerns of civil life, as in their dress, tables, and conversation, they affect to be as much English as possible," one visitor said. "There is no fashion in London, but in three or four months it is to be seen at Boston."

But Boston only looked like a displaced English port town. It differed in many ways. It had the highest literacy rate and the largest number of college-trained citizens of any town its size in the empire. Bookstores were a rarity outside London; Boston had several. Oxford and Cambridge universities monopolized higher education in England; Boston had its own college across the Charles River. A closed corporation dominated by the elite governed most English towns; a panel of selectmen chosen by the freemen at an annual town meeting ran Boston's affairs. The founding fathers had come to Massachusetts Bay to build a model city "upon a hill" for all Christendom to admire. Sailors and their doxies, the rising rich who wished "to be as much English as possible," and a growing secularism that made citizens as concerned for their pocketbooks as their souls had combined to dilute that sense of mission, but a remnant prevailed in citizens like Josiah Franklin. The church occupied a central role in his life, and when called upon he also served the public—one year overseeing the conduct of the markets, another as constable, still another supervising the collection of refuse from streets in his neighborhood.

Years would pass before Franklin sensed Boston's uniqueness. His memories were those of any boy growing up in a seaport town. His mother's preoccupation with a large family—she gave birth to a ninth child, Lydia, when Franklin was two and three years later to her last, Jane —left him free to roam the town. He exposed himself to the "promiscuous conversation" of the wharves, tramped through the salt marshes fronting on the bay, fished for minnows in convenient ponds. "I was generally a leader among the boys, and sometimes led them into scrapes," he recalled; "living near the water, I was much in and about it, learnt early to swim well, and to manage boats, and when in a boat or canoe with other boys I was commonly allowed to govern, especially in any case of difficulty."

His aspirations were those of any boy. When four and a half, with Queen Anne's War in progress, he yearned to be a soldier. Uncle Benjamin cautioned against this in one of the doggerel verses he forever passed along to the boy. "Believe me, Ben, it is a dangerous trade,/The sword has many marred as well as made." Later, when brother Josiah, a sailor, returned home after nine years' absence, Franklin "had a strong inclination for the sea; but my father declared against it." Josiah wanted to offer his youngest son as the tithe of his brood to the church, and when Franklin was eight he sent him to school to learn Latin. Less than a year later his father changed his mind, though Ben had progressed to the head of his class. He pulled him from grammar school and sent him to another to learn arithmetic and to write a neat hand. He told friends in the boy's presence that with a large family to rear he could not afford the expense of a college education, which would lead only to "the mean living many so educated were afterwards able to obtain." Such an explanation from one devoted to his church and the Puritan experiment hardly made sense. No matter, Franklin had to accept it in silence, but long before he came to relish the academic honors later heaped upon him he showed in oblique ways how much he resented, how deeply he had been hurt by, his father's decision. Soon after being taken from grammar school he talked of running away to sea. In the new school he hid a talent for figures by failing arithmetic, not once but twice. And he ridiculed the gift denied by calling Harvard a place for "dunces and blockheads" who learned "little more than how to carry themselves handsomely, and enter a room genteelly," and emerged "as great blockheads as ever, only more proud and self-conceited."

With the failure in arithmetic, Josiah Franklin withdrew his ten-year-old son from school and put him to work making soap and candles. The boy hated the work and after repeated hints of still "hankering for the sea," the apprehensive father looked around for a more agreeable trade that would keep him ashore. Franklin's "bookish inclination" suggested he might do well as a printer and so Josiah apprenticed his youngest son to his next youngest, James, who had recently set up in the business. "I stood out some time," Franklin recalled, "but at last was persuaded and signed the indentures when I was yet but twelve years old. I was to serve as an apprentice till I was twenty-one years of age, only I was to be allowed journeyman's wages during the last year. In a little time I made great proficiency in the business, and became a useful hand to my brother. I now had access to better books."

3

James Franklin learned the printing trade in London and there saved and borrowed (from his father) enough to return home in 1717 with a press and type and, at the age of twenty-one, open up his own shop. He took on his younger brother as an apprentice the next year, and thereby lost his reputation to history. "James Franklin remains eternally transfixed in the malice of his brother's *Autobiography*," it has been said. "This is the grim and sullen James whom posterity knows, but a different personality —gay and courageous—is recorded in the *Courant*."

He began the *New England Courant* during Benjamin's third year in the shop. Earlier he had printed the *Boston Gazette* for the town's postmaster—postmasters tended to publish newspapers because their job gave easy access to journals from abroad and also let them distribute their papers for nothing—but he lost that lucrative contract after forty issues.

In the lean year that followed he decided to publish his own newspaper. Friends tried to dissuade him, "one newspaper being in their judgment enough for America." But on 7 August 1721 the *Courant* came forth, a small sheet, less than the size of a piece of typewriter paper, printed in two columns on both sides. The printer promised to be neither pompous nor obsequious to authority. He sought "short pieces, serious, sarcastic, ludicrous, or otherways amusing; or sometimes professedly dull (to accommodate some of his acquaintance)."

The printer had few dull acquaintances. The liveliest young minds in Boston hung out in his shop. Among them were Matthew Adams, "who had a pretty collection of books"; John Checkley, a bookseller, apothecary, and an Anglican who nourished contempt for the Congregational clergy that dominated Boston's life; and Dr. William Douglass, the town's only university-trained physician and, though still in his twenties, the accepted leader of his profession. Douglass spoke with a Scotch accent so thick it invited jokes. "Maister," one parody went, "ye ken vary weel, that I canno spak Englis." He loved books and good talk and boiled over with acid judgments on any subject up for discussion. (He and Benjamin Franklin remained corresponding friends until the doctor "began to drink too much brandy in his old age" and died in 1752.)

The printer promised nothing would appear in the *Courant* "reflecting on the clergy (as such) of whatever denomination," but the opening issue indicated that a clergyman who strayed from the business of saving souls offered fair target. Cotton Mather had for weeks said that the epidemic of smallpox then sweeping through Boston could be contained by inoculation, that is, by inducing immunity in an individual by inserting live smallpox germs into an open incision. All the town's physicians but one—a sometime minister named Zabdiel Boylston—rejected the radical and untested preventative. Only Douglass dared to attack it publicly. He did so first in the *Boston News-Letter*, where he credited Mather with "a pious and charitable design of doing good," but censured Boylston for "*his mischievous propagating the infection* in the most public trading places of the town." Yet in the first issue of the *Courant* he took out after Mather in language the clergyman found unforgivable.

Mather, a well-meaning humanitarian, had earlier organized a "Society for the Suppression of Disorders" when he learned of "houses in this town where there are young women of a very debauched character." He had directed a relief program after the great fire of 1711, which consumed over one hundred houses. Now he crusaded for inoculation, and when Douglass objected that the "novel and dubious practice" had not been sufficiently tested to assure "its safety and consequences" he reacted as if the word of God had been traduced. He rallied the clergy behind his program and made it appear that the *Courant*'s objections were the work of the Devil.

Succeeding issues only convinced Mather that the simultaneous arrival of the *Courant* and smallpox made Boston a "town which Satan has taken a most wonderful possession of." As the death toll mounted—26 citizens died in August, 101 in September, 402 in October—the paper continued its lighthearted way, telling in one issue about a luminary of the town who enjoyed a night in bed with two sisters of ill-repute, in another of a man who had castrated himself and thus incensed "the looser sort of the female tribe." Tucked in the midst of these anecdotes, which young Franklin must have relished setting in type, were essays that spread a seditious doctrine—the clergy, lacking the power or talent, to "reform the present declining age, and render it more polite and virtuous," must relinquish its leadership to James Franklin and his friends. Mather quivered with anger and told all good citizens to drop their subscriptions to the *Courant*. The printer let it be known that Mather excepted himself from the injunction and every week sent a grandson to pick up the paper at the printshop. The call for a boycott, said James Franklin, shows that Mather aspires to "reign Detractor General over the whole province, and do all the mischief his ill nature prompts him to." Every offended answer from the clergyman brought a riposte from Franklin, until finally Mather wilted. "I cannot but pity poor Franklin," he said, "who tho' but a young man, it may be speedily he must appear before the judgment seat of God." Not long after that remark Mather had two Franklins on his hands, for in April 1722 the young apprentice, now sixteen, slipped the first of his Silence Dogood essays under the door of his brother's shop.

4

Even as a boy Franklin "was extremely ambitious" to become "a tolerable English writer." The first year in the printshop he composed a couple of ballads his father judged wretched but his brother, "thinking it might turn to account," had set in type and hawked about town. One, a pathetic account of the drowning of a lighthouse keeper and his family, "sold wonderfully." Though success "flattered my vanity," he published nothing more for nearly three years. He read instead of wrote, leading a somewhat lonely life in the process. While the rest of the shop went off to a long afternoon dinner, he stayed behind nibbling a vegetarian repast and reading, and after work he "sat up in my room reading the greatest part of the night."

Franklin had gorged on books longer than he could remember. As a child he absorbed the crisp, clean style of John Bunyan's *Pilgrim's Progress.* In those pages he learned about the Slough of Despond through which men must travel to reach the good life, and there, too, he met Lord Lechery and Sir Having Greedy, Mr. Legality, a shyster lawyer, and Mr. Say-Well, a bombastic professor—all gentlemen whom his own Bunyan-like creation Mrs. Silence Dogood looked upon with contempt. From Bunyan the boy retrogressed into a popular series of true adventure tales written by an English printer named Nathaniel Crouch. The brief lives ranged from the heroes and heroines (Crouch did not slight the role of women) of Elizabethan England through the age of Cromwell, but all of them made a single point—that "human freedom and progress were tied inextricably to the supremacy of Protestant power in the world."

Amid his father's books on religion Franklin turned up a copy of Plutarch's lives of the leaders of Greece and Rome, all, as Plutarch saw them, virtuous and public-spirited citizens. There also he found two books that showed how men could make the world a better place to live —Daniel Defoe's *Essay upon Projects* and Cotton Mather's *Essays to Do Good.* Defoe called for national reforms—the education of women, pensions for the aged, fire insurance, and such things—where Mather concentrated on the local scene. "Neighbors!" he exhorted, "you stand related unto one another. And you should be full of devices that all the neighbors may have cause to be glad of your being in the neighborhood." Care for the poor there, suppress "base houses," promote education, provide for widows and orphans, and be not concerned "if your opportunities to do good reach no further." Defoe made the deeper immediate impression, and Franklin quoted him at length in the Silence Dogood letters, but Mather's essays "perhaps gave me a turn of thinking that had an influence on some of the principal future events of my life."

In the printshop Franklin read whatever came his way—John Locke's *Essay Concerning Human Understanding,* James Greenwood's *An Essay Towards a Practical English Grammar,* John Tryon's vegetarian tract, *The Way to Health, long Life and Happiness,* Xenophon's *The Memorable Things of Socrates.* He dared, now beyond the eye of his father, to dip into deistical volumes like those of the Earl of Shaftesbury and Anthony Collins, who taught that men could be virtuous without being orthodox Christians, that God, the divine "mechanic," had created the universe but allowed it to operate without His intervention through revelations or miracles. By the age of sixteen Franklin was "a thorough deist."

On a shelf in the shop James Franklin had put the bound volumes of Addison and Steele's *Spectator* papers. The spectator, Sir Roger de Coverley, endorsed a standard of ethics strict enough to satisfy even Cotton Mather—decorum in dress, sedateness in language, fidelity in marriage, honesty in business—but in a style so graceful and witty that old thoughts appeared mint new. James Franklin and his friends thought they were patterning their contributions to the *Courant* after the style of the *Spectator* papers, but they were wrong. They wrote in a "native style" often on vulgar subjects that would have been shunned by Sir Roger de Coverley. They aimed, as Checkley put it, to speak to "men in a very easy and familiar manner, so that the meanest ploughman, the very meanest of God's people may understand them." Their essays, Perry Miller has said, "are more than colonial apings of Addison and Steele; they come from the streets of a trading and seaport town, out of that world which the official mind regarded with abhorrence, out of the mire and the stews where antiministerial sentiment was generated." Benjamin Franklin, too, thought he aped the *Spectator* papers, but his early style owed more to his brother James's influence than to Sir Roger de Coverley. Sir Roger would have never let someone lend "lubbers a helping hand," as Mrs. Dogood did, nor allow a man to earn his "bread by the sweat of his own brow." Nor would he sink to writing about a town's prostitutes or discourse, as Mrs. Dogood does, upon the words men use "to cover their folly" when they do not wish to be "known as *drunk.*"

The day after Franklin slipped the first of Mrs. Dogood's essays under the shop door he had "the exquisite pleasure" of hearing his brother and friends praise it and wonder who among the men of "learning and ingenuity" in town might have written it. Thereafter Mrs. Dogood spoke forth every two weeks in the *Courant.* The series lasted six months and Franklin kept his authorship secret until near the end. In the thirteenth essay one of the gallants about town told Mrs. Dogood *"that though I wrote in the character of a woman, he knew me to be a man,* but, continued he, *he has more need of endeavoring a reformation in himself, than spending his wit in satirizing others."* Perhaps the admonition came from James Franklin. The good lady appeared once more, then vanished, though her creator remained a year longer in the shop.

The essays vary in quality. A bright phrase or sentence illuminates them all, but only one, a superb satire on funeral elegies, deserves to survive. And they vary in tone—from a gentle ridicule of hoopskirts, those "monstrous topsy-turvy *mortar pieces*"—to the sarcastic observation that *"a little religion, and a little honesty, goes a great way in courts."* If Franklin had not penned "BF" next to the essays in his file of the *Courant,* they could have passed for those by his brother. Though an ingenious young man, he still looked at the world through James's eyes. When Silence Dogood remarked "I am naturally very jealous for the rights and liberties of my country, and the least appearance of an encroachment on those invaluable privileges is apt to make my blood boil exceedingly," it could have been James, as Abigail Afterwit, speaking. James Franklin may have been the "harsh and tyrannical" master his brother judged him, but something resembling a love-hate relationship must have existed between the two. As they were related in life, so, too, were their journalistic creations. Silence Dogood followed sedately behind in the path marked out by her old sister, Abigail Afterwit.

5

In January 1722 the *Courant*'s ridicule provoked Increase Mather to lament the passing of the day "when the civil government would have taken an effectual course to suppress such a cursed libel!" Six months later James Franklin twitted the government for laxness and thereby gave the legislature a flimsy excuse to jail him. While in jail he fell ill. He humbly confessed his folly "in affronting the government, as also his indiscretion and indecency," and after being certified by, of all people, Dr. Zabdiel Boylston, the inoculator, he received permission to exercise in the prison yard. During his confinement Benjamin Franklin ran the paper, "and I made bold to give our rulers some rubs in it, which my brother took very kindly. . . ." James returned to his shop a month later brassy as ever. "Better men than myself had been in prison before me," among them the late Governor Dudley, he told readers, "but I never could perceive that the jail stank a whit less for him."

Five months passed, and the *Courant* continued its irreverent way. In January 1723 the printer mocked pious hypocrites, who "*dissemble* and *lie, snuffle* and *whiffle*; and, if it be possible, they will overreach and defraud all who deal with them." Of all the knaves who plague the world, "the *religious knave* is the worst." Two days later the government announced that because the *Courant* continued to abuse religion and ridicule the clergy James Franklin must hereafter submit all copy for censorship. James flouted the edict, published one more issue, then, while dodging arrest, arranged for his brother's name to appear on the masthead as printer. The new management promised sedately to avoid "malicious scribbles and billingsgate-ribaldry" and to content itself with entertaining "the town with the most comical and diverting incidents of human life."

At this point James Franklin's life took a turn for the better. He married in February. The grand jury refused a few weeks later to bring charges against him. Publicity gained from the government's attack led to a sizable jump in the *Courant*'s circulation and number of advertisers; a shaky venture suddenly prospered. Only continuing differences with his brother marred life. Earlier, to make the transfer of the *Courant*'s title legal, James Franklin had turned over Benjamin's indenture contract "with a full discharge on the back of it," then exacted a new indenture for the remaining four years of the original apprenticeship. Benjamin doubted he would dare reveal the devious arrangement, and in the summer of 1723 demanded his freedom. Josiah Franklin tried to persuade the boy to abide by his contract; Benjamin refused. In the latter part of September under the cover of dark he absconded from Boston aboard a vessel bound for New York.

Even before Franklin's departure, James had let the *Courant* deteriorate into a drab sheet filled with tedious essays stolen from English journals. He kept the paper alive nearly two years longer, though all the old contributors had left. A flash of the old spirit showed in a satiric poem published in one of the last issues. He, a mere printer, unwelcomed by the Harvard-educated elite that ruled Boston, had tried with wit and reason to reform the town—true, without success, but "he wrote good sense," said James Franklin of himself, though he "never at the College did commence." After killing off the *Courant*, he left Boston to join his brother John in Newport, Rhode Island, and there opened a new printshop and began another newspaper. He died nine years later, at the age of thirty-five. Benjamin Franklin remembered all his life the blows his brother's "passion too often urged him to bestow upon me," but he also remembered that "he was otherwise not an ill-natured man; perhaps I was too saucy and provoking."

6

Franklin had the luck to be reared in Boston—and the good sense to leave it. He used the quarrel with his brother to justify what instinct told him to do. A Harvard elite ran the town. Those not members of the club had little chance to rise to wealth or power. The wit and ridicule in the *Courant* had changed nothing. Harvard might turn out genteel blockheads but those blockheads dominated Boston's life. A social structure as fixed as that in England blanketed the town. Josiah Franklin, a wise and able man, had no more chance in Boston than in Banbury to escape from the niche he believed God had assigned him. Nor, it appeared, did his sons. All were craftsmen, as his father's sons and his father's father's sons had been in England. Franklin expected more of life than what Boston had handed his family.

There were more immediate reasons for putting the town behind him: "I had already made myself a little obnoxious to the governing party; and from the arbitrary proceedings of the Assembly in my brother's case it was likely I might if I stayed soon bring myself into scrapes; and farther that my indiscreet disputations about religion began to make me pointed at with horror by good people, as an infidel or atheist."

Franklin visited Boston four times during the rest of his life, but only once, when out of a job and life looked hopeless, did he consider returning for good. Yet he always spoke fondly of the town. "The Boston manner, turn of phrase, and even tone of voice and accent in pronunciation all please and seem to refresh and revive me," he once said. He forever after thought of himself as a native of New England and would have agreed with the gentleman who called him a "citizen of Boston who dwelt for a little while in Philadelphia." A bill relating to Indian affairs drawn up for the Pennsylvania Assembly "was framed in imitation of a law of the same kind long in use in New England." A militia law pressed upon his adopted colony derived from New England. When he proposed a fast day to rouse the people of Pennsylvania and found no one knew how to word the proclamation, "my education in New England, where a fast is proclaimed every year, was here of some advantage." In London he sent to the press over the signature "A NEW ENGLANDMAN" a long, hot reply to a writer who had maligned Massachusetts. It delighted him when the Massachusetts legislature appointed him its agent in England. In all the letters back to Boston he spoke repeatedly of "my country" and "our charter rights," but the country and rights referred to were those of Massachusetts, not those of America. "And now that I am writing," he remarked a few years before he died to a friend in Boston, "it comes into my mind to inquire of you what light you find me to stand in among my country folks?"

CHAPTER

3

"A CONFUSED VARIETY OF DIFFERENT SCENES"

FRANKLIN'S *Autobiography* RELATES in detail his escape from Boston, his failure to find a job in New York, and his further trip to Philadelphia, where he had been told there was an opening in Andrew Bradford's printshop. "I have been the more particular in this description of my journey," he explains, "and shall be so of my first entry into that city, that you may in your mind compare such unlikely beginnings with the figure I have since made there."

"Though the honest autobiographer refuses to invent fictitious incidents," David Levin remarks, "he *actually creates himself as a character.*" Franklin was adept at this, losing himself in Silence Dogood or Poor Richard but never revealing the man behind the mask. He played these roles so effectively that at least two of his creations—Polly Baker, the mother of a houseful of illegitimate children, and William Henry, an escaped captive of Indians—were accepted as historical figures.

The Franklin of the *Autobiography* is another of his creations. The first half of the book, John Sanford writes, is a secularized version of Bunyan's *Pilgrim's Progress.* "His confessed *errata* are analogous to Christian's bundle of sins and to the giant Despair, over which he must prevail in order to gain the Heavenly City." Others did not fare so well on the journey. Several friends fell along the way into the Slough of Despond and other traps that entice the weak. Franklin as Christian appears more simple than he is. He plays down his learning, his amazing literary talent, portraying himself as an innocent abroad who learns only slowly to cope in a wicked world. He says nothing of his emotional life, the fears felt, the melancholy that must occasionally have overwhelmed him. But so skill-

fully does he tell the story that posterity, deprived of other records for
these years, has been forced to see them as he wished them to be seen.

At times, however, the events he relates can be viewed from an angle
that alters the picture. The escape from Boston was not that of a typical
absconding apprentice. Franklin left in comfort aboard a vessel bound for
New York. He must have carried the canceled indenture contract signed
by his brother, and so did not need to worry about being picked up as
a runaway by authorities. He arrived in Philadelphia with enough money
in his pockets not only to buy his famous breakfast of rolls but to pay for
room and board at a modest inn. He appeared bedraggled only because
a trunk full of fresh clothes had not yet come over from New York. Nor
did he arrive as just another printer. Andrew Bradford, publisher of
Philadelphia's *American Weekly Mercury,* read the *New England Courant*
with admiration. He had followed James Franklin's troubles with the
authorities closely and in one issue censured the leaders of Massachusetts
as "oppressors and bigots, who make religion the only engine of destruction of the people." He must have seen Benjamin Franklin's name on the
masthead while James languished in jail and had a high opinion of the
young man before he saw him set a stick of type.

Franklin reached Philadelphia on a Sunday morning. He could spot
superficial resemblances to Boston as he walked about the quiet streets.
A wooden platform in the center of town held a whipping post and
pillory like those at home. Hogs and dogs ran wild through the streets.
Dock Creek, a stream that curled through the heart of town, flanked by
stables and tanyards that used it for an open sewer, gave off a familiar
stench. Trash lay accumulated in the streets waiting for a heavy rain to
wash it away. Clouds of flies hovered over scattered piles of garbage.
Mosquitoes that thrived in nearby swamps buzzed everywhere, and in
the inn bedbugs and roaches lay waiting to torment the visitor. Out-
houses dotted every backyard.

These familiar sights aside, he could spot little else to remind him of
home. Gone were the squat frame houses he knew in Boston. In their
place stood narrow piles of light red brick built two or three stories high;
these Philadelphians called home. ("I say, give me a wooden one, that I
may swing a cat around in," a fellow New Englander remarked when he
saw the cramped houses.) Gone were Boston's twisting streets, supplanted by a giant gridiron pattern that shaped the town into a series of
squares stretching westward from the Delaware River. In Boston, citizens looked and spoke and even dressed like Englishmen. Here in the
space of an hour's walk Franklin could meet an Amish farmer arguing
in German with a shopkeeper, talk to a Jew, hear the brogue of a Scotch-

Irishman, visit a Catholic mass, or listen to a plainly dressed Quaker asking if "I can help thee." Quakers, a "remarkably grave and reserved people," dominated the town and imposed a sedateness upon it that made Boston seem debauched.

William Penn wanted a "green country town." He envisioned a city of great airy squares split into generous-sized lots surrounded with sufficient light and lawn to block the development of slums. Instead, the early settlers had subdivided the lots and cut through the expansive squares with dingy alleyways. Now it had a population of between six and seven thousand, but instead of spreading westward it continued to hug the banks of the Delaware. To a man from Boston it resembled a country town. The provincial legislature had no building of its own but met in a hired house or occasionally in the Friends' Meeting House. The town had no college and not even a good bookstore. None of its streets was paved. Along the waterfront Franklin could count only a piddling number of wharves—fifteen, a fourth the number in Boston. High Street Wharf, the town's pride, seemed diminutive compared to Boston's Long Wharf. Only the public market that stretched the length of two squares along High Street gave the town something to brag about.

As he walked the streets that Sunday morning, Franklin saw everywhere empty houses for rent, "which made me then think the inhabitants of the city were one after another deserting it." And they were. "Families who had lived well could scarce find means to purchase necessary provisions for their support," the legislature reported; "and therefore both artificers and traders were obliged to quit the country, in search of employment and sustenance elsewhere." All his life he would remember citizens coming to market that year to barter for provisions with their silver plate. Only seventy-nine vessels had entered and eighty-six cleared the port during the year, a drop of 40 percent in traffic from two years earlier and something like a tenth of the traffic in and out of Boston. Franklin could not have chosen a worse time to arrive in Philadelphia looking for a job.

2

Monday morning Franklin went over to Andrew Bradford's shop and found, as expected, business slow, no hand needed. Bradford, probably after praising James Franklin and glancing at the discharged indenture, took him over to Samuel Keimer, an eccentric who wore a long beard, worshiped God on Saturday, and had come to Philadelphia a year ago offering to teach "male Negroes to read the Holy Scriptures, etc. in a very *uncommon expeditious* and *delightful* manner," but now ran the only other printshop in town. They found Keimer composing an elegy directly from his head into type. He hired Franklin to print the elegy and after seeing he had a first-rate hand took him on full-time.

Franklin had worked for Keimer nearly a half year when one day the governor, Sir William Keith, strode into the shop, accompanied by John French, a political ally from Pennsylvania's sister colony, Delaware. Keith, a Scottish baronet, had become governor six years earlier, one of the last appointments William Penn made before drifting into death. He pleased the Quaker oligarchy until he proposed printing paper money to relieve the economic depression. The Quakers turned on him and a beleaguered Keith found himself spokesman for the people. "It is neither the great, the rich, nor the learned, that compose the body of the people," he said about the time Franklin arrived. Government "ought carefully to protect the poor, laborious, and industrious part of mankind." Keith determined to break the Quakers' hold on the colony. He called for naturalization of Germans then flooding into Pennsylvania. He orga-nized the Tiff Club to bring workingmen—"the new, vile people," a leading Quaker called them, no better than "a mob"—into politics. (Franklin once proposed to write a history of the club but never did. If he joined it, as seems likely, he kept the secret from posterity.) Now Keith needed only a printer to spread the gospel, and Franklin seemed the right man.

The governor, "with a condescension and politeness I had been quite unused to, made me many compliments, desired to be acquainted with me, blamed me kindly for not having made myself known to him when I first came to the place, and would have me away with him to the tavern where he was going with Col. French to taste, as he said, some excellent Madeira." Over wine the politicians promised Franklin they would push all public printing contracts his way after he had set up in business. And where would he get the money to open a shop? From his father, of course, who had recently sent word his son's sins were forgiven. "So it was concluded I should return to Boston in the first vessel with the governor's letter recommending me to my father."

When Franklin returned to Boston in the spring of 1724, after an absence of seven months, he had more in mind than persuading his father to back him in the printing business. He visited his brother's shop wear-ing "a genteel new suit from head to foot, a watch, and my pockets lined with near five pounds sterling in silver." James looked him up and down and without a word went back to work. Franklin, chatting nonchalantly with the other hands, found an excuse to produce "a handful of silver and spread it before them. . . . Then I took an opportunity of letting them see my watch; and lastly (my brother still grum and sullen) I gave them a piece of eight to drink and took my leave." When the mother tried to reconcile her sons, James said his brother "had insulted him in such a manner before his people that he could never forget or forgive it."

The humiliation handed James marked the high point of the trip home. His father said Governor Keith must be a man "of small discretion, to think of setting a boy up in business who wanted yet three years of being at man's estate." He also said he "had advanced too much already to my brother James." He did not say the obvious—that to help set Benjamin up in business would condone the wrongs done and insults meted out to his older brother. He suggested, perhaps with a light smile, that since Benjamin "had been so industrious and careful as to equip myself so handsomely in so short a time," he could surely save enough before he reached twenty-one to set himself up in business, "and that if I came near the matter he would help me out with the rest."

Back in Philadelphia Keimer supplanted James as the butt of Franklin's wit. "In truth, he was an odd fish, ignorant of common life, fond of rudely opposing received opinions, slovenly to extreme dirtiness, enthusiastic in some points of religion, and a little knavish withal." A foolish man, unquestionably, but hardly one deserving to be tortured and toyed with by a boy nearly twenty years his junior. "I used to work him so with my Socratic method, and trapanned him so often," Franklin recalled, "that at last he grew ridiculously cautious, and would hardly answer me the most common question, without asking first, *What do you intend to infer from that?*" Franklin agreed to grow a beard and keep Saturday as the Sabbath if Keimer adopted a vegetarian diet. "He was usually a great glutton, and I promised myself some diversion in half-starving him."

Outside the printshop Franklin found little to complain about. The governor continued "to like my company, had me frequently to his house," and promised to set him up with letters of credit to buy printing equipment in London. He courted Deborah Read, whom he had met when lodging in her parents' house, next door to Keimer's shop. Her mother squelched talk of marriage, "as I was about to take a long voyage, and we were both young," and, "perhaps, too, she thought my expectations not so well-founded as I imagined them to be." He made friends with others his age who were also "lovers of reading," and they had pleasant walks together "on Sundays into the woods near Schuylkill, where we read to one another and conferred on what we read." He especially enjoyed the company of James Ralph, an aspiring poet, also "ingenious, genteel in his manners, and extremely eloquent; I think I never knew a prettier talker." Weary of sniping from his in-laws, Ralph determined to leave his wife and child "on their hands" and go to London with Franklin.

Those who knew Franklin casually judged him a dispassionate man. Friends found that hardly an apt assessment of one who, like the Old Testament characters he admired, believed so much in revenge. Franklin rarely forgot an injury done to him and bided his time waiting for a chance to repay it. Once, when in his early sixties, a neighbor, Francis Alison, denied him a favor. "It is not amiss that the Reverend Doctor refused that privilege. We shall not want it," he told his wife. "Alison will in time want to cut off the tail of his lot to build on, and to have a passage to the street thro' ours. We may then remember his civility."

When Franklin, with Ralph as a companion, arrived in London at the end of 1725, he found he had been gulled by Governor Keith. The letters of credit Keith had promised to put in the ship's mailbag were not there. Instead of collecting equipment for a printshop, Franklin must find work to survive in the sprawling immensity of London. Yet, curiously, of all those who had handed him supposed or real injuries in his youth Keith is judged the most generously in the *Autobiography* written nearly a half century later. "It was a habit he had acquired," he said. "He wished to please everybody; and having little to give, he gave expectations. He was otherwise an ingenious sensible man, a pretty good writer, and a good governor for the people, tho' not for his constituents, the proprietaries, whose instructions he sometimes disregarded. Several of our best laws were of his planning, and passed during his administration."

3

Daniel Defoe once classified Englishmen thus:

The *great*, who live profusely.
The *rich*, who live very plentifully.
The *middle sort*, who live well.
The *working trades*, who labor hard but feel no want.
The *country people*, farmers, etc., who fare indifferently.
The *poor*, that fare hard.
The *miserable*, that really pinch and suffer.

Franklin on this, his first trip to England, spent a year and a half on Defoe's scale somewhere between those "that fare hard" and those "who labor hard but feel no want." If he had practiced the gospel later dispensed by Poor Richard, he could have saved enough during that time to buy the types and press he had come for. He immediately got a job in a printing house. Savings from his salary added to the twelve pounds brought in his pockets ought to have been enough to make a substantial down payment for his equipment. Instead, he ended the stay having to borrow money for passage home.

For several months he and James Ralph shared cheap lodgings near the printing house. Ralph borrowed from Franklin's nest egg while he looked vainly for work as a writer, and together they spent "a good deal of my earnings in going to plays and other places of amusement." Ralph took up with a young woman and moved in with her. Her earnings as a milliner were not enough to support him and her child, and in desperation he left the city to teach in a country school, a job so demeaning for a poet that he passed himself off as an American named Benjamin Franklin. From the country he sent Franklin installments of an epic poem and also asked his friend to keep an eye on his woman. Franklin did, and on one visit made advances "which she repulsed with proper resentment." Ralph, told of the *erratum*, "let me know he thought I had cancelled all the obligations he had been under to me."

Before the friendship ended Franklin dedicated to Ralph "a little metaphysical piece" entitled *A Dissertation on Liberty and Necessity, Pleasure and Pain,* a deistical tract printed at his own expense, and later listed as "another *erratum.*" It was a remarkable work for a nineteen-year-old. In it Franklin sees the universe a gigantic machine created as God wished it, "consequently *all is right*"; vice and virtue are "empty distinctions"; pain alone causes men to act and leads to pleasure ("The *pain* of confinement causes the *desire* of liberty. . . . The *pain* of labor and fatigue causes the *pleasure* of rest. . . . The *pain* of absence of friends, produces the *pleasure* of meeting in exact proportion," etc.); and God loves equally all creatures on earth, an insufferable doctrine to mankind perhaps, "but (to use a piece of *common* sense) our geese are but geese tho' we may think 'em swans; and truth will be truth tho' it sometimes prove mortifying and distasteful."

"By some means," said Franklin, a copy of the pamphlet fell into the hands of Dr. William Lyons, author of *The Infallibility of Human Judgment.* More likely, he sent it to Lyons. Its title came from an appendix in the fourth edition of the doctor's work, and he surely sought his reaction. Lyons "took great notice of me." He drew the young printer into a circle of physicians and surgeons, introducing him to Dr. Bernard Mandeville, author of *The Fable of the Bees* and "a most facetious, entertaining companion," and to Dr. Henry Pemberton, a fellow of the Royal Society then preparing under Newton's direction the third edition of the *Principia*. Pemberton "promised to give me an opportunity some time or other of seeing Sir Isaac Newton, of which I was extremely desirous; but this never happened."

After the break with Ralph, Franklin "began to think of getting a little money beforehand." He moved to a larger printing house, where "my uncommon quickness at composing, occasioned my being put upon all work of dispatch, which was generally better paid. So I went on agreeably." He swam Sundays in the Thames. He took trips into the country. At work he avoided the "muddling liquor" colleagues were addicted to and drank only water, but when in the company of friends like Dr. Lyons he sometimes suffered from "fits of indigestion brought on by indulgence at the table." Told a dose of the oil of wormwood would settle his stomach, he "went on sinning more freely than ever."

While in London Franklin kept touch with Thomas Denham, a merchant met on the voyage over. In the spring of 1726 Denham prepared to return to Philadelphia to open a store. Would Franklin like to join him in the business? "The thing pleased me, for I was grown tired of London," and "therefore, I immediately agreed on the terms of fifty pounds a year, Pennsylvania money; less indeed than my present gettings as a compositor, but affording a better prospect." Franklin sailed for Philadelphia on July 21 with Denham, who paid his passage.

The *Autobiography* gives nearly one-fourth of its pages to these early years after leaving Boston. Franklin exposes his *errata* without a blush, but nowhere reveals the frustration felt during this period. Franklin "harbored an early sense of originality and, in fact, superiority," knew that "his was the fate of an elect being." As a youngster he had written highly praised essays, managed a printshop, edited a newspaper. He saw the upper ranks of Boston society closed to him and so left, yet since then he found himself at every turn locked into the job of journeyman printer —the calling, as his father might put it, God had assigned him to. The friendship of a governor had not pried him from his niche. The deistical pamphlet carried him into a convivial circle in London, but he remained a journeyman printer. He sent Sir Hans Sloane, president of the Royal Society, a note—Sir Hans did not, as in the *Autobiography*, come "to see me"—offering to sell a purse made of asbestos and other American "curiosities"; Sloane bought the purse, but nothing more came of the meeting. Now he approached twenty-one, about to begin a new career yet no farther along than if he had stayed in Boston.

On the way back from London Franklin admitted that his life thus far had been "a confused variety of different scenes." The curtain would soon rise on a new scene. "Let me, therefore, make some resolutions, and form some scheme of action that, henceforth, I may live in all respects like a rational creature:

1. It is necessary for me to be extremely frugal for some time, till I have paid what I owe.
2. To endeavor to speak truth in every instance.
3. To apply myself industriously to whatever business I take in hand, and not divert my mind from my business by any foolish project of growing suddenly rich; for industry and patience are the surest means of plenty.
4. I resolve to speak ill of no man whatever, not even in a matter of truth."

4

Franklin arrived in Philadelphia on 11 October 1726. Deborah Read, "despairing with reason of my return," had married a potter, then quickly repented, "refusing to cohabit with him, or bear his name, it being now said that he had another wife"; but the husband vanished from Philadelphia before she could have the marriage annulled, and thus legally she still remained married. Governor Keith after being removed from office had stood for a seat in the Assembly and with the Tiff Club's backing won handsomely. Keimer, to Franklin's dismay, "had got a better house, a shop well supplied with stationery, plenty of new types, a number of hands, tho' none good, and seemed to have a great deal of business." Indeed, the whole town prospered. The depression had ended. Shipyards empty three years earlier now hummed with work. Trade had recovered and shipping in and out of the port had doubled. Immigrants from the Rhineland states and northern Ireland poured in, bringing hard money to add to the prosperity. Denham's store, and with it Franklin, seemed sure to succeed.

A reformed Franklin, with the *errata* cleansed from his life, celebrated his twenty-first birthday with a solemn letter to his favorite sister, Jane, warning that modesty "makes the most homely virgin amiable and charming," but "the want of it infallibly renders the most perfect beauty disagreeable and odious." He used part of a ten-pound Christmas gift from Denham to buy her a spinning wheel. In March 1727 both he and Denham fell ill. Franklin's distemper "very nearly carried me off." (Denham lingered for a year, finally dying in July 1728.) In the *Autobiography* he dismissed the brush with death lightly, saying he "was rather disappointed when I found myself recovering; regretting in some degree that

I must now some time or other have all that disagreeable work to do over again." At the time he felt otherwise. During the illness he reviewed his thoughts about God and in the coming year worked out a religious philosophy held to the rest of his life. His deistic pamphlet had denied any distinction between virtue and vice; pain alone drove men to act, seeking to relieve their uneasiness in pleasure. Now he saw that "without virtue man can have no happiness in this world," or as he later put it: "I grew convinced that *truth, sincerity,* and *integrity* in dealings between man and man, were of the utmost importance to the felicity of life." Earlier he envisioned the Creator as a remote being uninterested in His creatures on earth. It seemed senseless to direct prayers to Him. Now Franklin decided, "He is not above caring for us, being pleased with our praise, and offended when we slight Him, or neglect His glory." Only occasionally did he use the name God, then it was "good God." For one who would long feel the loss of Denham ("he counselled me as a father") and the absence of his own father ("I was . . . remote from the eye and advice of my father"), it seemed right to call Him "Infinite Father" or simply "Father." The names "Powerful Goodness," "O Creator," and "My Friend" also satisfied him. To escape the empty pieties dispensed by ministers, he devised a private service. It opened with a brief catechism, moved on to a "hymn to the Creator" taken from a passage in *Paradise Lost,* paused for a sermon drawn from "some book or part of a book discoursing on and exciting MORAL VIRTUE," and ended with thanks to "my good God."

Franklin had recovered by May 1727. Keimer tempted him "with an offer of large wages by the year to come and take the management of his printing," but he wanted none of that. He spent the next six months at loose ends, traveling over the town seeking a job as a merchant's clerk. Nothing turned up. Desperate for work, he reluctantly "closed again with Keimer" in October, back where he had started almost four years ago.

5

Franklin returned as Keimer's shop manager. He excelled as a pressman and compositor, could make engravings and even, in an emergency, mold new types. Also, "I made the ink, I was warehouseman, and everything; in short quite a factotum." Keimer had lured him back with a high salary to shape his "raw cheap hands" into craftsmen. That done, Franklin expected to be sent packing. "I went on, however, very cheerfully; put his printing house in order, which had been in great confusion, and brought his hands by degrees to mind their business and to do it better."

Life again turned agreeable. Keimer treated him civilly and the hands "all respected me." The master still worshiped on Saturday, leaving two days free to read, to visit with friends, and possibly to search out a girl for marriage. "I am about courting a girl I have had but little acquaintance with," he wrote in a commonplace book. "How shall I come to a knowledge of her faults and whether she has the virtues I imagine she has?" *Answer:* "Commend her among her female acquaintance."

Franklin admitted that the "hard-to-be governed passion of youth had hurried me frequently into intrigues with low women that fell in my way." Later, a letter on how to choose a mistress indicated he had given more than thought to the problem. Gossip about Franklin and women circled round him all his life. When he was fifty-eight, a piece of doggerel taunted:

> F——N, tho' plagued with fumbling age,
> Needs nothing to excite him.
> But is too ready to engage
> When younger arms invite him.

When Franklin was sixty-one, a youngster came upon him in London with a young girl on his lap in a compromising position. In his seventies he amazed Thomas Jefferson. "I have marked him particularly in the company of women where he loses all power over himself and becomes almost frenzied. His temperance would not be proof against their allurements were such to be employed as engines against him. This is in some measure the vice of his age, but it seems to be increased also by his peculiar constitution."

The gossip overlooked Franklin's affection for women as women, as individuals. He treated them as equals which, with his wit, may have been the reason this not handsome man appealed to them. Franklin delighted to flirt with any attractive young lady who came his way, but if he engaged in affairs after his marriage they were so discreet that not even his enemies could find evidence enough to use against him. The most specific hint that survives of possible extramartial affairs comes from John Adams, who reported that an English friend of Franklin's "now and then dropped to me some of Franklin's former confessions to him concerning his amours, which were curious enough." On that ambiguous note the matter of Franklin's love life must rest.

6

Not long after returning to Keimer, Franklin "formed most of my ingenious acquaintances into a club for mutual improvement, which we called the Junto." The club was his from the start, and remained so to the end. ("The Junto fainted last summer in the hot weather," a member wrote nearly thirty years later, "and has not yet revived; your presence might reanimate it, without which I apprehend it will never recover.") Most of the members were, like Franklin, in their early twenties, working men, bright, lovers of books, and witty (or if not witty then solid and sensible). The nucleus came from Keimer's shop—Hugh Meredith, an "honest, sensible" farmer's son, "something of a reader but given to drink"; Stephen Potts, another farmer's son, "a wit that seldom acted wisely"; George Webb, a former student at Oxford who had indentured himself to Keimer to pay for his passage to America.

From "ingenious acquaintances" about town came: William Coleman, a clerk "who had the coolest clearest head, the best heart, and the exactest morals of almost any man I ever met with"; William Parsons, a shoemaker whose hobbies were mathematics and astrology, "a wise man that often acted foolishly"; William Maugridge, "a joiner, a most exquisite mechanic, and a solid sensible man"; Nicholas Scull, a surveyor "who loved books and sometimes made a few verses"; and Thomas Godfrey, a self-taught mathematician whose demand for precision led to trifling over words and made him "not a pleasing companion." Only Robert Grace, "generous, lively and witty, a lover of punning and of his friends," could call himself a gentleman. A single sample of Grace's wit survives, a couplet tacked to the door of the chapel on his estate where he found his devout wife holding a small service:

> Your walls are thick, and your people are thin,
> The Devil's without, and Grace is within.

(Family tradition holds that when Franklin returned from England in 1775, a widower, he proposed to Grace's widow. She refused "to marry anyone whose religious opinions were so different from her own," but when sent for when Franklin was dying she rode over forty miles of mud-clogged roads to say goodbye.)

Franklin in his old age suggested that *Essays to Do Good* inspired him to form the club, and the debt to Cotton Mather's book has since been called "unmistakable." Later, when the Junto branched into civic projects, it did resemble a secularized version of the neighborhood Christian associations Mather called for. In the early years, however, it owed more to the social meetings of Dr. Lyons Franklin had attended in London. The Junto originally met on a Friday night in a Philadelphia tavern. Once a month the meeting opened with a poem "hum'd in consort by as many can hum it." Also each month, except during the winter, members met "of a Sunday in the afternoon in some proper place cross the river for bodily exercise." During regular meetings, according to one of the poets:

> Three queries in philosophy were first
> Gravely considered and at length discussed
> A declamation next was read in course
> Where keen wit did virtue's laws enforce
> Where strength of thought in lofty language shone
> Such as famed Swift or Addison might own.

The queries pricked the interest of young men eager to get ahead:

Hath any citizen in your knowledge failed in his business lately, and what have you heard of the cause?

Have you lately heard of any citizen's thriving well, and by what means?

Have you lately heard how any present rich man, here or elsewhere, got his estate?

Hath anybody attacked your reputation lately, and what can the Junto do towards securing it?

In what manner can the Junto, or any of them, assist you, in any of your honorable designs?

Have you any weighty affair in hand, in which you think the advice of the Junto may be of service?

Rarely did civic projects or concern for the welfare of the community intrude on these gatherings. During the week members pondered for discussion at the next meeting such questions as:

Does the importation of servants increase or advance the wealth of our country?

Can a man arrive at perfection in this life . . . ?

Wherein consists the happiness of a rational creature?

What is the difference between knowledge and prudence?

Does it not in a general way require great study and intense application for a poor man to become rich and powerful, if he would do it without the forfeiture of his honesty?

The club drove at the root of serious matters in a lighthearted way. Members did not hesitate while they paused for thought to "fill and drink a glass of wine," which "the witty bards [did] inspire/ With bright ideas and poetic fire." Franklin one evening opened on the ponderous subject of "the providence of God in the government of the world" in this manner: "You are all my intimate pot companions, who have heard me say a thousand silly things in conversation, and therefore have not that laudable partiality and veneration for whatever I shall deliver that good people commonly have for their spiritual guides."

Franklin relished the conviviality of these meetings all his life. "For my own part, I find I love company, chat, a laugh, a glass, and even a song, as well as ever," he wrote a member some thirty years later. "I am sure the Junto will be still as agreeable to me as it ever has been. I therefore hope it will not be discontinued as long as we are able to crawl together."

7

Franklin organized the Junto in the fall of 1727, about the time he found his services in the shop "became every day of less importance as the other hands improved in the business." In September Keimer tried to force him into cheaper terms. Failing that, "he grew by degrees less civil, put on more of the master, frequently found fault, was captious and seemed ready for an out-breaking." A month later "a trifle snapped our connections." Keimer from the street spotted Franklin craning out the shop window one afternoon searching for the source of a great noise near the courthouse. He hurled up a string of oaths which "nettled me the more for their publicity, all the neighbors who were looking out on the same occasion being witness how I was treated." Keimer continued the reprimands inside the shop, and after "high words had passed on both sides," Franklin quit on the spot, "and so taking my hat walked out of doors, desiring Meredith whom I saw below to take care of some things I left, and bring them to my lodging." Four years to the month had passed since he had run away from home. Back in his rooms Franklin decided to admit defeat and return to Boston.

CHAPTER

4

MAKING IT

Hugh Meredith's father staved off a return to Boston. He admired Franklin for persuading his son "to abstain long from dram-drinking" and offered to set him up in business if he took Hugh on as a partner. The New Printing-Office opened in the summer of 1728 in the first floor of a house rented on High Street opposite the market. The partners let the second floor to Thomas Godfrey and his family. Godfrey used a side of the shop for his glazier business and agreed to board the bachelors. The crates with the types and press from London had hardly been unpacked when a shoemaker Franklin knew brought in a farmer he had met on the street asking for a printer. Their first large job was printing the last forty sheets (one hundred sixty pages) of a history of the Quakers. Franklin said a friend got the partners the job, but he has been charged with "want of candor" in not admitting that "the patronage came from the poor, despised caricatured Keimer," who was printing the first one hundred thirty-four sheets of the history. They worked "exceeding hard" on the book, "for the price was low." Meredith ran the press while Franklin composed a sheet a day, often working until eleven at night before he had distributed the type from the sheet printed that day.

Franklin dreamed large from the start. Less than three months after the shop opened, when the firm had made no dent in the debt to Meredith's father and still lacked money to expand into stationery and book-selling, two profitable sidelines printers engaged in, he prepared to compete against Bradford's *American Weekly Mercury* with his own newspaper. Keimer got wind of the plan, and knowing the town could not support three newspapers announced in October he would soon be printing his own weekly, which came forth on Christmas Eve 1728 under the ponderous title *The Universal Instructor in all Arts and Sciences; and Pennsylvania Gazette.* He chose a bad time to begin, for "the freezing of our river has the same effect on news as on trade." Keimer admitted this in an ingenuous paragraph in the opening issue. "We have little news of consequence at present," he wrote. "In the meantime we hope our readers will be content for the present, with what we can give 'em, which if it does 'em no good, shall do 'em no hurt. 'Tis the best we have, and so take it."

To fill space Keimer plagiarized from an encyclopedia without bothering to read what he set in type. His fifth issue carried the article on abortion, an oversight Franklin did not let pass unnoticed. As the sedate Martha Careful, he warned Keimer in a letter to Bradford's *American Mercury* that "if he proceed farther to expose the secrets of our sex . . . to be read in all *taverns* and *coffee houses,* and by the vulgar, . . . my sister Molly and myself, with some others, are resolved to run the hazard of taking him by the beard, at the next place we meet him, and make an example of him for his immodesty."

For two months Franklin sought to entice readers away from Keimer's sheet by entertaining the public in Bradford's paper with essays signed "Busy-Body." An occasional shot infuriated Keimer, but the essays are otherwise forgettable, except one where Franklin poses as a lady named "Patience," who keeps a dry-goods shop. A friend on a visit lets her two pesky children "run about and do petty mischief" in the shop. "Sometimes they pull the goods off my low shelves down to the ground, and perhaps where one of them has just been making water. My friend takes up the stuff and cries *Eh! thou little wicked mischievous rogue! —But however, it has done no great damage: 'tis only wet a little;* and so puts it up upon the shelf again."

In March 1729 Franklin let Joseph Brientnall, a colleague in the Junto, continue as "Busy-Body" while he published in April *A Modest Enquiry into the Nature and Necessity of a Paper-Currency.* The theme would be the theme of his life, "enlightened self-interest"—what favors a tradesman like Franklin serves Pennsylvania, and what serves Pennsylvania benefits the empire, especially the mother country. The arguments used were those of Sir William Keith, who six years earlier had forced through the Assembly Pennsylvania's first issue of paper money. A new issue would invigorate commerce, raise the value of land, reduce interest rates. All sensible men favored paper money. Opposed were those who lacked the "courage to venture into trade," usurers who reaped excessive interest rates, the rich who wanted to keep down the price of land while they enlarged their holdings, lawyers who feared people "will have less occasion to run in debt and consequently less occasion to go to law and sue one another for their debts." Paper money schemes had failed in New England because of mismanagement. Pennsylvania's well-contrived plan would lead neither to inflation nor depreciation.

The pamphlet has been called "highly ingenious and effective as contemporary propaganda" but shot through with "hazy ideas regarding the amount of paper currency that can be issued without depreciation." But it served Franklin well. The Assembly thereafter bestowed favors upon him and his printing business because he had "been of some service" in getting a paper money bill passed in 1729.

Franklin kept an eye on the shop while ingratiating himself with the Assembly. He now stocked books, but only those sure to sell—Bibles, psalters, psalm books. He expanded into stationery and sold a variety of printed forms—bills of lading, powers of attorney, writs, apprentices' indentures, and the like. (Bills of lading customarily were headed "Shipped by the Grace of God." Some Philadelphians thought this sacrilegious; Franklin, surely with a smile, advertised his bills of lading "for sale at this office, with or without the Grace of God.") Meanwhile, Keimer approached bankruptcy. In June his creditors moved in, and the newspaper missed an issue. In September he announced that B. Franklin and H. Meredith of the New Printing-Office would hereafter publish the paper. He sold it "for a trifle," having nothing more than ninety subscribers to pass on to the new management.

2

The first issue of the paper edited by Franklin came out "with better type and better printed" on 2 October 1729, with Keimer's cumbersome title reduced to the *Pennsylvania Gazette*. Gone were the tedious excerpts from the encyclopedia; they contained "many things abstruse or insignificant to us." The printer promised "a good News-Paper" and hoped that "those gentlemen who are able will contribute towards the making this such." He also promised that "no care and pains shall be omitted that may make the *Pennsylvania Gazette* as agreeable and useful an entertainment as the nature of the thing will allow."

Franklin called Bradford's paper a "paltry thing"—witless, dull, badly printed—and thus it has since been characterized. It was none of these things. A printer who knew and admired Franklin said that "the typography of the *Mercury* was equal to that of Franklin's *Gazette*," nor was it notably inferior in content. Bradford more than held his own in subscribers and advertisers until he lost his job as postmaster, which he had used as a weapon in the circulation war with Franklin. Only when Franklin became postmaster in 1737 did the *Gazette* outstrip its competitor. By then Bradford, wealthy and old, no longer cared.

Franklin held that a newspaper editor should serve as a "guardian of his country's reputation, and refuse to insert such writings as may hurt it." Bradford, though no crusader for freedom of speech, had applauded James Franklin's attacks on Massachusetts leaders, and only a few weeks before the *Gazette* changed hands dared to publish a mild attack on the Assembly. The piece was cited as "a wicked and seditious libel, tending to introduce confusion under the notion of liberty, and to lessen the just regard due to persons in authority." Andrew Hamilton, then speaker of the Assembly, later famous as the Philadelphia lawyer who got John Peter Zenger acquitted, saw that Bradford cooled off in jail until he expressed remorse, which he quickly did.

Franklin dealt more delicately than Bradford with political affairs. His third issue obliquely praised the Assembly in a piece about a political battle going on in Massachusetts. The governor there demanded that the legislature grant him a "fixed and honorable salary"; but the representatives, though harried and intimidated, refused. The mother country should rejoice, said Franklin, that "her SONS in the remotest part of the earth, and even to the third and fourth descent, still retain that ardent spirit of liberty, and that undaunted courage in the defense of it, which has in every age so gloriously distinguished BRITONS and ENGLISHMEN from all the rest of mankind." These "spirited remarks," Franklin said later, "struck the principal people, occasioned the paper and the manager of it to be much talked of, and in a few weeks brought them all to be our subscribers." Andrew Hamilton thereafter particularly interested himself in the career of the young printer.

The *Gazette* as a rule stayed clear of controversial matter, favoring instead such items as:

And sometime last week, we are informed, that one Piles, a fiddler, with his wife, were overset in a canoe near Newtown Creek. The good man, 'tis said, prudently secured his fiddle, and let his wife go to the bottom.

From New York, we hear, that on Saturday se'nnight, in the afternoon, they had there most terrible thunder and lightning, but no great damage done. The same day we had some very hard claps in these parts; and 'tis said, that in Bucks County one flash came so near a lad, as, without hurting him, to melt the pewter button off the waistband of his breeches. 'Tis well nothing else thereabouts was made of pewter.

The same day an unhappy man, one Sturgis, upon some difference with his wife, determined to drown himself in the river; and she (kind wife) went with him, it seems, to see it faithfully performed, and accordingly stood by silent and unconcerned during the whole transaction. He jumped in near Carpenter's Wharf, but was timely taken out again, before what he came about was thoroughly effected, so that they were both obliged to return home as they came, and put up for that time with the disappointment.

Sometimes Bradford came in for a swipe ("When Mr. Bradford publishes after us, and has occasion to take an article or two out of the *Gazette*, which he is always welcomed to do, he is desired not to date his paper a day before ours . . . lest distant readers should imagine we take from him, which we always carefully avoid."), and so, too, did the printer:

Thursday last, a certain p——r ['tis not customary to give names at length on these occasions] walking carefully in clean clothes over some barrels of tar on Carpenter's Wharf, the head of one of them unluckily gave way, and let a leg of him in above his knee. Whether he was upon the catch at that time, we cannot say, but 'tis certain he caught a *Tartar*. 'Twas observed he sprung out again right briskly, verifying the common saying, *as nimble as a* bee *in a tarbarrel*. You must know there are several sorts of *bees:* 'tis true he was no *honey bee*, nor yet a *humble bee*, but a *boo bee* he may be allowed to be, namely B. F.

3

"At present I am much hurried in business," Franklin said early in the summer of 1730, but could have said any workday that year. He had help now—an apprentice and also Thomas Whitmarsh, a journeyman met in London—but the partnership with Meredith floundered. Worse, Meredith's father could not pay all he had promised to start the business; the creditor sued for his money. Franklin saw his "hopeful prospects" about to be dashed when two friends in the Junto—William Coleman and Robert Grace—separately offered to clear his debt. Once free of that burden he could be rid of Meredith, who "was often seen drunk in the streets, and playing at low games in the alehouses, much to our discredit." Meredith on his own offered to "leave the whole in your hands," and on 14 July 1730 the partnership was amicably dissolved. Six weeks later Franklin married Deborah Read.

Marriage had been on his mind for some time. Earlier, the wife of his companion in the Junto, Thomas Godfrey, the glazier with whom he still boarded, had off and on invited for dinner a girl she thought suitable for Franklin. In time "a serious courtship on my part ensued, the girl being in herself very deserving." Franklin by now counted many of the town's elite as friends or acquaintances, but a craftsman who spent his days covered with the grime of a printshop did not think to look among their kind for a wife. However, if he must marry a tradesman's daughter, he would drive a hard bargain. The dowry of his wife-to-be must be enough to pay off his debts. The parents of the girl Mrs. Godfrey had brought forth said they had no such sum. "I said they might mortgage their house in the Loan Office." They refused, hoping, Franklin thought, he and the girl would "steal a marriage, which would leave them at liberty to give or withhold as they pleased." Franklin ended the courtship, he and the Godfreys quarreled, and they moved away, leaving him the entire second floor to rattle around in.

Even among tradesmen's daughters Franklin could hardly be thought much of a catch. Though vigorous and healthy and a pleasant companion, no one called him handsome. The printing business was "generally thought to be a poor one." Then there was his illegitimate son William. He made no effort to hide his parenthood. "'Tis generally known here his birth is illegitimate and his mother not in good circumstances," a friend said of William some years later, but the report that his mother begs "bread in the streets of this city is without the least foundation in truth. I understand some small provision is made by [Franklin] for her, but her being none of the most agreeable women prevents particular notice being shown, or the father and son acknowledging any connection with her."

It was six months to a year after William's birth that Franklin took Deborah Read as his wife. No mention arose this time of a dowry to pay his debts, though his bride came to him as the daughter of a prosperous carpenter who owned two houses in the center of town. He had to be satisfied with someone willing to accept and rear William. Deborah was not handsome. Franklin later compared her to a large toby jar he had seen in England—"a fat, jolly dame, clean and tidy, with a neat blue and white calico gown on, good-natured and lovely." She was warmhearted and loved to talk. When Franklin's cousin and her husband moved to Phila-

delphia, Deborah clucked around them, "calling in as she passes by" and
entertaining Franklin "a deal when she comes home with what cousin
Sally does and what cousin Sally says and what a good contriver she is
and the like." She was a devout Anglican and somewhat prudish, judging
such things as theatergoing wrong. Visitors who caught her unawares
she would not see if "I was not fit to be seen." Her phonetically spelled
letters reveal a limited education: "I have to tell you sum thing of my
self, what I believe you wold not beleve of me oney I tell you my seleve.
I have bin to a play with Sister." But she moved easily among the elite
of Philadelphia; one of her close friends was Deborah Norris, daughter
of the patriarch Isaac Norris, I. She was a bright, lively companion and
Franklin's friends became hers. She was a marvelous cook, and once
when friends came to tea she shyly admitted, "We had the best buckwheat cakes that ever I made. They said I outdone my own outdoings."
Her occasionally sharp tongue led some to call her a scold; this did not
perturb Franklin. "Women of that character have generally sound and
healthy constitutions," he said, "produce a vigorous offspring, are active
in the business of the family, special good housewives, and very careful
of their husband's interest. As to the noise attending all this, 'tis but a
trifle when a man is used to it, and observes that 'tis only a mere habit,
an exercise, in which all is well meant, and ought to be well taken."

Franklin noted in a memorandum book that "D. Read came into the
house 23 September 1730," but the couple called September 1 their wedding day. No ceremony marked the occasion. Uncertainty whether
Deborah's first husband was dead forced them into a common-law marriage in order to avoid the charge of bigamy. Franklin began to prosper
the day she settled into his apartment above the printshop. He trusted her
judgment in all matters, for she "always knew what I did not know, and
if something escaped me, I was sure that it was precisely that which she
had seized." Publicly he pretended to be a frugal man but admitted to
friends in old age that "frugality is an enriching virtue, but a virtue I
never could acquire in myself; but I was once lucky enough to find it in
a wife, who thereby became a fortune to me." A final virtue goes unmentioned—Deborah adored her husband. Her love shines through all the
long, chatty, and wildly misspelled letters she sent by every ship when
he lived abroad during all but two of the last seventeen years of their
marriage. Long after passion might have cooled into affection she remarked how it pleased her to "read over and over again" what "I call
. . . a *husband's love letter.*"

Franklin pretended to be a husband pushed around by his wife—"my
dame being from home, and I quite master of the house," he once said,

inviting a friend to tea—but he ran his home with a tight rein. "Oh, my child," his wife wrote once when he was away, "there is great odds between a man's being at home and abroad, as everybody is afraid they shall do wrong, so everything is left undone." He could be brutally direct when she failed to toe the mark:

> That you may not be offended with your neighbors without cause [he wrote from England], I must acquaint you with what it seems you did not know, that I had limited them in their payments to you, to the sum of thirty pounds per month for the sake of our more easily settling, and to prevent mistakes. This making 360 pounds a year, I thought, as you have no house rent to pay yourself, and receive the rents of 7 or 8 houses besides, might be sufficient for the maintenance of your family. I judged such a limitation the more necessary, because you never have sent me any account of your expenses, and think yourself ill-used if I desire it; and because I know you were not very attentive to money-matters in your best days, and I apprehend that your memory is too much impaired for the management of unlimited sums, without danger of injuring the future fortune of your daughter and grandson. If out of more than £500 a year, you could have saved enough to buy those bills it might have been well to continue purchasing them. But I do not like your going about among my friends to borrow money for that purpose, especially as it is not at all necessary. And therefore I once more request that you would decline buying them for the future. And I hope you will no longer take it amiss to Messrs. Foxcrofts that they did not supply you. If what you receive is really insufficient for your support satisfy me by accounts that it is so, and I shall order more.

Another failing, not of her making, marred their marriage—she had difficulty bearing children. A large congenial family similar to the one he had been reared in would have delighted Franklin, but his wife was able to give him only two children—a son, Francis Folger, born in 1732, and a daughter, Sarah, born in 1743. The son died when four years old. Her inability to give Franklin a legitimate heir while constantly confronted by his illegitimate one led her in time to hate William. "Mr. Fisher, there goes the greatest villain upon earth," she remarked years later to an acquaintance as William passed through the house, then went on to denounce him "in the foulest terms I ever heard from a gentlewoman."

4

In 1730 Keimer sold out to David Harry, a journeyman in his shop, and left for Barbados. Franklin, "apprehensive of a powerful rival," offered Harry a partnership, which was rejected with scorn. A year later Franklin had accumulated enough money and self-confidence to expand in a bold way. He purchased—possibly from Harry, who soon followed Keimer to Barbados—a printing press and four hundred pounds of type and formed a silent partnership with his own journeyman, Thomas Whitmarsh, whom he sent to Charleston, South Carolina, to open a printshop and a newspaper there. Franklin would pay one-third of Whitmarsh's operating expenses and receive for his gamble one-third of the profits. At the age of twenty-five, with the nerve to match large dreams, he had begun to build what would soon become a network of printshops scattered through British America. The terms of these partnerships were embodied in contracts as precise as any drawn by a lawyer but written in Franklin's clear English. The partnerships "were all carried on and ended amicably, owing, I think, a good deal to the precaution of having very explicitly settled in our articles everything to be done by or expected from each partner, so that there was nothing to dispute. . . ."

Franklin later attributed his success to industry and frugality. There were other elements. He prospered in business to an extent because he enjoyed it, much as he relished a game of chess. Franklin regarded business as another form of chess, "a game played according to settled and known rules, wherein one could excel through application and skill," Paul Conner has remarked. The analogy between chess and business and the conduct of one's life led Franklin in time to write an essay on

The Morals of Chess

The game of chess is not merely an idle amusement. Several very capable qualities of the mind, useful in the course of human life, are to be acquired or strengthened by it, so as to become habits, ready on all occasions. For life is a kind of chess, in which we have often points to gain, and competitors or adversaries to contend with, and in which there is a vast variety of good and ill events, that are, in some degree, the effects of prudence or the want of it. By playing chess, then, we may learn:

1. *Foresight,* which looks a little into futurity, and considers the consequences that may attend an action; for it is continually occurring to the player, "if I move this piece, what will be the advantages of my new situation? What use can my adversary make of it to annoy me? What other moves can I make to support it, and to defend myself from his attacks?"

2. *Circumspection,* which surveys the whole chessboard, or scene of action, the relations of the several pieces and situations, the dangers they are respectively exposed to, the several possibilities of their aiding each other; the probabilities that the adversary may make this or that move, and attack this or the other piece; and what different means can be used to avoid his stroke, or turn its consequences against his.

3. *Caution,* not to make our moves too hastily. This habit is best acquired by observing strictly the laws of the game, such as, *If you touch a piece, you must move it somewhere; if you set it down, you must let it stand.* And it is therefore best that these rules should be observed, as the game thereby becomes more the image of human life, and particularly of war; in which, if you have incautiously put yourself into a bad and dangerous position, you cannot obtain your enemy's leave to withdraw your troops, and place them more securely; but you must abide all the consequences of your rashness.

And, lastly, we learn by chess the habit of *not being discouraged* by *present* bad appearances in the state of our affairs, the habit of *hoping for a favorable change,* and that of *preserving in the search of resources.* The game is so full of events, there is such a variety of turns in it, the fortune of it is so subject to sudden vicissitudes, and one so frequently, after long contemplation, discovers the means of extricating one's self from a supposed insurmountable difficulty, that one is encouraged to continue the contest to the last, in hopes of victory by our own skill, or, at least, of giving a *stalemate,* by the negligence of our adversary. And whoever considers, what in chess he often sees instances of, that particular pieces of success are apt to produce *presumption,* and its consequent inattention, by which more is afterwards lost than was gained by the preceding advantage; while misfortunes produce more care and attention, by which the loss may be recovered, will learn not to be too much discouraged by the present success of his adversary, nor to despair of final good fortune, upon every little check he receives in the pursuit of it.

Franklin gave no quarter to business opponents but none accused him of underhanded play. He took calculated risks. He attended to details.

When sent the wrong font of type and overcharged for it, he called the supplier's imposition "too much to bear, and therefore I do insist on his doing me justice, and refunding the additional sixpences; or he will forfeit the character he always bore with me, that of an honest man. I enclose you a piece of the newspaper for your satisfaction. Compare it with his specimen, and you will find what I say precisely true. The sum to be returned is £11 15s 6d for which when received please to give my account credit."

Franklin did not exaggerate the correspondence between chess and business, another reason why he prospered. In chess one did not have to exude sweetness, but a businessman, especially a printer "continually employed in serving all parties," must practice the art of pleasing. Franklin disciplined himself not to display his "fine parts"—"He's a fool that cannot conceal his wisdom," Poor Richard would say—or to speak "of ourselves and our own affairs." The ways for a businessman to please were clear: "Let his air, his manner, and behavior, be easy, courteous and affable, void of everything haughty or assuming; his words few, expressed with modesty, and a respect for those he talks to. Be he ever ready to hear what others say; let him interrupt nobody, nor intrude with his advice unasked."

Deborah Franklin made a large contribution to her husband's success. "She assisted me cheerfully in my business, folding and stitching pamphlets, tending shop, purchasing old linen rags for the paper makers, etc., etc." Under her shrewd attention the stationery shop expanded into a small general store that sold whatever came to hand—"good Rhode Island cheese and codfish . . . good live geese feathers . . . very good sealing wax . . . a likely Negro woman to be sold . . . James Austin's Persian ink . . . very good LAMPBLACK . . . very good chocolate . . . very good coffee . . . good writing parchment . . . choice English quills." From John Franklin in Newport came a shipment of "crown soap," a remarkable family product that cleansed delicate cloths that "suffer from long and hard rubbing," washed colored fabrics "apt to change by the use of common *soap,*" and gave men "by the sweetness of the flavor and the fine lather" a pleasurably smooth shave. Franklin used the shop to turn even adversity into profit. When his mother-in-law moved in, the *Gazette* announced that Widow Read "continues to make and sell her well-known ointment for the ITCH, with which she has cured abundance of people in and about the city for many years past."

Luck, too, had a part in his success. Bradford, "rich and easy," paid little attention to his affairs; Harry "dressed like a gentleman, lived expensively, took much diversion and pleasure abroad, ran in debt, and neglected his business, upon which all business left him." Cultivated friendships also paid off. Speaker Hamilton's influence brought the lucrative printing of an issue of paper money, previously done by Bradford, to Franklin in 1731. The same year the local lodge of the Masons welcomed him as a member. This close-knit fraternal group operated on the principle of "all for one, one for all." Members went out of their way to help one another. Possibly Franklin obtained from a fellow lodge member the loan needed to set Whitmarsh, also a Mason, up in business.

Franklin hid his burgeoning prosperity in public. "We kept no idle servants, our table was plain and simple, our furniture of the cheapest." He dressed modestly, lived frugally, still pushed a wheelbarrow through town to pick up paper or deliver a job. Profits went back into the business. He kept alert for any new opportunity to make money. In 1732, the year after he dispatched Whitmarsh to South Carolina, he hired a journeyman named Louis Timothee, a native of Holland who spoke and wrote French and German. Franklin now saw a chance to tap the potentially lucrative German-speaking population of Pennsylvania, which numbered something like a third of the colony's inhabitants. They lacked a newspaper, and in June 1732 Franklin announced the first issue of the *Philadelphische Zeitung* under Timothee's editorship. It would be published once a fortnight on Saturday, market day, when German farmers flooded the town. Franklin estimated he needed three hundred subscribers to break even. After two issues he had come nowhere near that goal; he dropped the experiment at once. The failure did not weaken his nerve. He immediately began work on another project, and in December the New Printing-Office announced: "JUST PUBLISHED FOR 1733: POOR RICHARD: AN ALMANACK."

5

Most colonial homes held little in the way of reading matter except the Bible and an almanac. One almanac differed little from another. Each carried a calendar with information about the phases of the moon, the conjunction of planets, when the sun rose and set—all interlaced with weather predictions and such useful facts as the reigns of the kings of England, the days when court met, distances between towns. All printers either sold, or, if they could latch onto a "philomath" (mathematician-astrologer) to compile the technical material, published almanacs. They were a profitable sideline. Bradford put out four and Keimer one when Franklin and Meredith opened their shop. Franklin enticed his tenant Godfrey to construct the *Pennsylvania Almanack* for him in 1730, and the next year added a second almanac put together by John Jerman. Godfrey and Jerman soon quarreled with Franklin, leaving him on short notice with no almanac for 1733. *Poor Richard's Almanack* came out late, only three days before the new year began.

Once again Franklin owed an unacknowledged debt to his brother James, who for several years had published the *Rhode-Island Almanack*, compiled by "Poor Robin." Other almanac makers took their work seriously and confined themselves to facts and figures. James Franklin broke with tradition and blended into his monthly calendars poetry, proverbs, aphorisms, and jests. The weather predictions were lighthearted. "It would have rained the 15th day [of September], but I had not room to write it." For November, " 'Tis cold, 'tis cloudy. Rain or hail,/ One of the four I hope won't fail." Franklin, with a touch of timidity in the first edition, followed the trail blazed by his brother. The weather predictions were cautious—"snow if not too warm" in early January, "windy and cloudy" for March, "more clear and pleasant weather comes in" mid-May. The aphorisms varied from the pedestrian ("Nothing more like a fool than a drunken man") to the genteelly earthy ("After three days men grow weary, of a wench, a guest, and weather") to the metaphorical ("He that lies down with dogs, shall rise up with fleas"). They appealed to common prejudices against professional men. "He's a fool that makes his doctor his heir," went one. Two beggars who claimed an oyster found along the road went to court. The judge's decision: *"A shell for him, a shell for thee,/ The middle is the lawyer's fee."*

The character of Richard Saunders distinguished Franklin's almanac. It took only a few lines of the preface to reveal him as a man like all men —much put upon. Others might offer their almanacs for the public's good; not he. "The plain truth of the matter is, I am excessive poor, and my wife, good woman, is, I tell her, excessive proud; she cannot bear, she says, to sit spinning in her shift of tow, while I do nothing but gaze at the stars; and has threatened more than once to burn all my books and rattling-traps (as she calls my instruments) if I do not make some profitable use of them for the good of my family. The printer has offered me some considerable share of the profits, and I have thus begun to comply with my dame's desire." Readers who doubted Saunders's authenticity were reassured on the last page by a note appended to a list of the principal kings of Europe: *"Poor Richard*, an American prince, without subjects, his wife being viceroy over him," born 23 October 1684, aged forty-nine years.

Poor Richard had doleful news for his readers in the opening page. Titan Leeds, a competing maker of almanacs published by Bradford, "must soon be taken from us," he said. "He dies, by my calculation made at his request, on 17 October 1733, 3 ho. 29 m. *P.M.* . . . . By his own calculation he will survive till the 26th of the same month. This small difference between us we have disputed whenever we have met these nine years past; but at length he is inclinable to agree with my judgment. Which of us is most exact, a little time will now determine." (Leeds, a man of little wit, foolishly snapped at the hook Poor Richard dangled. The next year he berated Saunders as a shoddy philomath. Richard announced Leeds indeed must be dead; his departed friend would never write a preface "in which I am treated in a very gross and unhandsome manner; in which I am called a *false predicter, an ignorant, a conceited scribbler, a fool, and a liar.*" When Leeds persisted in succeeding almanacs that he still lived, Poor Richard waved away the claim, for " 'tis plain to everyone that reads his last two almanacs . . . that they are not written with that *life* his performances used to be written with; the wit is low and flat; the little hints dull and spiritless. . . .")

Poor Richard's own wit and wisdom improved in later editions and soon the almanac was selling ten thousand copies annually and had become the most profitable item printed in Franklin's shop. Part of Poor Richard's appeal lay in his earthy bluntness: "Forewarned, forearmed, unless in the case of cuckolds, who are often forearmed before warned." Asked if predicting the weather was difficult, he remarked, "Alas! 'tis as easy as pissing abed." He disparaged dreamers curtly—"He that lives upon hope, dies farting." And of those who misused power he said: "Force shits upon reason's back."

Poor Richard may have been only another of his fictional creations, but Franklin believed in him. Forty years after the first almanac he told his daughter, soon to take charge of a household: "Study Poor Richard a little, and you may find some benefit from his instructions."

6

Franklin had made it by 1733, less than four years after the New Printing-Office had opened. Though not rich, he was well off. He set out to visit Boston with money again to clink in his pockets. He left in August and spent seven weeks seeing family and friends. On the return trip he stopped over in Newport to see John and James Franklin. The lines of communication with James had been reopened in the summer of 1732 when Franklin, posing as "Anthony Afterwit," published a piece in the *Gazette* about an aggrandizing wife. Anthony could have been either the husband or brother of Abigail Afterwit, the character created by James Franklin a decade earlier in the *Courant*. James reprinted his brother's piece in the *Rhode-Island Gazette*, where Patience Teacraft answered it; her reply soon found space in the *Pennsylvania Gazette*.

"Our former differences were forgotten, and our meeting was very cordial and affectionate," Franklin said after the visit with James. "He was fast declining in health, and requested of me that in case of his death which he apprehended not far distant [it came less than two years later] I would take home his son, then but ten years of age, and bring him up to the printing business. This I accordingly performed, sending him a few years to school before I took him into the office. His mother carried on the business till he was grown up, when I assisted him with an assortment of new types, those of his father being in a manner worn out. Thus it was that I made my brother ample amends for the service I had deprived him of by leaving him so early."

CHAPTER

5

"IMPROVING THE TASTE OF THE TOWN"

FRANKLIN ROSE AROUND FIVE each morning. The day began with exercise —a swim in the Delaware, a stint with dumbbells, or, in old age, an "air bath" in the nude. He shaved himself for the pleasure it gave and to avoid "the dirty fingers or bad breath of a slovenly barber." Each day he dressed in clean linen. A fastidious man who grew more so with age, he spoke up when customers in the shop spit on the hot stove, calling it a "filthy, unmannerly custom; for the slimy matter of spittle drying on, burns and fumes when the stove is hot," and it "smells most nauseously." He deplored sloppy penmanship and taught his children to write a clear "round hand," taking care to "make fair characters, and place them straight and even in the lines." He always used a sharp quill, good ink, and the best paper for his letters. Fastidiousness, too, influenced his literary style. The vernacularisms of Silence Dogood and the earthy remarks of Poor Richard vanished as he grew older. "*Spell* is a vulgar English word, therefore improper," he told a foreign friend. "It should have been after a warm *season*." When reprimanded for using an Americanism like "colonize," he promised to reform. "The *unshakeable*, too, tho' clear, I give up as rather low," he added. "The introducing new words where we are already possessed of old ones sufficiently expressive, I confess must be generally wrong, as it tends to change the language." It irritated him to see old words made to do new things. "NOTICE has been turned into a verb," he once complained. "ADVOCATE has had the same happen to it. And so, too, PROGRESS."

Once prepared for the day he addressed a prayer to the Powerful Goodness. He read for a while—"I rise in the morning and read for an hour or two perhaps, and then reading grows tiresome"—then break-fasted. He was too restless—"I have not the propensity to sitting still"—to be a contemplative man, and too gregarious. "Man is a sociable being, and it is for aught I know one of the worst of punishments to be excluded from society," he said. He went downstairs to the shop at eight and worked there until noon. Part of the two-hour break for lunch he worked on his accounts, part he gave over to reading; he still hoped to repair "in some degree the loss of the learned education my father once intended for me." He returned to the shop at two and stayed until six. After a light supper, he spent the evening visiting friends, playing chess, sometimes playing the violin. He especially enjoyed music.

His two sons, William and Francis, occupied a large part in his life. He justified indulging their whims by saying that it gave their countenances "a pleasant air" that would last through their lives. He glowed when "in the bosom of my family" surrounded by "little prattlers," and one of the greatest blows in his life came when Francis Folger Franklin died. To still gossip about the child's death, he published an open letter in the *Gazette* on 30 December 1736:

> Understanding 'tis a current report, that my son Francis, who died lately of the smallpox, had it by inoculation; and being desired to satisfy the public in that particular; inasmuch as some people are, by that report (joined with others of the like kind, and perhaps equally groundless) deterred from having that operation performed on their children, I do hereby sincerely declare, that he was not inoculated, but received the distemper in the common way of infection. And I suppose the report could only arise from its being my known opinion, that inoculation was a safe and beneficial practice; and from my having said among my acquaintance, that I intended to have my child inoculated, as soon as he should have recovered sufficient strength from a flux with which he had been long afflicted.
>
> B. FRANKLIN

He engraved on the child's tombstone, "The DELIGHT of all that knew him," and nearly a half century later still mourned for "my son Franky . . . whom I have seldom since seen equalled in everything, and whom to this day I cannot think of without a sigh."

Sunday mornings Franklin had to himself. Deborah attended the Anglican service at Christ Church, taking the children with her, and whatever apprentices then lived in were pushed off to their denomination's service. The apprentices inevitably tried to "evade going to meeting," said Franklin, the surrogate father. "I have brought up four or five myself, and have frequently observed, that if their shoes were bad, they would say nothing of a new pair till Sunday morning, just as the bell rung, when, if you asked them why they did not get ready, the answer was prepared, 'I have no shoes,' and so of other things, hats and the like; or if they knew of anything that wanted mending, it was a secret till Sunday morning, and sometimes I believe they would rather tear a little, than be without the excuse."

His social life was limited these days. He regularly attended the Masonic lodge meetings and the Friday evening gatherings of the Junto, but "spent no time in taverns, games, or frolics of any kind." He guarded his reputation with care but occasionally came close to losing it. One morning two fellow Masons entertained him and some friends with a tale of how they had pretended to induct an apprentice into the lodge. They said they planned "further diversions," and from one of them the boy later died. The *Gazette* reported the incident:

> We hear that on Monday night last, some people pretending to be Free Masons, got together in a cellar with a young man who was desirous of being made one, and in the ceremony, 'tis said, they threw some burning spirits upon him either accidentally or to terrify him, which burnt him so that he was obliged to take his bed, and died this morning. The coroners inquest are now sitting on the body.

Some accused Franklin of doing nothing to halt the hoax, indeed, of encouraging it by passing among his friends the blasphemous oath the boy had been forced to read. The accusations grew so sharp that he collected affidavits saying he "did neither approve of what had been *already* done . . . nor desire to be present at what was proposed to be *farther* done" to the boy. Gossip continued. Franklin took to print to defend himself. " 'Tis true I laughed (and perhaps heartily, as my manner is), at the *beginning* of their relation," he confessed, "but when they came to those circumstances of their giving him a violent purge, leading him to kiss T's posteriors, and administrating to him the diabolical oath which R—N read to us, I grew indeed serious, as I suppose the most merry man (not inclined to mischief) would on such an occasion." The defense had a hollow sound, for Franklin had read the oath aloud to all who wanted to hear it—"so many people flocked to my house for a sight of it, that it grew troublesome"—and he had done nothing to warn either the boy or his father of what lay in store. Nonetheless, the public seemed satisfied and the incident was soon forgotten.

2

The year 1733 marked the tenth since Franklin arrived in Philadelphia. Its population now equaled Boston's—around twelve thousand—but it remained a country town. "I assure you," a citizen complained, "that the merest trifle in the world will be made a town talk. Everything proper or improper, of a public or a private nature, is constantly bandied about in the two coffee houses." In 1730, 533 ships entered and 629 cleared the port of Boston, an enormous traffic compared to the some 165 vessels in and out of Philadelphia that year. The town still lacked a good bookseller. Citizens choked in dust as they walked along the unpaved streets, bridges crumbled in disrepair, thieves found it easy to slide past the ineffectual night watch. The moribund self-perpetuating council that governed the town showed little interest in making it a more amenable place to live. Here where few "have the advantage of good books, for want of which good conversation is still more scarce," said Franklin, there was much to be done about "improving the taste of the town."

He tried first through the *Gazette.* He closed its pages to "all libelling and personal abuse." He chose from London journals essays that pointed a sound moral and frequently printed similar pieces of his own that praised virtue and condemned vice. He even found a way to end a statement on literary style with an uplifting note: "I shall venture to lay it down as a maxim *that no piece can properly be called good, and well written, which is void of any tendency to benefit the reader, either by improving his virtue or his knowledge.* " The town's semiannual fairs called for a wrathful statement: They "corrupt the morals, and destroy the innocence of our youth; who are at such times induced to drinking and gaming, in mixed companies of vicious servants and Negroes."

The Masonic lodge resembled on a grander scale the club Franklin had created—secret, sociable, and devoted to members' "particular interests in business"—and after joining it he remodeled the Junto into a vehicle that launched "my first project of a public nature." Earlier he had suggested members might contribute books to form a library for the club. Though the offerings were fewer than expected, they filled one end of the room in the small building Robert Grace had given the group. The books were used but not always thoughtfully, and "for want of due care of them, the collection after about a year was separated and each took his books home again." Franklin rarely gave up because an experiment failed once; he tried it again from another approach. In the summer of 1731, the year he joined the Masons, he drew up plans for a subscription library. It would be called the Library Company and would open its doors one day a week for members to borrow books. "So few were the readers at that time in Philadelphia," Franklin recalled, "and the majority of us so poor, that I was not able with great industry to find more than fifty persons, mostly young tradesmen, willing to pay down for this purpose forty shillings each, and ten shillings per annum." But fifty proved enough, and in March 1732 the Library Company, with a capital of one hundred pounds, ordered from London forty-five books James Logan recommended it begin the collection with. (Logan probably also recommended Peter Collinson, a Quaker merchant, as its London agent.) By the end of the year "the mother of all the North American subscription libraries" had opened its doors. Two years later it had accumulated over two hundred and fifty books and twenty-five periodicals. In 1741 it had nearly four hundred volumes and over seventy members. But as it grew it ceased to be a library for working men. New members had to pay the substantial sum of nine pounds to join. The library had become the preserve of the city's elite, to which Franklin by then belonged.

The success of the Library Company led Franklin to turn his thoughts "a little to public affairs." He chose the right phrase, "a little," because business still absorbed most of his time, and three years passed before his next venture. Citizens who wanted to avoid their turn walking the night watch paid six shillings to the constables, who pocketed the money and for a drink or two in the taverns picked up substitutes; the substitutes more often than not continued to tipple through the night while supposedly walking their rounds. Franklin objected to "these irregularities" in a paper read to the Junto in 1735. He did not object to the tax for substitutes, no doubt having taking advantage of it himself, but he wanted it to be "proportioned to property" and used to hire "proper men to serve constantly in that business." He lobbied hard for the reform, but saw it acted on only after he entered the Assembly seventeen years later.

He had better luck with a call for volunteer fire companies, also put forth in 1735 in a paper read to the Junto. After passing remarks on the prevention of fires—don't carry hot coals about the house in an open shovel, prohibit "the detestable practice of putting wooden moldings on each side the fireplace," clean chimneys "frequently and more carefully," and fine chimney sweeps "if any chimney fires and flames out fifteen days after sweeping"—he focuses on the fighting of fires, in which Philadelphia wanted "order and method." He urges the town to form neighborhood clubs of fire fighters similar to those begun in Boston when he was a boy. Members would be trained for specific assignments: at the scene of a blaze "firewards" would "direct the opening and stripping of roofs by the axemen, the pulling down burning timbers by the hookmen, and the playing of the engines, and command the making of lanes, etc." The *Gazette* ran the essay. "A useful piece," friends said, but it took nearly two years to organize the first neighborhood club, the Union Fire Company. Another half year passed while the twenty members worked out a set of articles—as in his business ventures and "to leave nothing to dispute," Franklin insisted on such articles in civic projects—that satisfied all. They "obliged every member to keep always in good order and fit for use, a certain number of leather buckets, with strong bags and baskets (for packing and transporting goods) which were to be brought to every fire; and we agreed to meet once a month and spend a social evening together, in discoursing and communicating such ideas as occurred to us upon the subject of fires as might be useful in our conduct on such occasions." A half century later when virtually every able-bodied male property owner in the city belonged to a neighborhood fire company, Franklin doubted "whether there is a city in the world better provided with the means of putting a stop to beginning conflagrations; and in fact since those institutions, the city has never lost by fire more than one or two houses at a time, and the flames have often been extinguished before the house in which they began has been half consumed."

3

The year he spoke up for fire companies and a reformed night watch also saw Franklin enmeshed in his first public battle, one it took courage to fight and in which, win or lose, he risked much. His brother James would have been proud, for Benjamin refought on new ground what James had attacked earlier in Boston—an entrenched clergy determined to control the taste of the town. It was coincidental that James Franklin died in February 1735 as his brother launched into the Hemphill Affair.

Franklin made so much of the art of pleasing that few noticed the limits he imposed upon it. He never ceased to be his own man, particularly in matters of religion. At a time when Philadelphia demanded that a young man on the make attend church regularly, he spent Sundays at home. Yet he was devout, much more than he let the world know. In old age he confessed "with some emotion" that "he never passed a church, during public service, without regretting that he could not join in it honestly and cordially." This religious passion, for it can be called only that, so unsuitable in the Age of Reason, he kept veiled from the world, exposing it only occasionally, as during the Hemphill Affair.

After returning from England Franklin made an effort to come to terms with his Puritan upbringing. The Old Testament God his father worshiped in the Congregational Church, a revengeful, harsh God who predestined every man to a "calling," did not appeal to him. He replaced Him with a Benevolent Being. But he kept the rest of his Puritan heritage, if Puritanism is defined as "that firm tradition that required every Christian to venture into this world as a pilgrim, doing right for the glory of God."

Only a virtuous man could glorify God, and that set Franklin on a new quest—determining the qualities of a virtuous man. He explored the problem through the early 1730s and concluded that virtue and self-interest coincided. A man who practiced the virtues of temperance, sincerity, and resolution benefited himself and the world and surely pleased God. Franklin then constructed his famous list of virtues, twelve in number until a friend said "I was generally thought proud" and he added humility at the bottom. Each week he cultivated a single virtue, like a gardener who "works on one of the beds at a time," marking his failures with black dots on a chart. After thirteen weeks he wiped away the black dots and repeated the course. What appears as obeisance to a string of "petty commandments" seemed otherwise to Franklin. "All his experience," it has been remarked, "indicated that whether or not virtue and interest do coincide no other argument but that of self-interest will persuade men to act virtuously, and even that argument will not always persuade them."

In the midst of the course in virtue, the Reverend Mr. Samuel Hemphill, young, lively, and fresh from Ireland, came to town to assist the aging minister of the local Presbyterian meeting. Franklin, who saw little difference between Presbyterians and the Congregationalists he had been reared among, had earlier attended the meeting, but bored by the minister's "explications of the peculiar doctrines of our sect" and by sermons that aimed "rather to make us Presbyterians than good citizens," abandoned it for private devotions. When he heard that the new assistant minister brought life to the service, he returned, encouraged by the rumor Hemphill was "a vile heretic, a preacher of morality rather than dogma."

In April 1735 the synod charged Hemphill with preaching heretical doctrines. Franklin with unwonted warmth defended him in the *Gazette*. Traditionalists objected that Hemphill emphasized the duties of morality and touched too lightly on the importance of faith. "But surely *morality* can do us no harm," said Franklin. "Upon a supposition that we all have faith in Christ already, as I think we have, where can be the damage of being exhorted to good works? Is virtue heresy; and universal benevolence false doctrine, that any of us should keep away from meeting because it is preached there?" Hemphill played loosely with the Westminster Confession of Faith, concocted in Cromwell's time. Since we deny the infallibility of the pope, must we invest infallibility in a century-old doctrine? asked Franklin. Let us tolerate differences, "since 'tis an uncertainty till we get to heaven what true orthodoxy in all points is."

Though Franklin expected Hemphill would be found innocent, the church judged his preaching "unsound and dangerous." Franklin retorted with *Observations on the Proceedings Against Mr. Hemphill*, a line by line review of the trial containing harsh remarks on the clerical judges' "unChristian procedures," their "malice and envy." He dismissed the accusations against Hemphill as "trifling" and "groundless." The pamphlet had been delayed because the printer's sudden illness "unexpectedly continuing six or seven weeks has thus long retarded its publication." (Illness when under tension would mark Franklin's life.) Once recovered, his mind cleared of doubts, he attacked the clergy as had no one since James Franklin. In September he assailed "their pretending to be the directors of men's consciences." He said: "Nothing, in all probability, can prevent our being a very flourishing and happy people, but our suffering the clergy to get upon our backs, and ride us, as they do their horses, where they please." He also said:

> The generality of the clergy were always too fond of power to quit their pretensions to it, by anything that was ever yet said by particular persons; but, my brethren, how soon should WE humble their pride, did we all heartily and unanimously join in asserting our own natural rights and liberties in opposition to their unrighteous claims.

By now the battle had been lost. Someone discovered Hemphill had plagiarized his sermons. Franklin refused to abandon the field. In October he published *A Defense of Mr. Hemphill's Observations*, a vehement, passionate pamphlet resembling nothing he wrote until nearly thirty years later when censuring a massacre of innocent Indians. Even James Franklin would have winced at the vicious assault on the clergy, men filled "with malice, rancor, and prejudice in their hearts," stupid men, who reason by such syllogisms as:

> Asses are grave and dull animals,
> Our authors are grave and dull animals; therefore
> Our authors are grave, dull, *or if you will*, Rev. Asses.

These "Rev. Asses" manage evidence "by a *hocus pocus* slight of hand," they tell "a story of a cock and a bull." In a raging peroration they come forth as men willing "to stamp an appearance of sanctity upon animosity, false zeal, injustice, fraud, oppression, by their own open example as well as precept."

The outburst made little impression. With the revelation that Hemphill had stolen his sermons, the cause lost supporters. "On our defeat he left us, in search elsewhere of better fortune, and I quitted the congregation, never joining it after, tho' I continued many years my subscription for the support of its ministers."

4

Nothing can completely explain Franklin's rage—no other word will do—against the clergy in 1735. It owed something to James Franklin's similar rage in Boston, something to Benjamin's ecumenical approach to God, something to his distaste for dogmatism, something to his youth. He directed it, it should be noted, mainly against the Presbyterian clergy; Presbyterians again would be the target for his wrath in 1764, surely no coincidence. Regardless of why he felt the need to put his reputation on the line in the Hemphill Affair, his disgust with the clergy had abated by the time Philadelphia welcomed George Whitefield, a gentleman who would do more in a short time to improve the taste of the town than Franklin had in several years.

On 8 November 1739 the *Gazette* announced Whitefield's presence. He came wearing a "gown and wig white with powder and bushy," an ordained priest in the Church of England but allied to the Methodist wing of the church led by John Wesley. He had chosen Philadelphia as the first stop on a tour through the colonies to raise money for an orphanage in Georgia. Word of his eloquence swept through town and soon the churches could no longer hold his audiences. "On Thursday last," the *Gazette* reported, "the Rev. Mr. Whitefield began to preach from the Court House gallery in this city, about six at night, to near 6,000 people before him in the street, who stood in an awful silence to hear him; and this continued every night, 'till Sunday." After the Sunday farewell sermon, Whitefield left to preach his way across New Jersey and into New York, and America's first great religious revival, the Great Awakening, was under way.

The performance astonished Franklin. "The multitudes of all sects and denominations that attended his sermons were enormous, and it was matter of speculation to me who was one of the number, to observe the extraordinary influence of his oratory on his hearers, and how much they admired and respected him, notwithstanding his common abuse of them, by assuring them they were naturally *half beasts and half devils.*" But Franklin was not so overwhelmed to miss a chance to profit from the phenomenon. He made a point of meeting Whitefield and, as announced in the *Gazette,* got from him "copies of his journals and sermons, with leave to print the same; I propose to publish them with all expedition, if I find sufficient encouragement." Within the week he acquired two hundred subscribers. In the next two years Franklin printed eight volumes of Whitefield's journals and nine of his sermons and miscellaneous writings.

Whitefield returned to Philadelphia three times in 1740. By now most of the pulpits in town were barred to him. His eloquence aroused jealousy—as had Hemphill's—but his ecumenical appeal especially distressed sectarian clergyman as it attracted Franklin. In one sermon Whitefield asked Father Abraham how many Presbyterians lived in heaven. "None," came the answer. How many Quakers were there? "None!" How many Baptists? "None!" Who then lived in heaven? "Only good Christians," said Father Abraham. This appealing doctrine inspired the immense audiences. "The alteration in the face of religion here is altogether surprising," the *Gazette* reported in June, after Whitefield's second visit. "Never did the people show so great a willingness to attend sermons, nor the preachers greater zeal and diligence in performing the duties of their function. Religion is become the subject of most conversations. No books are in request but those of piety and devotion; and instead of songs and ballads, the people are everywhere entertaining themselves with psalms, hymns and spiritual songs. All which, under God, is owing to the successful labors of the Reverend Mr. Whitefield."

Franklin admired the changes wrought—they could do little but make the town a better place to live—but kept his distance from the revival. He had no part in promoting the huge "New Building" erected in 1740 as a hall for Whitefield. He opposed the asylum for orphans in Georgia, arguing it made more sense to build it in Philadelphia, where materials and workmen were handy and more than enough orphans to fill it. The resolute Whitefield "rejected my counsel, and I thereupon refused to contribute." (Once, though, he came carelessly to a sermon with a pocket full of money and, seduced by the oratory, "I emptied my pocket wholly into the collector's dish, gold and all.") Whitefield's technical skill fascinated Franklin—"every accent, every emphasis, every modulation of voice, was so perfectly well turned and well placed, that without being interested in the subject, one could not help being pleased with the discourse, a pleasure of much the same kind with that received from an excellent piece of music"—and that fascination helped to draw the two men into friendship. Franklin did not dissemble with Whitefield, making it clear he could not subscribe to much that traveled under the banner of Christianity. Having a lost soul for a friend only inspired Whitefield and gave further reason for keeping in touch. Shortly after leaving Philadelphia in November 1740 to continue the good work elsewhere, he sent back a brief note to Franklin: "Dear sir, adieu, I do not despair of your seeing the reasonableness of Christianity. Apply to God; be willing to do the divine will, and you shall know it." Franklin never succumbed, and though "a merely civil friendship," it remained "sincere on both sides, and lasted to his death."

5

While Franklin worked to improve the town and its taste, the town returned the favor, handing him two plums within the span of a year—clerkship of the Assembly in October 1736 and the local postmastership in October 1737. He got the job of postmaster by default. Bradford's refusal to turn in delinquent accounts forced his superior to replace him, and Franklin as the only other printer in town—printing offices were as much social centers as places of business—made him the obvious successor. Franklin accepted the post "readily, and found it of great advantage; for tho' the salary was small, it facilitated the correspondence that improved my newspaper, increased the number demanded, as well as the advertisements to be inserted, so that it came to afford me a very considerable income. My old competitor's newspaper declined proportionably, and I was satisfied without retaliating his refusal, while postmaster, to permit my papers being carried by the riders."

Speaker Hamilton arranged for the clerkship. Franklin tolerated the boredom of listening to debates in which he could take no part because "besides the pay for immediate service as clerk, the place gave me a better opportunity of keeping up an interest among the members, which secured to me the business of printing the votes, laws, paper money, and other occasional jobs for the public, that on the whole were very profitable."

Franklin enjoyed making money and while he never abandoned the pursuit, it never obsessed him. He had learned from chess that he who "loves money most shall lose; his anxiety for the success of the game confounds him." Status more than money fascinated him. Shortly before Whitefield came to Philadelphia Franklin revealed pretensions higher than those expected of a printer, pretensions that had nothing to do with improving the taste of the town. He asked his father in Boston if the Franklin family in England bore a coat of arms. "Your Uncle Benjamin made inquiry of one skilled in heraldry, who told him there is two coats of armor, one belonging to the Franklins of the north, and one to the Franklins of the west," Josiah Franklin answered. "However, our circumstances have been such as that it hath hardly been worthwhile to concern ourselves about these things, any farther than to tickle the fancy a little." But Benjamin Franklin did concern himself. He traced down one of the coats of arms, had a silver seal made that contained the heads of two lions, two doves, and a dolphin, and ever after used it on documents and to stamp the wax that closed his letters.

Clearly, Franklin aspired to be a gentleman. In January 1739 he rented the spacious house of Robert Grace, who had gone to Europe. He signed the lease with the high-sounding title of "B. Franklin, typographer." Only a few years ago he had been "clothed from head to foot in woolen and linen of my wife's manufacture." All that had changed now. He dined off china and the pewter tableware had been supplanted by silver, and only partly because his wife "thought *her* husband deserved a silver spoon and china bowl as well as any of his neighbors." Franklin liked to live and, especially, to dress well. Once when his wife and George, the family slave, were going through his clothes, they counted "at least twenty pair of old breeches" in the wardrobe. Early in 1739 a thief stole from the house a "coat lined with silk, four fine homespun shirts, a fine Holland shirt ruffled at the hands and bosom, a pair of black broadcloth breeches new seated and lined with leather, two pair of good worsted stockings, one of a dark color, and the other a lightish blue, a coarse cambric handerchief, marked with an F in red silk, a new pair of calf skin shoes, . . . and sundry other things." Franklin believed with Poor Richard that "wealth is not his that has it, but his that enjoys it."

CHAPTER

6

"LET THE EXPERIMENT
BE MADE"

THE WORDS OF AUGUR seemed written for Franklin and he knew them well:

> There be three things which are too wonderful for me,
> Yea, four which I know not:
> The way of an eagle in the air;
> The way of a serpent upon a rock;
> The way of a ship in the midst of the sea;
> And the way of a man with a maid.

Franklin kept to himself when he learned the way of a man with a maid, and the record is not much clearer when he began to explore other wonderful mysteries of the natural world. The asbestos purse carried to London, and used to meet the president of the Royal Society, hints at an early interest in natural philosophy, as science was then called, and so, too, does the seeking out of Dr. Henry Pemberton, Newton's friend and editor. *A Dissertation on Liberty and Necessity* reveals that Franklin at nineteen had absorbed the Newtonian conception of the universe. "How exact and regular is everything in the *natural* world!" he wrote, with a liberal use of exclamation marks that revealed his youthfulness. "How wisely in every part contrived! We cannot here find the least defect! Those who have studied the mere animal and vegetable creation, demonstrate that nothing can be more harmonious and beautiful!" But the Newtonian picture fascinated him then only for implications the world of men could draw from it, for he continues: "All the heavenly bodies, the stars and planets, are regulated with the utmost wisdom! And can we suppose less care to be taken in the order of the *moral* than in the *natural* system?"

The idea of natural philosophy as an end in itself could have sprung from discussions in the Junto—*Query:* "Whence comes the dew that stands on the outside of a tankard that has cold water in it in the summer time?"—or from James Logan, the lodestar of science in Philadelphia, to whom either Thomas Godfrey or Joseph Brientnall could have introduced Franklin. Logan was *the* patriarch of Pennsylvania. He had arrived with William Penn in 1682, serving as Penn's secretary. He stayed on to become the colony's guiding force for its first twenty-odd years, retired from politics to make a fortune in business, retired from business to pursue a fascination with the classics and natural philosophy. He bought the first edition of the *Principia* and taught himself higher mathematics in order to master its contents. Since then he had built up the finest scientific library in America. Though a forbidding, moody man, he welcomed those interested in science to his mansion just north of the city. Thomas Godfrey, then renting the apartment above Franklin's shop, went out to see him in 1729. He had taught himself to read Latin and wanted to borrow a copy of the *Principia.* It took only a short talk to see that Godfrey had an "excellent natural genius" for mathematics, and Logan opened his library to him. A year later Godfrey solved a problem that had long troubled sailors by inventing a device for finding longitude at sea. When Logan learned that the prize for such an invention offered by the Royal Society would go to John Hadley of London, he, staunch American, launched a fight to prove Godfrey's quadrant had been "not only made, but used at sea six months before J. Hadley's was seen or known." Convinced by affidavits, the Royal Society acknowledged Godfrey's claim and awarded him two hundred pounds—to be invested in a clock (in order to discourage Godfrey's indulging his fondness for drink).

Another of Logan's protégés was John Bartram, a local Quaker farmer who used his spare time to botanize. Logan taught him enough Latin to classify plants and read learned treatises, and though Bartram never became a systematic botanist, he soon had an international reputation as an assiduous and enterprising collector of plants and seeds. Joseph Brientnall recommended him to Peter Collinson, a London merchant, amateur horticulturalist, and member of the Royal Society, and soon letters and packets were passing between the two across the ocean. An introduction from Logan led to a correspondence with the great taxonomist Linnaeus. Franklin used the *Gazette* to raise money to finance Bartram's expeditions through the southern and back parts of the colonies.

In spite of ties with Philadelphia's natural philosophers, Franklin's interest in the field remained vicarious during the 1730s. The Royal Society published two of Logan's papers in its *Transactions,* one of which, "Experiments Concerning the Impregnation of the Seeds of Plants," won international praise; later the Society would publish papers by Brientnall and Bartram. None of these triumphs nor that of Godfrey with his quadrant induced Franklin to begin intensive experiments of his own. As a city man he found botany boring. His inability to learn higher mathematics, or his refusal to do so, closed off Newtonian physics as presented in the *Principia*. He could read Latin but not easily, and this blocked access to much of the work done since Newton's death. The route that led to natural philosophy can only be guessed at, but the iron fireplace Franklin invented in the winter of 1739 surely started him down the road.

The wonder is it took the economy-minded Franklin so long to invent the Pennsylvania Fireplace, as he called it. He estimated that five-sixths of the heat went up the chimney from regular fireplaces. They were inefficient and "next to impossible to warm a room with." Chimneys had been improved in recent years, and "tho' they keep rooms generally free from smoke," he said, "yet the funnel still requiring a considerable quantity of air, it rushes in at every crevice so strongly, as to make a continual whistling or howling; and 'tis very uncomfortable as well as dangerous to sit against any such crevice. Many colds are caught from this cause only; it being safer to sit in the open street." The more efficient Dutch iron stoves had an aesthetic flaw—"There is no sight of the fire, which is in itself a pleasant thing." Unvented German iron stoves failed to provide circulating air and this obliged people "to breathe the same unchanged air continually, mixed with the breath and perspiration from one another's bodies, which is very disagreeable to those who have not been accustomed to it."

Franklin designed an iron stove to sit on the hearth of a regular fireplace, and take up little space in the room. The fire burned in an open cradle as efficiently as other iron stoves and from an air box above "near ten barrels of fresh air are hourly introduced," allowing "the air in the room [to be] continually changed, and kept at the same time sweet and warm." In his pamphlet four years later Franklin drew on the works of European scientists to explain the principles behind his stove, quoting from Nicolas Gauger's *La Méchanique du Feu*, Martin Clare's *The Motion of Fluids, Natural and Artificial*, Jean Theophile Desaguliers's *A Course of Experimental Philosophy*. Several of the books quoted from were available only after he had invented the fireplace; he used them as scholarly dressing for what common sense and native ingenuity had led him to invent. Franklin's wide reading in science probably began sometime after June 1740, when the *Gazette* advertised "*a course of philosophical lectures and experiments*" to be given by Isaac Greenwood of Boston.

Greenwood had been Cotton Mather's most vociferous defender

when the *New England Courant* attacked him in 1721, and he may have reminded Franklin of this with a smile on the visit to Philadelphia. The year Franklin ran away from Boston Greenwood went to England to study under Desaguliers, a disciple of Newton. He returned to become the first Hollis Professor of mathematics at Harvard. A knack for popularizing Newton's ideas led to several public lectures in Boston, and in 1738, when Harvard dropped him from the faculty because of heavy drinking, he set out to earn a living as an itinerant lecturer. One lecture offered "various experiments concerning electrical attraction and repulsion," but if Greenwood influenced Franklin it was to expose him to an organized, scholarly approach to natural philosophy.

From the intensive reading program Franklin embarked on after Greenwood left town a single message emerged—a man with a good mind but untrained in mathematics need not be prevented from becoming a Newtonian philosopher. Newton's *Opticks* offered in readable English, unencumbered by a single mathematical formula, a bundle of fascinating hypotheses waiting to. tested by experiments. Desaguliers, Greenwood's mentor, said in *Natural Philosophy* that though the "truth" of Newtonian philosophy is "supported by mathematics, yet its physical discoveries may be communicated without" it. From Willem Jacob 'sGravesande's *Natural Philosophy* he learned that "many of the truths of Newtonian science could be apprehended without formal mathematics if every principle be illustrated by experiments." By the spring of 1743 when Franklin set out for Boston he had as sound a grounding in non-mathematical experimental science as any man in America.

2

In May of 1743 Franklin published over his name *A Proposal for Promoting Useful Knowledge among the British Plantations in America.* The timing owed something to boredom with life in Philadelphia. "We have seldom any news on our side of the globe that can be entertaining to you on yours," he told a London correspondent. "All our affairs are *petit.* They have a miniature resemblance only of the grand things of Europe. Our government, parliaments, wars, treaties, expeditions, factions, etc., tho' matters of great and serious consequence to us, can seem but trifles to you." One way to escape these trifles might be through a society "of virtuosi or ingenious men residing in the several colonies, to be called The American Philosophical Society; who are to maintain a constant correspondence" among themselves and also "with the ROYAL SOCIETY of

London and with the DUBLIN SOCIETY." All these communications would be handled by "Benjamin Franklin, the writer of this proposal," who "offers himself to serve the Society as their Secretary, till they shall be provided with one more capable."

The proposal revealed a man of large dreams. It also smacked of brashness and self-advertisement. Natural philosophers throughout America and England knew the names of Logan, Bartram, Brientnall, and Godfrey—all except Godfrey had had papers published by the Royal Society—but few beyond the boundaries of Philadelphia had heard of Benjamin Franklin. Later Franklin claimed full credit for "proposing and establishing a philosophical society," gliding over the fact that in 1739 John Bartram had suggested such a society of "ingenious and curious men" to study "natural secrets, arts, and sciences," and that when Franklin issued his broadside Bartram called the contents "our proposals," as they were.

Franklin had a reason for publishing his prospectus in May 1743. He would leave that month for his first visit to Boston in a decade. (The timing of the trip may have seemed strange to some in Philadelphia. Franklin's wife, who would be in charge of the shop and post office during his absence, was over six months pregnant. This would be their first child since Francis Folger Franklin died nine years before.) In the leisurely journey northward he could pass out copies of his broadside to all those interested. It would serve as a dignified letter of introduction to gentlemen everywhere.

And thus it happened that on the road in Connecticut Franklin met a natural philosopher named Cadwallader Colden, a Scotsman, a physician, and also surveyor general of New York. Colden was a botanist more skilled than Bartram (Linnaeus called him "Summus Perfectus"). He knew enough mathematics to have mastered the *Principia* and now was writing a treatise to explain "the cause of gravitation," a riddle that had eluded even Newton. Colden had only a short time to talk with Franklin —so short he failed to catch his name—but he drove away impressed. "I accidentally . . . fell into company with a printer, the most ingenious in his way without question of any in America," he wrote a friend in England, who replied, "I am sure it must be Mr. Franklin you mean, whose fame has long ago reached this part of the world, for a most ingenious man in his way."

Franklin spent the month of June in Boston. What he counted on being only a pleasant reunion with family and friends turned out, he said later, to be more. That summer Dr. Archibald Spencer, like Colden a Scotsman and a physician, gave in Boston a "Course of Experimental

Philosophy." Franklin attended the lectures. Spencer illustrated his sprightly survey of natural philosophy with experiments—"imperfectly performed, as he was not very expert," Franklin recalled, "but being on a subject quite new to me, they equally surprised and pleased me." He dated his interest in electricity from this time. A modern scholar doubts Franklin's recollection. In one experiment Spencer rubbed a long glass tube which, when placed near some leaves of brass, caused them to spring alive with "very brisk and surprising motions," according to a startled eyewitness. "Some would leap toward the tube, sometimes adhere and fasten to it, settle on its surface, and there remain quiet; and sometimes be thrown off from it with a great force." Professor Niels Heathcote has shown that this eyewitness copied his account from Francis Hauksbee's *Physico-Mechanical Experiments.* He suggests that Spencer's experiments were so "imperfectly performed" that they could have meant little to Franklin at the time and that only later, nudged from another direction, did he realize "the true character of the experiments he had seen." The fact that two years passed before Franklin began his own electrical experiments tends to support the point made.

3

When Franklin returned to Philadelphia early in July he found a letter awaiting him from Colden, eager to exchange thoughts with another lively mind. Franklin delayed answering until November. The "long absence" in New England, he explained, "put my business so much behind-hand, that I have been in a continual hurry ever since my return, and had no leisure to forward the scheme of the society." (He saw no reason to mention that on August 31 his wife gave birth to a girl whom they named Sarah but called Sally.) The philosophical society bloomed, so it appeared, that winter. When Dr. Spencer arrived at the end of April 1744 to repeat the lectures Franklin heard in Boston, it had nine members. After giving his course in Philadelphia, Spencer left with a bundle of Franklin's *Proposals* to distribute as he lectured down the coast and through the West Indies.

Though a second exposure to Spencer had still not aroused Franklin's interest in electricity, natural philosophy occupied more and more of his free time. He read widely but generally, touching all aspects of the field. He went through the works of Boerhaave, Boyle, Desaguliers, 'sGravesande, quoting from them all in the pamphlet on the Pennsylvania fireplace brought out in 1744. In letters that streamed between him and

Colden he touched on a variety of matters—perspiration and colds, the circulation of the blood, whatever at the moment attracted his attention. He even indulged the new hobby during business hours. When Dr. John Mitchell, a physician from Virginia fascinated with botany, passed through town, John Bartram brought him to the New Printing-Office. Franklin dropped his tasks. "We have been together all day," he wrote Colden. "We are to go to Mr. Logan's tomorrow, when I shall have an opportunity of knowing his sentiments of your piece on fluxions."

Colden had sent Franklin a copy of *An Explication of the First Causes of Action in Matter*, the masterpiece he hoped would win a seat in the pantheon of scientists alongside Newton. He wanted the opinion of the virtuosi of Philadelphia, especially Logan. Franklin dutifully passed the book among friends. None could understand it, including Logan. "Thus, tho' you should get no praise among us, you are like to escape censure," Franklin reported tactfully, "since our people do not seem to suppose that you write unintelligibly, but charge all to the abstruseness of the subject, and their own want of capacity."

Colden alone among friends outside Philadelphia urged Franklin not to give up the dream of a philosophical society. He suggested publishing a collection of papers by members to publicize the venture, and Franklin collected several, then dropped the project. By the summer of 1745 the society foundered. "The members," said Franklin, "are very idle gentlemen; they will take no pains." One member blamed Franklin for the failure. Bartram, too, may have referred to Franklin when he said the society would prosper "if we could but exchange the time that is spent in the club, chess, and coffee house for the curious amusements of natural observations." Franklin abandoned his dream, and it lay moribund until another generation of Philadelphians twenty years later resurrected it.

Franklin's interest shifted from the society to electricity in the summer of 1745 with the arrival of an essay from Collinson entitled "An historical account of the wonderful discoveries made in Germany, etc., concerning Electricity," which had appeared in the *Gentleman's Magazine* for April. The article revealed that "from the year 1743 . . . electricity became all the subject of vogue," and Franklin, with his curious concern for things fashionable, read on with interest—"princes were willing to see this new fire which a man produced from himself, which did not descend from heaven. Could one believe that a lady's finger, that her whalebone petticoat, should send forth flashes of true lightning, and that such charming lips could set on fire a house?" But the author saw electricity as more than a toy to amuse the public:

Electricity is a vast country, of which we know only some bordering province; it is yet unseasonable to give a map of it, and pretend to assign the laws by which it is governed.

But discover those laws and undreamed benefits might materialize:

It has been already discovered, or believed to be so, that electricity accelerates the motion of water in a pipe, and that it quickens the pulse. There are hopes of finding in it a remedy for the sciatica or palsy.

In passing, the author made a startling comparison. Electricity and lightning have "pretty much the same qualities," he said,

for it generally runs over the whole length of the solid bodies which it strikes, and it has been seen to descend along the wire of a steeple-clock from top to bottom, and the threads of the wire have been found at the bottom of the steeple, melted into thousands of small bits.

Along with the essay Collinson sent a glass tube similar to the one Dr. Spencer had used for his experiments. Franklin "eagerly seized the opportunity" to repeat Spencer's experiments, "and by much practice acquired great readiness in performing those also which we had an account of from England." At first the experiments only offered a chance to give alluring shows with Franklin the performing magician. "My house was continually full for some time, with people who came to see these new wonders. To divide a little this encumbrance among my friends, I caused a number of similar tubes to be blown at our glass house, with which they furnished themselves, so that we had at length several performers."

The experiments moved from the stage to the laboratory when Franklin learned that in 1746 Pieter van Musschenbroek of Leyden had discovered what came to be called the Leyden jar. Until now electricity could be accumulated only by rubbing a glass tube. This limited the scale and variety of experiments to be performed. The Leyden jar, for reasons then not clear, could accumulate or "condense" enough electricity to knock flat the unwary experimenter. By the winter of 1746–1747 Franklin had acquired a Leyden jar, and his electrical shows were more astonishing than ever. "Yesterday was the first time that I ever heard one syllable of thy electrical experiments," Logan wrote in February, "when John Bartram surprised me with the account of a ball turning many hours about an electrified body, with some particulars that were sufficiently amazing." What had been an amusing hobby verged on an obsession for Franklin. "For my own part," he confessed, "I never was before engaged in any study that so totally engrossed my attention and my time as this has lately done; for what with making experiments when I can be alone, and repeating them to my friends and acquaintance, who, from the novelty of the thing, come continually in crowds to see them, I have, during some months past, had little leisure for anything else."

4

Franklin conducted his early experiments with two friends from the Junto. Philip Syng used his skill as a silversmith to construct a delicate, tiny windmill with paper vanes rotating on a thin wire. He also devised a machine to rotate the glass tube and thus ease the tedious rubbing required to collect electricity. Thomas Hopkinson, a lawyer, "a gentleman possessed of many virtues, without the alloy of one single vice," and one of Franklin's closest friends, turned up an intriguing mystery in one of his experiments. He found that laying a slim needle atop an iron shot made it impossible to electrify the ball. The "wonderful effect" of "the power of points to *throw off* the electrical fire" amazed Franklin, and he could offer no explanation for it.

The experimenters found a number of other ways to de-electrify the iron ball—by sifting sand over it, by breathing upon it, by wafting smoke from a piece of burning wood over it. Sunlight focused upon the shot had no effect but candlelight did, "even tho' the candle is at a foot distance," said Franklin. "This difference between firelight and sunlight is another thing that seems new and extraordinary to us."

In the beginning Franklin assumed electricity to be a freak of nature created by rubbing an "electric" such as glass or amber. Gradually, he and his friends realized that "electrical fire is a common element," a "species of matter," that pervades the universe. Here Franklin thought he had discovered a phenomenon as extraordinary as gravitation. When the ice cleared from the harbor in the spring of 1747, an early ship brought from Collinson a packet of books on electricity with depressing news. From William Watson's *Experiments and Observations Tending to Illustrate the Nature and Properties of Electricity* and its *Sequel*, both published in 1746, Franklin learned that English experimenters had already judged electricity a common element in nature. "In this discovery, they were beforehand with us in England," he told Colden, "but we had hit on it before we heard it from them."

Isolation from the mainstream of European research in the long run helped Franklin. It left him with an open mind to draw conclusions from experiments uninfluenced by current thinking. European experimenters generally agreed that electricity was composed of two electrical fluids— one called "vitreous" (from the Latin word for glass), the other "resinous." Franklin, unaware of this when he began experimenting, argued from his own work for only one electrical fluid. To explain his view, he invented new terms. If A, standing on a wax mat that cuts off "his communication with the common stock" of electricity in the atmosphere, touches B, B thereupon becomes "electrised *positively; A negatively:* Or rather *B* is electrised *plus* and *A minus.*" Such terms implied that electricity could be measured, an insight that would in time revolutionize research in the field.

Behind the new terms lay a hypothesis that Franklin eventually elevated into a theory—that electricity was "not *created* by friction, but *collected* only." "This," it has been remarked, "is probably the first clear expression of the tremendously important generalization that electricity cannot be created or destroyed—a generalization that later came to be called the *principle of conservation of electrical charge.*" Another historian of science has remarked: "As a broad generalization that has withstood the test of two hundred years of fruitful application, Franklin's law of conservation of charge must be considered to be of the same fundamental importance to physical science as Newton's law of conservation of momentum."

Franklin pondered for several months the results of the winter experiments, then on 25 May 1747 put his findings in a long letter to Peter Collinson. He used Collinson, as had Logan, Bartram, and Brientnall before him, as a conduit to the Royal Society, where Collinson, a member, would read the letter aloud and, if past experience prevailed, it would be published in the *Transactions.* (Past experience did not prevail. William Watson commented favorably on the letter to the Society and read aloud *excerpts* from it, but none of it was published in the *Transactions.* The affront, which Franklin took it to be, rankled all his life.)

Through June and July Franklin worked on another long letter to Collinson. The rapid "progress made with you in electricity," he said, "half discourages me from writing," but in fact it hastened his pen and led to an egregious error in his findings. This report dealt with the Leyden jar, "Mr. Musschenbroek's wonderful bottle." Everyone who had worked with it knew the jar could store a charge strong enough to knock a man out, but no one had fathomed how or why this happened. Franklin's basic finding, that the jar contained both plus and minus charges of electricity, was correct and of great importance, but when he went on to say that the plus charge resided in the top of the jar and the minus charge in the bottom he erred. He should have said they lay on the "inside" and "outside" surfaces of the bottle.

Franklin mailed this second letter to Collinson on July 28. Normally he did not carry out electrical experiments during the humid summer months—dampness dispersed the electrical fluid through the atmosphere—but something nagged him about his report on the Leyden jar. Within two weeks he discovered he had been mistaken about the location of the plus and minus charges in the jar. Instantly he sent off a brief, hurried note to Collinson, dated August 24:

> On some further experiments since, I have observed a phenomenon or two that I cannot at present account for on the principles laid down in those letters, and am therefore become a little diffident of my hypothesis, and ashamed that I have expressed myself in so positive a manner. In going on with these experiments, how many pretty systems do we build, which we soon find ourselves obliged to destroy! If there is no other use discovered of electricity, this, however, is something considerable, that it may *help to make a vain man humble.* I must now request that you would not expose those letters; or if you communicate them to any friends, you would at least conceal my name.

Those few lines were the last Collinson would receive from Franklin on electricity for over a year and a half. Through this long silence Franklin continued his experiments, but having once released findings before rechecking them he would not again risk his reputation until absolutely certain about what he had to say.

CHAPTER

7

WAR AND THOSE
"DAMNED QUAKERS"

As AN OLD MAN Franklin said: "There never was a good war nor a bad peace." As a younger man he thought otherwise.

Whitefield's arrival in Philadelphia in 1740 coincided with news that war had broken out between England and Spain—the War of Jenkins' Ear. "On Monday," the *Gazette* reported on April 17, "our governor, attended by near two hundred gentlemen, came to the court house, where a vast concourse of people were assembled, and published the King's declaration of war against Spain. . . . The people expressed their joy in loud huzzas; and the cannon from the hill, and the ships in the harbor, were discharged. . . . Plenty of liquor was given to the populace; and in the evening they had a bonfire on the hill."

The pacifist Quakers controlled Pennsylvania politics, but Franklin doubted they could stifle the martial fever sweeping the province. "As a design against some of the rich Spanish settlements appears exceedingly agreeable to the people in general, and there is truly a great prospect of success, it is not doubted but a considerable body of men will be raised on this occasion, even in Pennsylvania."

The crown ordered Governor George Thomas to furnish men and supplies for an expedition to the Caribbean. He asked the Assembly to institute a draft for able-bodied men to satisfy the royal requisition. The Assembly refused. The governor resorted to the dubious device of urging indentured servants to leave their masters and join the army. Some two hundred and fifty did so at the peak of the harvest season. The success of the policy lost him support among non-Quaker farmers and in the Assembly it raised talk of forcing his resignation and petitioning the crown to take over the colony. Franklin, as clerk, sat silent through the debates. His sympathies lay with the governor and against the Quakers. Richard Peters, secretary of the province, and William Allen, scion of a wealthy Presbyterian family and son-in-law of Andrew Hamilton, served as the governor's lieutenants; both were fellow directors of the Library Company and friends of Franklin. But as the first major political battle shaped up since he began the *Gazette*, he had to proceed cautiously. Flagrant opposition to the Quakers might cost his clerkship and the profitable annual printing of the Assembly's laws and proceedings. Yet when his newspaper announced on September 18 that the governor had raised his companies and they "are all embarked," he dared give discreet support to the expedition. "The companies are all full, and the men cheerful and in good heart. They were reviewed by his honor the governor before they went on board, and performed their exercise to admiration."

The annual elections to the Assembly came soon after the troops sailed. The Quakers pictured Thomas as an arbitrary governor who, given a pliable Assembly, would burden the people with heavy taxes and enforced military service. They swept the election. Thomas warned the proprietors, who had left the Society of Friends for the Church of England and thus were no longer brethren, to expect nothing but trouble from the Quakers, especially the new generation of "young fry" now moving into politics, supplanting older, more conciliatory leaders like James Logan. "If you do not part with them, they will in the end part with you, for they publicly avow their design to throw the government into the hands of the crown, and from hence the more confusion the better, as that is the most probable way of bringing it about."

The war continued through 1741. Shortly before the elections Conrad Weiser, an Indian trader and greatly admired, appealed to his fellow Germans, in a letter printed by Franklin, to vote for candidates who would support defense measures. At the same time Logan told his brethren bluntly that government "is founded on force," and while he did not ask Friends to abandon their principles and engage in war they must not make it impossible for those willing to fight to do so. All Friends "who for conscience-sake cannot join in any law for self-defense [should] decline standing candidates at the ensuing election for representatives."

The letters only hardened resolve among the antidefense faction and increased tension on both sides. On election day in the city Richard Peters was accused of casting two ballots. Israel Pemberton, a far from meek Quaker leader, stepped into the scuffle that followed, only to be hit in turn by James Hamilton, one of the governor's supporters. The *Gazette* glided over the fracas silently, though it did report after the election that the Quakers still controlled the Assembly.

An even livelier election came in 1742. A gang of sailors, purportedly organized by William Allen, marched toward the courthouse, out to get the "Quaker sons of bitches." One of them along the way shouted, "By God, we'll kill Pemberton." When ordered back to their ships, another said, "You are damned Quakers, you are enemies to King George, and we will knock you all in the head." Franklin reported the riot in detail, though cleansed of the purple language. As the sailors were "mostly strangers," he wrote, "and had no kind of right to intermeddle with the election, and some ill consequence was apprehended if they should be suffered to mix, with their clubs, among the inhabitants, some of the magistrates, and other persons of note, met them, and endeavored to prevail with them to return peaceably to their ships, but without effect." It was a judicious account. The accusation that Allen had incited the riot went unmentioned. Pemberton, one of the "persons of note," could only be pleased by the rendering of his role.

The *Gazette* also reported that in the election "the majority in favor of the old Assembly was extraordinary." The Quakers had cemented their hold on the legislature and in the process forced Allen from his seat; he would not retrieve it for fourteen years. But he, Richards, and Franklin continued friends, united in their opposition to Quaker pacifism. The *Gazette* missed no chance to take good-humored jabs at the Quakers. In one issue it noted that Gilbert Tennent had baptized "eight adult persons" during one of his fire-breathing sermons, "who had been of the people called Quakers, one, as is said, a preacher. Mr. Whitefield had baptized three at the same place, when he was last in this city." An early issue of the *General Magazine*, a short-lived periodical Franklin published during the first half of 1741, affronted the Society of Friends with a manual of military exercises for recruits.

2

The War of Jenkins' Ear soon vanished into a broader conflict—the War of Austrian Succession Europe called it, renamed in America King George's War—which, as predicted, brought France into the action. Franklin followed the war more closely than most in Philadelphia, for in the early phase it bore heaviest upon New England. From its great garrison at the mouth of the St. Lawrence, Fort Louisbourg, France struck first at Nova Scotia. Governor Shirley of Massachusetts persuaded his legislature to authorize fifty thousand pounds for an expedition against the fort. In the harbor it overlooked nestled a flotilla of privateers that harassed American shipping as far south as Pennsylvania. He asked for aid—men, money, ships, or simply provisions—from all colonies, for this would be a completely American enterprise, initiated, planned, and undertaken with no help from the crown. Governor Thomas turned the request over to the Pennsylvania Assembly in late February 1745, commending "the undertaking publicly" but privately doing "all in his power to disappoint it," said Franklin. As the Assembly's clerk, Franklin listened to the Quakers behind closed doors admit they opposed the expedition because of their religious principles but refuse in their public reply to the governor to aid it because they had not been consulted in advance. "I think they ought to be open and honest and give the true reason, and not trifle in the manner they do," said Franklin in anger. "In short, the governor and Assembly have been only acting a farce and playing tricks to amuse the world."

When several of the members afterward told Franklin they wished the people of New England success, he gave a blunt reply. "I told them those people were as much obliged to them for their good wishes as the poor in the Scripture to those that say 'be ye warmed, be ye filled.' " What harm would it have done, he asked, to offer a few provisions? "That would be encouraging war," came the answer.

Franklin publicized the expedition heavily in the *Gazette*, until the town became as interested as he in the outcome. "Our people are extremely impatient to hear of your success at Cape Breton," he wrote his brother John in May. "My shop is filled with thirty inquiries at the coming in of every post." His reports emphasized how the distant fort endangered Pennsylvania. In one he reminded readers that a cruiser from Louisbourg "took four sail in a few days off our capes, to a very considerable value. What might we have expected from a dozen sail, making each three or four cruises a year? . . . It is therefore in their own NECESSARY DEFENSE, as well as that of all the other British colonies, that the people of New England have undertaken the present expedition against that place, to which may the GOD OF HOSTS grant success. *Amen.*"

In mid-July the town learned Louisbourg had fallen to the Americans. "'Twas near nine o'clock when the express came in," the *Gazette* reported, "yet the news flying instantly round the town, upwards of twenty bonfires were immediately lighted in the streets." Philadelphia celebrated all the next day, "and the evening concluded with bonfires, illuminations, and other demonstrations of joy." The Quakers refused to join in. "A mob gathered and began to break the windows of those houses that were not illuminated, but it was soon dispersed and suppressed."

Remorse, or something akin to it, soon struck the Assembly and it voted for "the King's use" in New England four thousand pounds "to be laid out . . . in the purchase of bread, beef, port, flour, wheat or other grain, or any of them, within this province." The governor's council advised him to reject the grant "as not being the thing he had demanded." He thought otherwise. "I shall take the money, for I understand very well their meaning: *other grain* is gunpowder." He used the money for that purpose and the Quakers, Franklin recalled, "never objected to it."

3

In 1746 King George's War touched Franklin more directly. One day his son William, now sixteen, "left my house unknown to us all, and got on board a privateer, from whence I fetched him." The father was embarrassed. "No one imagined it was hard usage at home that made him do this," he said. "Everyone that knows me thinks I am too indulgent a parent, as well as master." But, he added philosophically, "when boys see prizes brought in, and quantities of money shared among the men, and their gay living, it fills their heads with notions, that half distract them, and put them quite out of conceit with trades, and the dull ways of getting money by working." After all, Franklin himself had tried to run away to sea during Queen Anne's War.

But if his son must have a part in this war, let it be as a gentleman. Franklin arranged for him in June a commission as ensign in a company of volunteers headed for duty at Albany, whence it would join in an invasion of Canada. He hoped exposure to a northern winter would cool "his military inclinations," but this did not happen. "Billy is so fond of a military life, that he will by no means hear of leaving the army," his father reported. "We have good accounts of him from his captain and brother officers." William returned to Philadelphia on furlough in the fall of 1747 still enthusiastic for army life; the best the protective father could do was ask Cadwallader Colden in New York to "assist him with your advice or countenance."

At the time William was home on furlough it appeared that Philadelphia rather than Albany would be the next center of fighting. During the spring and early summer of 1747 French privateers had infested the waters off the Delaware capes. In July a raiding party from one sacked two plantations forty miles inside the capes. Stories swept about Philadelphia "that the French know our bay and river as well as we do," one man said, "that they are sure the Quakers will not consent to the raising fortifications, that there are no men-of-war upon the coast and that vast wealth may be got from the plunder of the city, and that some merchants and captains of ships in the French islands have actually concerted a scheme to be executed by six privateers of force against the city some time next year. . . . These accounts are handed about amongst the tradesmen and have made strong impressions on numbers." The governor's council pleaded with the Assembly to vote funds for raising a defense. The Quaker-ruled Assembly refused, saying "we hope there is no danger." One of the tradesmen especially "apprehensive of a visit from the French" was Franklin, and his fear made him bitter toward the Quakers. One day walking past a Quaker meeting house with William Allen, he "declared that more mischief was hatched in that place than in a meeting of JESUITS at St. Omers." He was only slightly less caustic in public. "Should we tell them," he wrote of the Quakers in the Assembly, "that tho' *they* themselves may be resigned and easy under this naked, defenseless state of the country, it is far otherwise with a very great part of the people; with *us*, who can have no confidence that God will protect those that neglect the use of rational means for their security?" He also snapped at the "great and rich" in the city, led by William Allen, who opposed defensive measures because they would cost too much.

Franklin made these remarks in November. Less than three months later Pennsylvania had nearly ten thousand men under arms, organized into over eighty companies; a fort had been built and equipped with cannon—all at a cost of nothing to the province—and "the prime mover," said the amazed James Logan, was Benjamin Franklin. As with his other projects, he had first conferred with friends on how to mobilize public opinion. "A scheme was formed" whereby Franklin, in the guise of a tradesman, would write a pamphlet attacking those who opposed defense measures "as people from whom no good could be expected, and by this artifice to animate all the middling persons to undertake their own defense in opposition to the Quakers and the gentlemen." The pamphlet came out on November 17 under the title *Plain Truth*. The country lay in danger, Franklin warned, not from disciplined troops but *"licentious privateers."* Conceive the horror they will inflict "when your persons, fortunes, wives and daughters, shall be subject to the wanton and unbridled rage, rapine, and lust of *Negroes, mulattoes* and others, the vilest and most abandoned of mankind. A dread scene!" The rich will flee, but "we, the middling people . . . cannot all fly with our families; and if we could how shall we subsist? No, we . . . must bear the brunt." What, then, is to be done? "All we want is order, discipline, and a few cannon," said

Franklin, following that reassuring statement with a marvelous image. "At present we are like the separate filaments of flax before the thread is formed, without strength because without connection; but UNION would make us strong and even formidable." The essay ended with a promise to the public that "the writer of it will, in a few days, lay before them a form of an ASSOCIATION for the purposes herein mentioned, together with a practicable scheme for raising the money necessary for the defense of our trade, city, and country, without laying a burthen on any man."

On November 21, Franklin met with one hundred and fifty tradesmen in a sail loft. He lauded them as "the first movers in every useful undertaking that had been projected for the good of the city—Library Company, fire companies, etc.," then read aloud his Plan of Association. All its features were appealing. A man was asked to supply himself only "with a good firelock, cartouche box, and at least twelve charges of powder and ball." If he had a sword or cutlass, fine, bring it along. He would be organized into a company of no more than one hundred men drawn from his own neighborhood. This, explained Franklin, "is intended to prevent people's sorting themselves into companies according to their ranks in life, their quality or station. 'Tis designed to mix the great and small together, for the sake of union and encouragement. Where danger and duty are equal to all, there should be no distinction from circumstance, but all be on the level." Company officers would be elected by their men, a novel feature Franklin imported from New England. Regulations would be laid down by a General Military Council composed of deputies from Associations throughout the province. Franklin had overlooked no detail. How would the money be raised to build a fort on the river and stock it with cannons and supplies? By a lottery. Ten thousand tickets would be sold at two pounds per ticket; three thousand pounds would be turned over to the Association and the rest distributed in 2,842 prizes.

The plan won instant approval from those in the packed sail loft; many wanted to enlist at once. "No," said Franklin, "let us not sign yet; let us offer it at least to the gentlemen, and if they come into it, well and good, we shall be the better able to carry it into execution." He met with the gentlemen two nights later in a coffee house. Earlier, Franklin had promised space in the *Gazette* for those who opposed his pamphlet or his plan. Allen, who had been expected to lead the opposition, had no objections now that he knew the Association would cost nothing. (Later he helped manage the lottery, sold tickets at his house, and when he won £312 in the drawing turned his winnings over to the Association.) With his authoritative backing, the Association won the gentlemen's full support.

The next night, November 24, some five hundred men gathered at the New Building to sign the Plan of Association. "The house was pretty full," Franklin recalled. "I had prepared a number of printed copies, and provided pens and ink dispersed all over the room. I harangued them a little on the subject, read the paper and explained it, and then distributed the copies, which were eagerly signed, not the least objection being made." By early December Franklin could boast that in the city alone "near eight hundred have signed the *Association*, and more are signing hourly." Most of the signers showed up for a mass rally at the courthouse on December 7, where Richard Peters said their "proceedings were not disapproved by the government." The next day the governor's council issued a proclamation for a fast day throughout the colony. Ministers were exhorted to ask God to "take this province under His protection." Franklin wrote the proclamation, again drawing on his youth in Boston, where such pronouncements were common fare.

Now that the people had been stirred to act, everyone but the strictest Quakers joined to make the city and province secure. The council asked the proprietors to contribute cannon; guns went on sale in shops "for a trifle"; the merchants petitioned the Admiralty for a warship in the bay and subscribed fifteen hundred pounds to buy cannons and arms in Boston. Later Franklin, Allen, and two members of the council went to New York to plead for cannons from Governor Clinton. "He at first refused us peremptorily," Franklin recalled; "but at a dinner with his council where there was great drinking of Madeira wine, as the custom at that place then was, he softened by degrees, and said he would lend us six. After a few more bumpers he advanced to ten. And at length he very good-naturedly conceded eighteen."

In the midst of all this Franklin had a satisfying note from James Logan. "I have expected to see thee here for several weeks," he wrote, "but it is probable thy thoughts of thy new excellent project have in some measure diverted thee, to which I most heartily wish all possible success. . . . Ever since I have had the power of thinking I have clearly seen that government without arms is an inconsistency. Our Friends spare no pains to get and accumulate estates, and are yet against defending them, though these very estates are in a great measure the sole cause of their being invaded. . . . Thy project of a lottery to clear £3,000 is excellent, and I hope it will be speedily filled; nor shall I be wanting."

Logan's support was important, for Franklin traveled over treacherous ground. To create a military force opposed by the legislature breached the law. It had been done twice before in America—in Virginia and New York—and history recorded those instances as Bacon's Rebellion and Leisler's Rebellion. Knowing this, Franklin kept Richard Peters informed of his plans and asked him to assure Thomas Penn that those in the enterprise "had nothing in view but the security of their lives and properties, and thought they were at the same time doing the proprietaries true service in defending the country by a voluntary association which the legislature had refused to do. . . ." Peters approved Franklin's work. Thomas Penn did not. "This Association is founded on a contempt to government and cannot end in anything but anarchy and confusion," he wrote Peters. Once the people learn to act "independent of this government," he asked, "why should they not act against it?" Citizens who raised their own army assumed a power that traditionally belonged to the king. This "I fear will be esteemed greatly criminal" by the British government, Penn said nervously. He had only recently gained a clear title to Pennsylvania and wanted nothing done there that would give the crown an excuse to deprive him of his immense piece of real estate. He objected, with reason, to the Association's making its own regulations through a self-chosen military council, unchecked by any legitimate authority. The council usurped "the king's power of ordering the militia, which you know our kings are very jealous of, and if it should be known to the ministers, would incline them to look with an evil eye over us on all applications." Finally, he suspected Franklin's motives. "He is a dangerous man and I should be very glad he inhabited any other country, as I believe him of a very uneasy spirit. However, as he is a sort of tribune of the people, he must be treated with regard."

Others, too—Peters and Allen among them—soon suspected Franklin's motives. He had none of the attributes of a demagogue, yet no one since William Keith a quarter of a century before had gained such a hold over the people. But how? He appeared an unremarkable man. He rarely forced his presence upon a group. "His voice was low, but his countenance open, frank, and pleasing," said one observer. He often sat silent in conversation, "unless he has some diverting story to tell, of which he has a great collection," said another. If in a talkative mood, "a natural and good-humored (not sarcastic) wit played cheerfully along and beguiled you into maxims of prudence and wisdom." He admitted, "I was a bad speaker, never eloquent, subject to much hesitation in the choice of words, hardly correct in language, and yet," he added, "I generally carried my point." This puzzling ability to carry his point frightened and angered the old guard, and as the Association took shape they wondered what he would do with the power he had suddenly accumulated.

The answer came when the threat of invasion by *"licentious pirates"* passed with the summer of 1748. Franklin did nothing to prevent the Association's companies from disbanding now that their reason for being had ended. His genial relinquishment of power allayed all suspicions, even those of Thomas Penn. "We are well pleased to find that the Association has had so good an effect," Penn wrote. "Their readiness to defend their country is very commendable, and it was with reluctance that we objected to anything done by persons that in general might intend nothing more than to defend themselves under their legal commanders."

Those who had feared Franklin during the crisis failed to see that creating the Association and serving as tribune of the people had been passing pleasures. He had outgrown Philadelphia. Before Penn's grudging compliments arrived he had retired from business and now dreamed of testing his talents on a larger stage. "In Europe the encouragements to learning are of themselves much greater than can be given here," he said wistfully. "Whoever distinguishes himself there, in either of the three learned professions, gains fame, and often wealth and power. A poor man's son has a chance, if he studies hard, to rise, either in the law or the church, to gainful offices or benifices; to an extraordinary pitch of grandeur; to have a voice in Parliament, a seat among the peers; as a statesman or first minister to govern nations, and even to mix his blood with princes." In October 1748, not long after the Association broke up, he wrote to an English couple: "By this time twelve-month, if nothing extraordinary happens to prevent it, I hope to have the pleasure of seeing you both in London."

CHAPTER

8

"I PASS MY TIME
AGREEABLY ENOUGH"

On 1 January 1748, shortly before his forty-second birthday, Franklin retired from business, turning over the shop and newspaper to his new partner, David Hall. Hall had come to him several years before highly recommended by William Strahan, a London printer. Franklin had planned to set him up with a shop in another town, "having all materials ready for that purpose," but when he saw that the young man could manage the shop and handle the newspaper he kept him on in Philadelphia. The new firm of Franklin and Hall would split profits down the middle for the eighteen years the partnership would last. Franklin's share would average six hundred and twenty pounds a year. The rest of his income would come from the rents of houses he owned in Philadelphia; from other printing partnerships in New York, Charleston, and Antigua; from the post office; and from the clerkship, though he kept this last mainly to know what went on behind the closed doors of the Assembly. Altogether his investments and posts brought in more than two thousand pounds a year, or over twice the governor's salary.

To mark the change in his life, he moved the family "to a more quiet part of the town." "For my own part, at present I pass my time agreeably enough," he told his mother after adjusting to retirement. "I enjoy (thro' mercy) a tolerable share of health; I read a great deal, ride a little, do a little business for myself, more for others; retire when I can and go [into] company when I please; so the years roll round, and the last will come; when I would rather have it said, *he lived usefully* than *he died rich.*"

The son assured Abiah Franklin, then in her mid-eighties, that "we read your writing very easily; I never met with a word in your letters but what I could readily understand; for tho' thy hand is not always the best, the sense makes everything plain." She had wondered if he still kept a Negro couple who had given him trouble. The woman, he said, "behaves exceeding well," and the man he had hired out to a printer, "who agrees to keep him in victuals and clothes, and to pay me a dollar a week for his work. . . . But we conclude to sell them both the first good opportunity; for we do not like Negro servants."

He clipped at least a year off the age when telling his mother about William, who in 1748 was eighteen and "a tall proper youth and much of a beau." In the summer of that year William had traveled to western Pennsylvania with Conrad Weiser. "He acquired a habit of idleness on the expedition," Franklin said, "but begins of late to apply himself to business, and I hope will become an industrious man. He imagined his father had got enough for him. But I have assured him that I intend to spend what little I have myself; if it please God that I live long enough. And as he by no means wants sense, he can see by my going on, that I am like to be as good as my word."

Daughter Sally, though still a child, "grows a fine girl, and is extremely industrious with her needle and delights in her books. She is of a most affectionate temper, and perfectly dutiful and obliging, to her parents and to all. Perhaps I flatter myself too much; but I have hopes that she will prove an ingenious sensible, notable and worthy woman, like her Aunt Jenney [Jane Mecom]."

Franklin's family lived as members of the gentry. Sally went to dancing school; soon she would be taking harpsichord lessons and studying French. He wanted William to study law in London and asked his friend Strahan to enroll the young man in the Middle Temple. (Strahan did in 1751, but six years passed before William took up residence.) He saw Deborah dressed like a lady, to judge from the belongings stolen from her in 1750, a partial list of which included "a double necklace of gold beads, a woman's long scarlet coat, almost new, with a double cape, a woman's gown of printed cotton, of the sort called brocade, very remarkable, . . . and sundry other goods." The theft offended Franklin enough to offer the then large sum of ten pounds for recovery of the goods. The robbery occurred soon after moving from the spacious house rented on the edge of town, where he had gone for peace and quiet, back to the center of the city. When one traded the countrylike atmosphere of Race Street for the soothing uproar of mid-town life a small price had to be paid.

2

Franklin did little or nothing in the way of electrical experiments through the first three-quarters of 1748. The Association occupied him until September, then he sank back to enjoy retirement or, more accurately, semiretirement. The small empire of printshops always called for attention. "Send 50 reams largest demi to Mr. Daniell, printer at Jamaica," he reminded Deborah when away from home. "Send 30 reams ditto to Peter Timothy. . . . Send the ream of thick blue paper to Parker."

The hours once given over to the shop passed in a variety of pleasant ways. Peter Kalm, a Swedish botanist and former pupil of Linnaeus, paid a long visit. The search for a Northwest Passage intrigued Franklin; he and Logan traded books on the subject that came their way. He read works on education and sent those, too, along to Logan. Collinson sent over a packet of the latest works on electricity. In a tardy note of thanks, Franklin said he had done little of late in electrical experiments, "but possibly may resume those inquiries this coming winter, as the approaching peace gives us a prospect of being more at ease in our minds."

Six months of silence followed that note. On 29 April 1749 he wrote two long letters—one to Collinson, the other to John Mitchell. Together they would have made a good-sized pamphlet. They differed from his earlier more informal reports. The paragraphs were numbered in the fashion used for papers printed in the Royal Society's *Transactions*. The letter to Collinson corrected misapprehensions of several English "electricians"—that the electrical fire, for instance, collected in the water of a Leyden jar. The water served only as a "conductor"—a term he coined —of the electrical fire. He also described "what we called an *electrical battery*"—his term, too—"consisting of eleven panes of large sash glass, armed with thin leaden plates," and joined together by wires in a way that all could be discharged together. He had constructed a parallel plate condenser, a device that is still standard and in common use.

During the winter of 1748–1749 Franklin acquired a new partner in science, Ebenezer Kinnersley, a Baptist clergyman and an ingenious experimenter. Kinnersley discovered that steam—like the humid air of a Philadelphia summer—disperses electrical fluid and prevents a Leyden jar filled with boiling water from being charged. Several delicate experiments performed with an "electrical thermometer," which he invented, revealed that electricity did not melt metals by "cold fusion." In the letter-essay to John Mitchell—entitled "Observations and Suppositions

towards forming a new Hypothesis for explaining the several Phae-
nomena of Thunder Gusts"—Franklin drew on an experiment "contrived by Mr. Kinnersley." "Lightning rends some bodies," concluded
Franklin. "The electrical spark will strike a hole thro' a quire of strong
paper." In other words, lightning and the electrical fire collected in a
Leyden jar were identical.

When Franklin's "very curious pieces" were read before the Royal
Society seven months later, they were "deservedly admired not only for
the clear intelligent style but also for the novelty of the subjects," Collinson reported. Still, the Society refused to publish either letter in the
Transactions. The affront had been carried too far for Collinson. "I am
collecting all these tracts together," he told Franklin, "with intention to
put them into some printer's hand to be communicated to the public."
And, he concluded, don't be put "out of countenance" by the "novelty
and variety" of your experiments. "Certainly something very useful to
mankind will be found out bye and bye."

3

The wait for the dry air of winter in which to conduct electrical
experiments gave Franklin a chance to collect his thoughts on electricity
and conceive new experiments. It also left time in the summer of 1749 to
stir up interest in a project that had long interested him—an academy to
educate the youth of Pennsylvania. He had broached the plan to Richard
Peters six years earlier; nothing had come of it then. Now the time
seemed ripe.

For the new campaign he revived techniques used to put across the
Association. First, he consulted friends, "of whom the Junto furnished
a good part." Next came persuasive arguments. "Numbers of our inhabitants are both able and willing to give their sons a good education, if it
might be had at home, free from the extraordinary expense and hazard
in sending them abroad for that purpose," said Franklin. "And this is the
more necessary now to be provided for by the English here, as vast
numbers of foreigners are yearly imported among us, totally ignorant of
our laws, customs, and language." The colony lacked good teachers,
having been "obliged frequently to employ in their schools, vicious imported servants, or concealed papists, who by their bad examples and
instructions often deprave the morals or corrupt the principles of the
children under their care." Finally, if the school succeeded it would
attract students from other colonies, "who must spend considerable sums
yearly among us."

Franklin floated a trial balloon in the *Gazette*, then unveiled the full plan in a pamphlet entitled *Proposals Relating to the Education of Youth in Pennsylvania*. The essay resembled nothing he had previously written. An avalanche of footnotes came within a line or two of pushing the text off nearly every page. He quoted liberally from Milton, Locke, and other learned Englishmen who censured "the *old method*" of educating youngsters. "For us, who are now to make a beginning, 'tis at least as easy to set out right as wrong; and therefore their sentiments are on this occasion well worth our consideration." It was an ingenious device—using Englishmen to endorse a system of education adapted to the American environment and little indebted to English precedents. Years ago Silence Dogood had ridiculed Harvard. Franklin's school would in no way resemble that adulterated version of Oxford and Cambridge. America needed something new.

First, students must be "frequently exercised in running, leaping, wrestling, and swimming." (In the footnotes Milton endorses exercise generally and Locke speaks up for swimming.) Their studies, says Franklin two pages and several footnotes later, must center on "things that are likely to be *most useful* and *most ornamental*, regard being had to the several professions for which they are intended." They will learn to write English in a fair hand and to speak it "properly, distinctly, emphatically; not with an even tone, which *underdoes*, nor a theatrical which overdoes nature." None of the students will be compelled to study the classical languages, "yet none that have an ardent desire to learn them should be refused; their English, arithmetic, and other studies absolutely necessary, being at the same time not neglected." The school seeks not to create learned gentlemen but to cultivate "that *benignity of mind*, which shows itself in *searching for* and *seizing* every opportunity *to serve* and *to oblige*; and is the foundation of what is called GOOD BREEDING; highly useful to the possessor, and most agreeable to all."

Thomas Penn objected to the proposed academy. People in London, he said, "think we go too fast with regard to the matter, and it gives an opportunity to those fools who are always telling their fears that the colonies will set up for themselves." But Franklin had little trouble getting twenty-four eminent Philadelphians to serve as trustees. They met in November and chose Franklin their president, but otherwise the meeting went badly for him. By his own count, three-fourths of the trustees were rich, conservative Anglicans, and not partial to experiments in education. Only a visionary could have expected their support for a scheme that played down the virtues of classical education. "The first instance of partiality in favor of the Latin part of the institution," Franklin reported, "was in giving the title of rector to the Latin master;

and no title to the English one." It hurt even more when "the votes of a majority carried it to give twice as much salary to the Latin master as to the English, and yet require twice as much duty from the English master as from the Latin, viz. £200 to the Latin master to teach twenty boys, £100 to the English master to teach forty!"

The school became less and less his. Like Cadwallader Colden he wanted it located in the country, because "the scholars will be freed from many temptations to idleness and some worse vices that they must meet with in the [city], and it may be an advantage to many children to be at a distance from their parents." But those who would endow the academy wanted it in the city and chose the now little used New Building built for Whitefield to house it. Franklin's conception was altered further by the owners of the New Building, who wanted a charity school within the academy to provide "instruction of poor children gratis, in reading, writing and arithmetic, and the first principles of virtue and piety."

Contributions nowhere neared the five thousand pounds Franklin announced in February 1750—two thousand would have been closer to the mark—but renovation of the lofty New Building went forward. "The care and trouble of agreeing with the workmen, purchasing materials, and superintending the work fell upon me," Franklin said. Richard Peters came to him with another worry. "I asked Mr. Franklin, who is the soul of the whole, whether they would not find it difficult to collect masters. He said, with an air of firmness, that money would buy learning of all sorts, he was under no apprehension about masters."

Franklin's interest in the Academy of Philadelphia slackened with the arrival of winter, and as if moving to the next act of a drama he resumed his electrical experiments. "They go on much slower in those discoveries at home, than might be expected," he said happily. He would soon send off to Collinson what he correctly regarded as his most important paper on electricity.

4

On 7 November 1749 Franklin noted in a journal kept for electrical experiments:

Electrical fluid agrees with lightning in these particulars: 1. Giving light. 2. Color of the light. 3. Crooked direction. 4. Swift motion. 5. Being conducted by metals. 6. Crack or noise in exploding. 7. Subsisting in water or ice. 8. Bending bodies it passes through. 9. Destroying animals. 10. Melting metals. 11. Firing inflammable substances. 12. Sulphureous smell. The electrical fluid is attracted by points. We do not know whether this property is in lightning. But since they agree in all particulars wherein we can already compare them, is it not probable they agree likewise in this? Let the experiment be made.

The experiments in the winter of 1749–1750 focused on the peculiar properties of pointed objects when put in contact with electrical fire, first noticed by Thomas Hopkinson four years earlier. "For the doctrine of *points* is very curious," said Franklin, "and the effects of them truly wonderful; and from what I have observed on experiments, I am of opinion, that houses, ships, and even towns and churches may be effectually secured from the stroke of lightning by their means; for if, instead of round balls of wood or metal, which are commonly placed on the tops of the weather cocks, vanes or spindles of churches, spires or masts, there should be put a rod of iron eight or ten feet in length, sharpened gradually to a point like a needle, and gilt to prevent rusting, or divided into a number of points, which would be better—the electrical fire would, I think, be drawn out of a cloud silently, before it could come near enough to strike; only a light would be seen at the point, like a sailor's corpusant [St. Elmo's fire]. This may seem whimsical, but let it pass for the present, until I send the experiments at large."

Nearly five months went by before Franklin felt confident enough to embody his "whimsical" idea in a paper to Collinson. The long essay, again with formally numbered paragraphs and a ponderous title—"Opinions and Conjectures concerning the Properties and Effects of the Electrical Matter, arising from Experiments and Observations made in Philadelphia, 1749"—opened with a description of the properties of electricity. ("The electrical matter consists of particles extremely subtile, since it can permeate common matter, even the densest metal, with such ease and freedom, as not to receive any perceptible resistance.") He went on to give with stunning clarity—"The most remarkable thing," an admiring layman wrote a few years after Franklin's death, "is the unparalleled simplicity and facility with which the reader is conducted from one state of the inquiry to another"—a full statement of all he had learned about electricity the past four years: that it was a single fluid; that it permeated the atmosphere; that it could be accumulated and discharged but not destroyed. It took several pages before he observed that pointed metal objects "have a property by which they *draw on* as well as *throw off* electrical fluid, at greater distances than blunt bodies can." Why this was so he did not know. "Nor is it of much importance to us to know the manner in which nature executes her laws; 'tis enough, if we know the laws themselves. 'Tis of real use to know, that china left in the air unsupported, will fall and break; but how it comes to fall, and why it breaks are matters for speculation. 'Tis a pleasure indeed to know them, but we can preserve our china without it."

It is one thing to conjecture "whether the clouds that contain lightning are electrified or not," another to prove it. Franklin now proposed an experiment to settle the question. "On top of some high tower or steeple, place a kind of sentry box big enough to contain a man and an electrical stand. From the middle of the stand let an iron rod rise, and pass bending out of the door, and then upright twenty or thirty feet, pointed very sharp at the end. If the electrical stand be kept clean and dry, a man standing on it when such clouds are passing low, might be electrified, and afford sparks, the rod drawing fire to him from the cloud. If any danger to the man should be apprehended (tho' I think there would be none) let him stand on the floor of his box, and now and then bring near to the rod, the loop of a wire, that has one end fastened to the leads; he holding it by a wax candle. So the sparks, if the rod is electrified, will strike from the rod to the wire and not affect him."

Franklin had written enough to shake the Royal Society awake, but he meant this paper to summarize *all* his opinions and conjectures about electricity. He moved on to report several experiments that proved electricity did not permeate glass—"*that we cannot, by any means we are yet acquainted with, force the electrical fluid thro' glass.*" He underlined the statement, for it contradicted the conclusions of all European experimenters. The remainder of the paper dealt mainly with the peculiar properties of glass. Finally, he pulled up short. "But I shall never have done," he said, "if I tell you all my conjectures, thoughts and imaginations on the nature and operations of this electrical fluid, and relate the variety of little experiments we have tried."

The abrupt ending made it appear Franklin had dashed off this long paper. Obviously, he had not. This was his masterpiece—"the fullest on the nature and operations of the electrical matter," he admitted—and he had probably completed the last of several drafts early in the summer of 1750 before he set off for Stratford, Connecticut, to woo Samuel Johnson, an Anglican clergyman, down to Philadelphia as master of the English school in the Academy; a strong man in that department would give ascendancy to Franklin's curriculum in spite of the trustees' preference for the Latin school. Johnson refused to commit himself—did Franklin still believe after the interview that money could "buy learning of all sorts"?—but the trip served as a vacation and gave a chance to ponder his ideas on electricity. On July 27, back in Philadelphia, he told Collinson he would soon mail a new paper about "our experiments on animals." Two days later he changed his mind and sent instead the long one with the cumbersome title. He knew Collinson was collecting the earlier papers into a book and wanted this one, rather than a trivial piece on experiments on animals, to round out the work.

5

Franklin, of course, knew that lightning could kill a man. He knew, too, that electrical fire (as he called it) collected in a battery of glass panes could kill a hen or a turkey; he and Kinnersley had done so in their experiments. He did not know first-hand what it felt like to be struck by a large charge of electrical fire until he made a mistake in an experiment two days before Christmas 1750. It was pure luck and his strong constitution that allowed him to survive; had he had a weak heart, he would have been killed. He described the accident in a precise, vivid report to his brother John. "I have lately made an experiment in electricity that I desire never to repeat," he wrote. "Two nights ago being about to kill a turkey by the shock from two large glass jars containing as much electrical fire as forty common vials, I inadvertently took the whole thro' my own arms and body, by receiving the fire from the united top wires with one hand, while the other held a chain connected with the outsides of both jars. The company present (whose talking to me, and to one another I suppose occasioned my inattention to what I was about) say that the flash was very great and the crack as loud as a pistol; yet my senses being instantly gone, I neither saw the one nor heard the other; nor did I feel the stroke on my hand, tho' I afterwards found it raised a round swelling where the fire entered as big as half a pistol bullet by which you may judge of the quickness of the electrical fire, which by this instance seems to be greater than that of sound, light and animal sensation. What I can remember of the matter, is, that I was about to try whether the bottles or jars were fully charged by the strength and length of the stream issuing to my hands as I commonly used to do, and which I might safely eno' have done if I had not held the chain in the other hand; I then felt what I know not how well to describe; an universal blow thro'out my whole body from head to foot which seemed within as well as without; after which the first thing I took notice of was a violent quick shaking of my body which gradually remitting, my sense as gradually returned, and then I thought the bottles must be discharged but could not conceive how, till at last I

perceived the chain in my hand, and recollected what I had been about
to do; that part of my hand and fingers which held the chain was left
white as tho' the blood had been driven out, and remained so eight or ten
minutes after, feeling like dead flesh, and I had a numbness in my arms
and the back of my neck, which continued till the next morning but wore
off. Nothing remains now of this shock but a soreness in my breastbone,
which feels as if it had been bruised. I did not fall, but suppose I should
have been knocked down if I had received the stroke in my head; the
whole was over in less than a minute.

"You may communicate this to Mr. Bowdoin [a Boston merchant and
fellow experimenter] as a caution to him, but do not make it more public,
for I am ashamed to have been guilty of so notorious a blunder; a match
for that of the Irishman, sister told me of, who to divert his wife poured
the bottle of gunpowder on the live coal; or of that other who being about
to steal powder, made a hole in the cask with a hot iron."

Thus did Franklin celebrate the end of 1750 and the approach of his
forty-fifth birthday.

CHAPTER

9

"HE AIMS AT GREAT MATTERS"

THE YEAR 1751 would be memorable for Franklin. On January 7, the day after his birthday, the Academy opened its doors. It soon flourished "beyond expectation." The trustees purchased two lots that flanked the New Building to prevent the school from "being crowded and our air taken away by future neighboring buildings." Thus far twenty-five hundred pounds had been spent, "but we have reason to think that in a few years the academy will maintain itself," Franklin said. "We have now above one hundred scholars, and the number daily increasing." He got the English master's salary raised to one hundred and fifty pounds and published another essay on his ideas for the English school, but the traditional curriculum continued to predominate. Franklin bided time, certain his views would eventually prevail.

Less than three weeks after the Academy opened he had another project going. Dr. Thomas Bond wanted a hospital for Pennsylvania. It would shelter the "lunatics or persons distempered in mind," two-thirds of whom he believed could be cured with proper care. It would also serve those "whose poverty is made more miserable by the additional weight of a grievous disease," those forced to "languish out their lives, tortured perhaps with the stone, devoured by the cancer, deprived of sight by cataracts, or gradually decaying by loathsome distempers."

When Bond approached possible contributors, they asked: "Have you consulted Franklin about this business? What does he think of it?" Bond, an old friend and fellow member of the Masons, the American Philosophical Society, and the Academy's board of trustees, called on Franklin, who, after listening to the scheme, said he liked it and agreed to help make it a reality.

Franklin saw that his usual techniques for raising money must be modified for the hospital, a project beyond the resources of private individuals. The government must help. But he found that members of the Assembly from the backcountry did not "relish the project; they objected that it could only be serviceable to the city, and therefore the citizens alone should be at the expense of it; and they doubted whether the citizens themselves generally approved of it." To meet the objections Franklin invented a new way to raise money—the matched gift. The Assembly would grant two thousand pounds for a hospital but only after an equal sum had been raised among the citizens. "The members who had opposed the grant, and now conceived they might have the credit of being charitable without the expense, agreed to its passage; and then, in soliciting subscriptions among the people, we urged the conditional promise of the law as an additional motive to give, since every man's donation would be doubled; thus the clause worked both ways. The subscriptions accordingly soon exceeded the requisite sum, and we claimed and received the public gift, which enabled us to carry the design into execution. . . . I do not remember any of my political maneuvers the success of which gave me at the time more pleasure, or wherein, after thinking of it, I more easily excused myself for having made some use of cunning."

Possibly Franklin used cunning in another way. The hospital campaign differed from others in that mainly Quakers supported and managed it. The Association had been sponsored by Presbyterians and other non-Quakers, the Academy largely by well-to-do Anglicans. Governor Hamilton, an Anglican and disliked by the Quakers, had signed the hospital bill into law reluctantly, convinced it would become a sectarian institution. The Quakers, in turn, omitted his name from the board of managers of the hospital and forced Franklin to go along with the gratuitous insult. (At least Thomas Penn thought he had been forced. "I believe Mr. Franklin had no intention to do a thing disagreeable to us," he said, "by leaving out the governor from being placed at the head of the visitation of the hospital, but no doubt many others had. . . .") Franklin may have allowed Hamilton to be slighted for a reason—he would soon stand for a seat in the Assembly. Quakers still controlled the legislature and, especially in the city, no man could win a seat without their support.

2

In April *Experiments and Observations on Electricity, Made at Philadelphia in America by Mr. Benjamin Franklin* was published in London. "I find you grow more and more famous in the learned world," Whitefield wrote. Franklin's aspirations rose markedly, and when he learned that Elliot Benger, postmaster general for the colonies, was dying, he saw no reason not to capitalize on his fame. He wanted the job, as did two friends— Cadwallader Colden and Dr. John Mitchell. Benger had mismanaged it, but in capable hands it ought to produce a substantial income and require little work once the department had been reorganized. The post also carried the prestige of being a royal official, and with a territory that stretched the length of the continent he would be able to travel where he wished on a government expense account. Franklin played down these attractions when asking Peter Collinson to work for his candidacy. In a day when postage was a considerable expense, letters to and from the postmaster general traveled free. The office would "be suitable to me, particularly as it would enable me to execute a scheme long since formed," he told Collinson, referring to the long since dead American Philosophical Society, "which I hope would soon produce something agreeable to you and all lovers of useful knowledge."

William Allen promoted Franklin for the post. He empowered his influential business correspondent in London to spend the "considerable sum" of three hundred pounds to improve Franklin's chances and searched out "his namesake, the worthy RALPH ALLEN, esq. of *Bath*," to work for the cause. It was a typical act of generosity on Allen's part. Earlier he had advanced a large sum to build the State House, a loan not repaid for thirty years. He had given more to the campaigns for the Academy and the hospital than anyone else. He had quietly subsidized the medical education in Europe of John Redman, now one of the city's leading physicians, and would later pay for the training abroad of a painter named Benjamin West and of another young man who would one day found the medical school of the University of Pennsylvania, Dr. John Morgan.

Franklin's political interests broadened as his aspirations rose. In May, he concerned himself with imperial affairs in a light but bitter essay. Parliament had forbidden the colonies to pass laws to prevent the importation of convicts from Great Britain, holding *"that such laws are against the public utility, as they tend to prevent the* IMPROVEMENT *and* WELL PEOPLING *of the colonies."* "Such a tender *parental* concern in our *mother country* for the *welfare* of her children, calls aloud for the highest *returns* of gratitude and duty," said Franklin. Let us show our thanks with a shipload of rattlesnakes, to be distributed gratefully around England, "but particularly in the gardens of the *prime ministers*, the *Lords of Trade*, and *members of Parliament;* for to them we are *most particularly* obliged." We are dutiful children, and "our *mother* knows what is best for us," he went on, putting a drain on his font of italics. "What is a little *housebreaking, shoplifting,* or *highway robbing;* what is a *son* now and then *corrupted* and *hanged,* a daughter *debauched* and *poxed,* a wife *stabbed,* a husband's *throat cut,* or a child's *brains beat out* with an ax, compared with this 'IMPROVEMENT and WELL PEOPLING' of the colonies!"

Franklin found another flaw in imperial management. The previous year's almanac had carried several pages of tables on births and deaths in and around Philadelphia, which led to the random thought that "people increase faster by generation in these colonies, where all can have full employ, and there is room and business for millions yet unborn." He said no more on the matter until 1751, when, in reaction against an act of Parliament that restricted the growth of the iron and steel industry in the colonies, he wrote "Observations concerning the Increase of Mankind, Peopling of Countries, etc." Here he applied to imperial policy the philosophy implicit in his essays on education—America is not Europe. The standard actuarial tables "formed on observations made on full settled old countries, as Europe," he said, will not "suit new countries as America." Here, where there is an abundance of land and a scarcity of labor, marriages "are more general, and more generally early than in Europe." Early marriages lead to large families, on the average twice the size of those in England. From some eighty thousand immigrants America's population has soared to over a million in little more than a century. "This million doubling, suppose but once in twenty-five years, will in another century be more than the people of England, and the greatest number of Englishmen will be on this side of the water. What an accession of power to the British empire by sea as well as land! What increase of trade and navigation!" How foolish, then, for Britain to restrain manufactures in her colonies, where there will always be a larger market than she can serve. "A wise and good mother will not do it. To distress, is to weaken, and weakening the children weakens the whole family."

Comments in a passing paragraph on slavery made Franklin the first to dismiss the institution as economically unsound. Some in Britain worried that the spread of slave labor would eventually let a manufacturing colony undersell the mother country. Dismiss the thought, said Franklin. "The labor of slaves can never be so cheap here as the labor of working men is in Britain," he wrote. "Anyone can compute it. Interest of money is in the colonies from 6 to 10 per cent. Slaves one with another cost £30 sterling per head. Reckon then the interest of the first purchase of a slave, the insurance or risk on his life, his clothing and diet, expenses in his sickness and loss of time, . . . expense of a driver to keep him at work, and his pilfering from time to time, almost every slave being from the nature of slavery a thief, and compare the whole amount with the wages of a manufacturer of iron or wool in England, you will see that labor is much cheaper there than it ever can be by Negroes here." In a postscript later omitted from all but the first printed edition, he observed that "the number of purely white people in the world is proportionably very small." Why, then, "increase the sons of Africa, by planting them in America, where we have so fair an opportunity, by excluding all blacks and tawneys, of increasing the lovely white and red?"

Despite the reference to the "lovely" redman, when Franklin talked of increasing mankind, he meant only his kind—the English-speaking Protestant white. He welcomed neither felons, Negroes, Catholics, nor the Germans flooding into Pennsylvania at the rate of several thousand each year. "This will in a few years become a German colony," he remarked in March 1751. "Instead of their learning our language, we must learn theirs, or live as in a foreign country." He amplified that thought in what appeared as an *obiter dictum* at the end of the essay but may have been one of the reasons that led to his writing it. "Why should the Palatine boors be suffered to swarm into our settlements, and by herding together establish their language and manners to the execution of ours?" he asked. "Why should Pennsylvania, founded by the English, become a colony of *aliens*, who will shortly be so numerous as to Germanize us instead of our Anglifying them, and will never adopt our language or customs, any more than they can acquire our complexion?" Though he cut this paragraph from later printings of the essay—not however, before it did him great harm—he held to his opinion in private. Though eastern counties had from six to eight members in the Assembly, Berks and York should be limited to one or two: because "a majority of Dutch lived in those counties, it was not proper to allow them to sit in the Assembly in an English government."

Franklin's startlingly accurate predictions—his "estimate that population in America would double every twenty or twenty-five years held substantially true until 1890, and his theory that English stock in the New World would outnumber Englishmen in the Old in one hundred years came true on schedule around 1851"—gave his essay a lasting fame that obscures its effect on contemporaries. The convincing forecast of America's inevitable growth planted the thought among English leaders that unless growth was held down by restraining acts of Parliament the colonies would soon be strong enough to declare their independence. The essay in the years ahead helped to justify the restrictive policies it sought to eliminate.

3

When Franklin decided in May 1751 to stand for a seat in the Assembly, he made a momentous decision. The electrical experiments would fix his reputation in history; the career in politics would nearly unfix it. Within fifteen years the list of those who hated him would be as long as his arm. On it would be several of his closest friends and heading it would be the proprietor, Thomas Penn.

Franklin had refused to run for the Assembly earlier; he stood for a seat in 1751 "against my inclination, and against my entreaties that I might be suffered to remain a private man." Later he said that an Assembly seat had become "more agreeable to me, as I was at length tired with sitting there to hear debates in which as clerk I could take no part, and which were often so unentertaining that I was induced to amuse myself.... And I conceived my becoming a member would enlarge my power of doing good. I would not, however, insinuate that my ambition was not flattered by all these promotions. It certainly was."

This hardly explains why an honor once dismissed was later accepted. In 1748 Franklin's Plan of Association had antagonized the Quaker community, which controlled the colony's political affairs and much of its wealth. ("Should we address that wealthy and powerful body of people, who have ever since the war governed our elections, and filled almost every seat in our Assembly?" he had asked of the Quakers in *Plain Truth*.) He probably could not have then won a seat in the Assembly; even if he had, once inside the chamber a majority of the members would have been arrayed against him. He chose instead to enter politics through another door—appointive office. In 1748 he accepted an invitation to join Philadelphia's city council, a self-perpetuating corporation. In 1749 the governor, with the approval of Thomas Penn, appointed him a justice of the peace. Franklin said later he did not like that post, and "finding that more knowledge of the common law than I possessed was necessary to act in that station with credit, I gradually withdrew from it." This sounds odd coming from one who could master almost anything he put his mind to and who could draw up a will or a complex partnership agreement, draft a bill, or compose a petition with a skill exceeded by few lawyers in the province. More to the point, the job was laborious, time-consuming, and unrewarding. The numerous petty disputes a justice dealt with made him as many enemies as friends. The city council, on the other hand, offered much prestige for little work and protected a man's reputation by meeting behind closed doors.

The Assembly offered these and other attractions and when in 1751 he received the proposal—"by me entirely unsolicited"—to stand for a seat, he accepted. By then he had smothered much of the Quaker animosity against him by his campaign for the hospital. He had worked closely on that project with Israel Pemberton, leader of the strictly pacifist Quakers. An alliance with the Quakers did not weaken the close tie with William Allen, leader of the non-Quaker or proprietary faction in the city, nor the friendly relations with the governor and with Thomas Penn, then working to help Franklin gain the job as postmaster general of the colonies. Franklin, in short, could run for the Assembly now knowing he would meet no serious opposition.

Even so, his election was staged to let him slip into the Assembly almost unnoticed. Franklin never revealed who backed his candidacy; he would only admit that "certain persons," unnamed, had proposed him. Some scholars credit Israel Pemberton for his election, others Isaac Norris, leader of the less rigid wing of the Quaker faction and the recently elected speaker of the Assembly. Neither man appears to have had a hand in it. Franklin stood for a seat left vacant in May by the death of William Clymer, a non-Quaker and a friend who had served as one of the lottery managers at the time of the Association. As with most by-elections, voting must have been light. The Assembly adjourned the day after the election. Not until August 13 could Benjamin Franklin, clerk, record that "Benjamin Franklin being returned a representative to serve in the Assembly for the city of Philadelphia, he was qualified and took his seat accordingly." Old friends now new colleagues honored him by appointing the hitherto unemployed twenty-one-year-old William Franklin the new clerk.

Franklin had joined a "club" as restricted and closely knit as his beloved Masonic lodge. Four times a year—in October, January, May, and August—it met behind the closed doors of a chamber in the State House large enough to seat the thirty members comfortably. (Later there would be less elbowroom when fifty-five gentlemen assembled in the same room as the Second Continental Congress.) Pennsylvanians "minded their own business," and paid attention to the Assembly only intermittently. Matters that interested the people—a new road, repair of a bridge, care of the poor—were handled by the county government, while the Assembly concerned itself principally with Indian affairs, paper money, and taxation. Indians had been no problem for several years; paper money was an issue too abstruse to arouse public interest; and taxes were virtually nonexistent. But though the Assembly had little to do, it could not be ignored: it was one of the most powerful legislatures in America. It disposed of every pence of provincial revenue collected from

the modest excise on spirits and from interests on loans made by the Loan
Office. When Franklin joined the legislature it had some fifteen thousand
pounds in the bank and an annual income of around seven thousand
pounds, none of which the governor or proprietors could touch, much
to their displeasure.

The Assembly's economic independence came about by accident. A
series of strokes had left William Penn paralyzed and speechless, and
years before his death in 1718 the colony had drifted along guided only by
local leaders. Not until 1746 did his sons, Thomas and Richard Penn, gain
clear legal title to the province. Thomas, as acting head of the family, set
about retrieving power usurped by the Assembly. Two forces drove him
to act. First, he wanted to put the colony on a paying basis. The books
showed that it was costing his family more to govern Pennsylvania than
it brought in in revenue. Second, the king's ministers had made it clear
that unless he reestablished control over the colony, the crown might take
it away from the family. Caught between an Assembly that proclaimed
control over provincial finances as a right and a crown that demanded
subjection of the Assembly to the executive, Thomas Penn would antago-
nize one side or the other, whatever he did.

Penn had twice visited the colony and knew its leading citizens well,
including Franklin, at whose shop he had often bought books and other
items. He returned to England in 1741, but after inheriting the proprietary hoped he would come back to Pennsylvania to serve as governor,
rather than send the customary deputy governor. He was liked and
respected in the colony. He took control of its affairs with a large hand-
icap—the Quaker oligarchy distrusted him for leaving the Society of
Friends for the Church of England. Nor did it help that he had also
abandoned his father's pacifist principles, a decision that led to a fight
with the Assembly three days after Franklin took his seat there.

Two years earlier rumors had drifted into Philadelphia that the
French were moving into the Ohio Valley, where local merchants were
expanding their trade with the Indians. Penn thought that a fort somewhere on the Ohio would contain the French menace and preserve Pennsylvania's interests in the area, and in February 1749 he offered to pay half
the estimated eight hundred pounds to erect one, plus one hundred
pounds toward its maintenance. The Assembly rejected the offer, preferring instead to win Indian goodwill with gifts. In the next two years it
dispensed over three thousand pounds for this purpose out of its own
pocket. In 1751 the Assembly asked the proprietor to share in this goodwill
program. He refused. Governor Hamilton reported his decision to the
Assembly on August 16. Franklin, surely impressed with the reasonable-

ness of Penn's call for a fort, signed a reply to the governor's message that rejected again the proprietor's offer to help build a fort. Rather, "we could wish our proprietaries had rather thought fit to join with us in the expense of those presents, the effect of which have at all times so manifestly advanced their interest with the security of our frontier settlements." Franklin three years earlier had stirred up Philadelphia to build a fort to protect the city. Now, three days in the Assembly, he advocated a Quaker program of love and friendship toward Indians and Frenchmen alike. It hardly made sense. William Allen must have wondered about his friend, with whom he had worked so hard to make the Association and the fort on the Delaware a reality. Franklin liked to say he often showed "an appearance of impartiality" in public affairs (it "gives a man sometimes much more weight when he would serve in particular instances"), but in his first important vote as an Assemblyman he made no effort at such an appearance. In a test of wills between executive and legislature he sided with the legislature, though it meant going against his better sense and accepting the Quakers' idealistic program over the proprietor's more reasonable one.

The question of how to deal with the Indians was, for the moment, minor compared to the fight over a new issue of paper money that came up a few months later. Parliament had recently forbidden New England to issue any more paper money. Pennsylvania went unmentioned in the act, and the Assembly expected its bill, calling for an issue of forty thousand pounds, would be accepted by the executive without hesitation. Instead, Hamilton rejected it, using the dubious arguments that it contravened British policy and that so large an issue might lead Parliament next to focus its restrictive policy on Pennsylvania. In a reply to the veto message that Franklin had a hand in, the Assembly reduced the amount of its proposed issue to twenty thousand pounds. The governor rejected the compromise. Unquestionably the colony needed a new issue of paper money, for the shortage of gold and silver was stifling trade. Previous issues, unlike those of the New England colonies, had been so well managed by Pennsylvania that there seemed slight chance that either Parliament or the king's advisers would look unkindly upon a new one. Yet the governor, without giving convincing reasons for his stand, refused to approve the measure.

The new issue of paper money, like previous ones, would offer more than a circulating medium. The interest on the bills would also produce a sizable income which, as in the past, would flow into the Assembly's hands. The governor dared not reveal that he had been ordered by Thomas Penn to sign no bill that failed to give control of all revenue raised to the executive. Penn asked only that his colony adhere to the practice in England, where Parliament voted on revenue-producing measures but the king and his ministers collected and spent the money. The Pennsylvania Assembly, however, though it presumed to emulate Parliament, had a different tradition. It claimed that it was the "natural right" of citizens "to dispose of their own money, by themselves or their representatives." Hamilton feared that if he revealed Penn's orders the Assembly would "bounce violently, and be very angry." His attorney general predicted that "the moment this instruction should be known it would occasion a down-right civil war in the province," and that "the governor and his friends would be publicly branded as deliverers up of the people's rights."

Hamilton chose to reject the Assembly's measure with flimsy arguments rather than face the issue. He only postponed the battle, for Thomas Penn was determined the Assembly should not dominate the government. Cutting the legislature down to size would be the first step in a sweeping reform program. In an early phase of the fight over paper money, which would go on for several years more, Richard Peters gave Penn an inkling of the sad state of his proprietary. "Your quit rents are shamefully in arrears," he wrote, "—your ferries out of your hands— your manor lords and appropriated tracts are settled . . . promiscuously. The Assembly [is] provoked by paper money being demanded and not likely to be granted—the sheriffs are the creatures of and subservient to the people—the juries without virtue in Proprietary disputes and no court of equity. While matters are in this situation it should be well considered where to begin and by what methods to proceed and who will undertake to manage—when this is agreed on order and steadiness may effect everything."

4

The year ended sadly for Franklin. James Logan, paralyzed by a series of strokes, died in his seventy-seventh year in the first week of November. A week later came a harder blow—Thomas Hopkinson, Franklin's closest friend, died at the age of forty-two. (He was the second charter member of the Junto to go; Thomas Godfrey had died two years earlier, his last years spent "continually muddled with drink.") Franklin ever after kept an eye on Hopkinson's widow and helped unobtrusively to rear her family. He later got the son Francis a sinecure from the crown and later still joined with him to sign the Declaration of Independence.

December brought the death of David Martin, rector of the Academy and the only man in Philadelphia Franklin judged a worthy chess opponent. With his death Franklin canceled an order for a book on chess placed with Strahan in London.

Thus ended 1751, the last year for the colonies under the Julian calendar. With eleven days dropped from the calendar in order to get in step with the Gregorian calendar long used by continental Europe, Franklin must hereafter celebrate his birthday on January 17. After explaining the reasons for the shift in calendar in the Preface to the almanac for 1752, Richard Saunders ended wishing "that this *new year* (which is indeed a New Year, such an one as we never saw before, and shall never see again) may be a happy year to all my kind readers. . . ."

CHAPTER

10

THE KITE

POLITICS IN 1752 still occupied a small part of Franklin's life, taking no more of it than when he served as the legislature's clerk. His routine remained much what it had been. He kept a close eye on the Academy, which now had three hundred students, about evenly divided among the Latin, English, and Charity schools. Francis Alison, a Presbyterian clergyman, ran the Latin school, but refused to serve as rector "or to have anything to do with the government of the other schools," which "obliges the trustees to more frequent visits." The hospital, too, took time. One month, in addition to the duties as a manager, he accompanied the physicians twice a week on their rounds. Friday evenings still went to the Junto, other evenings to meetings of the Masonic lodge, the Library Company's board of directors, the Academy's trustees, the hospital's board of managers, the city council, the Union Fire Company. Gaps in the day were filled with reading and long letters to friends in England and in other colonies. He still found time to take on new projects. In March he and Philip Syng sponsored the first insurance company in America—the Philadelphia Contributionship for the Insurance of Houses from Loss by Fire. (The seal designed by Syng, showing four united hands, led to the less pretentious nickname Hand-in-Hand.) Later in the year when a man named Charles Swain wrote from Maryland that he could find the Northwest Passage, Franklin, who had once collected and exchanged books on the subject with Logan, helped William Allen raise a thousand pounds to finance the search, and before the year ended could report that a "vessel is actually fitting for him to proceed . . . in the spring." (The *Argo*, under Swain's command, set out in March 1753 and after an abortive trip made a second search in 1754, again without success, yet without diminishing Franklin's certainty that such a passage existed.)

His mother died in May at the age of eighty-five. When confronted with the death of someone close, Franklin reacted with icy calm. Rarely did he say what the lost person had meant to him. Condolence came in a sentence or two of clichés. "She has lived a good life, as well as a long one, and is happy," he wrote of his mother's death, then went on to discuss business matters.

2

The month his mother died a Frenchman following a procedure outlined in *Experiments and Observations* tested and found true Franklin's hypothesis that lightning and electricity were one and the same. (It is a tribute to Franklin's grasp of the scientific method that he could design an experiment with such precision and clarity that a stranger three thousand miles away reading it in translation could carry it out and thereby transform a hypothesis into a theory.) Unaware of this, Franklin in June chose to test his hypothesis by flying a silk kite—silk was "fitter to bear the wet wind of a thunder gust without tearing"—into a thunderstorm.

As Carl Van Doren remarked years ago, "the episode of the kite, so firm and fixed in legend, turns out to be dim and mystifying in fact." At no time did Franklin say flatly *he* flew the kite. He left behind no firsthand account of the experiment. The *Autobiography* might have been expected to dwell on the event; Franklin mentions it there only in passing, after referring to the success of a French scientist in "drawing lightning from the clouds." "I will not swell this narrative with an account of that capital experiment," he writes, "nor of the infinite pleasure I received in the success of a similar one I made soon after with a kite at Philadelphia, as both are to be found in the histories of electricity."

The only known account of the experiment appeared fifteen years later in Joseph Priestley's *The History and Present State of Electricity*. Priestley unquestionably received his information from Franklin.

"The Doctor," Priestley wrote,

> having published his method of verifying his hypothesis concerning the sameness of electricity with the matter of lightning, was waiting for the erection of a spire [on Christ Church] in Philadelphia to carry his views into execution; not imagining that a pointed rod of a moderate height could answer the purpose; when it occurred to him that by

means of a common kite he could have better access to the regions of thunder than by any spire whatever. Preparing, therefore, a large silk handerchief and two cross-sticks of a proper length on which to extend it, he took the opportunity of the first approaching thunderstorm to take a walk in the fields, in which there was a shed convenient for his purpose. But dreading the ridicule which too commonly attends unsuccessful attempts in science, he communicated his intended experiment to nobody but his son who assisted him in raising the kite.

The kite being raised, a considerable time elapsed before there was any appearance of its being electrified. One very promising cloud had passed over it without any effect; when, at length, just as he was beginning to despair of his contrivance, he observed some loose threads of the hempen string to stand erect, and to avoid one another, just as if they had been suspended on a common conductor. Struck with this promising appearance, he immediately presented his knuckle to the key, and (let the reader judge of the exquisite pleasure he must have felt at that moment) the discovery was complete. He perceived a very evident electric spark. Others succeeded, even before the string was wet, so as to put the matter past all dispute, and when the rain had wet the string he collected electric fire very copiously. This happened in June 1752, a month after electricians in France had verified the same theory, but before he heard of anything they had done.

Franklin sailed the kite in June. There is no reason to doubt the date. It made no sense to risk the experiment after learning the French had verified his hypothesis. What is puzzling is the silence about an unequivocal triumph, a silence that lasted four months. Franklin generally did not speak of his experiments until months later, after double-checking results. The hasty report to Collinson of erroneous findings had bred caution. But the kite experiment differed from others. The findings were clear-cut and irrefutable—he had drawn electricity from the clouds. So far as he knew, no one else had confirmed his hypothesis, and one would expect him eager to transmit the news instantly to the world. But he said nothing—until October 19 in the *Gazette*—and then only described the experiment, said it had "succeeded in Philadelphia," but did not say that *he* had carried it out.

Such modesty was not like Franklin. Nor was it like him to keep buried "the exquisite pleasure he must have felt" when the silk threads of the kite string stood erect. When elated, Franklin confided in those he trusted. Some months after flying the kite he discovered that thunderclouds "are electrified negatively and the earth positively," a finding which, if true, was as momentous as the one about lightning. "This will seem a surprising position to you and to all mankind," he wrote to Collinson before he had verified the new hypothesis; "it will, when demonstrated, make a great alteration in our *theory,*" he added, meaning the theory about lightning. "You are the first I communicate this to, not only as a mark of my respect, but that you may consider if it has any relation to your principles. I only request that you would not divulge it at present."

Perhaps when Franklin learned that the French experiment with lightning antedated his own by a month he decided to withhold his news until he could profit from it. When he spoke of the kite in the *Gazette* in October, *Poor Richard* for 1753 was on the press. The last page carried a paragraph that would boost sales:

How to Secure Houses, etc. from LIGHTNING

It has pleased God in His goodness to mankind at length to discover to them the means of securing their habitations and other buildings from mischief by thunder and lightning. The method is this: Provide a small iron rod (it may be made of the rod-iron used by nailers) but of such a length that, one end being three or four feet in the moist ground, the other may be six or eight feet above the highest part of the building. To the upper end of the rod fasten about a foot of brass wire the size of a common knitting-needle, sharpened to a fine point; the rod may be secured to the house by a few small staples. If the house or barn be long, there may be a rod and point at each end, and a middling wire along the ridge from one to the other. A house thus furnished will not be damaged by lightning, it being attracted by the points and passing through the metal into the ground without hurting anything.

The puzzle here is: Why did Franklin wait, as he says he did, until September, some three months after flying the kite and just before releasing news of the experiment, to put lightning rods on his own house?

More curious is the manner in which he reported the experiment to Collinson. Normally his letters overflowed with details on how he carried out experiments. This time he mentioned only an enclosed clipping from the *Gazette* of "my kite experiment." Again he avoided saying *he* had flown the kite.

This studious sidestepping suggests the possibility he did not fly the kite. Earlier, in devising his experiment to draw lightning from the sky, Franklin raised the question of danger to the experimenter and answered: "I think there would be none." Since then he had been knocked out by a careless slip during an experiment. A man dealing with celestial lightning ran risks greater than the experimenter in a laboratory. Franklin knew this. For years the *Gazette* had studiously reported deaths from lightning in and around Philadelphia. Later he praised Thomas-François Dalibard "as being the first" who "had the courage to attempt drawing lightning from the clouds. . . ."

If Franklin did not fly the kite, who then did? Certainly not his son William, then in his early twenties. Franklin would no more have risked his son's life than his own. Perhaps a third man shared the vacant field that day and held the end of the kite string. If so, it had to be someone Franklin did not cherish, someone who would take orders, someone ignorant of the risks involved and in no position to claim credit for the results of the experiment, someone who, if injured in the experiment, or killed, would not be deeply missed. One of the young male slaves in Franklin's house would have fit these criteria perfectly.

"Every simple explanation of the kite mystery leaves it still confused," Van Doren has written. Perhaps to place a third person on that vacant field on the cloud-darkened afternoon in June 1752 clarifies the mystery no more than other explanations have. This much can be said —if a third person was there and flew the kite, Franklin ever after felt guilty about it. Something about the experiment all his life made him uneasy. That much is certain.

3

Several months after the kite experiment Franklin had another "exquisite pleasure," one he was willing to talk about—at length. This one was inspired by news from France. "The *Tatler* tells us," he wrote to a friend in New England,

> of a girl who was observed to grow suddenly proud, and none could guess the reason, till it came to be known that she had got on a pair of new silk garters. Less you should be puzzled to guess the cause when you observe anything of the kind in me, I think I will not hide my new garters under my petticoats, but take the freedom to show them to you, in a paragraph of our friend Collinson's letter last, viz.

—But I ought to mortify, and not indulge this vanity; I will not transcribe the paragraph. —Yet I cannot forbear. "If any of thy friends," says Peter, "should take notice that thy head is held a little higher up than formerly, let them know; when the grand monarch of France strictly commands the Abbé Mazéas to write a letter in the politest terms to the Royal Society to return the king's thanks and compliments in an extreme manner to Mr. Franklin of Pennsylvania, for the useful discoveries in electricity, and application of the pointed rods to prevent the terrible effects of thunderstorms, I say, after all this, is not some allowance to be made if the crest is a little elevated. There are four letters containing very curious experiments on thy doctrines of points and its verification, which will be printed in the new *Transactions*. I think now I have stuck a feather on thy cap, I may be allowed to conclude in wishing thee long to wear it. Thine P. Collinson." On reconsidering this paragraph, I fear I have not so much reason to be proud as the girl had; for a feather in the cap is not so useful a thing, or so serviceable to the wearer, as a pair of good silk garters. The pride of man is very differently gratified, and had his Majesty sent me a marshall's staff, I think I should scarce have been so proud of it as I am of your esteem.

The day he exulted about the praise from France he also boasted to Colden about the discovery that would surprise "all mankind." He had conceived an ingenious experiment to determine whether thunderclouds were electrified positively or negatively. Take two vials, one charged by a lightning rod, the other by friction; hang a small cork between them. "If both bottles then were electrified *postively*," he said, "the ball being attracted and repelled by one, must be also repelled by the other. If the one *positively* and the other *negatively*, then the ball would be attracted and repelled alternately by each, and continue to play between them as long as any considerable charge remained." On April 12, the day he revealed the French king's praise of his work, a "smart gust" passed over his house and he got a vial "charged pretty well with lightning." When he performed the experiment, "I beheld with great surprise and pleasure the cork ball playing briskly between them; and was convinced that one bottle was electrified *negatively.*"

Again he felt "exquisite pleasure." This time, the very day of his discovery, he sent word of it to Colden. Nearly a half year would pass before Collinson learned about it. Franklin repeated the experiment eight times in May, "always with the same success," he said later. "Yet notwithstanding so many experiments, it seems I concluded too soon; for at last,

June the 6th, in a gust which continued from five o'clock P.M. to seven, I met with one cloud that was electrized *positively*, tho' several that passed over my rod before, during the same gust, were in a *negative* state." A single experiment had destroyed his new hypothesis—that "*'tis the earth that strikes into the clouds*, and not the clouds that strike into the earth." Abashed, he dared now to say only that "for the most part" this seemed true.

He had still not resolved the contradictions four months later when, reversing previous practice, he sent the inconclusive results to Collinson. "These thoughts, my dear friend," he explained, "are many of them crude and hasty, and if I were merely ambitious of acquiring some reputation in philosophy, I ought to keep them by me, 'till corrected and improved by time and farther experience. But since even short hints, and imperfect experiments in any new branch of science, being communicated, have often times a good effect, in exciting the attention of the ingenious to the subject, and so becoming the occasion of more exact disquisitions and more complete discoveries, you are at liberty to communicate this paper to whom you please; it being of more importance that knowledge should increase, than that your friend should be thought an accurate philosopher."

4

On 30 November 1753 the Royal Society bestowed upon Franklin its highest award—the Copley Medal. The Society acknowledged Mr. Franklin "to be a very able and ingenious man" who "has a head to conceive and a hand to carry into execution, whatever he thinks may conduce to enlighten the subject matter of which he is treating." Upon receiving the medal Franklin responded with a graceful note:

> I know not whether any of your learned body have attained the ancient boasted art of *multiplying* gold; but you have certainly found the art of making it infinitely *more valuable*.

News of the award of the Society's gold medal had been brought from England by William Smith, then a friend. Four years later Smith accused Franklin of having plagiarized fame. Ebenezer Kinnersley was the "author of a considerable part of those discoveries in *electricity*, published by Mr. Franklin to whom he communicated them," said Smith. "Indeed, Mr. Franklin himself mentions his name with honor, tho' he has not been careful enough to distinguish between their particular discoveries. This, perhaps he may have thought needless, as they were known to act in concert. But tho' that circumstance was known here, it was not so in the remote parts of the world to which the fame of these discoveries have extended."

Smith had a point. Franklin often used the word "we" when recounting the experiments that had been conducted in Philadelphia, but not until 1769, eleven years after Smith's accusation, did he mention his collaborators. But Kinnersley would not stand for any reproof of his colleague and instantly defended Franklin in one of the most generous letters in the history of science written by one deprived of his just share of fame:

Sir,

I was very much surprised and concerned to see the account you have been pleased to give of my electrical discoveries, in page 639 of the *American Magazine*. If you did it with a view to procure me esteem in the learned world, I should have been abundantly more obliged to you, had it been done, so as to have no tendency to depreciate the merit of the ingenious and worthy Mr. Franklin in the many curious and justly celebrated discoveries he has made in electricity. Had you said that, being honored with Mr. Franklin's intimacy, I was often with him when he was making experiments, and that new discoveries were sometimes made when we were together, and at other times some were made by myself at home, and communicated to Mr. Franklin, this would have been really true, though it is what I never desired to have published. But to say, "That I am the author of a *considerable* part of those discoveries in electricity, published by Mr. Franklin"— the expression, from whomsoever you might have the intelligence, appears too strong. It may be understood to comprehend *more* than is strictly true, and therefore I thought myself obliged to take this public notice of it. If you will please, sir, to examine what Mr. Franklin has published on electricity, I think you will nowhere find that he appropriates to himself the honor of any one discovery; but is so complaisant to his electrical friends, as always to say, in the plural number, *we* have found out, or, *we* discovered, etc. As to his *not being careful to distinguish between the particular discoveries of each*: this perhaps was not always practicable; it being sometimes impossible to recollect in whose breast the thought first took rise, that led to a series of experiments, which at length issued in some unexpected important discovery. But had it been always practicable to distinguish between the particular discoveries of each, it was altogether unnecessary; as,

I believe, none of Mr. Franklin's electrical friends had the least thought of ever appearing as competitors for any of the honors that they have beheld, with pleasure, bestowed upon him, and to which he had an undoubted right, preferable to the united merit of all the electricians in America, and, perhaps, in all the world. I am, sir, your most obedient humble servant,

EBENEZER KINNERSLEY

CHAPTER

11

"JOIN, OR DIE"

"I THINK I HAVE NEVER BEEN more hurried in business than at present," Franklin remarked in May 1753, after five years of retirement. Between electrical experiments that month and the usual array of meetings, he finished copy for the upcoming edition of *Poor Richard* and attended the Assembly, where he sat on all important committees. In June, again between experiments and while clearing his desk in order to be free for a trip to New England on post office business—though still waiting to hear about the postmaster general appointment, he had recently been made comptroller of the American department—he visited the village of Lancaster to settle some matters with a printing partner there, arranged for his son William to manage the Philadelphia post office and his business affairs while away, and found time to welcome William Smith to Philadelphia.

Smith, a twenty-six-year-old Scotsman, came to New York in 1751 to tutor the sons of a Long Island country gentleman. The following year he published *Some Thoughts on Education,* which Franklin read "with great approbation," then in 1753 he elaborated those thoughts in *A General Idea of the College of Miranda.* "For my part, I know not when I have read a piece that has more affected me, so noble and just are the sentiments, so warm and animated the language," Franklin wrote the author, and though the young man planned to return soon to England for ordination in the Anglican Church he accepted an invitation to visit Philadelphia and tour the Academy. Franklin found him to be bright, well read, and good company. He invited Smith to accompany him on his trip as far as Connecticut, where with Samuel Johnson they could talk away the night about the best way to educate Americans. Smith proved a marvelous traveling companion. Before they parted Franklin gave him a warm letter of introduction to Collinson in London; in it he suggested that after ordination Smith might be persuaded to return to America as rector of the Academy. ("Mr. Smith's a very ingenious man," Collinson wrote later. "It's a pity but was he more solid, and less flighty." He continued to warn his friend about Smith's "warmth and fire," his immaturity, his lack of "judgment and understanding," but Franklin remained blind to the flaws.)

The New England trip lasted from June through August. Franklin suffered from the heat and had chosen to exchange the dreadful humidity of a Philadelphia summer for the sea breezes of Boston; he was rewarded with a cool and comfortable holiday. The highlight of the trip came on July 25 when Harvard awarded him an honorary degree as Master of Arts for his "great improvement in philosophical learning." It was a glorious occasion for Franklin, and twenty years later he was still relishing the "jolly conversation" he and the friends of his youth had had that day "over that well replenished bowl at Cambridge commencement."

2

Back in Philadelphia Franklin learned that a group of Indians wanted a conference with the leaders of Pennsylvania. The French in recent months had stepped up their attacks in the Ohio Valley against un-friendly tribes. The chiefs from that region, together with delegates from the Six Nations of the Iroquois, wanted reassurances that the English would aid in their resistance to French incursions. But they would ven-ture no closer to the white man's settlements than Carlisle, a Scotch-Irish village west of the Susquehanna. Hamilton commissioned Richard Pet-ers, Isaac Norris, and Franklin to represent the province at the conclave. The three hastened to Carlisle, arriving on September 26 to find more than a hundred Indians on hand.

The ritual of the conference fascinated Franklin. When the commis-sioners prepared to open negotiations the Indians demurred; they must wait for the presents coming from Philadelphia. The tribes from the Ohio Valley had suffered many losses from French raids and their chiefs "could not proceed to business while the blood remained on their gar-ments, and . . . condolences could not be accepted unless the goods intended to cover the graves, were actually spread on the ground before them." When the gifts arrived, Scaroyady, a chief of one of the Iroquois tribes that claimed suzerainty over the western Indians, spoke to his brethren. "We suppose that the blood is now washed off," he said. "We jointly . . . dig a grave for your warriors, killed in your country; and we bury their bones decently; wrapping them up in those blankets; and with those we cover their graves."

On the third day Scaroyady addressed the fidgety white men, who were eager to get on with the main business. "I desire you would hear and take notice of what I am about to say now," he said firmly. "We desire that Pennsylvania and Virginia would at present forbear settling on our lands, over the Allegheny hills. We advise you rather to call your people back on this side the hills, lest damage should be done, and you think ill of us." He wanted Pennsylvania to exert more control over the number and character of the traders sent among the Indians. "If only honest and sober men were to deal with us, we think they might afford the goods cheaper." The traders who come now bring too much flour and rum, not enough powder and lead. "The rum ruins us. We beg you would prevent its coming in such quantities, by regulating the traders. We never understood the trade was to be for whisky and flour. We desire it may be forbidden, and none sold in the Indian country."

The commissioners replied next day. They ignored the request that settlers be blocked from traveling over the mountains; they agreed on the need for closer supervision of Indian traders. The unregulated traders, they emphasized in their report to the governor, "by their own intemperance, unfair dealings, and irregularities, will, it is to be feared, entirely estrange the affections of the Indians from the English." The Indians got no promise of powder and guns with which to fight the French and of course none of military aid from a colony ruled by Quakers.

Franklin came away from his first exposure to Indian grievances with a simplified solution. Reform the Indian trade and all would be well. When in doubt how to proceed, he turned to New England for guidance. "If you can procure and send me your truckhouse law and a particular account of the manner of executing it, with its consequences, etc., so that we may have the benefit of your experience, you will much oblige me," he wrote a friend in Boston, "and if you have found it a useful law, I am in hopes we shall be induced to follow your good example." While waiting to hear, Franklin and Hall published *A Treaty Held with the Ohio Indians at Carlisle in October, 1753*, one of the most handsome volumes the New Printing-Office ever put out.

3

Soon after returning from Carlisle, Franklin learned that after two years of negotiations and support from William Allen and Thomas Penn he had been only partly successful in the bid for the job of postmaster general of the colonies. He won the post but had to share it with William Hunter, postmaster at Williamsburg and publisher of the *Virginia Gazette.* (For all that, he had been luckier than his friend Dr. Mitchell, who "was really bamboozelled per the office.") Allen offered to post Franklin's security bond but was told "Mr. Hunter has found security for them both." The salary of six hundred pounds, split two ways, would "be paid out of the money arising from the postage of letters" after all expenses had been covered. Franklin had said the income meant little to him. He now complained to his brother John that the office being divided "very much diminishes the profits." John reassured him. "I think if the post riders were regulated according to law you'd find the profits of one half amounting to more than the whole." Franklin marked the passage in John's letter and proceeded to act upon it. Before the year ended he had, with Hunter's concurrence, devised a set of instructions for all postmasters. They must take care in hiring post riders; if the riders dallied between stations the dereliction must be remedied. The rate schedule must be adhered to rigorously. Two months after undelivered letters had been advertised in the local press they were to be sent "to the General Post Office at Philadelphia as *dead letters.*" In the large towns letters not picked up at the local office would be hand-delivered for a penny. Within a year a letter mailed from New York on Monday reached Philadelphia the next day at 5 P.M. and service had been expanded from one to three weekly deliveries. The reforms were costly and "in the first four years the office became above £900 in debt to us," Franklin said, but in the fourth year they recouped their investment, and from then on sent a tidy sum to the home office after deducting their salaries. When "a freak of the minister's" removed Franklin from office in 1774, the American branch yielded a profit of three thousand pounds annually.

Franklin's instructions to the branch offices in 1753 established rules that would govern the operation of the American post office for over a century. At the same time he initiated an even more durable tradition: postmasterships became plums awarded to relatives, friends, and political allies. When Franklin became comptroller, William took over as Philadelphia postmaster, then as comptroller when his father moved up the ladder. Later, Franklin's printing partner in New York, James Parker, became comptroller when William sailed to London with his father. Meanwhile, Peter Franklin moved down from Boston to become Philadelphia's postmaster and brother John moved from Newport to assume the office in Boston. So it went as long as Benjamin Franklin ran the department.

4

Franklin and Hunter had worked out their plans for the department in the village of Baltimore, approximately halfway between the home base of each man. There Jonas Green, who had once worked in Franklin's shop and now published the *Maryland Gazette*, arranged to have him inducted into the Tuesday Club. A member preserved for posterity the quality of wit, fortified by wine, that prevailed at the meeting Franklin attended:

SECRETARY: . . . I would move that as this gentleman is to leave the club soon, he may, from a long standing, be transmogrified into an honorary member, as others before him have been.

JONAS GREEN: Why, Mr. Secretary, you would not have us dock the gentleman. I suppose the member, however he may stand now at this juncture, is as long as ever.

DEPUTY PRESIDENT: Ha, ha, ha, the long standing members methinks are waggish.

FRANKLIN: Long standing members, I think gentlemen, with submission, are not so properly waggish, because if they stand they cannot wag.

Refreshed by that exchange, Franklin arrived back in Philadelphia early in February 1754. Shortly after his return Governor Hamilton told the Assembly that Virginia was sending a company of militia under Lt. Col. George Washington, then twenty-one years old, to reinforce a makeshift fort at the Forks of the Ohio; Virginia would be pleased if Pennsylvania joined in the expedition. The Assembly haggled over whether the Forks of the Ohio lay within British territory, decided they did not, and refused to appropriate money for an expedition.

Hamilton also relayed word to the Assembly that the Board of Trade had asked Pennsylvania, along with all other colonies, to send delegates to Albany for a conference in June to cajole the Iroquois tribes from defecting to the French. The board hoped, too, a plan could be worked out whereby the colonies would jointly share the "expense and operations" of a campaign against the French. The governor wanted Richard Peters, John Penn, Isaac Norris, and Franklin to represent Pennsylvania at the conference. The Assembly approved the slate, then went on record against all "propositions for an union of the colonies in Indian affairs."

Early in May the governor reported to the Assembly that the French had captured Virginia's jerry-built fort at the Forks of the Ohio. They now controlled the entire Ohio Valley unless Washington could oust them. The *Gazette* reacted with a long account of events in the West that ended with an editorial probably by Franklin:

> The confidence of the French in this undertaking seems well-grounded on the present disunited state of the British colonies, and the extreme difficulty of bringing so many different governments and assemblies to agree in any speedy and effectual measures for our common defense and security; while our enemies have the very great advantage of being under one direction, with one council and one purse. Hence, and from the great distance of Britain, they presume that they may with impunity violate the most solemn treaties subsisting between the two crowns, kill, seize and imprison our traders, and confiscate their effects at pleasure (as they have done for several years past) murder and scalp our farmers, with their wives and children, and take an easy possession of such parts of the British territory as they find most convenient for them; which if they are permitted to do, must end in the destruction of the British interest, trade and plantation in America.

Common sense convinced Franklin that only a united America could keep the French at bay. But his vision of America outstripping Great Britain within a century called for more—the French must be ejected from the continent. Only then could the empire spread westward. As usual, Franklin tied his vision to personal interest. During the last trip to New England he had talked to gentlemen in Connecticut about settling the land beyond the Alleghenies. He agreed to negotiate with the Six Nations for a block of the territory over which they claimed suzerainty. The scheme must be kept secret, "as it may give notice to the French, and put them on taking some preventive measures; or stir up some persons at home to obtain a patent before we can take possession and make a settlement." His attendance at the Carlisle Indian conference, where chiefs from the Six Nations were on hand, offered the chance to put out feelers for the proposed purchase.

What could be gained by establishing new colonies in the West? They would secure the frontiers of the older colonies, promote Indian trade, prevent "the dreaded junction of the French settlements in Canada with those of Louisiana." Was the project feasible? Yes, "as there are already in the old colonies, many thousands of families that are ready to swarm, wanting more land," said Franklin. Also, "a great sum of money might be raised in America on such a scheme as this; for there are many who would be glad of any opportunity by advancing a small sum at present, to secure land for their children, which might in a few years become very valuable."

The sudden tightening of the French grip upon the West caused a change in plans. No private group nor even a single colony could overcome the French, but the united colonies could repel them and "they might easily, by their joint force, establish one or more new colonies, whenever they should judge it necessary or advantageous to the interest of the whole." Such were Franklin's thoughts on the eve of the Albany Congress.

5

The four commissioners, with Conrad Weiser along to interpret and negotiate with the Indians, set out on June 3 for the Albany Congress, leaving behind a defenseless colony. They paused in New York City to buy presents for the Indians; while there Franklin outlined a plan for a union of the northern colonies. "It would be a very strange thing, if six nations of ignorant savages should be capable of forming a scheme for such an union," he had once said, "and yet that a like union should be impracticable for ten or a dozen English colonies, to whom it is more necessary, and must be more advantageous." He saw no serious obstacle to implementing a colonial union, "for reasonable, sensible men, can always make a reasonable scheme appear such to other reasonable men, if they take pains, and have time and opportunity for it."

His plan called for a governor general appointed and paid by the crown and a Grand Council chosen by the assemblies of the northern colonies. The governor general could veto all acts of the Grand Council. Money to run the government would come from an excise on liquor collected by the colonies. Earlier, Franklin had said "a voluntary union entered into by the colonies themselves, I think, would be preferable to one imposed by Parliament." Now, with Pennsylvania on record against any kind of union, he thought any plan should be "sent home, and an act of Parliament obtained for establishing it."

The plan revealed a curious split in Franklin's political thinking. In Pennsylvania he had sided with the legislature in its battles against the executive. He opposed the governor having any say in the spending of money appropriated by the Assembly. Now he favored the executive sharing in the dispensation of all money collected. He also called for an executive whose salary would be paid by the crown, thus freeing him from a powerful legislative restraint, and he granted him an absolute negative of all legislation.

With the "Short Hints towards a Scheme for uniting the Northern Colonies" in his pocket, Franklin and his colleagues left New York City on Sunday evening, June 9. They had a leisurely trip up the majestic Hudson. Their sloop carried "a pipe of the oldest and best Madeira wine to be got . . . a barrel of good cider and two barrels of small beer" along with several sheep to provide fresh mutton. They reached Albany on June 17 and two days later the Albany Congress convened. Present were delegates from Pennsylvania, Maryland, New York, and all the New England colonies. Thomas Pownall, touring America on an investigatory trip for the Board of Trade, sat in as an unofficial observer. Absent was Virginia, a bad sign; without her concurrence any decision that touched her interests would lack authority.

Negotiations with the Indians opened on an embarrassing note, with the redmen heckling the English as cowards. "Look about your country and see. You have no fortifications about you," said one contemptuous chief. "Look at the French; they are men; they are fortifying everywhere. But, we are ashamed to say it, you are all like women, bare and open, without any fortifications." Franklin thought the powwows a waste of time. "Nothing of much importance was transacted with them; at least nothing equal to the expense and trouble of so many colonies," he said. "We brightened the chain with them, etc., and parted good friends; but in my opinion no assistance is to be expected from them in any dispute with the French, till by a complete union among ourselves we are enabled to support them in case they should be attacked."

Here Franklin dissembled, playing down concessions gained from the Indians to promote his Plan of Union. Under Weiser's skillful guidance, the Six Nations parted with an empire for four hundred pounds down and another four hundred to be paid "whenever the lands over the Appalachian hills should be settled." Franklin witnessed the deed that transferred enough land west of the mountains to create the two colonies he dreamed of.

Franklin spent most of his time at the congress working on a plan of union. The New England delegation arrived with its own scheme, drawn up by Thomas Hutchinson of Massachusetts. It called for a union of all the northern colonies except Pennsylvania, whose ruling Quakers would never sanction military operations against Indians. The central government would have little power, except in the military sphere. It could not levy taxes; all money would be requisitioned from the colonies. Hutchinson was an experienced politician and the weak central government he proposed was the most he thought could be exacted from the colonial assemblies.

Sometime during the first week of the congress Franklin and Hutchinson abandoned the limited scope of their plans and agreed with their colleagues that a union of *all* the colonies was "absolutely necessary for their security and defense." A committee headed by Hutchinson and including Franklin and Stephen Hopkins of Rhode Island, who would one day sign the Declaration of Independence with his colleague, was chosen to draw up a Plan of Union. Franklin, with his extraordinary ability to sway even such strong-minded men as these to his side, got the committee to back a plan that would create a true union of the colonies, no mere confederacy. The central government could tax, raise armies, wage war, and make peace. For colonies like Virginia whose charters granted them territory "from sea to sea," the government had power to reduce their boundaries "to more convenient dimensions," and in the newly acquired lands to make settlements and create new colonies. Any laws made by the government would be sent to the king for approbation, not to the colonial assemblies. The plan pleased Franklin. "It is not altogether to my mind, but 'tis as I could get it," he said, without specifying what he disliked about it; "for the sake of obtaining generals, you know one is sometimes obliged to give up particulars."

Franklin's reputation as a practical man has obscured the visionary whose schemes time after time failed because he dreamed too large and lost touch with reality. His Albany plan "sought to take a leap," Lawrence Gipson has remarked, when a small step was appropriate. Every change he persuaded colleagues to make to strengthen the loose union Hutchinson had proposed "lessened its chance of popular approval and acceptance in America." Hutchinson worked for the possible. Yet Franklin, the visionary, somehow persuaded Hutchinson and the other delegates, all seasoned politicians, to accept his plan—a gratifying tribute to a reasonable man's ability to sway other reasonable men to his side.

While debating the Plan of Union, the delegates learned the French had resoundingly defeated George Washington and now controlled all land west of the Appalachian Mountains to the Mississippi River. If the news convinced doubters at Albany of the need for a strong union and hastened acceptance of Franklin's plan, it had no similar effect upon the colonial legislatures. All rejected it. "The governor of Pennsylvania in sending it down to the Assembly," Franklin recalled, "expressed his approbation of the plan 'as appearing to him to be drawn up with great clearness and strength of judgment, and therefore recommended it as well worthy their closest and most serious attention.' The House, however, by the management of a certain member [Isaac Norris, who had voted for the plan at Albany] took it up when I happened to be absent, which I thought not very fair, and reprobated it without paying any attention to it at all, to my no small mortification."

Still, Franklin did not abandon hope. "Our Assembly were not inclined to show any approbation of the Plan of Union," he wrote a friend, then hinted what he expected, "yet I suppose they will take no steps to oppose its being established by the government at home." To help convince the government at home he composed a long essay entitled "Reasons and Motives for the Albany Plan of Union" which he gave to Thomas Pownall, who promised to send it to the Board of Trade. A few days later Franklin—with William Hunter as a companion—vanished from Philadelphia for half a year.

6

The trip, a long overdue inspection of the American postal system, had been mapped out for some time. Franklin hoped "to be at home in the winter, the season for electrical experiments," then visit the South in the spring. He estimated they "must travel at least 3,000 miles before we sit down at home again."

The itinerary called for making Boston their headquarters and working outward on brief trips to branch offices through the autumn. That plan had to be discarded. "Poor Mr. Hunter is relapsed into his last summer fever, and has kept his bed these eight days, frequently delirious, and watchers attend him every night," Franklin reported in mid-October. "This has prevented our journey to Piscataqua, and very much disconcerts our measures." A month later Hunter's fever had dropped but "left him under an obstinate disorder in his bowels."

Franklin, however, remained in good health and passed the days pleasantly. He struck up a friendship with Gov. William Shirley, one of the ablest royal officials in America, and the two argued amiably about the Plan of Union. Shirley thought it would be more acceptable to the crown if the Grand Council as well as the president general were appointed by the home government. He thought that continental taxes should be laid on America by Parliament. Franklin disagreed. "I apprehend, that excluding the *people* of the colonies from all share in the choice of the Grand Council, will give extreme dissatisfaction, as well as the taxing them by act of Parliament, where they have no representative." Americans, he went on, "are likely to be better judges of the quantity of forces necessary to be raised and maintained, forts to be built and supported, and of their own abilities to bear the expense, than the Parliament of England at so great a distance." Furthermore, they are not represented in Parliament, and "it is supposed an undoubted right of Englishmen not to be taxed but by their own consent given thro' their representatives." Did Franklin favor Americans holding seats in Parliament? Shirley asked. Yes, "provided they had a reasonable number of representatives allowed them; and that all the old acts of Parliament restraining the trade or cramping the manufactures of the colonies, be at the same time repealed." He went on to state the goal he would seek for the next twenty years. "I should hope, too, that by such an union, the people of Great Britain and the people of the colonies would learn to consider themselves, not as belonging to different communities with different interests, but to one community with one interest, which I imagine would contribute to strengthen the whole, and greatly lessen the danger of future separations."

As he watched the colonies one by one reject his plan—Massachusetts dismissed it peremptorily on December 14—Franklin finally admitted that none of the colonies "will act upon it so as to agree to it, or to propose any amendments to it." He said: "Everybody cries, a union is absolutely necessary; but when they come to the manner and form of the union, their weak noodles are presently distracted. So if ever there be an union, it must be formed at home by the ministry and Parliament. I doubt not but they will make a good one, and I wish it may be done this winter."

7

Hunter refused to mend. The "obstinate disorder in his bowels" left him barely able to sit up in bed. On December 30, Franklin left Hunter to recuperate in Boston and set out to continue the inspection tour. Several friends accompanied him, one of them Catharine Ray, a handsome twenty-four-year-old girl he had recently met at a relative's house. Franklin had made advances toward her which she rebuffed. Once sure he could not conjure her into bed, it satisfied him to enjoy her company. "Your favors come mixed with the snowy fleeces, which are as pure as your virgin innocence," he said later in a letter, "white as your lovely bosom—and as cold. But let it warm towards some worthy young man, and may heaven bless you both with every kind of happiness."

The trip began badly. A blacksmith for an exorbitant price supposedly put steel shoes on the horses before the party left. "But he never did it, for as soon as we set out from Boston, I perceived the horses to slip on the ice," Franklin reported back to his brother John. "We were obliged to alight and lead them, and they could no more stand than if they had been shod with skates, but were upon their knees and noses every step." The blacksmith "had shown such a strict regard to the old *moral law* in the Eighth Commandment, *Thou shalt not STEEL,*" said Franklin, "I rather take him to have been a thief, and if he minds any Scripture, 'tis that in the Revelations, *Let him that hath stole*, STEEL *no more*, and so the rascal only cheats."

Franklin spent the end of January and all of February ambling through Rhode Island and across Connecticut, checking on postmasters, pausing at New Haven to hear a stately oration in Latin which formally bestowed an honorary degree Yale had awarded him two years earlier. "I left New England slowly, and with great reluctance," he said. "Short days' journeys, and loitering visits on the road, for three or four weeks, manifested my unwillingness to quit a country in which I drew my first breath, spent my earliest and most pleasant days, and had now received so many fresh marks of the people's goodness and benevolence, in the kind and affectionate treatment I had everywhere met with. I almost forgot I had a home; till I was more than halfway towards it; till I had, one by one, parted with all my New England friends and was got into the western borders of Connecticut among mere strangers. Then, like an old man, who, having buried all he loved in this world, begins to think of heaven, I begun to think of and wish for home; and as I drew nearer, I found the attraction stronger and stronger, my diligence and speed increased with my impatience. I drove on violently, and made such long stretches that a very few days brought me to my own house, and to the arms of my good old wife and children, where I remain, thanks to God, at present well and happy."

In Philadelphia Franklin saw that if the choice were to join or die, the colonies must die; they would not join. Nor would the mother country prod them toward union. "The crown disapproved it," he said later, "as having too much weight in the democratic part of the constitution; and every assembly as having allowed too much to prerogative. So it was totally rejected." Franklin erred. The crown and Parliament had considered Franklin's Plan of Union and a number of others and rejected them all—not because of their "democratic parts" but because of the "ill consequence to be apprehended from uniting too closely the northern colonies with each other, an independency upon this country to be feared from such an union." The ancient principle of "divide and rule" prevailed.

Franklin died thinking the American Revolution could have been avoided if his plan had been accepted. "For the colonies, if so united, would have really been, as they then thought themselves, sufficient to their own defense," he said in his last year, "and being trusted with it, as by the plan, an army from Britain, for that purpose would have been unnecessary. The pretenses for framing the Stamp Act would then not have existed, nor the other projects for drawing a revenue from America to Britain by acts of Parliament, which were the cause of the breech, and attended with such terrible expense of blood and treasure."

Franklin was wrong. The colonies and the mother country were right to reject his plan. It had a deadly flaw—a failure to define the scope of the king's power in the contemplated union. It took eleven years after independence before the colonies, now states, accepted a union similar to the one Franklin had proposed at Albany, long before anyone was ready for it. He saw what must be in the future but misjudged what the present would accept.

CHAPTER

12

"THE RASHEST GOVERNOR
I HAVE KNOWN"

EN ROUTE TO BOSTON in the fall of 1754 Franklin met Robert Hunter Morris, who had just arrived from England with a commission in his pocket that made him the new governor of Pennsylvania. Franklin had known him for some years "intimately," but except that both enjoyed chess they shared little in common. Morris had been born to wealth. His father as governor of New Jersey had made the son chief justice of the colony, a post he still held. Now in his mid-fifties, he remained unmarried and the father of four illegitimate children—"a kind, amicable, sensible man, but with a wrong turn of mind."

At their meeting in New York, Morris asked if Franklin thought he "must expect an uncomfortable administration."

"No," said Franklin, "you may on the contrary have a very comfortable one, if you will only take care not to enter into any dispute with the Assembly."

"My dear friend," said Morris, "how can you advise my avoiding disputes. You know I love disputing; it is one of my greatest pleasures. However, to show the regard I have for your counsel, I promise you I will if possible avoid them."

Franklin at the time considered himself on good terms with everyone in the Pennsylvania government. While in New York he came upon a man who boasted he could teach "even a veteran scrawler to write fairly in thirty hours." Franklin sent him along to Richard Peters, whose handwriting was execrable, "for tho' we are about to have a new governor, and they say a new Assembly, I do not desire to see a new secretary. I only think it convenient that what he writes may possibly be read." But while in Boston Franklin began wondering about his friendly ties with the executive. He learned in a letter from Collinson that someone in the government had prejudiced Thomas Penn against him. "I know not why he should imagine me not his friend," Franklin replied, "since I cannot recollect any one act of mine that could denominate me otherwise. On the contrary, if to concur with him, so far as my little influence reached, in all his generous and benevolent designs and desires of making his province and people flourishing and happy, be any mark of my respect and dutiful regard to him, there are many who would be ready to say I could not be supposed deficient in such respect." Penn's displeasure distressed Franklin. "I much fear from a letter Mr. Franklin showed [me]," a mutual friend wrote the proprietor months later, "that our friend Collinson is part of the innocent cause of Franklin's conduct. He told Franklin that you could not be persuaded to think him your friend."

The possibility of mending his reputation with the proprietor seemed dim when Franklin returned home in March 1755. The governor had not restrained his love of disputing, and the Assembly, which had first claim on Franklin's allegiance, was arrayed against him. Earlier, when revealing that the mother country was sending Gen. Edward Braddock with two regiments to remove the French from the Ohio Valley, Morris had demanded an appropriation to buy supplies for the troops. The Assembly, as usual, had said it would not vote for the raising of any money unless it controlled the spending of it. Acrimony between legislature and governor reached a high point on January 7 when the Assembly sent a petition to the king asking him to take over Penn's colony. Franklin called the petition "ill-judged and ill-timed."

2

Braddock and his troops landed in Virginia on February 19. He had expected to find wagons and supplies at the staging area in Winchester; he found nothing. He had assumed a road was being cut through the wilderness to the Forks of the Ohio; not a tree had fallen. On February 28, he sent a blistering letter to Governor Morris, censuring the Pennsylvania Assembly for its "pusillanimous and improper behavior" and threatening "unpleasant methods" to get what he wanted. Morris passed the letter on to the Assembly on March 18, adding some gratuitous insults of his own. The Assembly found the letter "most alarming." Franklin, with the interests of colony, continent, and empire in mind, argued that his colleagues this once must bend to the governor's desire and give him a supply bill he would sign. The Assembly refused. It sent up a bill to raise twenty-five thousand pounds, but it would dispense all money received. The governor sent the bill back.

Franklin devised an ingenious way out of the impasse. Earlier, Josiah Quincy had arrived from Massachusetts to plead for aid in his colony's projected expedition against the French entrenched at Crown Point. Franklin "advised Mr. Quincy what strings to touch in his discourses with each of [the assemblymen], drew up for him his remonstrance to the House, supported and enforced it in the House, and when they became willing to give" proposed a scheme to satisfy Massachusetts and Braddock and at the same time circumvent the governor. The Assembly would borrow fifteen thousand pounds from the Loan Office, but only two-thirds of the money would go to Massachusetts; the remaining third would be used to outfit Braddock. Such a loan—unusual but not illegal—did not require the governor's approval. It would be paid back out of the excise which the Assembly controlled. Franklin had gratified the Quakers by letting them demonstrate "their readiness to comply with the demands of the king as far as we are capable consistently with our religious and civil liberties," but the governor, said one of them, "was extremely mortified by the success of this proceeding." He and his friends, Franklin learned, "are angry with me for disappointing them by that means, of a fresh accusation against the Quakers."

Early in the evening of April 8 Governors Shirley of Massachusetts and DeLancey of New York arrived in town to pick up Governor Morris and then push on for a conference in Virginia with Braddock. Shirley insisted that Franklin, as head of the post office, must join the group in order to work out with Braddock "the mode of conducting with most celerity and certainty the dispatches between him and the governors of the several provinces." Franklin had just returned from a long trip and in the few weeks home had been much occupied with business. He did not want to go. Friends in the Assembly said he must; under the guise of talking about postal business he could correct the "violent prejudices" Braddock had conceived against the Pennsylvania legislature.

Travel invigorated Franklin, and this trip proved the rule. No problem ever so preoccupied him that he put aside enjoying life or satisfying his curiosity. On the road through Maryland he noticed a small whirlwind of dust traveling toward his party. After it had passed by, "the rest of the company stood looking after it," he said later, "but my curiosity being stronger, I followed it, riding close by its side, and observed its licking up, in its progress, all the dust that was under its smaller part. As it is a common opinion that a shot fired through a waterspout will break it, I tried to break this little whirlwind by striking my whip through it, but without any effect." When the whirlwind left the road, Franklin raced after it through the woods. "I accompanied it about three-quarters of a mile, till some limbs of dead trees, broken off by the whirl, flying about, and falling near me, made me more apprehensive of danger, and then I stopped." After trotting back to his party, he asked the host if the phenomenon was common in Maryland. *"No,"* said the host, *"not at all common; but we got this on purpose to treat Mr. Franklin."*

Franklin found that Governor Morris had filled Braddock and his officers with "violent prejudices" against the Assembly. "Such is the infatuation and obstinacy of the people I have to deal with, or at least their representatives that tho' their country is invaded and everything they enjoy depends upon removing the French from their borders, yet I could not persuade them to act with vigor at this juncture, or even to grant supplies expected by the Crown," Morris had told the general in one letter. In another he accused Philadelphia merchants of selling the food and war supplies to the French that made their invasion possible. Franklin denied the accusations and convinced Braddock Pennsylvania would support his expedition. Soon the general was spilling out confidences.

"After taking Fort Dusquesne," the short, stocky officer remarked one day, dribbling snuff over his waistcoat as he chatted away, "I am to proceed to Niagara; and having taken that, to Frontenac; if the season will allow time; and I suppose it will; for Dusquesne can hardly detain me above three or four days; and then I see nothing that can obstruct my march to Niagara."

"To be sure, sir," Franklin answered cautiously, "if you arrive well before Dusquesne, with these fine troops so well provided with artillery, that place, not yet completely fortified, and as we hear with no very strong garrison, can probably make but a short resistance. The only danger I apprehend to obstruction to your march, is from ambuscades of Indians, who by constant practice are dextrous in laying and executing them. And the slender line near four miles long, which your army must make, may expose it to be attacked by surprise in its flanks, and to be cut like a thread into several pieces, which from their distance cannot come up in time to support each other."

"These savages may indeed be a formidable enemy to your raw American militia," Braddock said with a smile, "but upon the king's regular and disciplined troops, sir, it is impossible they would make any impression."

Braddock was an honest man, but "a little more ability and a little less honesty on the present occasion might serve our turn better," an aide said of him. William Allen, who did not meet the general but probably formed his opinion through Franklin, reported him to be a man "of a mean capacity, obstinate and self-sufficient, above taking advice, and laughed to scorn all such as represented to him that in our wood country, war was to be carried on in a different manner from that in Europe."

Franklin thought the general "presumed too much," but held his tongue.

Braddock presumed less the day Franklin prepared to return home. The general learned that of the two hundred wagons and twenty-five hundred horses promised for his expedition, hardly a tenth that number had been procured, "and not all of those were in serviceable condition." Amazed, he threw up his hands, "declared the expedition was then at an end, being impossible, and exclaimed against the ministers for ignorantly landing them in a country destitute of the means of conveying their stores, baggage, etc., not less than 150 wagons being necessary." Franklin commiserated with Braddock. What a pity, he said, that the army "had not been landed rather in Pennsylvania, as in that country almost every farmer had his wagon." The general swung round at the remark and said:

"Then you, sir, who are a man of interest there, can probably procure them for us; and I beg you will undertake it."

Franklin asked what terms he could offer Pennsylvania farmers. The general said he wanted fifteen hundred pack horses plus one hundred and fifty wagons equipped with four horses each and a driver. He would pay two shillings per diem for each pack horse, fifteen shillings per diem for the equipped wagons. Franklin said the terms were generous. Braddock commissioned him to carry out the mission, and on the morning of April 23 turned over eight hundred pounds in cash. Franklin headed that day for Lancaster, in the center of Pennsylvania's richest farming country. There he prepared a broadside to be scattered throughout the counties of Lancaster, York, and Cumberland. It was among the most ingenious pieces he ever composed. It played first on *fear:*

> It was proposed to send an armed force immediately into these counties, to seize as many of the best carriages and horses as should be wanted, and compel as many persons into the service as would be necessary to drive and take care of them.
>
> I apprehended that the progress of a body of soldiers thro' these counties on such an occasion, especially considering the temper they are in, and their resentment against us, would be attended with many

and great inconveniencies to the inhabitants; and therefore more willingly undertook the trouble of trying first what might be done by fair and equitable means.

An appeal to *greed* came next:

> The people of these back counties have lately complained to the Assembly that a sufficient currency was wanting; you have now an opportunity of receiving and dividing among you a very considerable sum; for if the service of this expedition should continue (as it's more than probable it will) for 120 days, the hire of these wagons and horses will amount to upwards of thirty thousand pounds, which will be paid in silver and gold of the king's money.

The risks will be slight:

> The service will be light and easy, for the army will scarce march above 12 miles per day, and the wagons and baggage horses, as they carry those things that are absolutely necessary to the welfare of the army, must march with the army no faster, and are, for the army's sake, always placed where they can be most secure, whether on a march or in camp.

Franklin had the broadside translated into German, and directed the next paragraph particularly to those readers:

> If you are really, as I believe you are, good and loyal subjects to his Majesty, you may now do a most acceptable service, and make it easy to yourselves. . . . But if you do not do this service to your king and country voluntarily, when such good pay and reasonable terms are offered you, your loyalty will be strongly suspected; the king's business must be done.

Next came a disclaimer—"I have no particular interest in this affair; as (except the satisfaction of endeavoring to do good and prevent mischief) I shall have only my labor for my pains"—then one more threat, again aimed at the German-speaking farmers:

> If this method of obtaining the wagons and horses is not like to succeed, I am obliged to send word to the general in fourteen days; and I suppose Sir John St. Clair, the Hussar, with a body of soldiers, will immediately enter the province. . . .

"I cannot but honor Franklin for the last clause of his advertisement," one reader remarked, knowing that to cast St. Clair in the guise of a

Hussar would recall for every German farmer the notorious cavalrymen who had pillaged the Rhineland valley.

On Monday, April 28, Franklin began to hire wagons and drivers at Lancaster; on May 1 he was in York repeating the performance while his son scoured Carlisle, appealing to the Scotch-Irish farmers of Cumberland County. In two weeks Franklin and son had procured 150 wagons and 259 horses and more were coming in daily.

Franklin returned to Philadelphia on May 12 to resume his seat in the Assembly. Colleagues unanimously thanked him for all he had done, but Morris, in a passion to strike at the Quaker-led legislature, passed over the achievements and censured the Assembly for refusing to aid the British army. It pleased a Quaker who had always regarded Franklin as an enemy to see the governor's message animate "Franklin so effectually that I am in hopes it will engage him to act steadily and zealously in our defense." Actually, Franklin had not yet committed himself to the Quakers or against the governor. "I am heartily sick of our present situation," he told a friend; "I like neither the governor's conduct nor the Assembly's, and having some share in the confidence of both, I have endeavored to reconcile 'em, but in vain, and between 'em they make me very uneasy. . . . If my being able now and then to influence a good measure did not keep up my spirits, I should be ready to swear never to serve again as an Assemblyman, since both sides expect more from me than they ought, and blame me sometimes for not doing what I am not able to do, as well as for not preventing what was not in my power to prevent."

The return to Philadelphia did not slow Franklin's work for the British army. He spent the rest of May rounding up laborers to build a road from the frontier down to Braddock's encampment. He got the Assembly to send each of Braddock's officers gift packages that included, along with a horse to carry him, parcels of tea, coffee, a Gloucester cheese, a keg of butter, two gallons of Jamaican rum, two cured hams, six pounds of rice, and two dozen bottles of Madeira wine. Braddock, having found his man, continued to press requests on Franklin, who had soon spent over a thousand pounds of his own money to fulfill them. A heat wave struck Philadelphia early in June and Franklin collapsed. As he was "not well enough to go about the town," people continued to come to his house seeking help and advice.

On June 21 the Assembly responded to a new request from the governor for money to aid Braddock with a bill to raise fifteen thousand pounds. However, it rigged the bill to produce a surplus of two thousand pounds that it alone could spend. The governor rejected it, and the Assembly soon after adjourned. Franklin distributed blame for the stalemate equally between governor and Assembly. "Did you never hear this old catch?" he asked a friend:

> There was a mad man, he had a mad wife
> And three mad sons beside;
> And they all got upon a mad horse
> And madly they did ride.

"'Tis a compendium of our proceedings, and may save you the trouble of reading them."

Outwardly Franklin and Morris remained on good terms during the great quarrel. "Franklin," the governor said one day, coming upon him in the street, "you must go home with me and spend the evening. I am to have some company that you will like." The evening went well. In the "gay conversation" over wine after supper, the governor jokingly said "he much admired the idea of Sancho Panza, who when it was proposed to give him a government, requested it might be a government of *blacks*, as then, if he could not agree with his people he might sell them."

"Franklin," asked one of the guests, "why do you continue to side with these damned Quakers? Had not you better sell them? The proprietor would give you a good price."

"The governor," Franklin answered, "has not yet *blacked* them enough."

The witty riposte allowed the evening to continue pleasantly, but buried within the reply lay a commitment Franklin seemed unaware of. He still professed to like "neither the governor's conduct nor the Assembly's." Morris doubted his detachment. He has "very out of the way notions of the power of the people," Morris wrote to Thomas Penn, "and is as much a favorer of the unreasonable claims of American assemblies as any man whatever."

3

Shortly after Franklin rounded up wagons for Braddock, his wife complained to a visitor that "all the world claimed a privilege of troubling her pappy . . . with their calamities and distresses. . . ." Still, Franklin found time to enjoy himself. On May 28 he attended a ceremony for laying the cornerstone of the Pennsylvania Hospital he had done so much to create. A few days later Governor Morris sent him a letter of praise from General Braddock. Franklin had copies made to pass among friends. On June 24 the Masons celebrated Saint John the Baptist Day with more pomp than Philadelphia had ever seen, "no less than 160 being in the procession, in gloves, aprons, etc., attended by a band of music," according to an observer of the parade. "Mr. Allen, the Grand Master, honoring them with his company, as did the Deputy Grand Master, Mr. Benjamin Franklin, and his son, Mr. William Franklin, who walked as the next chief officer. A sword bearer with a naked sword drawn headed the procession. They dined together elegantly, as it is said, at their hall upon turtle, etc."

Governor Morris on July 3 jostled the town's serenity by clamping a thirty-day embargo on all shipping to prevent merchants from trafficking with the enemy, as many were doing. He acted only after the Assembly refused to do so. Franklin had not adjusted to this bold assumption of authority when news arrived from England that gave further reason to seethe against the governor. Though Franklin's electrical experiments were known, the Royal Society had not yet elected him a fellow—and would not until 29 April 1756. But on June 12 it had so honored Robert Hunter Morris, who, so far as Franklin knew, had contributed nothing to the world of natural philosophy.

This humiliation had still not been digested when on July 18, around three o'clock in the afternoon, an express rode into town with shocking news—Braddock's army had been routed and Braddock himself killed; wagons and horses had been abandoned and the remaining troops under Col. Thomas Dunbar were fleeing back toward Philadelphia. On receiving the news, "the governor sent in haste for me, to consult with him on measures for preventing the desertion of the back counties," Franklin recalled. "I forget now the advice I gave, but I think it was, that Dunbar should be written to and prevailed with if possible to post his troops on the frontiers for their protection, till by reinforcements from the colonies he might be able to proceed on the expedition."

Details of the disaster filtered in over the weekend. On Wednesday, July 23, a mob assembled "in great numbers, with an intention of demolishing the mass house belonging to the Roman Catholics, wherein they were underhand excited and encouraged by some people of higher rank." While a group of Quakers sought to calm tempers, "the magistrates met and with a good deal of difficulty prevailed with the mob to desist."

The next day the governor called the Assembly into special session. The shaken deputies responded by voting the immense sum of fifty thousand pounds for defense. The money would be raised by an unprecedented tax on all land within the colony. The bill went to the governor on August 2. He sent it back three days later asking for a small change. "His proposed amendment," Franklin said, "was only of a single word;

the bill expressed that all estates real and personal were to be taxed; those of the proprietaries *not* excepted. His amendment was: for *not* read *only.*" The rejection stunned the Assembly. The French and Indians seemed about to overrun the colony, yet the proprietors refused to share in the defense of the land, the bulk of which belonged to them. In England not even the king's lands were exempt from taxation. True, the Assembly refused to allow the proprietors a hand in the choice of tax assessors and gave no assurance the levies would be made without prejudice, but these to the Assembly seemed carping objections.

Since returning from New England, Franklin had drafted the Assembly's messages to the governor. All had been dignified and respectful. Their tone shifted now, becoming "tart, and sometimes indecently abusive." Those who said Franklin lacked passion had only to read the messages. His reply of August 8 called Morris the "hateful instrument for reducing a free people to the abject state of vassalage." Thomas Penn came off no better. "How odious it be to sensible manly people to find *him* who ought to be their father and protector, taking advantage of public calamity and distress, and their tenderness for their bleeding country, to force down their throats laws of imposition, abhorrent to common justice and common reason!" His reply of August 19 attacked the governor for lacking that "*spirit of government, that skill,* and those *abilities,* that should qualify him for his station." Again Thomas Penn came off no better—"though a subject like ourselves, would *send* us out to fight *for* him, while he keeps himself a thousand leagues remote from danger! Vassals fight at their lord's expense, but our lord would have us defend his estate at our own expense! This is not merely vassalage, it is worse than any vassalage we have heard of; it is something we have no adequate name for; it is even more slavish than slavery itself."

The words sounded odd from the professed mediator between legislator and executive, but they were Franklin's and he meant them all. "The substance of these late inflammatory messages," William Smith wrote the proprietor, "I have often had from him as his real sentiments."

Just when politics, once a pleasant hobby, began to swallow up the days, a crisis in Franklin's private affairs intervened. With Braddock's defeat farmers who had leased wagons and horses to the army besieged Franklin, who had given his bond to all. Their claims "amounted to near £20,000, which to pay would have ruined me." He asked his friend Shirley, the current commander-in-chief of the army, to pay the claims, "but he being at a distance an answer could not soon be received. Some of the impatient, suspicious farmers "began to sue me." Colonel Dunbar, who had fled from the battlefield with the remains of Braddock's army, did not help matters by reneging on a promise to discharge three farmers' indentured servants. "He promised me, that if the masters would come to him at Trenton, where he should be in a few days on his march to New York, he would there deliver their men to them. They accordingly were at the expense and trouble of going to Trenton, and there he refused to perform his promise, to their great loss and disappointment."

Franklin had been harassed before without losing his self-control, but now a new ingredient had been added to his political life and he did not like the taste of it. "A number of falsehoods are now privately propagated to blast my character, of which I shall take no notice till they grow bold enough to show their faces in public," he said. "Those who caressed me a few months since, are now endeavoring to defame me everywhere by every base art." He worried most about the gossip in England, where he had taken care to build his reputation. He had reason to worry. Governor Morris—"He is, I think, the rashest and most indiscreet governor that I have known," Franklin had said of him during one of his own indiscreet moments—had told one of the king's ministers that Franklin had written the "very abusive messages" so "highly reflecting upon the proprietaries and plainly calculated to render them odious to the people." Peters, Smith, and others had made sure Thomas Penn knew who had "poisoned the people against your family." "I abhor these altercations," the depressed Franklin said, "and if I did not love the country and the people, would remove immediately into a more quiet government, Connecticut, where I am also happy enough to have many friends."

Franklin no longer seemed himself. While being slandered, he told Catharine Ray that "many more people love me now than ever did before." (He had the wit to add that the people only "say they love me; they *say so*, as you used to do; and if I were to ask any favors of them, would, perhaps, as readily refuse me. So that I find little real advantage in being beloved, but it pleases my humor.") To another friend he spoke vaguely of having the means to defeat his enemies "and shall use those means in due time." He talked mysteriously to William Smith about "a scheme," but "what that scheme is, time must show," Smith reported to Penn.

The network of friends built during twenty-five years in Philadelphia began to unravel in September 1755. For six years he had attended meetings of the city council regularly. Now, unsettled by the cool treatment from colleagues, he stopped going. One close friend, William Smith, drafted a petition to the king to "interpose your royal authority that this important province . . . may be put into a posture of defense," and another, William Allen, circulated it about the city. As old friends lined up against him, they were pushing Franklin into an alliance with the Quakers he had never sought.

CHAPTER

13

"THE PEOPLE HAPPEN
TO LOVE ME"

IN OCTOBER 1755 Franklin planned to leave for Virginia on post office business; he had never been south and looked forward to the trip. The Assembly adjourned in mid-month and would not meet until December, "when I hope to be home again." Then on October 25 came the news all Pennsylvania had feared since Braddock's defeat. "Just now arrived in town an express from our frontiers, with the bad news that eight families of Pennsylvanians were cut off last week about twenty miles above Harris's Ferry in the new purchase near Shamokin," Franklin wrote. "Thirteen men and women were found scalped and dead; and twelve children are missing, supposed to be carried away." Franklin, as one of the commissioners in charge of a one-thousand-pound emergency fund, immediately ordered six hundred guns with ammunition to the frontier "to supply such as are without and unable to buy for themselves." The next day he fell ill, "confined to my room and bed most of the time" until just before the Assembly reconvened in special session on November 3. The governor pressed two requests on the members—pass a bill to create a militia and another to raise money, and do "not waste your time in offering me such bills as you must know . . . it is not in my power to consent to."

The Assembly ignored the warning. It sent up a money bill he could not sign. The bill, which Franklin had a large hand in drawing up, provided for raising sixty thousand pounds, to be paid by a tax on all estates, the proprietors' included. The governor sent it back with a blunt note: since the Assembly seemed bent on doing nothing he and his council were leaving for the frontier to see what *they* could do to save the province. Shortly before the note arrived the Assembly had been even more harshly chastised by an impressive visitor—the Indian chief Scaroyady, who warned that unless his warriors and other Indians friendly to Pennsylvania received arms all would desert to the French. Earlier, the Assembly had told the governor Indian discontent stemmed from maltreatment by non-Quaker government officials. Send a wagonload of presents and their friendship would be regained. Scaroyady said only if the presents were guns would all be well.

The Assembly still refused to provide for the colony's defense until the proprietors agreed to share in the cost. It "had reason to believe" the people stood behind it, Franklin wrote in reply to the governor's message, "that in the midst of their distresses they themselves do not wish us to go farther." Then, in a sentence he would quote many times in the years ahead, he added: "Those who would give up essential liberty, to purchase a little temporary safety deserve neither liberty nor safety." The message avoided a personal attack on the governor; it blended moderation with firmness. "We being as desirous as the governor to avoid any dispute on that head, have so framed the bill as to submit it entirely to his Majesty's royal determination, whether that estate has or has not a right to such exemption." If the king later judged it unlawful to tax the proprietors' lands, all money would gladly be refunded. "We cannot conceive anything more fair and reasonable than this."

The moderate tone appealed to the governor. He agreed the dispute in the end must "be determined by his Majesty." He suggested a bill taxing the proprietary estates, but with a clause suspending its execution until the king had given his approval. That meant, of course, months must go by before taxes could be collected from the proprietors. He ended accusing the Assembly of being little "affected with the miseries and distresses of our bleeding country." This from a man whose roots and wealth lay in New Jersey did not sit well with Franklin. "As we are most of us natives of the country, and all of us have our estates and other more valuable connections in it," he wrote in the Assembly's reply, "and the governor is a stranger among us, it should seem, we think, at least probable, that we may be even *more* deeply affected with its distresses than he is."

In the midst of the fight over money, Franklin on November 19 introduced a bill entitled *An Act for the better ordering and regulating the Military Force of this Province.* It proposed for the first time in Pennsylvania's history the creation of a militia. The armed force would resemble the Association—composed only of volunteers and with all officers elected by the men. But the Association had been created outside the law; the militia would be backed by the government. The Assembly debated the bill for two days, altered the title to emphasize that only *"such as are willing and desirous to be united for Military Purpose within this Province"* need join the militia, then passed it with only four dissenting votes. The governor said it contained much "of a very extraordinary nature" and would "never answer the purpose of defending this province," yet he would sign it into law. Privately, he said it had been passed with "no other view but that I should refuse it and then to raise a clamor against me on that account, but as it is of such a nature as cannot be carried into execution, I have disappointed them, and given my consent to it." True, by exempting pacifists and calling for the election of officers by their men "the militia act violated fundamentals of British military practice and was in no way a defeat for any but the most rigid pacifists," but Morris had been carried away by his suspicion of the Assembly. Franklin had not devised the bill as a political trick to embarrass the governor. He offered it as a well-meant gesture, the best that could be pried from Quaker colleagues. Nor did he think his bill could not be "carried into execution." The Association had worked; why would not a voluntary militia work?

On Monday, November 24, the governor handed the Assembly a surprise. He said that Thomas Penn in a letter just received had offered a "free gift" of five thousand pounds to the war effort. While the Assembly pondered whether to accept the gift in lieu of taxing the proprietors' estates, a new element entered into their calculations that night. Some seven hundred frontiersmen marched into town. The backcountry men milled about the streets next morning while the Assembly met with their leaders, who were told the governor had invaded the liberties of the people. One of the frontiersmen said his people "did not know that their liberties were invaded, but they were sure their lives and estates were," and that they hoped the Assembly would "dispute no longer but send the governor such a bill as he could pass."

On November 27, as the frontiersmen headed home, the Assembly passed a supply bill that accepted the proprietor's gift and taxed all estates in the colony but his. It conceded another point. Hitherto the House controlled disbursement of all tax money. That raised under the new bill could be spent only with the approval of a committee composed of two members from the governor's council and five from the Assembly. The bill elated Morris; it enraged Franklin. By their "mean selfish claim of a right to exemption from taxes," said Franklin, the proprietors "have brought on themselves infinite disgrace, and the curses of all the continent." To have lost the fight was humiliating; to have lost it to Morris was unbearable. "If we cannot have a governor of some discretion (for this gentleman is half a madman)," Franklin said, "fully empowered to do what may be necessary for the good of the province and the king's service, as emergencies may arise, this government will be the worst on the continent."

Franklin and the Assembly soon learned they had been gulled into concessions. Penn's gift of five thousand pounds was comprised of quit-rents he had been unable to collect. He had turned over bad debts for the Assembly to collect. Caught between what he thought to be a half-mad governor and a penurious proprietor, Franklin saw no choice but to beg the king to take over the colony. Rumors soon circulated about town that the Assembly would send him to London on such a mission. But nothing could be done until the bleeding colony had been restored to health.

2

Early in December Philadelphia learned Indians had scalped nearly all the inhabitants of Gnadenhutten, a Moravian village on the northern frontier not far from Bethlehem. The committee of seven commissioners chosen to disburse money raised by the supply bill took charge of defense measures in consort with the governor. "We meet every day, Sundays not excepted," Franklin said. The committee sent one hundred guns with a hundred pounds of powder and four hundred pounds of lead to the frontier on December 5 and with them a promise that three hundred armed men would soon follow.

The commissioners thought the best way to secure the frontier "was to carry the war into the enemy's country, and hunt them in all their fishing, hunting, planting, and dwelling places." Franklin suggested that "large, strong, and fierce" dogs accompany the soldiers. "In case of meeting a party of the enemy, the dogs are then to be all turned loose and set on. They will be fresher and fiercer for having been previously confined, and will confound the enemy a good deal, and be very serviceable." George Croghan, a leading Indian trader, advised the commissioners "that by a chain of forts the frontier should first be in some degree secured before we acted offensively"—a plan similar to the one advanced some time ago by Thomas Penn but rejected by the Assembly.

The commissioners accepted this advice and voted to send James Hamilton and Franklin to the embattled frontier to choose spots for erecting the blockhouses. "Think of suitable officers for raising and com-manding men to be kept in the province pay," Franklin wrote William Parsons of Easton, "for Mr. Hamilton does not know the people your way; nor do I know who to recommend. He will bring some blank commissions with him." Parsons had been an original member of the Junto, but his allegiance to the governor and proprietor had caused a rift in the long friendship with Franklin. Soon after the militia bill had been signed by the governor, Franklin had written asking that party differences be put aside: "let you and I use our influence to carry this act into execution." Parsons agreed to a truce.

Franklin believed that "if people are but well disposed, a good use may be made" of the Militia Act. Before leaving for the frontier he presented his case in "A Dialogue between X, Y, and Z, concerning the present state of Affairs in Pennsylvania." In the dialogue Franklin, posing as "X," said the militia resembled the Association, only now we may *"lawfully* do in this affair what we then did *without law."* The act uniquely fit American circumstances. Those who ridicule the election of officers by their men should remember, said "X," that "this mode of choice is . . . agreeable to the liberty and genius of our constitution." Did the law violate English custom? Yes, "X" admitted, but the king has the power "to grant *additional* liberties and privileges not used in England, but suited to the different circumstances of different colonies." Did the law violate an act of Parliament dealing with militias? Yes, the Assembly has "varied a little from that part of the Act of Parliament, in favor of liberty; they have not given the sole power of making those Articles of War *to the governor* as that act does *to the king;* but have joined with the governor, for that purpose, a number of officers to be chosen by the people." The nimble "X" brought his opponents around, "but hang me," said "Z" at the end, "if I'll fight to save Quakers." Ah, Franklin answered much as he had when defending the Association, only more pungently —"you won't pump ship, because 'twill save the rats, as well as yourself."

The dialogue appeared on December 18. That same day Franklin and his son, whom he trusted for advice on military matters, set out for Bethlehem with James Hamilton, Joseph Fox, a militant Quaker from the Assembly, fifty mounted troops, and three wagonloads of supplies. The first night out they stopped at a country inn. Franklin asked the landlady to air the damp bedsheets. "Half an hour afterwards, she told us the bed was ready," he reported back to Deborah, "and the sheets *well aired.* I got into bed, but jumped out immediately, finding them as cold as death, and partly frozen. She had *aired* them indeed, but it was out upon the *hedge.* I was forced to wrap myself up in my great coat and woolen trousers, everything else about the bed was shockingly dirty."

When the party arrived at Bethlehem the next day it surprised Franklin "to find it in so good a posture of defense." Surprised, because he thought the Moravians were pacifists. An act of Parliament had specifically exempted them from military duty. "It seems they were either deceived in themselves or deceived the Parliament," Franklin remarked. "But common sense aided by present danger, will sometimes be too strong for whimsical opinions."

Satisfied Bethlehem could take care of itself, though swollen thrice its size by refugees, the party moved on the next day to Easton. There they found chaos—a terrified village short of food, jammed with refugees. "All business is at an end, and the few remaining starving inhabitants in this town are quite dejected and dispirited," Franklin said in one of his news reports to Philadelphia, which the *Gazette* printed as they came in. He commissioned William Parsons a major in the provincial troops. (Provincial troops, Franklin explained to a puzzled Englishman, are "regularly enlisted to serve for a term, and in the pay of the province; and do nothing but bear arms like your regulars. The *militia* follow their respective callings at home, muster only on certain days to learn discipline and are to be ready in case of invasion, etc. by any great force; but are of little use in hunting Indians; and therefore all the colonies in such wars hire men for the purpose who are fitter for it, and make it their business.") He ordered Parsons "immediately to raise and take into pay for one month a company of foot consisting of twenty-four men" to protect the village.

The commissioners and their escort spent ten days in Easton. The nights were frigid, and Franklin asked Deborah to send up a nightgown to replace one that he had lost. Now that he had become "much more tender," he slept in winter in "a short calico bedgown with close sleeves and flannel close-footed trousers." New Year's Day found the party in Reading, another village of log houses on the western edge of the northern frontier. There they met Governor Morris and his party, on a tour of inspection. The plan had been for the two groups to travel westward for a parley with some friendly Indians assembling at Carlisle. But on 3 January 1756 word arrived that Indians had routed a detachment of troops sent to Gnadenhutten. Morris, "fearful that the whole country will fall into the enemy's hands," proposed "that one of the commissioners return to Bethlehem and Easton, and there give fresh directions to the troops and post them in the best manner for the protection of the remaining inhabitants." The commissioner chosen—Franklin.

He reached Bethlehem on January 7. "We found this place filled with refugees, the workmen's shops and even the cellars being crowded with women and children," he told Morris. "And we learnt that Lehigh township is almost entirely abandoned by the inhabitants." He spent a week in Bethlehem organizing its defenses, conscripting soldiers to march back to Gnadenhutten, dispatching "wagons loaded with bread and some axes" to beleaguered hamlets. He gave all he could, but he also made demands, once threatening "to disband or remove the companies already posted for the security of particular townships, if the people would not stay on their places, behave like men, do something for themselves and assist the province soldiers."

On January 13 Franklin left Bethlehem with one hundred and thirty men and seven wagons hauling stores and equipment. He expected to be gone two to three weeks building forts in the vicinity of Gnadenhutten, which lay twenty miles from Bethlehem and just north of the Lehigh Gap. They reached Gnadenhutten three days later. "Here all round appears nothing but one continued scene of horror and destruction," one man wrote. "Where lately flourished a happy and peaceful village is now all silent and desolate, the houses burnt, the inhabitants butchered in the most shocking manner, their mangled bodies for want of funerals exposed to birds and beasts of prey and all kinds of mischief perpetrated that wanton cruelty can invent."

The expedition arrived shortly after noon on Sunday. By nightfall the men had enclosed the camp with a musketproof breastwork and got "up some shelter from the weather." All day Monday, Franklin reported to the *Gazette*, "it rained, with so thick a fog, that we could not see round us, so as either to choose a place for a fort, or find materials to build it. In the night it cleared up, and this morning we determined, marked out the ground, and at ten o'clock set the men to work, and they have worked with such spirit, that now, at half past three in the afternoon, all the logs for the stockade are cut, to the number of four hundred and fifty, and being most of them more than a foot in diameter, and fifteen feet long." Awed by the axemen's speed, Franklin timed them and found that two men working on a fourteen-inch-thick tree could fell it in six minutes. "The Reverend Mr. Beatty is with us," he added for the devout among his readers, "and we have regular prayers morning and evening. We went to prayer before we began to work, all the men being drawn up to receive orders and tools." He did not add that they also received a ration of rum after prayers, thus the reason for "all the men" attending.

Five days later they finished the fort, one hundred and twenty-five feet long, fifty feet wide. "This day we hoisted your flag," Franklin wrote his wife on January 25, "made a general discharge of our pieces, which had been loaded, and of our two swivels, and named the place *Fort Allen* in honor of our old friend." (William Allen, no longer a friend, refused the flattering honor as the peace offering Franklin meant it to be; he continued to revile him at every chance.) Work had already begun on two more stockades flanking Fort Allen fifteen miles on each side. Franklin expected them to be completed within the week.

His wife extended herself to make certain "dear Pappy" did not suffer on the frontier in the midst of winter. "We have enjoyed your roast beef, and this day began on the roast veal; all agree that they are both the best that ever were of the kind," Franklin told her. "The apples are extremely welcome, and do bravely to eat after our salt pork; the minced pies are not yet come to hand, but suppose we shall find them among the things expected up from Bethlehem on Tuesday; the capillaire [an orange-flavored syrup] is excellent, but none of us having taken cold as yet, we have only tasted it."

Franklin had some five hundred men under his command scattered along the frontier. He also had complaints from settlers drifting back to their homesteads to deal with. "Here are ten Lehigh people buzzing me in both ears while I write," he remarked to one correspondent. "I thought to have wrote you a long letter," he said to another, "but here comes in a number of people, from different parts, that have business with me and interrupt me; we have but one room, and that quite public." His self-control awed the men. "Mr. Franklin will at least deserve a statue for his prudence, justice, humanity, and above all for his patience," one of them said. "It is impossible to convey you an idea of the temper of these people who are daily endeavoring to impede all measures for their own safety and studious of nothing but to improve the general calamity to their own private interest."

Early in February Franklin received "a letter from the governor, acquainting me that he had called the Assembly, and wished my attendance there, if the posture of affairs on the frontiers was such that my remaining there was no longer necessary. My friends, too, of the Assembly pressing me by their letters to be if possible at the meeting, and my three intended forts being now completed, and the inhabitants contented to remain on their farms under that protection, I resolved to return." He turned his command over to an experienced Indian fighter and on February 4 an escort carried him to Bethlehem, where he stayed overnight. "The first night being in a good bed, I could hardly sleep, it was so different from my hard lodging on the floor of our hut at Gnadenhutten, wrapped only in a blanket or two." The next day, traveling at top speed, he reached Philadelphia late at night. Later he explained why he had hurried back: "When I was on the frontier last winter, a great number of the citizens, as I was told, intended to come out and meet me at my return, to express their thankful sense of my (small) services. To prevent this, I made a forced march, and got to town in the night, by which they were disappointed, and some little chagrined." Also, he was ill, "with a pain and giddiness in my head."

3

Franklin rested only a day after his return. On February 7 colleagues in the Assembly placed him on a committee to draft an objection to the impressment of indentured servants into the royal army. Early the next week came news his brother John had died. As usual, Franklin had little to say about the death of someone close. "As our number grows less, let us love one another proportionably more," he remarked in a letter to his sister Mecom, then turned to other matters.

The Indian raids continued through February. When told by an acquaintance in Bethlehem that the people "are afraid of going to their plantations," Franklin shot back a testy reply. "If they have no regard to it, but run away in so shameful and cowardly a manner every time an Indian or two appears in any part of the province, and abandon their plantations, I believe the government will not think it worthwhile to keep up those guards merely to secure empty houses and uncultivated fields, but will demolish the forts, withdraw the companies from your frontier, and send them to other parts to defend a better and more manly people." Furthermore, he went on, government allowances for refugees cease with the arrival of this letter, "for some of them, as long as they can live in idleness with you, and be fed, will think little of returning to their places, or of the duty of caring and laboring for their own livelihood."

The letter's sharpness owed something to a new fight forced upon Franklin. In his absence a militia regiment for Philadelphia had been formed. The governor dallied signing the *elected* officers' commissions and did so only after being hung in effigy. He had not, however, blocked the creation of an independent extralegal company, organized, ironically, along lines laid down in Franklin's Plan of Association. The issue at stake —which wing of the government, executive or legislative, would control the provincial military force—came to a head on February 12 when the militia regiment elected Franklin its colonel. (This time, for reasons kept to himself but tied, perhaps, to a confidence gained on the frontier, he accepted the honor.) If Morris refused to sign his commission, he risked a riot. If he signed it, friends warned that Franklin would end up running the colony, using the militia to elect an Assembly he could "turn and twist as he pleases." After two weeks' delay and "against all reason and without advice," Morris signed the commission. Richard Peters, convinced his sometime friend was a dangerous man, believed the governor would "lose all character" for his decision. Peters, seeking petty revenge, told Franklin upon turning over the commission to him, he must take his oath of office four days hence before his regiment, which must then stand in review.

With such short notice, the review as expected went badly, to Franklin's humiliation. One critic wondered "whether between six and seven hundred men *and boys,* a great part of whom had never appeared at any former muster, can with any propriety be called a well-trained regiment of a thousand men?" Franklin did not improve matters by afterward marching his men through town to the Academy building, where a group had gathered to coordinate plans for additional independent companies. The meeting, forewarned, adjourned before the regiment arrived, but it hardly reassured his enemies to know Franklin would stoop to confront a peaceful meeting with an array of troops. He was accused of acting like "CROMWELL."

A second review promised the public had to wait until a three-foot snowfall had been cleared from the streets. This one went well. Each company performed complicated maneuvers, then came the artillery "with four *neatly painted* cannon, drawn by some of *the largest and most* stately horses in the province," after which "upwards of one thousand able-bodied effective men" marched through the city. The regiment "accompanied me to my house," Franklin recalled, "and would salute me with some rounds fired before my door, which shook down and broke several glasses of my electrical apparatus."

The next day, March 19, Franklin set out on his long postponed trip to Virginia on post office business. That morning "twenty officers of my regiment with about thirty grenadiers, presented themselves on horseback at my door just as I was going to mount, to accompany me to the ferry about three miles from town. Till we got to the end of the street, which is about two hundred yards, the grenadiers took it in their heads to ride with their swords drawn, but there they put them up peaceably into their scabbards, without hurting or even terrifying man, woman, or child; and from the ferry where we took leave and parted, they all returned as quietly to their homes." Franklin recounted the episode in detail because he had heard it had given "great offense to some folks," specifically Thomas Penn, who had learned of it from Richard Peters. A "silly affair," Franklin admitted, dismissing it. "The people happen to love me. Perhaps that's my fault." The people did "happen to love" Franklin. Peters confessed that two-thirds of the normally conservative

Anglicans in Philadelphia "are gone off . . . in favor of him and his politics."

4

Franklin left for Virginia driving a chaise and accompanied by his slave Peter, who rode alongside. En route Peter came down with a fever and a pain in his side. Franklin had him bled, then pushed on with Peter riding in the chaise "wrapped up warm, as he could not bear the motion of the horse." At Fredericktown Peter "went immediately to bed and took some camomile tea." The half day's pause to let Peter recuperate passed pleasantly. Col. George Washington, an acquaintance first met at Braddock's camp, rode into town, returning from a visit to New England. The two colonels exchanged news about the war against the French and Indians. On March 21 Washington rode on toward home; Franklin and Peter, "about again and almost well," took a boat down Chesapeake Bay. "We were only Sunday night and Monday night on the water," he reported back to Deborah. Tuesday morning about ten o'clock they arrived off the landing of William Hunter's place near Hampton, Virginia, "where I was received in the most obliging manner." The next day Hunter and Franklin rode forty miles up a finger of the bay to Williamsburg. Everything along the way fascinated Franklin. Less than four days after leaving Philadelphia "I find myself in the midst of spring; peaches on the trees as big as kidney beans, and asparagus on the tables they say they have had three weeks." He refreshed himself when they stopped to eat with crab apple cider, and years later remarked that "I do not find that England anywhere produces cider of equal goodness with what I drank frequently in Virginia made from those crabs."

Franklin, like the countryside, bloomed. "I have been well," he reassured Deborah from Williamsburg, "quite clear of the dizziness I complained of, and gay as a bird, not beginning yet to long for home, the worry of perpetual business being fresh in my memory." He refused to worry about war or politics or even to make plans. "I may return up the bay by water, or go to New York in the man-of-war if she goes soon; or perhaps get horses here, and ramble up thro' the country to Annapolis."

Straightening out postal accounts swallowed up the days in Williamsburg, but time remained for socializing in the evenings. Franklin found "the people extremely obliging and polite." He met a lawyer named George Wythe who twenty years later would sign the Declaration of Independence with him. On April 2 William and Mary College awarded

Franklin an honorary degree. Three days later he and Hunter rode thirty-five miles into the countryside. "We have almost finished our business together and wait only for the arrival of the next post with some accounts from the northern offices," he told Deborah.

Franklin found it hard to tear himself away from this leisurely life, knowing nothing pleasant awaited in Philadelphia. Over a month passed before finally, on May 10, he arrived back home. He must have yearned at once for Virginia, for the day after his return Richard Peters and William Smith joined to oust him as president of the Academy's board of trustees. Peters supplanted him in the office. The gratuitous insult rankled all Franklin's life. "The trustees had reaped the full advantage of my head, hands, heart and purse, in getting through the first difficulties of the design," he said later, "and when they thought they could do without me, they laid me aside." But the Academy suffered even more from the rash act. With Peters and Smith, both Anglican ministers, running it, Quakers and Presbyterians took their children away and within six months enrollment dropped from two hundred to one hundred and twenty-five students. Smith ignored these figures and gloated that "the church by soft and easy means daily gains ground in [the Academy]. Of twenty-four trustees, fifteen or sixteen are regular churchmen. . . . We have prayers twice a day, the children learn the church catechism."

It wounded, too, to learn about the time he returned from Virginia that William Smith had written several notorious pamphlets and newspaper articles censuring the Assembly and Franklin. Though he and Smith had openly disagreed politically, Franklin had trusted him as a friend with as much confidence as he gave to any man. From May 1756 on he ceased to speak with William Smith.

Once before, Franklin had been so nearly overwhelmed by political infighting that he had talked briefly of leaving Pennsylvania for Connecticut. Now he dreamed of running even farther away. "I sometimes wish, that you and I were jointly employed by the crown to settle a colony on the Ohio," he wrote George Whitefield a month and a half after returning to the strife in Pennsylvania. "I imagine we could do it effectually, and without putting the nation to much expense. But I fear we shall never be called upon for such a service. What a glorious thing it would be, to settle in that fine country a large strong body of religious and industrious people! What a security to the other colonies; and advantage to Britain, by increasing her people, territory, strength and commerce. Might it not greatly facilitate the introduction of pure religion among the heathen, if we could by such a colony, show them a better sample of Christians than

they commonly see in our Indian traders, the most vicious and abandoned wretches of our nation? Life, like a romantic piece, should not only
be conducted with regularity, but methinks it should finish handsomely.
Being now in the last act, I begin to cast about for something fit to end
with. Or if mine be more properly compared to an epigram, as some of
its few lines are but barely tolerable, I am very desirous of concluding
with a bright point. In such an enterprise I could spend the remainder
of life with pleasure; and I firmly believe God would bless us with
success, if we undertook it with a sincere regard to His honor, the service
of our gracious king, and (which is the same thing) the public good."

5

Franklin and his militia law had been ridiculed during his absence,
and the rancor increased as the French and Indians stepped up their
attacks in April and May. From the western frontier where he had gone
to supervise the building of blockhouses Governor Morris sent back a
stream of dire reports. The unrelenting bad news, however, had an effect
Franklin could applaud. On June 4 "all the stiff rumps except one," he
said, referring to the pacifist Quakers who "could be suspected of opposing the service from religious motives, have voluntarily quitted the Assembly." Anglicans eager to support the war filled the empty seats. Richard Peters did not cheer the change. "They are mere Franklinists," he
said.

About this time Franklin heard from Thomas Pownall that England
had dispatched an army to America under the command of Gen. John
Campbell, Lord Loudoun. Pownall would come over as the general's
secretary extraordinary. He and Franklin had met two years earlier when
Pownall, then a traveling observer for the Board of Trade, had visited
Philadelphia. Franklin did not at first take to the bright, hot-tempered,
ambitious, and somewhat officious young man—he was thirty-four—but
when they met again at the Albany Congress they became friends. Pownall did not approve of proprietary governments; some suspected Franklin's aversion toward him "ceased and they became intimate" when this
prejudice emerged. Pownall asked Franklin to be in New York when
Lord Loudoun arrived. Pownall wanted the general's initial impression
of the situation in Pennsylvania to come from Franklin rather than his
opponents. Franklin did not keep Pownall's letter secret; soon after he
received it Richard Peters and William Allen expressed alarm at the
proposed meeting in letters to Thomas Penn. Governor Morris sought

to undercut Franklin's reputation in a letter to the then commander-in-chief of British forces in America, William Shirley. He hoped Lord Loudoun would not "countenance in any shape, a man that has in so remarkable a manner obstructed the king's affairs." Earlier, Morris had written to London saying that Franklin had been remiss in his duties as deputy postmaster general.

The vanguard of Loudoun's army dropped anchor off Sandy Hook in mid-June. Franklin hurried at once to New York, only to find that the ship carrying Loudoun and Pownall lay far behind. He had to wait five weeks for their arrival. "He seems to me very well fitted for the charge he has undertaken," Franklin remarked after several conferences with the general, "and I promise myself the king's affairs on this side will prosper in his hands." (Later he would call him indecisive, weak, and frivolous.)

Loudoun, on July 27, after only four days in New York, sailed up the Hudson to inspect the situation at Albany. Franklin returned to Philadelphia the next day and revealed himself as an "intimate" of the new commander-in-chief. He had further news—a new governor was on the way to replace Morris.

CHAPTER

14

OLD TROUBLES WITH A
NEW GOVERNOR

THE NEW GOVERNOR, a small, delicate-looking man named William Denny, arrived in New York in mid-August 1756. He was forty-seven years old and in spite of appearances a professional army officer. A Philadelphia pleased to be rid of Morris rolled out a carpet for Denny that stretched to New York. Richard Peters hastened there to escort him back. A contingent of Quakers headed by Israel Pemberton met Denny at Princeton and another body of citizens led by Robert Hunter Morris waited upon him at Bristol. Troops mustered at the county and city lines hailed his arrival and in the center of town Franklin drew up his regiment for review.

At the festive inauguration on August 20 Denny wore a plain brown coat, the first hint of his miserly character caught by no one at the time. That evening at a banquet the Assembly presented the new governor with a gift of six hundred pounds. "After dinner, when the company, as was customary at that time, were engaged in drinking," Franklin said later, "he took me aside into another room, and acquainted me that he had been advised by his friends in England to cultivate a friendship with me, as one who was capable of giving him the best advice, and of contributing most effectually to the making his administration easy." What Morris later observed of Denny—"when with men he ought to fear he is quite open, concealing nothing and most of all so after a hearty glass"—Franklin caught that evening. "The drinkers finding we did not return immediately to the table, sent us a decanter of Madeira, which the governor made liberal use of, and in proportion became more profuse of his solicitations and promises." Franklin replied with bromides. He was "much obliged" for the governor's "professions of regard," he would do "everything in my power to make his administration as easy to him as possible," and so forth.

Denny could not have come to Pennsylvania at a worse time. On August 14 the French captured Oswego, the key fort on the New York frontier, a loss so crucial only a year after Braddock's defeat that it would soon lead the British to send over thirty thousand troops to America. On August 17 the Assembly learned that Fort Granville, one of its western strongholds, had been burned to the ground and other forts on the Pennsylvania frontier lay exposed to the enemy. If the troops, long unpaid, disbanded, the road would lay open for the French and Indians to march on Philadelphia. Denny asked the Assembly for a supply bill of sixty thousand pounds. He received one promptly. It excluded the governor from any control over expenditures and also provided the House with a handsome slush fund to use as it wished. Denny rejected it, as he had to if he adhered to Penn's instructions. The Assembly grumbled several days, but with survival of the colony at stake it backed down in mid-September and gave the governor a bill he could sign but for only half the amount he had asked for.

Two weeks later came the annual October elections. Franklin and leaders in the proprietary camp agreed that the military crisis called for a political truce. They settled on a slate of candidates for the eight seats of the city and county of Philadelphia, three allotted to proprietary men, the rest to Franklin's clique. There would be no campaigning. One of the proprietary candidates was William Coleman, the close friend who had helped set Franklin up in business years ago. All the proprietary candidates lost on election day. One of the victors, not on the compromise slate, was Joseph Galloway, a "noisy" young man of twenty-five, William Franklin's best friend and a warm admirer of the father. Richard Peters blamed the proprietary defeat on the Quakers, who "were never more assiduous nor more of their young people avowedly busy" campaigning for their people. A recent historian has said Franklin "sabotaged the compromise" out of hatred for the proprietors and in order to bring his protégé Galloway into the Assembly. The evidence is ambivalent. If Franklin reneged on the truce at the expense of a friend, Coleman never knew it. The two continued friendly, and seven months after the election Franklin named Coleman one of the executors in his will.

Still, if an unsavory deal seems unlike Franklin, so, too, does the relentless hate for the proprietors he manifested at this time. "Tho' at present I have not the least inclination to be in their good graces," he wrote a month after the election, "I have some natural dislike to persons who so far *love money*, as to be *unjust* for its sake. I despise their *meanness* (as it appears to me) in several late instances, most cordially, and am thankful that I never had any connection with them, or occasion to ask or receive a favor at their hand." Here Franklin conveniently forgot that Thomas Penn had helped him gain the postmaster generalship. "I am sometimes ashamed for them," he went on, "when I see them differing with their people for trifles, and instead of being adored, as they might be, like demi-gods, become the objects of universal hatred and contempt. How must they have managed when, with all the power their charter, the laws and their wealth give them, a private person (forgive your friend a little vanity, as it's only between ourselves) can do more good in their country than they, because he has the affections and confidence of their people, and of course some command of the people's purses. You are ready now to tell me that popular favor is a most uncertain thing. You are right. I blush at having valued myself so much upon it. I have done."

2

Shortly after he took office Denny pleased the Assembly by lifting the embargo imposed by Morris on all shipping. Lord Loudoun, infuriated, ordered him to restore it, but the governor allowed the Assembly to procrastinate over a new bill while the illicit trade continued apace. "I know not what to say about the governor," Richard Peters remarked, appalled at the man Penn had sent over. "He is a trifler, weak of body, peevish and averse to business and, if I am not mistaken extremely near if not a lover of money." Robert Hunter Morris had lingered in Philadelphia long enough to make an equally severe judgment. "He is extremely slow and formal in everything else as well as business, which he seems to hate, and from that cause things are much in arrears and will be much more so soon. He sees nobody, has no company at his house, dines and sups alone, goes not out."

Franklin despised the man but got along with him better than most because, Peters thought, he and the Assembly did with the governor *"what they please."* Denny, probably with a push from Franklin, had written Thomas Penn urging him to accede to a tax on his lands. The day after the election Franklin accompanied the governor on an inspection tour of the frontier. They found things "in a deplorable condition," the people everywhere pleading for soldiers to protect them. Their desperation came at an embarrassing moment for Franklin. News had recently arrived that the king had disallowed his militia act, calling it "in every respect the most improper and inadequate to the service which could have been framed and passed and is rather calculated to exempt persons from military service than to encourage and promote them."

Denny did not like to be pried away from the plush isolation of the governor's mansion, but early in November Franklin and others forced him out—to attend an Indian conference at Easton. If he must go, then it would be in splendor, accompanied by an imposing body of troops. And thus Denny arrived at the meeting site, a drab huddle of log houses, "with colors flying, drums beating and music playing, *and all the honor due to a person of his rank*," according to the official minutes, whose author crossed out the snide final clause.

The conference lasted ten days. Discussion revolved mainly around the so-called Walking Purchase, made in 1737 when the proprietors bought from the Indians a parcel of land whose boundary would extend as far as a man could walk in a day. The purchase was "walked off" by a swift runner who traveled along a route cleared of underbrush. No one raised the charge of fraud until nearly twenty years later at the Easton conference. There Franklin, in collusion with Israel Pemberton, manipulated the protagonists—Governor Denny and the Indian chief Teedyuscung, who lived soaked in alcohol—so effectively that "the charge has never died," according to one historian, "despite the fact that a crown investigation did not substantiate it, that Teedyuscung himself later retracted it, and the particular Indians he had said were the sufferers (those Delawares who had moved to the Ohio country) disclaimed any interest in the matter and tried to consign it to oblivion." For Pemberton the "fraud" explained why the Indians maurauded the frontiers, and it would absolve Quakers of responsibility for Pennsylvania's military unpreparedness. Franklin had another purpose. He planned to use the charge in the campaign then taking shape in his mind to deprive the Penns of their colony.

Early in the conference Denny, serving as Franklin's mouthpiece, for he had written the speech, said to the Indians: "As we are now met together at a council fire kindled by us both, and have promised on both sides to be free and open to one another, I must ask how that League of Friendship came to be broken? Have we, the governor or the people of Pennsylvania, done you any kind of injury?" The Indian interpreter, Conrad Weiser, had pleaded with Denny not to ask that question, saying it "was a very absurd one in the Indian light, for they wanted nothing but forgiveness, and old friendship restored."

Teedyuscung, prompted by Pemberton, gave the expected answer. "This very ground, that is under me," he said, stamping the earth, "was my land and inheritance, and it is taken from me by fraud."

Denny, still speaking Franklin's words, said: "Tell me what will satisfy you for the injustice you suppose has been done you in the purchase of lands in this province; and, if it be in my power, you shall have immediate satisfaction, whether it be justly due to you or not." Teedyuscung said he would give the matter thought, and on that note the conference ended.

Franklin had never before spoken against the Walking Purchase nor had he put much faith in the Quakers' conciliatory policy toward the Indians. He believed that we shall never "have a firm peace with the Indians till we have well drubbed them." Now, however, filled with rage toward the proprietors, he not only accepted the Quaker view but went so far as to suggest that *all* recent troubles on the frontier had arisen because "the Delawares were grossly abused in the Walking Purchase," an injury imposed upon them by "the proprietors."

3

The arrival of Lord Loudoun's army had not slowed the French advance. After the fall of Fort Oswego, Loudoun revised his strategy, deciding now to strike at the enemy by sending a prong of his army through Pennsylvania. In October he alerted Governor Denny that a contingent of six hundred men, under the command of Col. Henry Bouquet, would arrive in Philadelphia early in December. The city must provide quarters for them. Denny made a quick survey. The Pennsylvania Hospital could handle up to five hundred men, but the board of managers, headed by Franklin, refused to open its doors to the army. The city council refused to rent vacant houses. Homeowners refused to take even officers into their houses. This "ill-humor spreading itself everywhere" owed something to selfishness but more to the rumor that the arriving soldiers brought smallpox with them.

The Assembly, with one quartering bill already disallowed by the king, drew up another "exactly conformable" to an act of Parliament. It provided for troops to be quartered in public houses. It was a devious measure. Though Philadelphia had 117 taverns, they were small and incapable of handling an influx of six hundred men. Moreover, the bill offered tavern owners only fourpence per diem for every soldier quartered, a rate at which they would lose money, and fined them five pounds for every man they refused to billet. The Assembly for years had complained that the proliferating public houses were ruining Philadelphia's high moral tone. The crisis at hand gave the House a chance to put a large number of owners out of business under the guise of obeying the British army. The Assembly's bill passed December 3. Denny returned it unsigned, noting that it contained passages identical to those in the act disallowed by the king. The Assembly cut the offensive passages. Denny knew the public houses could not accommodate the soldiers but signed the bill as something better than nothing. The day he signed the troops marched in, arriving as "a very deep snow fell, succeeded by a sharp frost." They were jammed into the public houses, where many of them had only straw for beds and no access to a fire. Within a few days over one hundred and twenty men were seriously ill, a large number of them with smallpox.

Though the fear prevailed "that the whole town would soon become a hospital," the hospital still refused to accept the soldiers as patients. The governor issued Colonel Bouquet a warrant that gave the army the right to quarter men in private homes. This threw the Assembly "into a ferment," and for the first time in Pennsylvania's history it met on Sunday. The Assembly judged itself blameless and chose a committee led by Franklin to confer with the governor and his council. The meeting occurred on December 20. Franklin made "large professions of the good disposition of the House for the army." The usually malleable Denny, stung by the treatment to an army he had served in so long, said the Assembly had been "indecent, frivolous, and evasive," and he demanded "that quarters be instantly provided." The committee self-righteously insisted "that the House could only prepare laws; they had no power to execute them." It saw no need to quarter troops in private houses "since there was room enough in the public houses of the suburbs, and neighboring towns, and other towns in the province," an oblique admission that those of Philadelphia did not suffice.

Denny responded that Lord Loudoun had said he wanted his troops together in Philadelphia. And what about the sick soldiers? he asked.

The committee said a special hospital would be created for them "at the province's expense."

Ah, said Denny, you have done something at last, but "with an ill grace."

"Upon the whole," said one sympathetic to the governor, "there was an abundance of heat, passion and rudeness, on the part of the committee," but of all the members Franklin, unused to such talk from Denny, used the harshest language. He made "several indecent and rude expressions," and according to Richard Peters he "behaved with great rudeness and insolence," calling the governor at one point "in express terms, a mere Bashaw or worse."

Three days later the Assembly said it still thought the public houses could cope with the problem, "if the law were properly executed," then turned its back on the matter by adjourning for ten days. A survey by the army that same day revealed that at least eighty-three soldiers were ill housed, some with no beds. Colonel Bouquet told Denny that quarters in private houses must be provided within a week for an additional five hundred new troops. Lord Loudoun, watching all this from New York, now determined to make an example of Pennsylvania. Comfortable quarters, including a decent ration of firewood and beer for every soldier, must be provided for his men at once, and "if the number of troops now in Philadelphia are not sufficient, I will instantly march a number sufficient for that purpose, and find quarters to the whole." Denny got this word on Christmas night. The next day he summoned those responsible for the colony's war effort, the provincial commissioners, one of whom was Franklin. They grumbled over the ultimatum but made no move to back down until, said Richard Peters, Franklin inexplicably "expressing his sentiments in favor of a total compliance, the rest immediately changed their tone." A sour mood at once turned sweet. The hospital agreed to inoculate all soldiers who had not had the smallpox and put a vacant building at the disposal of those "sick of that distemper." All troops would "be quartered in town," and "if the whole number of beds cannot be provided by the first of January, at least one hundred should be provided, filled with soft hay or straw or chaff, and covered with a blanket, besides sheets and blankets for covering." Later Colonel Bouquet hinted to Peters "that had he applied directly to B. F. and not to the governor matters would have been done at first to Lord Loudoun's satisfaction." But then, Peters added of Franklin, "this is actually all he aims at."

4

The Assembly on 22 January 1757, in response to information from Denny that over one hundred thousand pounds would be needed to meet the costs of war, sent him a bill to raise that sum through a tax on *all* lands in the province. The governor said he sympathized with the Assembly's desire to make the proprietors share in the cost of defense, but to protect the five-thousand-pound bond posted when he accepted his post he must adhere to his instructions. He rejected the new supply bill. On the morning of January 28, the Assembly marched in a body through the streets of Philadelphia—"to alarm everybody with the sight and occasion," said Peters—and handed the governor a remonstrance detailing its grievances. That done, it returned to the State House and that afternoon resolved to send Franklin to England "to solicit a removal of the grievances we labor under by reason of proprietary instructions, etc." The proprietor used his instructions, it said, "to deprive the Assembly and people of their rights and privileges, and to assume an arbitrary and tyrannical power over the liberties and properties of his Majesty's liege subjects." The Assembly saw itself "an English representative body" with all the rights and privileges of the House of Commons.

Franklin wanted to leave for England before river and bay froze over, but in February Lord Loudoun asked him to delay his departure. He planned a conference of colonial leaders in mid-March in Philadelphia and wished Franklin there, "as I know your presence will be of great use in forwarding whatever shall be found necessary to be done." Possibly Bouquet's observation that nothing moved in Pennsylvania without Franklin's blessing prompted this remarkable request from the commander-in-chief of the royal forces in America to a local assemblyman.

The colonies represented at the conference promised to join in a coordinated military operation against the French, but this meant little without the cooperation of that peculiar "country" Pennsylvania, the keystone colony. Loudoun "talked over the situation of this country and the deplorable state it appears to be in" with Franklin. Later, in a joint conference with Franklin and Denny, he found neither man "agreed in the facts which the other alleged" but that Franklin appeared better informed. Impressed, he asked Franklin for a memorandum answering the governor's objections to the supply bill. In the memorandum, he admitted the bill did not assure fair taxation of the proprietor's estates, but this could be remedied. He said, choosing the words with care, that the governor had "always had the disposal of all presents to Indians," and the Assembly "never claimed any power of this kind," but this hardly answered the objection that the Assembly constantly meddled with Indian relations, as it had. He also said "the Assembly have great respect for their present governor," a half-truth at best. (The Assembly "treat him with *contempt*, which he bears," said Peters of the governor.) The trouble lay with his council, "men who are looked upon as enemies to the House and to the people."

Events rather than goodwill or reason resolved the crisis on March 21, when Denny learned of a threat to Fort Augusta by eight hundred French and Indians and that the men there "refused to do duty for want of pay." Denny consulted Loudoun, Loudoun consulted Governor Dinwiddie of Virginia, and word came down that Denny "should for this time" break his instructions, and "pass the bill as it was presented by the

Assembly." And so it was done. It especially angered Thomas Penn when he heard the news through Peters that Loudoun had forced the retreat upon Denny because he had taken "Mr. Franklin's reflections on the council for facts."

5

Franklin spent the two weeks after Loudoun's conference ended preparing for the trip to England. He sent his unmet friend William Strahan in London a warning to "look out sharp, and if a fat old fellow should come to your printing house and request a little smouting, depend upon it, 'tis . . . B. Franklin."

He expected to be gone at least a year. For his partner Hall he went through the records and drew "a red line over all such accounts in this book, as are either settled or not like to be recovered." He made his "trusty and loving friend and wife, Deborah Franklin, to be my true and lawful attorney" in his absence. He appointed his wife's nephew-in-law, William Dunlap, the local postmaster and left precise instructions for him. Dunlap "should have a little book" for all receipts. Deborah depended upon him "to pay her, every Monday morning, the postage of the preceding week, taking her receipt for the same, and retaining only your commission of ten per cent." He collected letters to be delivered and favors to be performed in London. Israel Pemberton gave a restrained letter of introduction to Dr. John Fothergill, a leading Quaker in London. Pemberton explained privately to Fothergill that Franklin as a politician might "be capable of removing some difficulties" for Pennsylvania but Quakers "as a religious society" could "expect little more from him than . . . has been made by some others."

Joseph Galloway would serve as Franklin's lieutenant in the Assembly and he, too, received orders. "I leave some enemies in Pennsylvania, who will take every opportunity of injuring me in my absence. However, as they are my enemies, not on my own private account, but on that of the public, I seem to have some right to ask the care of my friends, so watch 'em and guard my reputation and interest as much as may be from the effects of their malevolence." With Franklin would go his son William, and their two slaves, Peter and King. William would study law at the Middle Temple, where Strahan had enrolled him six years earlier. He was leaving with mixed feelings, being deeply in love with a beautiful young woman named Elizabeth Graeme, and though the romance had been "overcast, threatening a wrecking storm," he still called her his "charmer."

Franklin, son, and servants left Philadelphia on April 4. A dozen friends accompanied them to Trenton, where they spent a convivial evening. Roads clogged with the mud from a spring thaw made the rest of the trip a tedious struggle. In New York, Franklin found that rumors of a French fleet hovering somewhere off the coast had led to orders from Loudoun that no ship should leave for England until a protective convoy had been assembled. Franklin used the spare time to appoint James Parker, his printing partner in New York, comptroller of the postal system. He composed an epitaph for the tombstone of his parents. He warned his wife to stand clear of a family quarrel in Boston swirling around Sister Douse—she, old, infirm, and poor, felt put upon—then stepped in himself. "As *having their own way*, is one of the greatest comforts of life, to old people, I think their friends should endeavor to accommodate them in that, as well as in anything else," he wrote Sister Mecom.

A stream of orders that revealed something of his life at home and the preciseness of his mind flowed back to Deborah:

> Send me the Indian sealskin hussif, with all the things that were in it. . . . In the right hand little drawer under my desk, is some of the Indian lady's gut cambric; roll it up as you would a ribbon; wrap it in paper, and put it into the hussif with the other things.
>
> Among my books on the shelves there are two or three little pieces on the game of chess; one in French bound in leather, 8vo. One in a blue paper cover, English; two others in manuscript; one of them thin in brown paper cover, the other in loose leaves not bound. If you can find them yourself, send them; but do not set anybody to look for them. You may know the French one by the word ECHECS in the title page.
>
> In my room, on the folio shelf, between the clock and our bed chamber, and not far from the clock, stands a folio called *The Gardner's Dictionary* by P. Miller. And on the same side on the lowest shelf, or lowest but one, near the middle, and by the side of a little partition, you will find standing, or rather lying on its fore edge, a quarto pamphlet, covered with blue paper called *A Treatise on Cyder-Making*. Deliver those two books to Mr. Parker.

Franklin saw Loudoun several times in New York, where his lordship lived in accustomed splendor, served by a retinue of servants he had brought from home. During one week he and his staff drank nineteen dozen bottles of claret, thirty-one dozen of Madeira, a dozen bottles of Burgundy, four bottles of port, and eight bottles of Rhenish. "His lordship has on all occasions treated me with the greatest goodness," Franklin reported back to Philadelphia, "but I find frequently that strong preju-

dices are infused into his mind against our province. We have too many
enemies among ourselves; I hope in time things will wear a better face."
The respect Loudoun acquired for Franklin in Philadelphia diminished
during the layover in New York. After further acquaintance he confided
to his diary that Franklin was not to be trusted.

By the end of April Franklin, too, had become disenchanted with
Loudoun. The general talked daily of dispatching the convoy for England, then each day postponed its departure. "'Tis an uneasy situation;
but we must have patience," Franklin said. He used up a small part of
the time on his hands writing a new will. All his brothers and sisters and
their progeny shared in it. Sister Douse's mortgage was willed to Sister
Mecom, but Sister Douse "must be never disturbed in the possession of
the said house and lot during her life." Two small houses he owned near
Boston went to nephew James Franklin. A fifty-pound loan to nephew
Benjamin Mecom was forgiven. And so on. The bulk of the estate went
to his immediate family. William would receive a building lot and "my
pasture ground," all his library and manuscripts, his air pump, "all my
natural curiosities," and a thousand pounds. The same amount of cash
went to Sarah and to Deborah, who also would get his two houses and
lots, and all the household goods. Wife and children would share the
income from his partnership with David Hall. Yale College, instead of
the Academy that had removed him as president of its board of trustees,
would receive his electrical apparatus. "And I will that my Negro man
Peter and his wife Jemima, be free after my decease." The will ended
with the same paragraph that concluded his will of 1750:

> And now humbly returning sincere thanks to GOD, for producing
> me into being, and conducting me hitherto thro' life so happily, so
> free from sickness, pain and trouble, and with such a competency of
> this world's goods as might make a reasonable mind easy; that he was
> pleased to give me such a mind, with moderate passions, or so much
> of his gracious assistance in governing them; and to free it early from
> ambition, avarice and superstition, common causes of much uneasi-
> ness to men: That he gave me to live so long in a land of liberty, with
> a people that I love; and raised me, tho' a stranger, so many friends
> among them; bestowing on me, moreover, a loving and prudent wife
> and dutiful children: For these, and all his other innumerable mercies
> and favors, I bless that BEING of BEINGS who does not disdain to care
> for the meanest of his creatures. And I reflect on those benefits re-
> ceived, with the greater satisfaction, as they give me such a confidence
> in his goodness, as will, I hope, enable me always in all things to

submit freely to his will, and to resign my spirit cheerfully into his hands, whenever he shall please to call for it; reposing myself securely in the lap of God and Nature, as a child in the arms of an affectionate parent.

At the end of May Loudoun had still not given orders for the convoy to depart. "I have been very low-spirited all day," Franklin said; "this tedious state of uncertainty and long waiting has almost worn out my patience." However, a few days later Franklin, son, and servants were allowed to board their ship, which dropped down to Sandy Hook and anchored amid the fleet. There they lingered two more weeks while Loudoun dallied with decision. The boredom finally overwhelmed Franklin and he "got drunk one day" according to the captain of the packet, "and talked plain language." Finally, on June 20, eleven weeks after Franklin left Philadelphia, the fleet sailed. Twenty-seven days later Franklin reached England, where he would live for five years.

CHAPTER

15

"A CORDIAL AND THOROUGH CONTEMPT"

WILLIAM FRANKLIN SUMMARIZED THE TRIP nicely: "In general, we were highly favored with winds, were several times chased, and met with no accident, except the night before our arrival, when we narrowly escaped running ashore on the Rocks of Scilly, owing to our not having discovered the light ashore till it was almost too late to avoid them."

The final moments at sea moved his father to write: "About nine o'clock the fog began to rise, and seemed to be lifted up from the water like the curtain at a playhouse, discovering underneath the town of Falmouth, the vessels in its harbor, and the fields that surrounded it. A most pleasing spectacle to those who had been so long without any other prospects, than the uniform view of a vacant ocean!"

They reached Falmouth on July 17, a Sunday morning. "The bell ringing for church," Franklin wrote Deborah soon after touching shore, "we went thither immediately, and with hearts full of gratitude, returned sincere thanks to God for the mercies we had received; were I a Roman Catholic, perhaps I should on this occasion vow to build a chapel to some saint; but as I am not, if I were to vow at all, it should be to build a *lighthouse*."

Into the packet with the letter to Deborah went the copy for his twenty-seventh and last edition of *Poor Richard's Almanack*, which he had worked on during the voyage. The preface this time consisted of a long speech to a market-day audience by a character named Father Abraham. The speech blended maxims and aphorisms culled from previous almanacs into a promise that men who worked hard, were prudent and frugal, would become rich. The people listened attentively, but once

Father Abraham had finished they "immediately practiced the contrary, just as if it had been a common sermon," Poor Richard remarked ruefully; "for the vendue opened, and they began to buy extravagantly, notwithstanding all his cautions, and their own fear of taxes." Under the title *The Way to Wealth* the speech would become the most popular of all Franklin's writings—and the most harmful to his cherished reputation. Ever after he would be remembered more as the mouthpiece of strait-laced, materialistic Father Abraham rather than of the witty, earthy Poor Richard.

Since Franklin had achieved wealth, he no longer needed to heed Father Abraham's advice. He set out for London with son and servants in the luxury of a hired carriage. The ten-day trip began as a leisurely sight-seeing venture, but ended, when either boredom or restlessness set in, in a final dash of seventy miles in a single day. On the previous trip to London Franklin had arrived as one of Defoe's "*poor*, that fare hard." This time he rolled in ranked somewhere between "the *middle sort*, who live well" and "the *rich*, who live very plentifully." He and his son put up the first night at the Bear Inn. Notes went out to Peter Collinson and William Strahan, and the next morning the three who had never met during more than twenty years of friendship did so at last. Collinson, now sixty-one, had been a prosperous merchant and well-known member of the Royal Society when he and Franklin began to correspond, but Strahan then had been only another of London's struggling printers. Now he could boast of publishing Dr. Johnson's *Dictionary* and was "in such a way as to lay up £1,000 every year from the profits of his business, after maintaining his family and paying all charges."

Lodgings for the Franklins had been arranged in Craven Street, off the Strand, with Mrs. Margaret Stevenson, a widow, and before the week ended they settled in there. Mrs. Stevenson was Franklin's age and in all ways much like Deborah—plump, good-natured, an efficient manager, and an abysmal speller. She had a bright, eighteen-year-old daughter named Mary but called Polly, who lived as a companion to an elderly aunt in a village some ten miles from London. After several queries from Deborah about the living arrangements, Franklin would say only "we have four rooms furnished, and everything about us pretty genteel, but living here is in every respect very expensive."

Expensive, yes, mainly because Franklin indulged himself during the first month in London, as if to wash from memory the lowly life endured on the last visit. Among the expenses listed for August were:

shoemaker's bill	2–11–0
wigmaker's bill	10–10–6
tailor's bill	45–9–2 1/2
shoemaker's bill	1–16–0
watch at auction	4–0–0
for mending sword and blade	1–2–0
2 pair silver shoe and knee buckles	2–12–6
2 razors and case	0–17–0

In later months £6 6s went for having his portrait painted and £7 for a chessboard. Intermingled in the accounts were reminders of constant "loans to Billy."

Between shopping tours Franklin found time for business. Soon after arriving he saw Dr. John Fothergill, who agreed to arrange a meeting with the proprietors, Richard and Thomas Penn. A friend of Collinson's carried him to see Lord Granville, then president of the powerful Privy Council. When Granville understood Franklin had come to England to stop Penn from imposing binding instructions on his governor, he spoke bluntly about instructions in general, royal and proprietary.

"Those instructions are not like little pocket instructions given to an ambassador or envoy, in which much may be left to discretion," he said. "They are first drawn up by grave and wise men learned in the laws and constitutions of the nation; they are then brought to the Council Board, where they are solemnly weighed and maturely considered, and after receiving such amendments as are found proper and necessary, they are agreed upon and established. The Council is *over all* the colonies; your last resort is to the Council to decide your differences, and you must be sensible it is for your own good, for otherwise you often could not obtain justice. The King in Council is THE LEGISLATOR of the colonies; and when his Majesty's instructions come there, they are LAW OF THE LAND; *they are,*" repeated Granville, "the Law of the Land, and as such *ought to be* OBEYED."

Franklin sat stunned. "I told his lordship this was new doctrine to me. I had always understood from our charters, that our laws were to be made by our assemblies, to be presented indeed to the king for his royal assent, but that being once given the king could not repeal or alter them. And as the assemblies could not make permanent laws without his assent, so neither could he make a law for them without theirs." Granville told Franklin he "was totally mistaken."

The disturbing aspect of the exchange, a scholar has remarked, was that neither man "had been aware of the other's conceptions, and neither had been touched by the other's arguments. Their reactions portended trouble for the empire, which could be averted only by statescraft of a high order on the British side, along with tolerance and good will."

Franklin knew that if Granville's views reflected those of the government, negotiations with the proprietors were certain to fail. Instead of reporting the conversation back to the Assembly, Franklin let nearly two years pass before revealing it.

2

The first meeting with Thomas Penn took place less than three weeks after Franklin arrived in London. Present were Penn and Ferdinand John Paris, his solicitor. Franklin called Paris "a proud angry man"; a less prejudiced observer admitted he "had a peculiar talent at slurring the characters of his antagonists." He was also exceedingly able. He could match Franklin in political adroitness and because he "had an uncanny ability to expedite business at the public offices" could outmatch him in manipulating the government to serve his client. He had been the Pennsylvania agent in London for several years before transferring his allegiance to Penn and knew its affairs as well as Franklin.

Paris had been warned about Franklin by Robert Hunter Morris. "He is a sensible artful man, very knowing in American affairs, and was his heart as sound as his head, few men would be fitter for public trust," Morris wrote. "But that is far from being the case. He has nothing in view but to serve himself, and however he may give another turn to what he says and does, yet you may be assured that is at the bottom, and in the end will show itself."

Thomas Penn, too, had been warned—by Richard Peters. "Certain it is that B. F.'s view is to effect a change of government, and considering the popularity of his character and the reputation gained by his electrical discoveries which will introduce him into all sorts of company he may prove a dangerous enemy. Dr. Fothergill and Mr. Collinson can introduce him to the men of most influence at court, and he may underhand give impressions to your prejudice. In short, heaven and earth will be moved against the proprietors." Penn took the warning lightly. He knew something about British political life Franklin had yet to learn. "I think I wrote you before that Mr. Franklin's popularity is nothing here, and that he will be looked very coldly upon by great people," he told Peters. "There are few of any consequence that have heard of his electrical experiments, those matters being attended to by a particular set of people," he added, "but it is quite another sort of people, who are to determine the dispute between us."

Franklin and Penn met in August as old acquaintances. Penn had lived several years in Pennsylvania. He had used Franklin's shop to have bookplates printed, books bound, and he had subscribed to the *Gazette*. Now fifty-five years old and still a handsome man, he dressed richly and divided his time between a town house and his country estate. He had waited until the age of forty-nine to marry, and then to a wealthy, good-looking, intelligent woman twenty-eight years his junior who during their affectionate marriage would give him eight children. Penn had inherited a bankrupt estate. "I want to have every debt due from my family paid," he said soon afterward, stating his credo. "To this end I shall ever think myself obliged to serve the public both with my person and my pocket, but I never desire to have views so noble, extensive and benevolent as my father, unless he had left a much larger fortune, because these views, though good in themselves, yet by possessing so much, led him into inconveniences which I hope to avoid."

As one who ranked somewhere between the "*rich*, who live very plentifully" and "*great*, who live profusely," Penn must have held a touch of disdain for B. Franklin, printer, but if so he kept the feeling hidden. The first meeting went amicably—"we spoke of things generally," Penn reported, "my brother being in the country on a tour, I did not think it proper to do otherwise." During the meeting Penn told Franklin "it was absolutely necessary to have what he demanded in writing." At the next meeting, on August 20, Franklin came with a short paper entitled "Heads of Complaint." He considered it an informal agenda for discussion and failed to address it to the proprietors, an *erratum*, he would learn later, more grave than any listed in the *Autobiography*. In the paper he asked that the deputy governor be given the "use of his best discretion." As the man "on the spot, he can better judge of the emergency state and necessity of affairs than proprietaries residing at a great distance." He objected to instructions that excluded "the greatest part" of the proprietary estates from a land tax.

At subsequent meetings in September the proprietors told Franklin several points in the "Complaint" concerned the royal prerogative and they must therefore consult the king's attorney general and solicitor general for advice. "This they would endeavor to obtain as soon as possible, having already stated a case and laid it before those gentlemen for their consideration." Unknown to Franklin, Paris had sent the royal officials a series of legitimate but "loaded" questions. For example, could the proprietors "lawfully restrain their lieutenant governor's power and authority by instructions?" Had Franklin known of the questions he would have seen at once, after the conversation with Lord Granville, his case was doomed.

3

Perhaps he sensed that in jousting with Paris and Penn he had ventured beyond his depth. In the midst of the negotiations he fell ill with "a violent cold and something of a fever." He recovered long enough to plant two essays in the London press defending Pennsylvania and the Quakers, then "I had another severe cold, which continued longer than the first, attended by great pain in my head, the top of which was very hot, and when the pain went off, very sore and tender." Dr. Fothergill came when Franklin turned "now and then a little delirious." He bled the patient at the back of the head and that seemed to ease him. Franklin thought himself well enough in October to sit for his portrait wearing a dressing gown and to venture out once or twice. He fell ill again. Dr. Fothergill "grew very angry" with him. Mrs. Stevenson "nursed me kindly," and Peter, the slave whom Franklin and his wife had worried might give trouble in London, "was very diligent and attentive." Finally, after enduring the mysterious illness for nearly two months, "I was seized one morning with a vomiting and purging, the latter of which continued the greater part of the day, and I believe was a kind of crisis to the distemper, carrying it clear off; for ever since I feel quite lightsome, and am every day gathering strength; so I hope my seasoning is over, and that I shall enjoy better health during the rest of my stay in England."

He was well enough by mid-November to see the Penns again. He came to complain that troops raised to range the frontiers had been kept in the forts by Governor Denny. Penn immediately sent "peremptory orders" to Denny to use the rangers for the purpose they had been trained. A few days later Paris told Franklin that the proprietors would be pleased "to use their utmost endeavors to promote any such application" he might make to the crown for aid to Pennsylvania. When later in the month Thomas Penn heard from Franklin that the Admiralty had not stationed a warship at the mouth of Delaware Bay to protect shipping, he persuaded the authorities to send one. The proprietors, in short, made it clear that on all matters except that of instructions to their governor they wanted to work with Franklin for the welfare of Pennsylvania. Franklin admitted they "always treated him with great civility."

Then came a meeting in mid-January 1758. The issue discussed centered on the appointment of commissioners to regulate the Indian trade. The Assembly insisted that the governor could have no say in the matter. Conversation began with a misunderstanding on Thomas Penn's part.

Franklin said the Assembly's bill was modeled on that of Massachusetts, where the General Court—that is, both houses of the legislature—made such appointments. Penn, thinking the General Court equated with the appointed council in Pennsylvania, said he approved the Massachusetts method, and when the Assembly passed a bill along those lines he would give it his sanction. Nothing Franklin said could convince Penn he did not know what he was talking about. Franklin then said, probably with some heat, that if the House of Commons could name commissioners without the king's approval, the Pennsylvania Assembly had the same right, given to it by William Penn in his Charter of Privileges of 1701. Thomas Penn thought the comparison inapt, "that we were only a kind of corporation acting by a charter from the crown and could have no privileges or rights but what was granted by that charter, in which no such privilege as we now claim was anywhere mentioned."

It has been pointed out that Penn's "position was logical and soundly based in English constitutional theory, and it was one that his long experience with officials in the English government had confirmed." Franklin found it neither logical nor sound. "Your father's charter," he answered, "expressly says that the Assembly of Pennsylvania shall have all the power and privileges of an assembly according to the rights of the freeborn subjects of England, and as is usual in any of the British plantations in America."

"Yes," said Penn, "but if my father granted privileges he was not by the royal charter empowered to grant, nothing can be claimed by such grant."

"If then your father had no right to grant the privileges he pretended to grant, and published all over Europe as granted, those who came to settle in the province upon the faith of that grant and in expectation of enjoying the privileges contained in it, were deceived, cheated and betrayed."

If the settlers "were deceived, it was their own fault," Penn said, uttering this last, according to Franklin, "with a kind of triumphing laughing insolence, such as a low jockey might do when a purchaser complained that he had cheated him in a horse. I was astonished to see him thus meanly give up his father's character and conceived that moment a more cordial and thorough contempt for him than I ever before felt for any man living—a contempt that I cannot express in words, but I believe my countenance expressed it strongly. And that his brother was looking at me, must have observed it; however, finding myself grow warm I made no other answer to this than that the poor people were no lawyers themselves and confiding in his father did not think it necessary to consult any."

When Thomas Penn later heard about Franklin's report of the meeting he insisted he had said or done nothing "in any manner, as my brother tells me, that could give any cause of offense." Franklin felt otherwise. Thus far he had told friends in the Assembly little about the negotiations with the Penns, but the day after this meeting he put discretion aside and sent a full account home, including the reference to Penn as "a low jockey." "I begin to think I shall hardly be able to return before this time twelve months," he wrote his wife a week after the interview. "I am for doing effectually what I came about; and I find it requires both time and patience." A month later, still raging, he hoped "the proprietors will be gibbeted up as they deserve, to rot and stink in the nostrils of posterity."

4

In March Franklin received good news—that "inveterate scribbler," William Smith, "has at length wrote himself into a jail." Smith had published some libelous remarks on the Assembly, and in January he stood trial before the legislature, "deprived of the common modes of defense by those violent and ignorant men," said William Allen, "who claim all the powers of the House of Commons, and greatly go beyond them." Allen, as chief justice, refused to grant Smith a writ of habeas corpus because "our pious Assembly" would only have recommitted him to jail, "for they seem to know no bounds to their power and are resolved to crush every man that dares oppose them in turn." Later, after the Assembly adjourned, Allen issued the writ, which freed Smith after four months in prison, but meanwhile he had organized a defense fund that would allow Smith to petition the crown for redress. The petition reached London in March, brought by former governor James Hamilton. The hearing, set for April 20, was, said Franklin, "looked upon by everybody as an open declaration of war" between him and the proprietors. Ferdinand John Paris headed Smith's counsel, and though Franklin hired lawyers to present the Assembly's case he directed the presentation at every step.

Paris dressed his case with invective, painting an Assembly dominated by Quakers whose ire had been raised by a clergyman of the Church of England who promoted measures of defense for a beleaguered colony, but the burden of his brief rested on a single statement—"the Assembly of Pennsylvania was not a Parliament nor had anything near so much power as the House of Commons had." Franklin's counsel dismissed the attack on the Quakers as rubbish—they no longer controlled

the legislature—then bore in on the central point—the Assembly had all
the powers and privileges of the House of Commons and in jailing Smith
did no more than Commons would have done in similar circumstances.
The issue involved more than local politics in Pennsylvania. It concerned
all America, for, counsel held, following Franklin's lead, "all representative bodies must have incident to them the powers exercised by the
Assembly."

At stake were two conceptions of the American assemblies. Neither
side dared predict the outcome of the momentous question. As Paris
remarked, the members of the board "are but young in office, are cautious
how they act."

5

Supervising the case against Smith had involved prodigious labor
under a tight deadline. Franklin had paused in April to buy equipment
for electrical experiments, but otherwise had relaxed little. Early in May
he took a week off to visit Cambridge University. His health and spirits
improved there and when invited to attend the commencement in July,
he and William "went accordingly, were present at all the ceremonies,
dined every day in their halls, and my vanity was not a little gratified by
the particular regard shown me by the chancellor and vice chancellor of
the university, and the heads of the colleges."

After the commencement, Franklin and son, with Peter in attendance, toured the countryside searching out Josiah Franklin's homestead
and any surviving members of the clan. They found Mary Fisher, a
daughter of Josiah's brother Thomas, who was "five years older than
Sister Douse, and remembers her going away with my father and his then
wife, and two other children to New England about the year 1685." A visit
to Ecton, where Josiah Franklin had been reared, turned up a bundle of
family anecdotes. The chatty wife of the village rector "carried us out
into the church yard and showed us several of their grave stones, which
were so covered with moss that we could not read the letters till she
ordered a hard brush and basin of water, with which Peter scoured them
clean, and then Billy copied them."

In Birmingham Franklin looked up his wife's relatives, sending home
a long report on all he met. One, a Mrs. Salt, "is a jolly lively dame; both
Billy and myself agree that she was extremely like you; her whole face
has the same turn, and exactly the same little blue Birmingham eyes."
They spent a week in Birmingham, traveling "continually on the foot,

from one manufactory to another, and were highly entertained in seeing all the curious machines and expeditious ways of working." Every morning before they left their inn for sight-seeing some member of Deborah's clan stopped by to visit, to drop off a letter or a present for one of the Reads who had emigrated to Pennsylvania. Franklin entered each of their names in a notebook. After he left town one of the relatives came "twenty miles on foot to see us, a little angry with his Uncle Joshua for not informing him of us when we were in town." He wanted "his name put down in my book among the rest of the family." Deborah was assured all her relatives were "industrious, ingenious, working people and think themselves vastly happy that they live in dear old England."

Franklin returned to London the end of July, spent some time putting his affairs in order, then in mid-August traveled with William to Tunbridge Wells, a fashionable spa. After taking the waters for a week or so, he left William behind and went back to London. William, who was studying law at the Middle Temple but now on vacation, planned further travels with friends. Franklin at the end of the summer justified his own traveling as a way "partly to recover my health, and partly to improve and increase acquaintance among persons of influence." He deluded himself if he thought those met to be persons of influence. Most of his acquaintances had little weight in government. Outside London he circulated mainly among craftsmen, businessmen, and intellectuals. In the city he saw much of Collinson, Fothergill, and Strahan, and also Richard Jackson and Dr. John Pringle. Pringle served as the queen's physician but had little influence among politicians. Jackson was an eminent barrister, a favorite with such literary lights as Dr. Samuel Johnson, but the best he could do in a political way was introduce Franklin to second-string politicians. Several times Franklin tried to see William Pitt but never got beyond the antechamber of his secretaries.

The doors of those at the top were closed to an extent because Thomas Penn did what he could to keep them closed. After learning Franklin had called him "a low jockey," Penn promised that "from this time I will not have any conversation with him on any pretense." He carried a copy of Franklin's indiscreet letter to Lord Halifax, the powerful president of the Board of Trade, and to "some other people, to show how well disposed this man is to settle differences."

Dr. Fothergill had mixed feelings about Franklin but watched the net close round him in dismay. "His reputation as a man, a philosopher and a statesman, only seem to render his station more difficult and perplexing," he wrote to Israel Pemberton. "You must allow him time, and without repining. He is equally able and solicitous to serve the province, but his obstructions are next to insurmountable. Great pains had been taken, and very successfully, to render him odious and his integrity suspected, to those very persons to whom he must first apply. These suspicions can only be worn off by time, and prudence." In the meantime, Franklin did not let the obstructions confronted, the frustrations endured, depress him. "The agreeable conversation I meet with among men of learning, and the notice taken of me by persons of distinction, are the principal things that soothe me for the present," he said.

He spent much of his spare time shopping for family and friends. Before illness made him housebound he found time to buy a crimson satin cloak for Deborah of "the newest fashion," and one of black silk for Sally. Later for Deborah and her friend Goody Smith he bought two books of Common Prayer in large-size print, "so you will both of you be reprieved from the use of spectacles in church a little longer." In another box went "a newest fashioned white hat and cloak" for Sally and sundry other "little things," such as "a pair of buckles, made of French paste stones, which are next in luster to diamonds." He promised her, too, a harpsichord if he could find a good one at a reasonable price. Things fashionable meant much to Franklin. Deborah had sent over portraits of herself and Sally, and Franklin planned to have them copied with one of himself into a family portrait: when the limner told him such paintings "never look well, and are quite out of fashion," he abandoned the project.

Franklin pretended to care little for food, saying he ate whatever was put before him. Yet he seemed to be often hungry in his letters. In one he asked for "some pippins for myself and friends, some of your small hams, and some cranberries," and in another he suggested his wife neglected him. "Goodies I now and then get a few; but roasting apples seldom; I wish you had sent me some; and I wonder how you, that used to think of everything, came to forget it." Roasting apples seemed about the only thing forgotten. Every ship arriving from Philadelphia brought a box of "goodies" along with her latest installments in a stream of letters. She worried constantly about her "dear Pappy," and Franklin spent much space in his own letters reassuring her. Yes, yes, "my shirts are always well aired as you directed." Yes, "your kind advice about getting a chariot I had taken some time before." Yes, "Peter behaves very well to me in general, and begins to know the town so as to go anywhere of errands."

Franklin tried to keep control of his family from afar. He praised one of Sally's letters as "the best wrote that of late I have seen of hers. I only wish she was a little more careful of her spelling," he added. "I hope she continues to love going to church and would have her read over and over again *The Whole Duty of Man* and *The Lady's Library.* "The difficulties with the Penns went unmentioned, except once when he wanted to use his wife as a conduit for gossip and referred to it obliquely. He had heard the proprietors were searching for a new governor. This news "was to have been kept a secret from me," Franklin wrote, "so you may make a secret of it too, if you please, and oblige all your friends with it."

<h1 style="text-align:center">6</h1>

Franklin had handed the proprietors his "Heads of Complaint" in August 1757, but not until November 1758 did the Penns receive the opinions of the attorney and solictor generals on the grievances. They advised the Penns to reject all except the one concerning taxation of the proprietary estates. Ferdinand John Paris so informed the Assembly in a message dated November 27. The passage dealing with taxation was a masterpiece of obfuscation:

> However, to take off all pretense of clamor, they are very ready to have the annual income of their estate inquired into, and are as ready to contribute whatever the said sum shall fall short of their proportion of what has been laid on the inhabitants in general, for every part of their estate, that is in its nature taxable.

Franklin the next day asked for clarification of these remarks. What did the proprietors mean by "inquired into"? What was their just "proportion"? What parts of their lands were taxable? The Penns refused to answer the questions. Instead, hoping to force Franklin's recall, they wrote the Assembly of his "disrespect" toward them—on a matter of the greatest importance he had turned in to the Honorable Proprietors a paper entitled "Heads of Complaint," but "neither dated, signed, or addressed to any person"—but they remained agreeable "to enter into free conference on all these several subjects with any persons of candor, whom you shall authorize for that purpose." They also sent Paris round to Franklin's lodgings to tell him the proprietors no longer wished to continue any correspondence or negotiations with him. After the visit Paris said that Franklin upon receiving this message "answered not a word, looked as if much disappointed, and took no notice of him when he went out." It has been remarked that Franklin "had not endured such a string of personal indignities since the abrasive apprenticeship of his Boston youth under his brother James."

CHAPTER

16

"I AM A BRITON"

HE HAD PLANNED an alternate course of action long before the rebuff from the Penns. After Paris presented Smith's case at the hearing in April 1758, Franklin asked Richard Jackson, who was "esteemed the best acquainted with our American affairs, and constitutions, as well as with government law in general," to find out how much Pennsylvania's rights and privileges would be altered under a royal government. Jackson's report called for caution. He warned that the Assembly's demand for full control of all monies collected would be "determined against them, both by the Privy Council and the Parliament." He opposed pressing the Penns for "a formal decision at present, if at all." However, he did think Parliament and the crown would support the Assembly in a land tax on the Penns' estates. Also, and this was what Franklin wanted to hear, he thought none of the Assembly's powers would be diminished by any parliamentary act calling for royal assumption of the colony. But remember, he warned at the end, whatever the crown wished to do it would "always be able to support and carry in Parliament."

After the Penns cut communications, Franklin determined to deprive the proprietors of their colony—not of their estates but of their political power in Pennsylvania. This course, it has been remarked, "offered an opportunity to visit Old Testament vengeance" on the Penns. Vengeance certainly spurred Franklin on, but he also saw a principle involved. "I believe it will in time be clearly seen by all thinking people," he said, "that the government and property of a province should not be in the same family. 'Tis too much weight in one scale."

Franklin did not see royal government as a panacea for Pennsylvania's ills. (A year earlier Poor Richard had observed that "the royal crown cures not the headache.") Nor did he count on a generous conception of American rights and privileges from the king's ministers. "The prevailing opinion, as far as I am able to collect it, among the ministers and great men here, is," he told Isaac Norris, "that the colonies have too many and too great privileges; and that it is not only the interest of the crown but of the nation to reduce them. An absolute subjection to orders sent from hence in the shape of instructions is the point to be carried if possible." Indeed, he knew of one minister, Lord Halifax, president of the Board of Trade, who wanted to set up military governments in the colonies. But he also knew of a strong feeling among the king's ministers that "the Parliament would establish more liberty in the colonies than is proper or necessary, and therefore [the ministers] do not care the Parliament should meddle at all with the government of the colonies." That convinced Franklin "our best chance in an application is directly to Parliament." For Franklin, scarred from his battles with the Pennsylvania executive, no legislature would do wrong to the people.

It was an ingenious plan but, as he must have seen, one filled with revolutionary implications. It called for Parliament to meddle in matters it had hitherto stayed clear of—the government of the empire. And there were other hazards, "for tho' there are many members in both houses who are friends to liberty and of noble spirits, yet a good deal of prejudice still prevails against the colonies; the courtiers think us not sufficiently obedient; the illicit trade from Holland, etc. greatly offends the trading and manufacturing interest; and the landed interest begin to be jealous of us as a corn country, that may interfere with them in the markets to which they export that commodity." How could these prejudices be overcome? Jackson suggested he get elected to the House of Commons, which could easily be managed, and work from within. Franklin rejected that tactic, because "I am too old to think of changing countries, am almost weary of business, and languish after repose and my America."

Instead, he told Galloway and Norris that the Assembly must "petition the crown to take the government into its own hands." He assured them, though he had no right to, that such a petition would be "very favorably heard." Meanwhile, he would be busy *removing the prejudices that art and accident have spread among the people of this country* against us, and obtaining for us *the good opinion of the bulk of mankind without doors.*" Thomas Penn knew the workings of the British government better than Franklin and worried little about a propaganda campaign. What worked in Philadelphia would fail in London. "Appealing to the public will displease the administration," he said, "and for that reason I shall not practice it but let them write what they please."

Franklin opened with an oblique attack in September 1758, using Maryland to illustrate the defects of proprietary government. William Strahan published the piece in his *London Chronicle*. In March 1759 Franklin subsidized publication of *An Enquiry into the Causes of the Alienation of the Delaware and Shawanese Indians*, a damning attack on the proprietary Indian policy, especially the Walking Purchase, and written by a young Philadelphia neighbor of Franklin's, Charles Thomson. (Conrad Weiser had called the pamphlet "a notorious lie" and the author "a scoundrel and an ignorant fellow," and noted that one of the censured transactions with the Indians had been witnessed by "Mr. Benjamin Franklin.") In June came *An Historical Review of the Constitution and Government of Pennsylvania*, a work Franklin thought would "engage the attention of many readers, and at the same time efface the bad impressions received of us." Franklin "looked over the manuscript," but, so he said, "was not permitted to alter everything I did not fully approve." The work claimed that the rights of Pennsylvanians, identical to those of all Englishmen, had been steadily diminished over the years by the proprietors. It sought to give "Parliament and ministry a clearer knowledge and truer notion of our disputes." Franklin hoped it would "spread and confirm among our people, and especially in the rising generation, those sentiments of liberty that one would wish always to prevail in Pennsylvania." Though not the author of the book (it is not clear who was), he dedicated it to the Speaker of the House of Commons, "and I flatter myself we shall after its publication stand in a much fairer light." He was wrong. The book sold poorly in London and Philadelphia. It impressed no one of importance in or out of the British government.

2

By early 1759 Franklin had become a familiar figure to the doorkeepers of London's government buildings, and by then he appeared to have mastered the intricacies of the political machinery. He missed no trick to smooth the way for the causes he pled, listing among his expenses the "customary New Year's gifts, and Christmas presents to doorkeepers and clerks of the public offices, tavern dinners for the lawyers and our other friends at hearings, coach hire, etc. . . ." He moved about at a steady pace that never seemed hurried yet never slackened through the long day. His schedule had forced him to forgo sending copy for the previous year's almanac, though he had "collected many materials which only wanted putting together," and he confessed early in 1759 he probably would not find time to work up the material for the upcoming edition. "If I do not correspond so fully and punctually with you as you expected," he explained to his partner Hall, "consider the situation and business I am in, the number of correspondents I have to write to, the eternal interruptions one meets with in this great city, the visits one must necessarily receive and pay, the entertainments or amusements one is invited to and urged to partake of, besides the many matters of use and importance worth a stranger's while to inquire into who is soon to return to his own country, and then if you make a little additional allowance for the indolence that naturally creeps upon us with age, I think you will be more ready to excuse me."

The countless treks down marbled corridors, the long hours spent waiting in ministers' antechambers, produced no triumphs in 1759. The year opened unpleasantly with the arrival in London of Smith the Libeller, as Franklin called him, come to push for a decision on his petition against the Assembly that had jailed him. In February, while Smith was "dancing attendance" upon ministers, Franklin submitted to the Privy Council Teedyuscung's petition against the notorious Walking Purchase, prefacing it with a request that all purchases of land from the Indians by the proprietors (including the one he had witnessed at Albany) be reexamined by the crown. In April Parliament authorized a subsidy of two hundred thousand pounds to be divided among the colonies according to their contributions in the war against the French and Indians. Franklin immediately submitted an account for Pennsylvania alone that exceeded by some eighteen thousand pounds the total authorization for all the colonies. On May 15 he spoke on Teedyuscung's petition before the Board of Trade and felt he had scored several points against the Penns' solicitor, Paris, and that the board looked kindly upon the arguments he had presented. Two weeks later he appeared before the board again, and again thought he made a good impression defending the Assembly's bill for regulating the Indian trade.

The first bad news came early in June when the Board of Trade refused to censure the proprietors' land purchases and said Teedyuscung's petition called for further investigation. The next setback came at the end of the month when the Privy Council censured the Assembly for jailing William Smith. True, Smith had published a libelous statement, but he could not be jailed "for a contempt to any former Assembly" that had adjourned sine die. Besides, contrary to what Franklin had argued, "inferior assemblies" like that of Pennsylvania "must not be compared, either in power or privileges, to the Commons of Great Britain." The elated Smith, after collecting a doctor's degree in divinity from Oxford, returned to Philadelphia to gloat. Franklin, who had predicted that if the Privy Council "censure anything in the conduct of the Assembly, it will be modes and not essentials," said nothing.

Government business slowed down as summer approached and officials drifted to their country estates. Early in August, Franklin and William left on a trip that would last three months and cover nearly fifteen hundred miles. They were attended this time only by Peter. Franklin explained the situation to his wife:

> Peter continues with me, and behaves as well as I can expect in a country where there are many occasions of spoiling servants, if they are ever so good. He has as few faults as most of them, and I see with only one eye, and hear only with one ear; so we rub on pretty comfortably. King, that you inquire after, is not with us. He ran away from our house, near two years ago, while we were absent in the country; but was soon found in Suffolk, where he had been taken in the service of a lady that was very fond of the merit of making him a Christian, and contributing to his education and improvement.

Father, son, and Peter spent August in Derbyshire "among the gentry there to whom we were recommended," then moved on to Manchester and Liverpool. "The journey agrees extremely well with me; and will probably be many ways of use to me," Franklin reported from Liverpool. In Sheffield he bought his wife two saucepans, "which instead of being tinned within, are plated with silver, that will not melt off like the tin. The biggest cost me two guineas, the smallest 17s. I flatter myself they will please you."

September found them in Edinburgh, which they used as a base from which to fan out on sight-seeing trips through the Scottish countryside. William Strahan came up from London to make sure they met such friends of his as David Hume and Adam Smith. William, of whom Strahan was especially fond, made an excellent impression. He was, said one dinner guest, "open and communicative, and pleased the company better than his father; and some of us observed indications of that decided difference of opinion between father and son which, in the American war, alienated them altogether."

The highlight of the trip came in October at the estate of Lord Kames, Scotland's most eminent jurist. The Franklins arrived back in London on November 2, ending "six weeks of the *densest* happiness I have met with in any part of my life."

3

While Franklin toured Scotland, General Wolfe defeated the French at Quebec. The fall of that city opened all Canada to the British. "No one can rejoice more sincerely than I do on the reduction of Canada," Franklin told Lord Kames; "and this, not merely as I am a colonist, but as I am a Briton. I have long been of opinion that the foundations of the future grandeur and stability of the British empire, lie in America; and tho' like other foundations, they are low and little seen, they are nevertheless, broad and strong enough to support the greatest political structure human wisdom ever yet erected. I am therefore by no means for restoring Canada. If we keep it, all the country from St. Lawrence to Mississippi, will in another century be filled with British people; Britain itself will become vastly more populous by the immense increase of its commerce; the Atlantic sea will be covered with your trading ships; and your naval power thence continually increasing will extend your influence round the whole globe, and awe the world! If the French remain in Canada, they will continually harass our colonies by the Indians, impede if not prevent their growth; your progress to greatness will at best be slow, and give room for many accidents that may forever prevent it. But I refrain, for I see you begin to think my notions extravagant, and look upon them as the ravings of a mad prophet."

In London Franklin found a strong sentiment to return Canada to the French when the peace came and take, in its place, Guadeloupe, a French island in the West Indies rich in sugar and other tropical products. He also heard wherever he went "that to keep Canada would draw on us the envy of other powers, and occasion a confederacy against us; that the country is too large for us to people, not worth possessing, and the like. These notions I am every day and everywhere combating and I think not without some success." The jousting with Penn had revived on the return to London and Franklin might have said no more on Canada if he had not suddenly in February 1760 come down with "an epidemical cold." The distemper gave him a headache that would not go away and a constant feeling of giddiness. On February 21 he parted with eight ounces of blood from the back of his head, then three days later with sixteen more ounces, "which was of great service; but that and physic left me a little weak." By mid-March he had "grown a little thin, which I do not dislike," but felt "pretty well-recovered," well enough to use the leisure time in bed to write a long essay on Canada that came out in April under the title

The Interest of Great Britain Considered. To say, as has been suggested, that it might have been more aptly entitled *The Interest of Greater America Considered with Regard to Britain* misses Franklin's point—that Britons at home and those from overseas like himself were involved in a common cause "in which the interest of the whole nation is directly and fundamentally concerned."

In the offhand remarks to Lord Kames, Franklin revealed "a more grandiose vision of the American future than any other man of his generation." His pamphlet—clearly a piece of propaganda that ignored such staggering problems as how to govern the huge accession or how to deal with a populace of French-speaking Catholics—sought to convince those who shaped imperial policy that it was in the interest of Great Britain to make a reality of that vision. Indeed, not to do so might endanger the empire. If the land west of the Appalachian Mountains was left in the hands of the French, the Americans penned along the seacoast, most of them farmers, will soon "surpass the number that can subsist by the husbandry" and turn to manufacturing. If, on the other hand, those western lands were opened to settlement, it "must take some centuries to fulfill, and in the meantime this nation must necessarily supply them with the manufactures they consume, because the new settlers will be employed in agriculture." Leaving France in control of its holdings on the American continent, he warned, is "neither safe nor prudent." Great Britain need not fear the power of an expanded American empire. Jealousy among the colonies is so great that even when their survival would seem to depend upon it, "they have never been able to effect such an union among themselves, nor even to agree in requesting the mother country to establish it for them." But, he added slyly:

> When I say such an union is impossible, I mean without the most grievous tyranny and oppression. . . . While the government is mild and just, while important civil and religious rights are secure, such subjects will be dutiful and obedient. The waves do not rise but when the winds blow.

Before turning it over to the printer, Franklin showed his manuscript to Richard Jackson, whose judgment he respected. Jackson suggested inserting a flattering comment on Lord Halifax, the powerful, anti-American president of the Board of Trade, in the hope that "it might induce him to look with a more favorable eye on the colonies." Halifax thereupon became a gentleman "as much distinguished by his great capacity, as by his unwearied and disinterested application" to American affairs. Strahan printed one thousand copies of the pamphlet, which Franklin paid for. It sold well.

4

At the time the recuperating Franklin wrote the pamphlet on Canada he talked of returning home, "as I think our affairs here will now soon be brought to a conclusion." Strahan pleaded with him to stay in England. "I gave him, however, two reasons why I could not think of removing hither," Franklin wrote his wife. "One, my affection to Pennsylvania, and long established friendships and other connections there. The other, your invincible aversion to crossing the seas. And without removing hither, I could not think of parting with my daughter [i.e., his wife] to such a distance."

Franklin thought "our affairs" would soon be decided one way or another because in January 1760 Thomas Penn asked the Privy Council to review eleven of the Assembly's acts. Penn thought them unconstitutional because they contravened his instructions to the governor. One of the acts challenged called for taxation of the proprietary estates. Another, the Agency Act, authorized Franklin to collect whatever sum the government allocated to Pennsylvania for its contributions to the war effort and place the money in the Bank of England for use by the Assembly. This act especially angered Penn because it gave full control of the money to the Assembly. It, along with the others, had been signed into law after the Assembly slipped Governor Denny a three-thousand-pound bribe. In challenging the eleven acts, Penn forced Franklin into a battle that could make or break his reputation. Disallowance of all the acts by the Privy Council would mean a decisive defeat for the Assembly and loss of the power it had usurped from the executive. Approval of them all would mean Franklin could return home a hero. He refused to predict the outcome of the battle: "I have not all the confidence I could wish, that what appears right and reasonable to me, may easily be made appear the same to others."

Except during the weeks of his illness the fight occupied all Franklin's working hours from February through August. The first set of hearings, before the Board of Trade, began on May 21 and lasted for three days. The proprietors' lawyers opened with an attack on the Assembly's usurpation of executive powers, its "almost rebellious declarations" against certain royal instructions, and its numerous "other acts of avowed democracy." They accused the legislature, correctly, of using bribery to get the bill taxing proprietary estates signed into law. Franklin's lawyers denied the bribery charge. They argued "that the assessors were honest and discreet men, under an oath to assess fairly and equitably," and that it was ludi-

crous to think they could or would ruin the proprietors. The Board of
Trade handed down its judgment a month later. It said that when the
Assembly spent public money it usurped "one of the most inviolable
prerogatives of the executive power, not countenanced by any example
of the British representatives." In spite of those harsh words it thought
Pennsylvania should be paid for its war services "with as few delays as
possible," and therefore recommended approval of the Agency Act, even
though disposition of the money was "reserved solely to the Assembly,
independent of the proprietaries." It accepted the "grand principle," as
Franklin called it, that the proprietary legitimately could be taxed, but
because the Assembly bill was so loosely written it recommended disallowance. All told, it recommended approval of four of the acts challenged
and disallowance of seven.

These recommendations went to the Privy Council's Committee for
Plantation Affairs, whose judgment would be final. Hearings before that
body were held at the end of August and lasted two days. During the
hearings Lord Mansfield, one of the committee, beckoned to Franklin and
the two went to a nearby room while the lawyers continued to argue.
Could Franklin assure him that the proprietary estates would be fairly
taxed? Lord Mansfield asked.

"Certainly," Franklin said.

"Then," said Lord Mansfield, "you can have little objection to enter
into an engagement to assure that point."

"None at all," said Franklin.

The agreement soon after drawn up stated that the lands to be taxed
must be "defined with precision, so as not to include the unsurveyed
wasteland belonging to the proprietaries"; that unsettled lands owned by
the proprietors would be taxed no higher than similar lands owned by
others; that all rents due to the proprietors must be paid in sterling.
Franklin and Robert Charles, the Assembly's permanent agent in London, signed a pledge that the Assembly would carry out these and other
provisions of the agreement. A week later, on September 2, the Privy
Council issued its report. It disallowed six of the eleven challenged acts,
but among those approved were the Agency Act and an amended supply
act allowing the proprietary lands to be taxed.

Who won the great battle? Franklin and the Assembly gained a clear-
cut decision on only the Agency Act. Thomas Penn, who had earlier
resigned himself to some kind of taxation on the family lands, thought
the compromise on that issue a fair one. And the concession that rents
must be paid in sterling, something he had tried to get for over thirty
years, was a major victory. The implications in the Board of Trade and

the Privy Council reports that both royal and proprietary instructions must be adhered to by the Assembly and that the Assembly had the right only to levy taxes, not to dispose of the money collected, were clear-cut decisions against Franklin and the legislature.

All the issues that brought Franklin to England had now been decided with finality by the highest power in England, the king's Privy Council. All but one—the right to tax the proprietary estates—had been decided against him. His affairs were now concluded. He could return home, or so it would seem.

CHAPTER

17

"WE HAVE NOT KEPT HIM"

HE COULD RELAX now that "the long litigation" between the Assembly and the Penns had ended, and shortly after the Privy Council handed down its judgment Franklin and his son began a six-week holiday through western England and Wales. In Birmingham they visited the shop of John Baskerville, printer and type designer, and performed electrical experiments with Matthew Boulton, designer of an efficient steam engine. In Bristol they saw a relative of Collinson's, to whom Franklin had been introduced as "a very sensible knowing gentleman of an original turn and genius; of great modesty; and rather deliberate in communicating the treasures of his mind, than forward in displaying his ability." While taking the waters at Bath they learned that George II had died and that his twenty-two-year-old grandson had ascended the throne as George III.

When Franklin returned to London early in November, he found that the government had allotted Pennsylvania £26,618 14s 5d for its contribution to the war effort, something considerably less than the bill of over £218,000 he had submitted but still a tidy sum for the Assembly to play with. He had planned to put the money in the Bank of England, where the Pennsylvania Loan Office could draw upon it, but this "being contrary to their rules," he had to deposit it in his own name, which meant he must linger in England to honor all drafts on the sum. Franklin advised the Assembly to put the money in stocks, "which will certainly at a peace produce a profit of near 20 per cent besides intermediate interest." The Assembly accepted the suggestion, but the governor vetoed it. The Assembly by Franklin's lights could do with the money as it wished. He ignored the governor's veto and in December 1760 bought fifteen thousand pounds' worth of stock. Early in 1761 the Assembly told Franklin not to make more investments. He ignored that order, too, assuming that as the man on the scene he knew better than the legislature the right course to follow. By mid-summer he had parlayed the parliamentary grant into a sum with a face value of thirty thousand pounds. He planned to cash the nest egg in when peace with France was declared.

Except for handling the Assembly's investment, Franklin spent little time on public matters in 1761. He wrote only one essay for the press, a deft piece that urged England not to hurry into a peace with Spain until certain of gaining something worthwhile from the war. He resumed a neglected correspondence on scientific matters. He entertained visitors with electrical experiments, dined out regularly with friends, and generally enjoyed himself.

Thomas Penn watched from a distance and remarked with disdain that Franklin was spending his time "in philosophical, and especially in electrical matters, . . . and musical performances on glasses." The electrical shows that had astonished Philadelphia were repeated for English friends on a "machine" brought from home. It threw sparks for the new audience "judged . . . to be nine inches," Franklin said. "So powerful a machine had then never been seen in England before, as they were pleased to tell me." The musical shows were performed on an instrument he invented and called the armonica, "in honor of your musical language," he told an Italian friend. Anyone could produce musical tones by rubbing the lips of wine glasses with a moist finger. Franklin's instrument brought order and precision to the haphazard art. He had glass spheres blown that varied in size from nine to three inches in diameter. The spheres were pierced at either end and by varying the size of the holes could be tuned exactly. After being tuned, they were mounted on a spindle and installed in a portable case. The glasses were rotated by pumping a treadle attached to the spindle. "The instrument is played upon by sitting before the middle of the set of glasses as before the keys of a harpsichord, turning them with the foot, and wetting them now and then with a sponge and clean water," he said. "The advantages of this instrument are that its tones are incomparably sweet beyond those of any other."

Between armonica concerts and electrical shows, the days passed so agreeably that Franklin forgot about home. Letters to his wife shrank to notes, then ceased altogether during the first half of 1761. "As to Benjamin Franklin, I cannot on all the inquiry I could make in London find out where nor how he spends his time, excepting it be in travel about and seeing the curiosities of the country," an acquaintance from Philadelphia remarked. "I find Dr. Fothergill, John Hunt, and most other Friends here in London have no extraordinary opinion of him nor any good he has done or intends to do our country, and greatly admire at his continuance here. I know he is looked upon on our side of the water as a second Sir William Pitt; perhaps their eyes may be opened in time and they may see clearer."

Late in the summer the peace negotiations with Spain collapsed. William Pitt resigned as prime minister, and in his place came Lord Bute. British politicians despised Bute as an interloper from Scotland and deplored his influence over the new young king. With Bute's rise to power the stock market plummeted. Franklin apparently viewed the decline as temporary. He did not cancel a trip to the Continent in August with his son and Richard Jackson. He would have set out less lightheartedly if he had known that the Assembly was about to draw on him for twenty-five thousand pounds, a sum the now shrunken parliamentary grant did not come close to equaling.

2

Franklin and Jackson wanted to be back in London for the coronation of George III. That left only a month to tour and Franklin on this, his first visit to the Continent, intended to make the most of it. The party visited all the principal cities of Holland and Belgium, pausing in none longer than three or four days. Franklin's reputation had gone before him, and the eminent entertained the tourists wherever they went. Prince Charles of Lorraine welcomed them in Brussels and showed his apparatus for carrying out experiments devised by Franklin. At Leyden they visited Professor Musschenbroek, inventor of the Leyden jar. "At The Hague we received great civilities from Sir Joseph Yorke, our ambassador there, with whom we dined in company with most of the foreign ministers," William reported home. "We dined also at Count Bentinck's, who is at the head of the nobility in Holland."

William alone left an account of the trip. The magnificent Catholic cathedrals "surpassed anything I had ever seen before or conceived." The antiseptic cleanliness of Holland pleased him, the only "disagreeable circumstance" being the people's fondness for smoking. "I don't recollect that I saw more than one Dutchman without a pipe in his mouth, and that was a fellow who had hung in chains so long that his head had dropped off. Their very children are taught smoking from the moment they leave sucking, and the method they take to teach them is, to give them when they are cutting their teeth, an old tobacco pipe which is smoked black and smooth to rub their gums with instead of coral."

The return across the Channel was a landlubber's nightmare. William vomited up "every bit of gaul I had in my body," though he wished to save "a little for my enemies." He said nothing on how his father and Jackson fared during the trip. They reached London in time for the coronation. Jackson and Franklin watched from seats they had purchased along the procession route weeks earlier. William, with connections better than his father's, wangled a ticket that allowed him to walk in the procession and into Westminster Abbey, where the crowning took place.

3

Two unpleasant setbacks dimmed the pleasure of the coronation for Franklin. The first concerned his post as deputy postmaster general of America. News of the death of William Hunter, with whom he had shared the office for eight years, reached London early in October, accompanied by a request from Francis Fauquier, governor of Virginia, that John Foxcroft of that colony be appointed to fill the vacancy. Franklin immediately sent a strong letter to the head of the London office. He insisted there was no vacancy to fill. "The commission I have had the honor so recently to receive," he wrote, "grants the whole office, powers and salary to *the survivor* of the two persons therein appointed; and therefore, notwithstanding the decease of Mr. Hunter, there is properly no vacancy; unless you should think fit to make one by revoking that commission, which when my long and faithful service of twenty-four years in the post office is considered, I hope will not be done."

Franklin dropped all pretense of modesty in order to persuade his superior that the three hundred pounds that once went to Hunter should now come to him. "During the greatest part of that time, I had the burthen of conducting the whole American office under others, with a very slender salary; and it has been allowed, that the bringing the office to what it is, from its former low insignificant state, was greatly owing to my care and management. And now that in the course of things some additional advantage seems to be thrown in my way, I cannot but hope it will not be taken from me in favor of a stranger to the office; especially as Governor Fauquier has in his disposition many places of profit in his government as they fall, and therefore cannot long want an opportunity of gratifying the services of his secretary." The reasonable argument could not be refuted, but it could be ignored. The wishes of a respected royal governor weighed more to the bureaucratic mind than those of Franklin. John Foxcroft got the post.

The second unsettling event came in November, when Franklin began receiving bills from the Pennsylvania Loan Office. These could be paid only by unloading the now depreciated stock he had invested in. During the month he had to sell his original investment of £15,000 at a loss of £1,363 2s 6d. Worse lay ahead. On 4 January 1762 Britain declared war on Spain and the stock market collapsed. Every ship from Philadelphia that month brought further bills for Franklin to pay. When he had sold all the stock, his loss stood just short of four thousand pounds. He turned to his bankers, Henton Brown and Sons, and asked for a loan to cover the bills coming in. They refused. He turned next to two mercantile firms, Sargent and Aufrere and Barclay and Sons, which had been chosen to handle the next parliamentary grant, coming in February, and asked them to advance a loan that would be repaid out of that grant. Thomas Penn stepped in at this point, saying such an arrangement would be illegal without the approval of both the Pennsylvania Assembly and Governor Hamilton. Both firms rejected Franklin's request on January 13. Just when Penn could almost taste the pleasure of revenge, John Sargent pulled Franklin from the fire. Sargent had been friendly with Franklin since his arrival in England five years before. On January 15 his firm reversed itself and told Franklin it would cover all unpaid bills "without accepting any security other than that which we know we have in your character."

It may have been coincidental, but in the midst of what could have proved to be the greatest financial disaster of his life and possibly, if the accusation of misusing public funds were leveled at him, the greatest humiliation, Franklin told friends he was "preparing to return and propose taking passage in the first man-of-war that goes to any part of North America in the ensuing spring or summer."

4

Trouble in an old form came in March when William Smith arrived in London on a fund-raising mission. The Academy founded by Franklin had been transformed into the College of Philadelphia, with Smith as its provost. The trustees had sent him to England to raise an endowment for the school. They had told him to see Franklin for advice before approaching anyone for gifts. The two men, who had not spoken for five years, met on March 22. Franklin, in an affable mood, promised to draw up a list of possible donors but would do no more. He wanted to use his remaining time in England visiting among old friends.

A month later Franklin traveled to Oxford to receive an honorary doctorate of civil law. While there he learned that three years earlier when Oxford had made Smith a doctor of divinity—it always pleased Smith his doctorate preceded Franklin's—he had remarked in a letter to an official of the university that it would debase the institution's reputation to award a degree to Franklin. The revelation put Franklin in a "great dudgeon." Back in London he arranged a meeting with Smith, asking Strahan to be present as a witness. After he read the offending letter aloud, Smith admitted it "contained many particulars in which he had been misled by wrong information, and that the whole was written with too much rancor and asperity." He promised to retract "what was false in it," not now, but "in a day or two." The day or two passed with no retraction. Franklin then set out to ruin Smith's fund-raising mission. Smith told how he went about it. "An eminent Dissenter called on me," he said in a letter to Richard Peters, without revealing what had provoked Franklin, "and let me know that Dr. Franklin took uncommon pains to misrepresent our Academy, before he went away, *to sundry of their people*, saying that it was a narrow, bigoted institution put into the hands of the Proprietary party as an engine of government; that the Dissenters had no influence in it (though, God knows, all the professors but myself are of that persuasion), with many things grievously reflecting upon the principal person concerned in it; that the country and province would readily support it if it were not for these things; that we have no occasion to beg, and that my zeal proceeds from a fear of its sinking and my losing my livelihood."

After learning of Franklin's campaign to defame him and the Academy, Smith, equally petty, spread the word about London that Franklin's reputation at home had sunk to zero, that all his friends had turned on him, that the Assembly would censure him for the way he had conducted his mission in England. Only later did Franklin reveal how much this gossip disturbed him. It made him all the more eager to return home. But one large piece of unfinished business remained before he could leave England. When completed, it would serve as a wonderful revenge on both Thomas Penn and William Smith and make the five years in England a great success, if not for Pennsylvania, at least for himself.

5

Sometime in 1760 Franklin toyed with a new way to deprive Thomas
Penn of his colony. After William Penn's death, ownership passed to his
second wife and the sons of that union. Some people, Franklin among
them, thought the arrangement illegal, that the colony really belonged to
Springett Penn, grandson of the founder by his first wife. If it could be
proved that Springett Penn, in 1760 an emaciated young man of twenty-
one suffering from consumption, had been wrongfully deprived of his
inheritance; if he could be induced to sue for recovery of his property;
if, once recovered, he would sell the colony for twelve thousand pounds,
an acceptable price to William Penn years earlier when Pennsylvania was
still a fragile enterprise—all these ifs fulfilled would clear the way for the
crown to take over the province. Franklin considered this farfetched plan
to the point of consulting lawyers and cultivating Springett Penn, but he
never pursued it wholeheartedly. It was one of several options investi-
gated in a desperate effort to deprive Thomas Penn of his colony. By 1762
Franklin had resigned himself to the tedious strategy of stirring up sympathy for Pennsylvania among members of Parliament. His connections
with those who set policy and ran the government were virtually nonexistent until sometime after 1760 when he established a friendship with
Lord Bute.

Bute was a charming, handsome Scotsman who upon the accession of
George III became one of the most powerful men of the realm and one
of the most hated. Through a close friendship with George's mother—
rumored to be adulterous but probably was not—he became the young
man's tutor. When George came to the throne, Bute had become master
of his "mind and heart—guide, philosopher, friend, paragon, seat of all
wisdom and virtue." Politicians shuddered at his power over the young
king. That and his being an outlander from Scotland caused him to be
despised.

"The precise nature of Franklin's relationship with Bute is one of the
major mysteries of his career," it has been remarked. It is not clear when
or how the two met. Collinson, whose interest in botany had brought a
friendship with Bute, could have introduced them. Dr. Pringle, Bute's
personal physician, may have brought them together. It is clear that the
friendship was close with both Bute and his wife. (Franklin promised her
ladyship to search out a variety of American seashells when he returned
home; he kept the promise, only to hear when she thanked him "that your

seas afforded none of any value.") In later years when Englishmen every-where reviled Bute Franklin stood by him.

Bute became the king's chief minister in May 1762. Earlier in the year it had been determined to recall the current governor of New Jersey. The post had been offered to Thomas Pownall, Franklin's friend since the Albany Congress. Pownall turned it down. Quite likely he may have mentioned to Franklin that the post lay vacant. Why not put William Franklin's name in for the job? New Jersey was one of the few colonies where it was not unusual to choose an American for governor. Not one of the diamonds, perhaps, in the British tiara of colonies, but an excellent training ground for a young man of parts. Young Franklin was bright, charming, and able, and though at thirty-two the few jobs he had held came from his father's beneficence no one among the British upper class considered this a drawback. And now as never before he needed a steady income. He had fallen in love with a handsome young lady named Eliza-beth Downes and wanted to marry her. (He had also fathered an illegiti-mate son of whom his father was unaware; William Strahan, whom William confided in, arranged for the child to be reared in a foster home.)

Pushing through the appointment of a royal governor called for tact, patience, and immense skill. A host of government bureaus had to be consulted. Clerks had to be bribed to speed documents across their desks. New instructions had to be collected from the Treasury department, the Admiralty, the Board of Trade, and other concerned bureaus. In a town that thrived on political gossip, Franklin campaigned for his son's ap-pointment so quietly that later one of the Penns complained that "the whole of this business has been transacted in so private a manner, that not a tittle of it escaped until it was seen in the public papers; so that there was no opportunity of counteracting, or, indeed, doing one single thing that might put a stop to this shameful affair." By the end of July 1762 Franklin had been assured the post would go to his son. Now at last he could return home knowing he had enhanced his own prestige—winning a royal governorship for one's illegitimate son was no small feat—and at the same time had humiliated Thomas Penn, who would have fought the appointment with all his power if he had known what was going on.

6

What had Franklin accomplished during his stay in England? "I can-not find that his five years' negotiation at a vast expense to the province, hath answered any other purpose with respect to the public than to get every point that was in controversy determined against them," Governor Hamilton wrote when he heard Franklin was returning but before he knew of William's appointment as governor of New Jersey. "Yet what is this to Mr. Franklin? Hath it not afforded him a life of pleasure, and an opportunity of displaying his talents among the virtuosi of various kingdoms and nations? And lastly hath it not procured for himself the degree of Doctor of Laws, and for the modest and beautiful, his son, that of master of arts, from one of our most famous universities? Let me tell you, those are no small acquisitions to the public, and therefore well worth paying for."

Friends in Britain had more charitable judgments on his stay among them. William Strahan to the end tried to hold him in London. "Dear Straney," Franklin wrote from Portsmouth in late July, while waiting for his ship to sail, "I value myself much on being able to resolve on doing the right thing, in opposition to your almost irresistible eloquence, secretly supported and backed by my own treacherous inclinations." The departure left "Straney" inconsolable. "I know not where to find his equal, nor can the chasm his departure leaves in my social enjoyments and happiness ever be filled up. There is something in his leaving us even more cruel than a separation by death; it is like an *untimely death*, where we part with a friend to meet no more, *with a whole heart*, as we say in Scotland."

David Hume, whom Franklin had met through Strahan, sent a graceful note after learning his friend was heading home. "I am very sorry that you intend to leave our hemisphere," he wrote. "America has sent us many good things, gold, silver, sugar, tobacco, indigo, etc. But you are the first philosopher, and indeed the first man of letters for whom we are beholden to her. It is our own fault that we have not kept him. Whence it appears that we do not agree with Solomon, that wisdom is above gold; for we take care never to send back an ounce of the latter, which we once lay our fingers upon."

One of the last of Franklin's notes before the ship sailed went to Lord Kames. "I am going from the old world to the new; and I fancy I feel like those who are leaving this world for the next: grief at the parting; fear of the passage; hope of the future."

To an English friend he hinted how much he would miss the friends he had made during the past five years. "Of all the enviable things England has, I envy it most its people," he said. "Why should that petty island, which compared to America is but like a stepping-stone in a brook, scarce enough of it above water to keep one's shoes dry; why, I say, should that little island enjoy in almost every neighborhood, more sensible, virtuous, and elegant minds than we can collect in ranging one hundred leagues of our vast forests?"

Why, then, did Franklin depart? To rebuild the reputation that Smith gossiped was in disrepair? Perhaps, but hardly a matter of importance if he had stayed in England. To be reunited with his wife and friends in Philadelphia? No hint that this entered the decision appears in his writings. To put his affairs in order so that he could return to live out his life among his British friends? Most likely. Before he left Franklin confided to at least one friend, Dr. Pringle, that he was "determined . . . to return to England."

Franklin sailed on August 24. His son remained behind in London, waiting to receive his royal commission as governor and then to marry Miss Downes. On the day Franklin's ship left Portsmouth, Strahan's *London Chronicle* announced the appointment of William Franklin as governor of New Jersey. An appalled William Smith carried the news at once to Thomas Penn. Together they concocted a plan to get the appointment rescinded. Penn would urge a friend in the ministry, probably Lord Halifax, and two officers he knew in the Treasury department who were close to Lord Bute to put pressure on the prime minister. They must tell Bute that William Franklin was *illegitimate*, a fact of common knowledge in Philadelphia but apparently unknown in London. Two of William Allen's sons, then in London studying law, would verify this information.

The reactions of Lord Bute and his advisers are not on record—Bute, descended from a bastard branch of Scotland's royal family, probably smiled at the news—but on September 1 the Privy Council approved William Franklin's appointment. On September 4 he married Elizabeth Downes while William Smith spread the word about London that William Franklin was a bastard.

CHAPTER

18

"I COULD NOT WISH A MORE
HEARTY WELCOME"

FRANKLIN REACHED PHILADELPHIA on 1 November 1762. He arrived with "a little touch of the gout," but this hardly marred the homecoming. In a rare display of openness he revealed how uneasy he had been about his reception in letter after letter to friends back in England. "I . . . had the pleasure to find all false that Dr. Smith had reported about the diminution of my friends," he wrote Jackson. "My house has been filled with a succession of them from morning to night almost ever since I landed to congratulate me on my return; and I never experienced greater cordiality among them." To Strahan he boasted that "my fellow citizens while I was on the sea, had, at the annual election, chosen me unanimously, as they had done every year while I was in England, to be their representative in Assembly; and would, they say, if I had not disappointed them by coming privately to town before they heard of my landing, have met me with five hundred horse. Excuse my vanity in writing this to you, who know what has provoked me to it." Five days later he told Collinson that he found "my friends as cordial and more numerous than ever," and again to Strahan that "I could not wish for a more hearty welcome." Friends were punctilious to address him as "Dr. Franklin." The new title came more slowly from the lips of others.

Deborah had moved during his absence—across Market Street from one rented house to another, newly built, only a short distance from the building where she had been reared and where Franklin had boarded when he came to Philadelphia years ago. The high rent—eighty pounds a year—amazed him, but otherwise he had no comment. He spent the first week home unpacking. From one crate came the harpsichord long promised to Sally. The armonica, he found with relief, had crossed the ocean intact, not a glass cracked, and a few evenings after returning he gave a concert on it. He hung Lord Bute's picture in the sitting room and told visitors how well he knew that great man. A hint of how well came with the next ship from London, which brought word that William had been appointed governor of New Jersey. The news appalled Governor Hamilton. It "occasioned a universal astonishment," he said, for young Franklin "is perhaps a man of as bad a heart as I ever was acquainted with. He would certainly make wild work without his father's experience and good understanding to check and moderate his passion."

The Assembly convened on 10 January 1763. Franklin served on eleven committees during the nine-week session. In February he submitted his expense account for the nearly six years in England. The care he took to draft the account indicated the trepidation felt about its reception. The House accepted it without a quibble, agreeing to pay him five hundred pounds for each of his years abroad. This, added to the four thousand pounds Franklin had lost on his investment of the parliamentary grant, unmentioned in the journal, meant that his mission had cost the substantial sum of seven thousand pounds sterling, or over ten thousand pounds when translated into Pennsylvania currency. Franklin spoke of the generous treatment in letters to Strahan and Jackson. "This I mention to you," he said, "because I hear that Mr. T. Penn has insinuated to Mr. Collinson that I had embezzled the public money, and made use of it in my private affairs in England; and possibly the same may have been intimated to you and others of my friends."

Franklin reveled in the hearty welcome received, but otherwise he did not seem pleased to be back in Philadelphia. He complained that the cost of living had "greatly advanced in my absence; it is more than double in most articles; and in some 'tis treble." The British army had pumped some eight hundred thousand pounds into the colony's economy, with the result that "our tradesmen are grown as idle, and as extravagant in their demands when you would prevail on them to work, as so many Spaniards." He missed the bustle of a great city. Here, he said, "the streets seem thinner of people, owing perhaps to my being so long accustomed to the bustling crowded streets of London." Local politics dealt with petty matters; he urged Strahan to keep him posted on the political happenings in London, for "you have an opportunity of hearing them all, and no one that is not quite in the secret of affairs can judge better of them." Imperial affairs, especially the progress of the war, occupied his attention. He rejoiced to hear of the capture of Havana and predicted it would "contribute a due share of weight in procuring us reasonable terms of peace; if John Bull does not get drunk with victory, double his fists, and bid all the world kiss his a——e." He rejoiced again in late January when he learned that a preliminary peace with France gave Canada to England. "I congratulate you on the glorious peace we have made," he told a friend, "the most advantageous to Great Britain, in my opinion, of any our history has recorded."

To Strahan he confessed what he would have told no one in Philadelphia. "God bless you and let me find you well and happy when I come again to England; happy England!" he wrote five weeks after his return. "In two years at farthest I hope to settle all my affairs in such a manner as that I *may* then con eniently remove to England, provided we can persuade the good woman to cross the seas. That will be the great difficulty; but you can help me a little in removing it."

2

William Franklin and his new wife arrived in Philadelphia on February 19. The winter crossing had been dreadful. William would not have wished even the "devil, nay Parson S[mith] to experience a winter passage like ours." During one storm "a great sea broke thro' our cabin windows and did considerable damage to our stores and baggage." A river clogged with ice obliged the couple "to land 150 miles from Philadelphia and travel about 100 in an open one-horse chair, as no other carriage was to be had, the weather extremely severe." Word raced ahead that the couple had arrived, and when they reached Chester, a village a few miles south of Philadelphia, "a considerable number of gentlemen, with my father and sister, came out to meet us and escort us into the city."

Young Franklin and his wife rested four days in Philadelphia, then on February 23 father and son, leaving their wives behind, set out for New Jersey. Franklin went along as a proud father eager to see his son inducted into office. Also he hoped his presence would allay any grumbling about William's appointment by such as Robert Hunter Morris, still chief justice of the colony. Franklin had attacked Morris, a native of New Jersey, as an interloper in Pennsylvania politics; Morris with reason could now direct the shaft at William. Franklin may have been uneasy, too, that there might be "some remonstrance upon this indignity" of having an illegitimate son handed to them as governor, as one man predicted there would be. "If any *gentleman* had been appointed it would have been a different case."

Father and son headed for Perth Amboy. Though only a village of two hundred houses on Raritan Bay, it served as the capital for East Jersey, with Burlington, twenty miles from Philadelphia, the capital for West Jersey. This tradition of two capitals dated from the time when the colony had been divided between its two proprietors. The crown allowed the tradition to continue when it took over the province. The legislature held alternate sessions in each town, but the governor could choose which he preferred for his official residence.

The Franklins spent the first night at Trenton. The next morning they found the Delaware River "hard and firm, and we got well over." On the opposite side Sir John St. Clair, the "Hussar" once with Braddock's army who had elected to stay in America, "came to us and very obliging offered his chariot and four for the rest of the journey." After resting overnight at New Brunswick, they approached Perth Amboy in a snowstorm, but "notwithstanding the great inclemency of the weather," a troop of horse and a number of gentlemen in sleighs rode out to escort them into town. There, "amidst a numerous concourse of people," William Franklin took the oath of office as the twelfth governor of New Jersey, "and the whole was conducted with as much decency and good decorum as the severe season would possibly admit of."

The Franklins lingered a week at Perth Amboy, where the father "had the pleasure of seeing [William] received everywhere with the utmost respect and even affection of all ranks of people," then moved on to Burlington to repeat the induction ceremony. Again "the greatest demonstrations of joy" greeted them. On March 5 father and son left for Philadelphia "attended by the principal gentlemen of Burlington." Though William had refused at each capital to reveal where he would make his official residence no one doubted he would choose Burlington, so close to home and father. He did so two months later.

It took the people of New Jersey only a short while to accept the opinion Strahan had rendered earlier on William—that he had "a solidity of judgment not very often to be met with in one of his years." The legislature raised his salary two hundred pounds in an early session. He appeared to be without flaws—tall, handsome, quick-witted, intelligent, and married to a lovely, poised woman. Even Robert Hunter got along well with him.

But the son had lived too long in his father's shadow to be immediately his own man. When Robert Hunter Morris died in 1764 William filled the vacancy without consulting the home government, as required. Franklin sought to smooth away the error. "I could wish to hear that the appointment is confirmed at home," he wrote Jackson. "A word from you, properly placed, may do the business." A word from Jackson did not do the business. The Board of Trade rescinded the appointment and ordered Governor Franklin to replace his man with one of its own choosing. The young governor came from under the shadow only after his father had returned to England. Later, when Franklin admonished him for some action from across the ocean, William dared to snap back: "It is impossible for you at so great a distance to be acquainted with every circumstance necessary to form a right judgment of the expediency or inexpediency of particular transactions." William still addressed his letters to "Honored Father," as Franklin always had to his father, but the docile son had vanished forever.

3

No one ever called Franklin mercurial or flighty, yet at times only such words seem fitting to explain his actions. He arrived home determined, so it appeared, to return to London as quickly as possible. Yet a month after the trip to New Jersey William predicted that "my father will never be induced to see England again," for he is "now building a house to live in himself." William thought he had decided to stay because "my mother is so entirely averse to going to sea," but that seems unlikely. What, then, prompted the decision? It has been suggested that the handsome settlement from the Assembly for his years in England "crystallized in Franklin's mind a plan perhaps long thought of, but which never before had seemed to lie within the realm of possibility." Deborah's mother had died the previous year. Franklin now owned her two houses that fronted on Market Street and the long lots that stretched behind them. He already owned several adjacent lots. Using the Read houses to block out the noise of Market Street, he conceived in his mind a building surrounded by gardens and trees, large and airy as a country home but still at the center of the city's life, in walking distance of the State House, the London Coffee House, the post office, the printing shop.

Early in April Franklin gave ninety-six pounds to Robert Smith, the carpenter-architect who had designed Nassau Hall in Princeton, "toward my house," and seven months later another eighty pounds. He hired his friend Samuel Rhoads to supervise the construction and made six hundred pounds available "as occasion requires to carry on my building." The house became the grand creation of his life. Every detail inside and out concerned him, and when in London in 1765 it was hard to tell from his letters which occupied him more, the house or the Stamp Act crisis. He deluged his wife with instructions:

The blue mohair stuff is for the curtains of the blue chamber. The fashion is to make one curtain only for each window. Hooks are sent to fix the rails by at top, so that they may be taken down on occasion.

I almost wish I had left directions not to paint the house till my return.

I could have wished to have been present at the finishing of the kitchen, as it is a mere machine, and being new to you, I think you will scarce know how to work it. The several contrivances to carry off steam and smell and smoke not being fully explained to you. The oven I suppose was put up by the written directions in my former letter. You mention nothing of the furnace. If that iron one is not set, let it alone till my return, when I shall bring a more convenient copper one.

Let me have the breadth of the pier, that I may get a handsome glass for the parlor.

I think you cannot have cellar enough. Are the vaults made?

As to oiling the floors, it may be omitted till I return, which will not be till next spring. I need not tell you to take great care of your fires.

Two years later he still fussed:

I suppose the blue room is too blue, the wood being of the same color with the paper, and so looks too dark. I would have you finish it as soon as you can, thus: paint the wainscot a dead white; paper the walls blue, and tack the gilt border round just above the surbase and under the cornish. If the paper is not equal colored when pasted on, let it be brushed over again with the same color; and let the papier mache musical figures be tacked to the middle the ceiling; when this is done, I think it will look very well.

Deborah nearly broke his heart with her report of the first dinner party in the new house. "You tell me only of a fault they found with the house, that it was too little; and not a word of anything they liked in it. Nor how the kitchen chimneys perform; so I suppose you spare me some mortification, which is kind."

4

At the same time Franklin was building his house he pursued another dream. During the trip through New Jersey he had talked in Princeton to Samuel Finley, president of the College of New Jersey. Finley wanted to found a colony west of the Allegheny Mountains. He had also spoken with members of the Coxe family, who asked him to recommend someone in England to track down a grant of western lands acquired by their ancestor Daniel Coxe many years ago.

Franklin had convinced himself by the time he returned from New Jersey that America would soon be swarming west. He told Jackson: "There are already several schemes on foot among the people in different parts of this and the neighboring provinces for removal westward, and great numbers show a strong disposition to go and settle on the Ohio or Mississippi, but they want heads to form regular plans of proceeding. I am convinced that a new colony that should be placed within Coxe's bounds . . . would have a more rapid progress in population than any heretofore planned."

Franklin had dreamed of a western colony for nearly a decade. In England he and Jackson had often talked about "the proper constitution of government to be obtained, and the modes of settling" the wilderness. He, John Sargent, and others had associated in a scheme to get a grant of land from the crown. They had talked dreamingly of the west mainly late at night in front of a warm fire or when the port was being passed. Now that the peace treaty with France had been signed, they could act. "Since all the country is now ceded to us on this side the Mississippi, is not this a good time to think of new colonies on that river, to secure our territory and extend our commerce," Franklin asked Jackson in a long letter written soon after returning from New Jersey; "and to separate the Indians on this side from those on the other, by intervening settlements of English, and by that means keep them more easily in order? What think you now of asking for a slice of territory . . . ?" And so on for several pages.

All this went to Jackson. To Strahan he said nothing about his dream of western settlement. He was busy putting his affairs in order, he told Strahan, and "I trust I shall see you before you look much older." In the mail that brought this letter to Strahan came the one from William telling of his father "building a house to live in himself." Strahan must have wondered why a man building a house for himself would leave it to retire in England.

5

The post office called for Franklin's attention in the spring of 1763. There were now forty-eight offices strung out from Falmouth (Portland),

Maine, to Norfolk, Virginia, and Franklin had visited none of them for six years. The home office had reprimanded him and his new colleague, John Foxcroft, for their lax control of the American operation. It reminded them their job was "rendering correspondence in the vast empire of North America of the greatest use to his Majesty's subjects, and at the same time to improve the revenue of it." To that end, every postmaster must submit full accounts regularly as those in England did. Once again Franklin patiently explained that America was not England, that what worked in the mother country did not necessarily fit conditions here.

"The advantage of the office to a postmaster in these countries has been in many places so inconsiderable that the office is not sought after as in England," he told his superior in London. Here "we were glad to find an honest careful man who would at our request undertake it, to oblige us and his neighbors. Such persons would remit us money from time to time as it arose in their hands, and when it suited with their leisure draw out and send us their accounts, but if rigidly required to do it at certain periods, would decline the service and desire us to provide some other person to undertake it. We were therefore under some necessity of tolerating these omissions, and content ourselves with obtaining a settlement when we could." For those offices that are profitable enough to "become valuable," he added, "we can insist more absolutely on a regularity in the execution of the office; and shall do it; but as in this growing country there is a continued necessity of erecting new offices in places, and we do not see how it can be avoided."

Franklin left for Virginia in mid-April. In Williamsburg, after he had retrieved four hundred pounds from William Hunter's estate due to the home office, one of the relatives approached him with a personal problem: Hunter had left behind an illegitimate son. Would Franklin oversee his education in Philadelphia? Franklin replied in a way that explained why so many men were bound to him in deep affection. "I am sensible that the care of the education of young persons is attended with trouble, and like other old men I begin in most things to consult my ease," he said. "But I shall with pleasure undertake the charge you propose to me, if it be, as I suppose it is, agreeable to his other friends, for I loved his father truly, and think it a duty to perform the request of a friend deceased, who living would I am sure have thought little of any trouble in obliging me."

Franklin and John Foxcroft toured the post offices throughout Virginia and then headed northward. They were back in Philadelphia preparing to set out for a tour of the northern offices early in June. Just before they left Franklin learned that "the Indians on the Ohio have broke out again, scalped a number of people, and seized some horse loads of goods." Franklin supposed the uprising was "occasioned by the mere

relish they acquired in the last war for plunder." He was concerned with
the effect it would have on his plans for western settlement. The Indians
must be "prudently prepared for such things, or they cannot succeed,"
he wrote Jackson. A few days later in New York City he found all talk
centered on the uprising. By then it was known that every western fort
but the ones at Detroit and Pittsburgh had fallen to the Indians. General
Amherst, with whom Franklin dined one afternoon, thought that French
troops in the west unaware that peace had been declared had incited the
Indians. "But others here say," Franklin remarked, "the Indians are
disgusted that so little notice has lately been taken of them, and are
particularly offended that rum is prohibited, and powder dealt among
them so sparingly. They have received no presents. And the plan of
preventing war among them, and bringing them to live by agriculture,
they resent as an attempt to make women of them, as they phrase it; it
being the business of women only to cultivate the ground; their men are
all warriors." Whatever the cause, he thought that "we stooped too much
in begging the last peace of them; which has made them vain and insolent;
and that we should never mention peace to them again, till we have given
them some severe blows, and made them feel some ill consequence of
breaking with us."

Franklin kept a close watch on the news from the West the rest of the
summer and until he returned to Philadelphia in November. But he did
not become so preoccupied as to forget to enjoy himself or tend to business. He visited friends and relatives in and around New York constantly
during the three weeks spent there. Between visits he and Foxcroft
worked out plans for a packet service between the West Indies and New
York and a postal service to Quebec. At the end of June he had his
daughter Sally brought to the city from Perth Amboy, where she had
been visiting her brother the governor. She was now nearly twenty years
old and her father had determined, despite Deborah's reluctance to let
her go, to show her off to relatives in New England. In Boston Franklin
would lodge with his sister Jane Mecom, but Sally would stay with his
niece and her husband, Jonathan Williams, because they had "a harpsichord, and I would not have her lose her practice; and then I shall be more
with my dear sister."

Franklin, Sally, and Foxcroft set out by water early in July for Newport. They spent three days there, then headed for Boston overland. They
had planned to stop overnight with Catharine Ray, the lively young lady
Franklin had flirted with ten years earlier and who was now married to
William Greene, but on the road Franklin injured his shoulder and the
short stay extended into several days. After resuming the trip, he assured
the Greenes in a thank-you note that "the soreness in my breast seems

to diminish hourly. Rest and temperance I ascribe it to chiefly, tho' the bleeding, etc. had doubtless some share in the effect."

The party reached Boston on July 20 and settled in for what turned out to be a two-and-a-half-month stay. The comforts of home his solicitous sister could not provide Franklin had brought with him. He had, for instance, become accustomed to the bright, clear light of wax candles— "I am now so used to it, I cannot well do without it"—and Deborah, who did not need to be told how to please her "pappy," had slipped a packet of them in his trunk.

Boston served as a headquarters from which Franklin and Foxcroft fanned out on short trips to inspect post offices. On a visit to Portsmouth, New Hampshire, Franklin again injured himself, this time more seriously. "I am almost ashamed to tell you that I have had another fall, and put my shoulder out," he wrote Catharine Greene. "It is well reduced again, but is still affected with constant tho' not very acute pain. I am not yet able to travel rough roads, and must lie by a while, as I can neither hold reins, nor whip with my right hand till it grows stronger." Meanwhile he kept posted on the Indian uprising, which he now thought, as General Amherst had earlier, had been caused by the French "before they had heard of the peace between the two nations; and will probably cease when we are in possession of what is there ceded to us." Strahan filled him in on the latest news in British politics and only touched lightly on his loneliness: "Not an hour have I spent on cribbage since you left us, nor shall it cost me one till your return, which I hope you still *seriously* think of." Franklin did not disillusion his friend. "No friend can wish me more in England than I do myself," he said. "But before I go, everything I am concerned in must be so settled here as to make another return to America unnecessary."

The second week in October Franklin at last felt well enough to start for home. The day before he left he took time to do one more favor for a friend. "Herewith you have the recipe you desired," he wrote James Bowdoin:

To make milk punch

Take 6 quarts of brandy, and the rinds of 44 lemons pared very thin; steep the rinds in the brandy 24 hours; then strain it off. Put to it 4 quarts of water, 4 large nutmegs grated, 2 quarts of lemon juice, 2 pound of double refined sugar. When the sugar is dissolved, boil 3 quarts of milk and put to the rest hot as you take it off the fire, and stir it about. Let it stand two hours; then run it thro' a jelly-bag till it is clear; then bottle it off.

On the way home Franklin spent two days with Joshua Babcock, who lived in Westerly, Rhode Island. "I perceive the artifice of your eloquence, which in some degree saves me from being carried away by its force," Franklin had written from Boston. "You promise me the communication of some new philosophical discovery. Then you pique my pride by challenging me at drafts, and insinuate that I have not the courage to meet you. Then you work upon my fears, by your prophecies and auguries, threatening me with mischief and misfortune if I travel any other road. All this is very good in its place; but you omit an argument that weighs much more with me, the happiness I should enjoy in your conversation and in some true, ancient, cordial hospitality, with which you and good Mrs. Babcock always entertain your friends."

From Rhode Island Franklin jogged at a leisurely pace through Connecticut, where over the years he had accumulated many friends, but also where the "excessively strict observation of Sunday" both irritated and amused him. He complained to a friend there "that a man could hardly travel on that day among you upon his lawful occasions, without hazard of punishment." In Holland, where the people were as fat and prosperous as those of Connecticut, Sundays were given over to "plenty of singing, fiddling, and dancing," he said, "which would almost make one suspect that the Deity is not so angry at that offense as a New England justice."

In New Haven Franklin and Foxcroft found that the postmaster had bilked their department out of more than three hundred pounds. The rest of the trip passed uneventfully. William traveled twenty miles out of Burlington to escort them to his home, and after a night with him, Franklin, Sally, and Foxcroft arrived back in Philadelphia on Saturday evening, November 5. Except for a brief rest after the trip to Virginia, Franklin had been on the road nearly seven months. "That I have not the propensity to sitting still that you apprehend," he had told Strahan before leaving Boston, "let my present journey witness for me, in which I have already traveled eleven hundred and forty miles on this continent since April and shall make six hundred and forty miles more before I see home."

Franklin found a new governor on his return home. Young John Penn, son of Richard, nephew of Thomas, had just arrived from London. He also found that the Indian uprising had enmeshed Pennsylvania in a multitude of troubles.

CHAPTER

19

"RUNNING FAST INTO ANARCHY AND CONFUSION"

RUMORS CIRCULATED THROUGH THE CITY shortly after Franklin's return that the backcountry was bitter "because the authorities are taking no adequate measures for defense" against the Indians. If Philadelphia did not soon act, the people there might "come to the city in droves and destroy everything in *revenge.*" If the gossip made Franklin uneasy, no sign appeared in his correspondence. He told sister Mecom, with good-humored sarcasm, his pleasure being home, for here "I am allowed to know when I have eat enough and drank enough, am warm enough, and sit in a place that I like, etc., and nobody pretends to know what I feel better than I do myself." The pain from his fall had waned, but "still some weakness in my shoulder" remained, enough to make him indecisive about future plans. Second thoughts about creating a colony in the West occurred to him. There, he said, "I could have been of use in procuring settlers; but begin to think myself too old to engage in new projects that require time to become advantageous." As to London, "I am not coming over," he told Collinson, but the message differed in another letter written the same day. "Now I am returned from my long journeys which have consumed the whole summer, I shall apply myself to such a settlement of all my affairs, as will enable me to do what your friendship so warmly urges," he wrote Strahan. "I have a great opinion of your wisdom (Madeira apart) and am apt enough to think that what you seem so clear in and so earnest about, must be right. Tho' I own, that I sometimes suspect my love to England and my friends there seduces me a little, and makes *my own* middling reasons for going over appear very good ones. We shall see in a little time how things will turn out." Franklin sounds devious in these contradictory statements to Collinson and Strahan, and so his enemies would have judged him if they had read the letters. But what they took for guile often, as here, reveals only indecisiveness, a side of his personality that has passed unnoticed though it manifests itself frequently.

Shortly after his return Franklin called on John Penn, and whenever they met about town "in various places at dinner, and among the commissioners for carrying on the war," he treated him with respect. The governor was a known quantity. He had lived three years in Pennsylvania as a young man. In 1754 he had attended the Albany Congress with Franklin. He was now thirty-five and gave every sign of being a capable governor. "I had but an indifferent opinion of him whilst he was with us formerly," William Allen said, but now "he is very much esteemed by everybody here and is thought to be a very worthy honest gentleman. . . ." Franklin promised friends he would "give no occasion" for a quarrel with Penn. "For though I cordially dislike and despise the uncle, for demeaning himself so far as to backbite and abuse me to friends and to strangers, as you well know he does, I shall keep that account open with him only, and some time or other we may have a settlement."

In mid-December Philadelphia learned that the Indians had raised the siege on Fort Detroit. Franklin had mixed reactions to the news. "I only fear we shall conclude a new peace before those villains have been made to smart sufficiently for their perfidious breach of the last; and thereby make them less apprehensive of breaking us again hereafter," he said. "And yet perhaps 'tis best to conclude the war as soon as possible; for tho' it may be that these colonies, if they were united in their measures, and would exert their united strength, could fill the Indian country with so many and such strong parties, as to ruin them in one summer, and forever deter them from future attempts against us. Yet we see and know that such union is impracticable." General Amherst had asked those colonies threatened by Indians to raise and clothe one thousand men each to march against them. Pennsylvania alone "complied fully and heartily," Franklin reported to Jackson. Thus, he said, colonies potentially strong "are in effect weak; and shall remain so, till you take some measures at home to unite us."

The governor had asked the Assembly to comply with General Amherst's request on December 20. On December 21 he told the Assembly that the previous week a band of fifty-seven armed frontiersmen had murdered in their huts near Lancaster six Indians "who have lived peaceably and inoffensively among us, during all our late troubles." No one, Franklin included, sensed Pennsylvania verged on the greatest crisis in its history as a colony.

2

The massacre of the six Indians had occurred on December 14. On December 28 Penn learned that "upwards of a hundred" frontiersmen— the Paxton Boys they would be called—had the previous day ridden into Lancaster and slaughtered fourteen more Indians who had been placed for their safety in the workhouse. During the second massacre the murderers had boasted that their next stop was Philadelphia, where one hundred and forty peaceful Indians had been brought for protection. This second massacre, and Lancaster's placid reaction to it, outraged Franklin. The "barbarous men" committed their atrocity "in defiance of government, of all laws human and divine, and to the eternal disgrace of their country and color," he said, "then mounted their horses, huzzaed in triumph, as if they had gained a victory, and rode off—*unmolested!*"

Rumors floated in from the backcountry that five hundred, a thousand, perhaps two thousand frontiersmen were gathering to march on Philadelphia. Pennsylvania verged on civil war. The split was not simply between town and country. Presbyterians and Germans in the city sympathized with their religious and ethnic counterparts in the backcountry. Workingmen also identified with the frontiersmen. In the backcountry, frustrations that had been accumulating for over a generation were boiling over in a rage directed against Quakers generally and their policy of coddling Indians with gifts and against the Quaker-dominated Assembly and its policy of limiting the back counties to less than their share of seats in the legislature.

The governor acted with dispatch after learning of the second massacre. He asked the British commander-in-chief to place all royal troops in Pennsylvania under the governor's orders "to support civil authority." He issued a proclamation demanding that the murderers be brought to justice and offered a reward for their arrest. He ordered that the Indians harbored within the city be sent to New York under a guard of British soldiers. When the Assembly, prodded by Franklin, asked him to bring all civil officials in Lancaster to Philadelphia to explain why the murderers had not been apprehended, Penn sensibly refused, realizing this would only further inflame the frontier people. The refusal disgusted Franklin, who saw the governor using a crisis to build a political following in the back counties. At no time during the days that followed did Franklin reveal either sympathy or understanding for the grievances of the backcountry. His sense of decency had been so outraged by the

senseless slaughter of innocent Indians that he could think of nothing but
atonement for the atrocity. The creation of a western settlement intrigued Franklin as a dream, but the reality of such a settlement close to
home repelled him.

Governor Penn's best efforts failed to cope with the crisis. New York
refused to allow the Indians sent from Philadelphia inside its borders;
royal troops marched them back and on January 24 installed them in
barracks in the center of town. There the Indians sat, a red flag to entice
the frontiersmen into the city.

Franklin, appalled as he watched "the spirit of killing all Indians,
friends and foes, spread amazingly thro' the whole country," wrote a
pamphlet to "check this spirit." It resembled nothing he had previously
published on public affairs, and only once before, during the Hemphill
Affair, had he exposed the unbridled anger exhibited in *A Narrative of the
Late Massacres.* . . . The evil that has been done, ran one sentence, "cannot
be covered, the guilt will lie on the whole land, till justice is done on the
murderers. THE BLOOD OF THE INNOCENT WILL CRY TO HEAVEN FOR VEN-
GEANCE." The peroration seemed lifted from the Old Testament:

> O ye unhappy perpetrators of this horrid wickedness! Reflect a mo-
> ment on the mischief ye have done, the disgrace ye have brought on
> your country, on your religion, and your Bible, on your families and
> children! . . . Think of the mild and good government you have so
> audaciously insulted; the laws of your king, your country, and your
> GOD, that you have broken; the infamous death that hangs over your
> heads: For JUSTICE, though slow, will come at last. All good people
> everywhere detest your actions. You have imbrued your hands in
> innocent blood; how will you make them clean? The dying shrieks
> and groans of the murdered, will often sound in your ears; their
> spectres will sometimes attend you, and affright even your innocent
> children! Fly where you will, your consciences will go with you:
> Talking in your sleep shall betray you, in the delirium of a fever you
> yourselves shall make your own wickedness known.

On Saturday, February 4, the city learned that men "from all parts
of our frontier, . . . armed with rifle guns and tomahawks," were marching on Philadelphia. The governor called for a mass meeting of citizens
in the State House yard for four o'clock that afternoon, and some three
thousand tramped through a "driving cold rain" to attend. Penn told
them of the threat from the west and urged all to arm themselves and join
one of the nine military companies Franklin was organizing. That night
riders fanned out from the city "up the different roads to observe the

motion of the rioters, and to bring intelligence of their approach." All ferries on the Schuylkill River were ordered pulled to the Philadelphia side; someone overlooked the boat at Swede's Ford, fifteen miles up the river. The Paxton Boys found it.

Sunday saw the whole town up and about early. Cannons were installed in newly built ramparts around the army barracks. An embarrassing number of Quakers put aside pacifist principles and joined the military companies, but few Germans and fewer Presbyterians were seen carrying weapons. At midnight bells rang throughout the city, signaling the approach of the rioters. The governor, Franklin said later, "did me the honor, on an alarm, to run to my house at midnight, with his councillors at his heels, for advice, and made it his headquarters for some time." What followed blended into a blur for Franklin—"running, all night, with our governor, and my rest so broken by alarms on the other nights, that the whole week seems one confused space of time, without any such distinction of days, as that I can readily and certainly say, on such a day such a thing followed."

The Paxton Boys installed themselves north of the city in the village of Germantown. There on Monday morning a group of clergymen from the city visited them. They entreated the men to return home and warned that any move on the city would be answered with gunfire. Back in the city a number of Quakers urged the governor to order an attack on the rioters' encampment. Penn refused. Instead, he approved a plan to send a delegation of seven prominent citizens, Franklin among them, to negotiate with the frontiersmen. The party rode out at five o'clock the next morning and spent the day in prolonged and often spirited talk.

The men from the backcountry "frankly confessed," a Quaker assemblyman reported, "they had set out, with full purpose to kill every Indian in the barracks, having been invited and encouraged by many considerable persons in Philadelphia, and that they should meet with no opposition in the execution of their design, but now being informed the Indians were under the protection of the king's troops they professed so much loyalty to his Majesty that they would not lift a hand against them—a very poor thin guise this, to cover the disloyal principles of the faction, which appears to be a Presbyterian one—that society throughout the province being tainted with the same bloody principles with respect to the Indians and of disaffection to the government."

The Paxton Boys agreed to disperse the next day if their leaders might present the backcountry's grievances to the governor and the Assembly. On Wednesday morning, February 8, the leaders rode into Philadelphia accompanied by an armed bodyguard of thirty frontiersmen. Franklin wanted the Assembly to receive the emissaries and administer a public tongue-lashing to them. Penn rejected that plan, preferring to appease rather than humiliate the men. He received them courteously and listened to their grievances in private.

On February 11 Franklin said: "At present we are pretty quiet, and I hope that quiet will continue." No hope had a smaller chance to be realized. The backcountry's uprising unleashed hatreds within Pennsylvania that would flourish unabated for years to come. The Assembly did nothing to ease the tension. It received the frontier's list of grievances coolly when the governor passed them along and for the next twelve years ignored them. Though William Penn's Charter of Privileges, which Franklin had quoted so often to Thomas Penn in London, said that all counties should have not less than four members in the Assembly, all backcountry counties continued to be limited to two deputies. "The back people have a right to complain that they are not sufficiently represented," William Allen, then on a visit to London, remarked when he heard of the uprising. "But even that should be done in a lawful way, and not by force of arms; for that will make in the end the cause, otherwise very justifiable and good, a very dangerous and bad one."

3

"And within twenty-four hours," Franklin remarked a month after the uprising, "your old friend was a common soldier, a counsellor, a kind of dictator, an ambassador to the country mob, and on their returning home *nobody* again. All this has happened in a few weeks!" The emphasis on *"nobody"* underscored the hurt Franklin felt when the governor ceased to seek his advice or to confer with him after the crisis passed. (In his report to Uncle Thomas, Penn failed even to mention Franklin's name.) This rebuff to the most powerful man in the colony, the man he had leaned on heavily in time of danger, would color all Franklin's reactions in the weeks that followed.

Looking back a month after the uprising, Franklin said he suspected the governor's partisan motives the day the leaders rode into town to present their grievances. "The Assembly's proposal of joining with the governor in giving answer to the remonstrance presented by the deputies of that mob, was rejected," he said, "tho' intended merely to add weight to that answer, by showing that the government was unanimous. He said nothing about the public humiliation the Assembly planned to hand the leaders. The governor chose instead, Franklin added bitterly, "to give his answer separately, and what it was is a secret; we only learn that they went home extremely well satisfied with the governor, and are soon expected down again." Penn apparently saw more clearly than Franklin the depth of feeling among Presbyterians and Germans throughout the colony against Quakers and the Quaker-controlled Assembly. When the governor dropped "all inquiry after the murderers," whom Franklin wanted hunted down and brought to trial, he was thought to be playing on the people's prejudices in order to strengthen the hand of the executive. True, perhaps. Equally true, the governor may have wished his colony well and sought to ease tension with leniency. Franklin, isolated from the governor's confidence, refused to concede this.

Only gradually did Franklin sense the wave of hate for Quakers that washed over the colony. "Would you believe it," he asked in astonishment some time after the rioters had returned home, "that they are charged here, not with offending the Indians, and thereby provoking the war, but with gaining their friendship by presents, supplying them privately with arms and ammunition, and engaging them to fall upon and murder the poor white people on the frontiers?" The "bitter enmity" toward Quakers soon exploded into a vicious pamphlet war. Franklin despaired for his "darling" Pennsylvania, to the point where he lost all perspective. "The mobs," went one hyperbolic judgment, "strike a general terror, and many talk of removing into other provinces, as thinking both their persons and properties insecure." The backcountry, having been stirred awake, refused to go back to sleep, but no more mobs threatened the city. Instead it resorted to flooding the Assembly with petitions listing grievances. One with several hundred signatures arrived five yards long, another "of the same tenor . . . will be lodged fifteen yards long," with "more daily coming in." The Assembly ignored them all.

While the petitions rolled in and the pamphlet war continued the Assembly behind closed doors dealt with a crisis of another kind. The sum of fifty thousand pounds had to be raised to pay for the troops promised to the British commander-in-chief. The legislature earlier had assured the governor that it "was truly desirous to avoid every occasion of disagreement with his honor," and the bill it sent up on February 24 showed its willingness to adhere to the agreement Franklin had worked out with the Penns and the Privy Council in London. The new issue of paper money would not be legal tender for the "proprietaries' sterling rents." The proprietors' "unappropriated lands" were "explicitly exempted from taxation." But two points in that agreement the Assembly failed to comply with. These, said Franklin—"that the best of the proprietor's located uncultivated lands should be taxed no higher than the worst of the people's; and that his town lots should be exempted from all tax—these the House thought too unjust to be complied with." A lot Thomas Penn had recently sold currently paid "near £7 tax," Franklin observed, "which in the proprietors' hands would not (being to be rated as unimproved land) pay more than seven pence half penny. And this not owing to any improvement, but merely the change of owner." The provisions unquestionably contradicted "common justice and common sense," but Franklin had put his name to them. Now that the Assembly had flouted them, he could only hope the governor would not insist upon their enforcement. If he and the governor had been speaking to one another, a compromise of some sort might have been worked out. But they were not speaking to one another. On March 7 Governor Penn returned the Assembly bill unsigned and "with an absolute refusal."

The governor garnished the insult five days later by sending back two other bills unsigned. One, dealing with the militia, had, as in the past, called for the election of all officers by their men. Penn objected to that, holding, correctly, that by British tradition the executive must approve all military appointments. The other, which provided for the erection of a lighthouse, he had no objection to other "than that the House have, by inserting the officer's name for collecting the duties thereby imposed, without even consulting him [the governor] in the appointment or nomination of such officers, made an infringement on the prerogatives of the crown, with which he is entrusted."

These two rejections infuriated Franklin. He now saw a conspiracy afoot—unrest in the backcountry being stirred "by the governor's party, to awe the Assembly, and compel them to make such a militia law as the governors have long aimed at." As to the lighthouse keeper's job—"a trifle"; the Assembly would gladly have let the governor substitute another name. The House had "a sincere desire to continue on good terms with the governor," he said, but now "I foresee an immediate breach."

The impasse with the governor provoked Franklin into a bitter denunciation of not just John Penn but of mankind. "Do you please yourself with the fancy that you are doing good?" he asked on March 14 in a long letter to Dr. John Fothergill. "You are mistaken. Half the lives you save are not worth saving, as being useless; and almost the other half ought not to be saved, as being mischievous. Does your conscience never hint to you the impiety of being in constant warfare against the plans of Providence? Disease was intended as the punishment of intemperance, sloth, and other vices; and the example of that punishment was intended to promote and strengthen the opposite virtues. But here you step in officiously with your art, disappoint those wise intentions of nature, and make men safe in their excesses. Whereby you seem to me to be of just the same service to society as some favorite first minister who out of the great benevolence of his heart should procure pardons for all criminals that applied to him. Only think of the consequences!"

If Fothergill wondered what prompted these depressing observations, the explanation came in the next paragraph, where Franklin recounted the events of the past several weeks. "In fine," he concluded, "everything seems in this country, once the land of peace and order, to be running fast into anarchy and confusion. Our only hopes are, that the crown will see the necessity of taking the government into its own hands, without which we shall soon have no government at all."

The day he wrote Fothergill the Assembly gave Governor Penn an amended supply bill but with none of the objections removed. Penn returned it unsigned. The House insisted it had "complied to the best of their understanding" with the agreement Franklin had signed in London. On March 24 the House sent a blistering reply to the governor, then unanimously approved a string of twenty-six resolutions that listed its grievances against the proprietary and concluded "that the powers of government, ought in all good policy, to be separated from the power attending that immense property, and lodged where only it can be properly and safely lodged, in the hands of the crown." With this "necklace of resolves," as Franklin called them, on the record, the Assembly adjourned until May, "in order to consult their constituents, whether an humble address should be drawn up, and transmitted to his Majesty, praying that he would be graciously pleased to take the people of this province under his immediate protection and government. . . ."

CHAPTER

20

"MR. FRANKLIN DIED LIKE
A PHILOSOPHER"

THOSE WHO DISTRUSTED FRANKLIN invariably suspected the motives behind his projects. When he called for the crown to take over Pennsylvania they assumed he sought revenge on Thomas Penn, the antagonist who had consistently bested him over the past seven years, or that he saw the chance to win the post of royal governor for himself. Franklin said that he worked only to promote what was best for the empire and Pennsylvania. And it would not be so much a *"change of government,"* he insisted, but "rather and only a *change of governor,* that is, instead of self-interested proprietaries, a gracious king! His Majesty, who has no views but for the good of the people, will thenceforth appoint the governor, who unshackled by proprietary instructions, will be at liberty to join with the Assembly in enacting wholesome laws." Privately, he added that this was more than a local issue, that he favored the crown taking over all the colonies, for standardized governments in America would promote the unity he had been calling for during the past ten years.

On 29 March 1764, five days after the Assembly adjourned, Franklin set out to convince the people Pennsylvania's salvation lay in royal government. That day the press published the Assembly's "necklace of resolves," and three thousand copies of a broadside by Franklin explaining those resolves were distributed. He also drafted a petition to the king to take over the province, had it translated into German, and, missing no trick, drew up a slightly reworded version to appeal to Quakers. Two days later came a mass meeting of citizens in the State House yard. After a long speech by Joseph Galloway, who promised that "the way from proprietary slavery to royal liberty is easy," the petitions were passed out and the campaign was officially under way.

Franklin meanwhile found time to open a second front among friends in England. "You will endear yourself to us forever if you can get this change of government completed," he wrote Jackson, enclosing a copy of the petition. He asked Strahan to insert the Assembly's resolves in his newspaper, *The London Chronicle*, in order to "prepare the minds of those in power for an application that I believe will shortly be made from this province to the crown, to take the government into their own hands." To strengthen his case he painted a dismal scene to English friends. "We continue in great disorder here," he said in one letter. "We are now in the utmost confusion, tumults threatened and daily expected," he said in another, and in a third he warned that if the king refused to take over the colony "many talk of quitting the province, and among them your old friend."

He also found time to produce a pamphlet, which came out in mid-April under the title *Cool Thoughts on the Present Situation of Our Public Affairs*. The tone, dispassionate and reasonable, contrasted with the feeling displayed in his letters. He conceded that in the battle between proprietary and Assembly "there are *faults on both sides*, every glowing coal being apt to inflame its opposite." The Penn family and those they appointed as governors were no "worse men than other rulers," he said. "I suspect, therefore, that the cause is radical, interwoven in the constitution, and so become of the very nature of proprietary government; and will therefore produce its effects, as long as such governments continue." (Franklin asked Strahan to reprint the pamphlet, which he did, with minor revisions. "Dear Mr. Strahan," Franklin later wrote—no longer plain "Straney"—"I have of late fancied myself to write better than ever I did; and farther, that when anything of mine is abridged in the papers or magazines, I conceit that the abridger has left out the very best and brightest parts.")

Franklin launched his fight confidently against an opposition in disarray. Those who had sniped at him in the past were out of action. James Hamilton, the former governor, lay ill in his country mansion; Richard Peters, William Smith, and William Allen were all in England. An Assembly, the supposed voice of the people, united against the proprietary strengthened his confidence. But Franklin misjudged both the battle and the opposition. The absence of old leaders in the proprietary faction meant less now with new ones coming to the fore. Young John Dickinson's power as a speaker had already undercut Joseph Galloway's leadership in the Assembly. George Bryan, up to now a crony of Galloway's and his able ally in the legislature, feared Presbyterians like himself might be forced to support an established Church of England under a royal government; his opposition would hurt. Presbyterians, virtually to a man, opposed royal government and so, too, did a majority of Germans. The proprietary government had done nothing to win their love, but it had let them alone to live and worship as they pleased, which no one could be certain would hold true under a royal government. Quakers, who in recent years had rarely differed with Franklin, now divided. Isaac Norris, speaker of the Assembly, showed no enthusiasm for a change. It would not do to say "Isaac's rage is predominant against his new enemy," Galloway, whose tactical skill and eloquence had undercut his leadership. Quakers in Pennsylvania lived with more freedom than their brethren in England, and Norris feared they would lose some of their extraordinary privileges under royal government.

Hindsight revealed the scope and intensity of the opposition to Franklin's scheme, but in the spring of 1764 he could smell only victory in the air and pushed ahead confidently with his campaign.

2

The Assembly adjourned in March "expressly to consult their constituents" on the proposed petition to the king. When it reconvened on May 14, the governor sent back with a long list of objections the supply bill handed him in March. On May 22 the Assembly abruptly gave in to all his demands; the king and his ministers must see it as a compliant rather than a refractory body and that it had the interests of the empire uppermost in mind. The arrival of the petitions for royal government that had been circulating the past seven weeks helped to sugarcoat the pill the Assembly had swallowed. Franklin glowed as he glanced over the some 3,500 names on them, but he glowed without reason. Nearly half the signers lived in or about Philadelphia, an area that held about 8 percent of the 250,000 people who lived in Pennsylvania. The backcountry had yet to be heard from.

On May 23 the Assembly voted "by a great majority" (27 to 3) that a committee be created to draw a petition to the king to take over the colony. The next day John Dickinson, a tall, thin, thirty-two-year-old bachelor who had studied law in the Middle Temple and now had one of the most lucrative practices in Philadelphia, rose to speak against the decision. His normally pale complexion was paler than usual, for he had pulled himself from a sickbed to talk this day. He did not speak as one of Franklin's inveterate enemies. Indeed, on the requested revisions of the supply bill he had been "one of the *first* and *warmest* to declare my *fixed resolution*, not to admit of the governor's construction of the stipulation he disputed with us." Let us resent unjust demands, "but let our resentment bear proportion to the provocation received." No more than four or five hundred pounds in taxes is involved here. Before taking a great leap in the dark, let us first ask the king to judge the quarrel between us and the proprietors. "Let us take a cast or two of the dice for smaller matters before we dip deeply," he said. "If we *are* to *play* with the *public happiness,* let us act at least with *as much* deliberation as if we were *betting* out of our private purses."

Look at the risks in this great gamble. William Penn's Charter of Privileges bestows privileges upon the people of Pennsylvania greater than those enjoyed anywhere else in the empire. "We here enjoy that best and greatest of all rights, *a perfect religious freedom.*" The Assembly suffers no checks from a council "instituted in fancied imitation of the House of Lords." It sits upon its own adjournment and has a hand in the disbursement of all public funds, a power denied even to Parliament. The people elect their own sheriffs and coroners. "Any body of men acting under such a charter, must surely tread on slippery ground when they take a step that may be deemed a surrender of that charter."

Dickinson spoke for nearly two hours. Joseph Galloway rose at once to answer. Dickinson had raised the specter of the king imposing a standing army on the colony. He had hinted the Church of England might become the established, state-supported church. He had remarked it would be the king's ministers, not the gracious king himself, who would rule the province, and "since the gale of ministerial favor has in *all seasons* blown propitious to proprietary interests, why do we now fondly flatter ourselves that it will *suddenly* shift its quarter?" To all this Galloway had a simple answer: "The royal government shows its limits; they are known and confined; and rare it is, that any attempts are made to extend them. But where proprietary power will terminate, where its limits will be fixed, and its encroachments end, is uncertain."

Galloway had spoken only a few minutes when "it was observed that the speaker was so ill, that it was proper to adjourn." Isaac Norris may have feigned illness. He opposed the petition to the crown and may have wanted the Assembly members to return to their lodgings with Dickinson's arguments fresh in mind. If this was his purpose, Governor Penn demolished the tactic with incredible ineptness. The next day he demanded several more changes, all petty and technical, in the wording of the supply bill. An enraged Assembly rejected the request with a blunt note, then, with all thought of conciliation washed from their minds, proceeded to discuss the petition to the king. Isaac Norris stepped down from the chair to explain why he opposed it. The next day, unnerved that he must sign as speaker a document he disapproved of, Norris sent the Assembly a note saying that "the long sitting of yesterday and the bad night I have had in consequence of it" had left him exhausted and too ill to attend. The House thereupon chose a new speaker—Benjamin Franklin. Governor Penn confirmed the election that afternoon. The Assembly, again "by a great majority," formally approved the petition asking the king to take over Pennsylvania. A week later it waived its "important parliamentary rights relating to money bills" and accepted all the governor's requested changes in the supply bill, hoping this final retreat would make a good impression upon the king and his ministers.

The debate over an issue that concerned the welfare of over a quarter of a million people had, as usual, been conducted behind closed doors. No one doubted the propriety of this, but some thought secrecy carried too far when Franklin refused to allow a copy of the petition to be entered into the Assembly's journals or to be printed in the press. Not to allow the people of Pennsylvania to see exactly how the Assembly gambled with their future Franklin regarded as a matter of "no great importance."

Shortly after it had passed the Assembly, Franklin sent the petition to Jackson in London, asking him to present it to the King-in-Council. "They would fain have sent me home with this petition," he said, but "I am very unwilling the public should by that means be put to any unnecessary expense" when Jackson could just as well do the job. Was Franklin being deceitful or simply indecisive when he wrote thus to Jackson? "I believe (but you best not mention it) that you will see my father in England shortly," William Franklin had written to Strahan a month earlier, and two weeks after the letter to Jackson he wrote again: "My father seems to be preparing in earnest for a voyage to England."

3

Those for a change in government dominated the battle until early June, when William Smith returned from London and set about organizing the opposition. Now petitions castigating Franklin's proposal circulated throughout the colony. Dickinson's speech of May 24 was published with a preface by Smith. Probably he also had a hand in other pamphlets soon streaming from the press, a number of them vitriolic attacks on Franklin. "I bore the personal abuse of five scurrilous pamphlets, and three copper-plate prints, from the proprietary party, before I made the smallest return," Franklin said later. His "return" came the second week of August in the form of a long preface to an essay by

Galloway attacking Dickinson's now famous speech.

The opposition gained another leader on August 13, when William Allen returned from England. Franklin paid a visit "to congratulate him on his arrival, intending it as an overture," he said. Allen rejected the peace offering. Instead, in the presence of a large company he announced in a booming voice that while in England Richard Jackson had told him it would cost one hundred thousand pounds for the government to buy Pennsylvania from the Penn family, which "Parliament will oblige us to pay, and saddle us besides with a salary to be paid by us to a king's governor of £5,000 sterling per annum more."

The £100,000 figure staggered Franklin. "I can scarcely conceive that you sent me such a message nor can I believe that so absurd a thing would be proposed by the ministry, that we should pay the purchase money for the government, unless we were to buy it for ourselves," he said. Allen, purposely or not, had misunderstood Jackson, who had said only that the cost in legal fees, bribes, and other incidentals would be enormous. But the general tenor of Jackson's remarks Allen had not misinterpreted, and Franklin knew this. Jackson had told Franklin that the application to the crown "will in the end meet with success," but added "I mean if kept up, perhaps for a course of years, and this I have frequently I think convinced Mr. Allen of." He had also warned that power in time might fall to a man less "good and gracious" than George III. "I think, therefore, that for the present, if the Proprietary is disposed to give way, it may be better, till future misconduct on his part makes it necessary, to delay presenting the petitions."

Allen had still more embarrassing gossip to relay to Franklin and the other guests. In the Assembly Franklin had often said that "the present ministry are desirous of vesting the government of this province advantageously in the crown." Not so, said Allen. He reported that Lord Halifax, the powerful president of the Board of Trade, had called the Assembly's resolves for a change of government *"rebellion!"* He said, too, that Lord Mansfield had told Thomas Penn: "Now is your time to make a good bargain for yourself. Put these refractory people into our hands and we'll soon make them feel the difference between a proprietary and a royal government!"

Franklin already had evidence that Thomas Penn was using his influence with members of the ministry to thwart him. Lord Hyde, his superior in the postal department, had warned him in a letter that "all the officers of the crown are expected to assist government," whether royal or proprietary, and that the ministry would only look with disfavor upon any "person who shall embroil government." Franklin had a jaunty answer to the rebuke—others could do as they wished, but he for one "was not to be *Hyde-bound.*" But privately he worried. He wrote General Bouquet that "my enemies (for God has blessed me with two or three, to keep me in order) are now representing me at home as an opposer and obstructer of his Majesty's service here." After detailing his services to the crown during the past decade, he asked the general for a letter of commendation. "My having such a letter to produce on occasion, may possibly be of considerable service to me."

Through August the reputation Franklin cherished took a drubbing. The pamphlet writers accused him of buying honorary degrees and of passing off Ebenezer Kinnersley's electrical experiments as his own. They reminded the public of his illegitimate son. They pictured him as a man who hated Presbyterians—"Piss-brute-tarians" one of his followers called them—and despised Germans. In the essay *On the Increase of Mankind* he had asked: "Why should the Palatine boors be suffered to swarm into our settlements, and by herding together establish their language and manners to the exclusion of ours?" He cut the remark from the second edition of the essay, but someone recalled it during the campaign and had the sentence translated into German, with the word "boors" rendered as "bauerntolpels" or blockheads. One of Franklin's people retranslated it into "bauerns" or peasants, but the damage had been done.

On September 10, with the election only three weeks away, the Assembly convened for a short session. The opposition presented petitions against a change of government with fifteen thousand signatures, over four times the number Franklin's faction had gathered. William Allen urged his colleagues to recall their petition to the king, "but as far as I can perceive without the least effect," Franklin reported. He warned the Assembly that "the king's little finger we should find heavier than the proprietor's whole loins," but, said Franklin, "the bugbears he would frighten us with, are rather laughed at."

4

A few days before the election Allen remarked that Franklin seemed "very gloomy and thoughtful." He had reason to be. The opposition had boxed him into a corner from which he saw no way to escape. They had constructed an appealing ticket—a blend of Anglicans, Presbyterians, and Germans—while he offered only old, familiar, and mostly Quaker faces to the public. Rumors circulated in the city that Thomas Penn had instructed the governor to accept the Assembly's interpretation of how the proprietary estates should be taxed. Both Allen and Smith knew of this concession but withheld it from the people. Franklin thought "they keep them back in hopes the next election may put the proprietaries in a condition not to need the proposing them." Actually, no one thought of reneging on the concession, but to admit before the election that Franklin and his friends had been right on the taxation issue would assure their victory and continued control of the Assembly.

A deeper reason for Franklin's gloomy countenance concerned the trend of imperial affairs, which only in the autumn of 1764 began seriously to disturb him. For nearly a year Jackson had warned from London of Parliament's determination to lay taxes upon the colonies to pay for the royal troops stationed there. "I am not much alarmed about your schemes of raising money on us," Franklin replied placidly. "You will take care for your own sakes not to lay greater burthens on us than we can bear; for you cannot hurt us without hurting yourselves. All our profits center with you, and the more you take from us, the less we can lay out with you." When the new taxes in the Revenue Act of 1764 went into effect, to be collected by an enlarged force of customs officers, he was still not especially disturbed. "Undoubtedly the illicit trade ought to be stopped," he said, "and if all this strictness is necessary to that end, I have the less objection to it." Poor Richard for 1765 called the new taxes unwise but not illegal. Generally, "my political faith is, that what our superiors think best for us, is really best," said Poor Richard. Yet obviously Americans lacked the cash to pay for the new levies. In that case, we must "endeavor to do without the things we shall, perhaps, never be able to pay for; or if we cannot do without them or something like them, to supply ourselves from our own produce at home."

Even when Jackson warned that Parliament considered levying a stamp duty, which would tax virtually every piece of paper—newspapers, wills, playing cards, the list was endless—that circulated in the colonies, Franklin reacted calmly. "Your objection to internal taxes is undoubtedly just and solid," he said, but while Jackson called the proposed stamp duty unconstitutional Franklin merely thought it impractical. "When any tax for America is proposed in your Parliament, how are you to know that we are not already taxed as much as we can bear?" he asked. "If you choose to tax us, give us members in your legislature, and let us be one people." While dodging a public stand on the stamp duty, it was embarrassing to read in his own newspaper shortly after Parliament had temporarily shelved the proposal that "had not WILLIAM ALLEN, Esq., been here [in London], and indefatigable in opposing it, and happily having made acquaintance with the first personages in the kingdom and the greatest part of the House of Commons, it would inevitably have passed this session." It was even more embarrassing to be reminded that while Franklin took a benign view of the new imperial policy Thomas Penn led the fight against it in London. "Our people are very unjust to Mr. Penn in their thoughts of him," Allen reported in a letter detailing Penn's efforts to block the stamp duty. "He is really anxious for our welfare and takes great pains to promote our interest."

When Allen warned of the dangers posed by the crown and Parliament—"we are to be their grand milch cow"—Franklin replied mildly, "The cat can yield but her skin." His resignation owed something to the wounds inflicted during the scurrilous campaign. "I begin, as I grow old," he remarked in June as the worst of the pamphlets against him were appearing, "to be more willing than I used to be, that the world should take its own course, without my officiously intermeddling with its affairs." Also, he had convinced, or deluded, himself into believing that the mother country would do nothing to harm the welfare of her colonies, for any policy that injured American prosperity would in time hurt England. But as the months passed and he sensed the ill effects of the new imperial policy, he still could not raise his voice in opposition. He found himself on the wrong side of a popular issue but forced to stay silent. As deputy postmaster general and a royal servant he risked losing his post by opposing royal policy. More important, to join with Allen and Dickinson and the despised Penn on this issue would in effect concede many of the arguments they had raised in their opposition to assumption of Pennsylvania's government by the crown. Allen had warned that the king's little finger would weigh heavier upon the colony than all the proprietor's loins, and the prophecy seemed about to be fulfilled.

Franklin dealt with the dilemma by ignoring it, though by early autumn despair seeped through his letters. "Nothing is now talked of all over America but frugality and economy, abating the use of West India and English luxuries, particularly the former," he wrote Jackson on September 25, the day Allen had remarked on his gloomy countenance. Now he admitted that Poor Richard's proposal for supplying "ourselves from our own produce at home" was a fantasy. How could America clothe itself when "our sheep have such small fleeces, that the wool of all the mutton we eat will not supply us with stockings"? (Later, with good-humored exaggeration, he would tell the people of England that "the very tails of the American sheep are so laden with wool, that each has a car or wagon on four little wheels to support and keep it from trailing on the ground.") But dejected as he was, Franklin could not bring himself

to oppose the imperial program, particularly with the election less than
a week away.

5

The election was held on Monday, October 1. Franklin's slate of
candidates was called the Old Ticket, the proprietors' the New Ticket.
Two men appeared on both tickets, thus leaving a field of fourteen for
the eight seats representing the county of Philadelphia. Two other tickets
competed for the city's two seats. Franklin was on both the city and
county slates.

One of the key aides promoting the Old Ticket was William Franklin,
who left the governor's mansion in Burlington "to keep open house at
Germantown in favor of his father and Mr. Galloway," a critic reported.
"He was several days there canvassing among the Germans and endeavoring to get votes by propagating the most infamous lies he could invent;
he is as bad as his father." It was wondered if this were "a conduct
becoming a king's governor?"

A week before the election William Allen said "both sides seem confident of success; but from what I hear, there will be a change of the
members. I shall not intermeddle, nor be in the town the day of the
election; I hope the peace will be preserved; yet, from the mutual heats,
it is to be feared there will be warm work. The serious Friends seem to
be dissatisfied with the intention to change the government . . . ; the
younger folks are, I think, too much under the influence of that disturber
of the peace, Franklin, and all his creatures."

The polls at the courthouse opened at nine in the morning, and the
steps leading into the building were "so crowded till between eleven and
twelve at night," an observer remarked, "that at no time a person could
get up in less than a quarter of an hour from his entrance at the bottom,
for they could go no faster than the whole column moved. About three
in the morning, the advocates for the New Ticket moved for a close, but
(Oh! fatal mistake) the old hands kept it open, as they had a reserve of the
aged and lame, which could not come in the crowd and were called up
and brought out in chairs and litters, etc., and some who needed no help,
between three and six o'clock, about two hundred voters. As both sides
took care to have spies all night, the alarm was given to the New Ticket
men. Horsemen and footmen were immediately dispatched to Germantown, etc., and by nine or ten o'clock they began to pour in, so that after
the move for a close, seven or eight hundred votes were procured; about

five hundred, or near it, of which were for the New Ticket, and they did not close till three in the afternoon, and it took them till one next day to count them off."

Nearly four thousand votes were cast in the day and a half of balloting, a record in Pennsylvania elections. Franklin lost both in the city and the county. Four out of six of his candidates went down with him. Though fewer than 130 votes separated Franklin from John Dickinson, who led the ticket for the contested seats, he ran thirteenth in a field of fourteen. Even his protégé Galloway outpolled him by eleven votes. Galloway, suffering his first defeat, *"agonized in death* like a mortal deist who has no hopes of a future existence," but "MR. FRANKLIN died like a philosopher." He called it "quite a laughing matter" that the proprietary faction had "carried (would you think it!) above one thousand Dutch from me," but the defeat rankled. In a less jaunty mood he accused his opponents of "numberless falsehoods propagated as truths, and the many perjuries procured among the wretched rabble brought to swear themselves entitled to a vote."

The proprietary faction made few gains outside the county and city of Philadelphia. The Old Ticket still commanded a two-thirds majority in the Assembly. With little difficulty it voted down a new attempt to get the petition to the king rescinded in the first session after the election. Then shortly after Governor Penn left town the Franklinists pulled a maneuver they knew twisted parliamentary procedure out of shape. A proprietary partisan later told Thomas Penn what occurred: "A day or two after the governor left town, Mr. Norris resigned the chair on account of his indisposition of body, and Mr. Fox was elected Speaker. The House then proceeded to business notwithstanding they were informed that it was first necessary to present their new Speaker and that the governor would return in a few days to give them an opportunity of doing it. They absolutely insisted that the presenting a Speaker was mere matter of form; that the person chosen to the chair was as instantly their Speaker and the House immediately qualified to do business, and immediately appointed Franklin assistant agent to Mr. Jackson, and voted that he should be paid out of the next money which should be raised on the public."

The vote was 19 to 11 to send Franklin to England, though he had so recently been discredited at the polls. An embittered Dickinson protested in the press. He held that Franklin's "fixed enmity to the proprietors will preclude all accommodation of our disputes with them," that he "is very unfavorably thought of by several of his Majesty's ministers," that the recent election had shown him to be "extremely disagreeable to a very great number of the most serious and reputable inhabitants." William Allen, of whom a friend said at the time, "I am afraid the frenzy has seized him," exhausted his vocabulary of invectives to describe Franklin, calling him "this inflammatory and virulent man . . . the most unpopular and odious name in the province . . . a very bad man . . . one delirious with rage, disappointment and malice . . . this ungrateful incendiary."

Stung by the accusations, Franklin publicly exulted at the honor handed him. "And what comfort can it afford you," he asked his opponents, "when by the Assembly's choice of an agent, it appears that the same, to you obnoxious man (notwithstanding all your venomous invectives against him) still retains so great a share of the public confidence?"

Why had the Assembly committed itself to the considerable expense of sending Franklin to London when it already had there Richard Jackson, who had proved to be an able agent? The day of the appointment, the governor announced that the proprietor had accepted the Assembly's interpretation on the taxing of his estates. Withholding the news until after the election may have struck some members as a cheap political trick and encouraged them to offer Franklin a consolation prize for his defeat. Allen later told Thomas Penn that he thought some members favored sending Franklin to serve "as a rod to hang over you to bring you to agree to their measures." And still others thought Franklin in London could better fight the proposed stamp duty, which was to be revived in the coming year, even though he had not spoken against it.

And why did Franklin, nearing sixty, wish to endure another long ocean trip and absence from home? For one thing, he missed London. Every letter to friends there pleaded for full reports on the latest political developments. He missed being at the center of great events. Now he had a chance to return on an all-expense-paid trip. He had, too, a chance to put his humiliating defeat behind him; if in London he could effect a change in the government he could return home in triumph. But the opportunity to make a reality of a larger dream dwarfed all other reasons for going. Since 1751 Franklin had been developing ideas for imperial reform—union of the colonies, representation in Parliament, tighter management of Indian relations. In the 1750s the ministry was uninterested; now it seemed to be. "If the Ministry was ready to put a new policy into effect," Professor Hanna has written, "an obvious first step was to remove proprietary governments and establish a unified system of royal administration. Franklin expected that both England and the colonies would have to make concessions: America must stop or be stopped from illegal trade and smuggling, and England must find some way to give American interests formal recognition in Parliament or even in the Ministry. In this momentous undertaking . . . the Ministry needed information and guidance. Would not this be a priceless opportunity for an able, far-seeing American spokesman?"

Twelve days after the Assembly's appointment Franklin set out for England. In the haste to depart before winter froze over the river, he had to borrow a woolen nightgown from a friend. His departure was made an affair of state. Some three hundred friends accompanied him down to the village of Chester, where his ship was anchored. Cannon hauled from the city were fired as he was rowed out to the *King of Prussia* by a crew of ten from the White Oaks Company, while the watching throng on shore sang to the tune of "God Save the King" an anthem composed for the occasion:

> O Lord our God arise,
> Scatter our enemies,
>   And make them fall.
> Confound their politics
> Frustrate such hypocrites,
> *Franklin* on thee we fix,
>   God save us all.

"In short," said a pleased spectator, "the respect that was paid to this great and truly deserving patriot, can hardly be set forth, nor the joys shown on the occasion, be expressed."

CHAPTER

21

"O, *FRANKLIN*, *FRANKLIN*, THOU CURSE!''

FRANKLIN ARRIVED AT PORTSMOUTH on 9 December 1764 after a swift but stormy passage. Word went back immediately he had made the dangerous winter crossing safely; he learned later the news "occasioned . . . great and general joy" in Philadelphia, "the bells rang on that account till near midnight, libations were poured out for your health, success, and every other happiness." The Quakers, Governor Penn remarked sourly, "ran about like mad men to acquaint such of their crew of the joyful tidings as they imagined had not heard it before. People as they met in the streets shook hands, and wished one another joy upon this great event."

Franklin made the seventy-two-mile trip to London in a single "short winter day." He found the house in Craven Street empty of Mrs. Stevenson "and the maid could not tell where to find her, so I sat me down and waited her return, when she was a good deal surprised to find me in her parlor."

Since political business would remain at a standstill until Parliament convened in January, Franklin expected to have a month to enjoy his London friends before settling down to work. Instead, he spent most of the time housebound, as he had after the previous crossing—this time with "a most violent cold," so severe it "worried me extremely." A harsh cough wracked his chest and his arms pained so greatly that several weeks passed before he could "put on and off my clothes." He was still on the mend when on 2 February 1765 he, Jackson, and two other colonial agents visited George Grenville, chancellor of the Exchequer, hoping to dissuade him from the plan to impose a stamp duty upon the American colonies.

Franklin came to detest Grenville and all his judgments upon him were filtered through his prejudice. The most balanced assessment by a contemporary of this difficult man, whom the king said had "the mind of a clerk in a counting-house," was written by his cousin:

> He had nothing seducing in his manners. His countenance had rather the expression of peevishness and austerity. . . . He was to a proverb tedious . . . he was diffuse and argumentative, and never had done with a subject after he had conceived your judgment till he wearied your attention—the foreign ministers complained of his prolixity which they called amongst each other, the being *Grenvilisé.* The same prolixity rendered him an unpleasant speaker in the House of Commons. . . . Yet though his eloquence charmed nobody, his argument converted. . . . The abundance of his matter, his experience of the forms and practices of the House . . . his accurate knowledge of the laws and history of his own country . . . his wariness never to suffer himself to be drawn out beyond the line he had prescribed to himself . . . his skill upon all matters of finance, of commerce, of foreign treaties, and above all the purity of his character . . . gave him . . . weight. . . . He never took notes; he never quitted his seat for refreshment in the longest debates, and generally spoke the last, when his strength and his memory served him to recollect every argument that had been used, and to suffer scarce a word of any consequence to escape his notice. . . . He was a man born to public business, which was his luxury and his amusement. . . . His prudence bordered on parsimony.

A modern scholar has remarked that Grenville, "alone among the British statesmen, before the American Revolution, offered a comprehensive plan which demonstrated true imperial statesmanship and a deep understanding of the British constitution." He faced all the problems Franklin had ignored in his pamphlet on Canada—"absorbing the new conquests into the empire, settling a satisfactory financial basis for doing so, and, indirectly, creating better order among the older colonies by pulling them more firmly into the imperial orbit of the British constitution." He had not adopted the plan for a stamp duty hastily. Royal officials in America told him the people there would accept a stamp duty and Franklin, who thought so too, did not disillusion him. Grenville consulted Lord Mansfield, the eminent jurist who worked out the compromise between Franklin and Penn for taxing proprietary estates; Mansfield told him Parliament had a right to tax the colonies.

When Franklin's group of agents walked into Grenville's office, they spoke to a minister who for the moment could not be checked by the king; George III was then enduring his first bout with insanity. Franklin urged the minister to continue using the old system of requisition upon each colony to pay for the royal troops in America rather than a stamp duty. Could the agents guarantee that the colonies would comply with the requisitions? Grenville asked. They could not, and knew well that in the past several had failed to meet their assigned quotas. The meeting ended with Grenville promising to consider a more palatable plan for raising money if the agents could suggest one.

In the week that followed Franklin drew up a scheme for a continental loan office similar to the one that worked effectively in Pennsylvania. It would loan out on "good security" at 5 percent interest paper money which would circulate as legal tender. The merits of the scheme were many. The royal government, as had Pennsylvania's, could "by the interest of these loans meet some public outlays without laying new taxes. And since specie is very scarce, and these bills circulate as money, by these loans many poor colonists are put into position to acquire the necessary cattle, farm equipment, etc., and to cultivate their fields properly." It would give America a continental currency which would promote both commerce and unity among the colonies. "It will operate as a general tax on the colonies and yet not an unpleasing one," Franklin said, meaning that only those who wished to use the paper money had to do so. But it would be a tax, and though less onerous than a stamp duty nonetheless a tax authorized by Parliament. Galloway, more alert to the mood of the colonies, kept Franklin's proposal secret when he learned of it, for "in the present temper of Americans, I think, it would occasion great clamors." Fortunately, the scheme was rejected, as Franklin must have known it would be, for both Grenville and Parliament were on record as opposed to paper money circulating as legal tender. A continental loan office, like the Plan of Union, would appear reasonable and practical to later generations, but to politicians of the day on both sides of the water they were shot through with flaws, the product of a visionary mind rather than a man of affairs.

Though Franklin knew the stamp duty would bear hard upon him personally—"I think it will affect the printers more than anybody"—he abandoned opposition to it and "stood entirely neuter till he saw which way the cause would be carried, and then he broke out fiercely on the side of America," a fellow agent who disliked him said. A modern scholar, more generous, suggests that because the petition for royal government "was his first consideration and Grenville's support promised to be invaluable," he could not afford to offend the minister. "Franklin saw the stamp duty as a minor matter, a necessary price for royal government and other reforms. His acceptance of it was an earnest expression of his willingness to assist the government at home."

The king, once again well, signed the Stamp Act on 22 March 1765. It would go into operation in November. "We might as well have hindered the sun's setting," Franklin wrote home. "That we could not do. But since 'tis down, my friend, . . . let us make as good a night of it as we can. We may still light candles." To help light the night for his printshop he had shipped off a huge order of paper to Philadelphia. Cut these large sheets in half, he told David Hall, and you will halve the stamp tax on them without seriously reducing the size of the newspaper. (Franklin outsmarted himself. When the government announced newspapers in America could be printed only on special prestamped paper the entire shipment had to be sent back to England.)

Shortly after the Stamp Act passed Franklin heard that "Mr. Grenville was desirous to make the execution of the act as little inconvenient and disagreeable to the Americans as possible; and therefore did not think of sending stamp officers from hence, but wished to have discreet and reputable persons appointed in each province from among the inhabitants, such as would be acceptable to them." Did Mr. Franklin have in mind anyone for what would be lucrative posts? He suggested John Hughes for Pennsylvania, William Coxe for New Jersey, and Zachariah Hood for Maryland. All were accepted, an indication of the regard Grenville held for Franklin. The appointment of Hughes, a leader in the Assembly's fight to deprive the Penns of their colony, embarrassed Thomas Penn, who had opposed the Stamp Act more vigorously than had Franklin. He complained to Grenville, but the appointment remained unchanged. Franklin had reason to feel pleased with himself in early April as news of the Stamp Act traveled over the ocean toward Philadelphia.

2

Franklin hoped after passage of the Stamp Act to press on with the Assembly's petition to the king, but April found him working to block passage through Parliament of a bill authorizing military commanders in America to quarter troops in private houses. He and Thomas Pownall devised a compromise that gave colonial governors power "to hire vacant buildings and fit them up as temporary barracks," which would be stocked with rations and refreshments for the troops out of funds appropriated by the legislatures. With Grenville's blessing the amended bill passed the House of Commons on May 3. Franklin, pleased with his handiwork, claimed credit for the modified bill. Later, when it proved both unworkable—legislatures could thwart it by refusing to appropriate funds to build the barracks and stock them with rations—and resented by the colonies as an indirect tax upon them, Franklin saw flaws unnoticed earlier and scaled down his role.

The day the revised act passed he was suffering an attack of gout that would keep him housebound for a fortnight. When able to move without wincing, he renewed the assault upon the proprietors. "Our petition, which has been becalmed for some time, is now getting underway again, and all appearances are for us," he remarked in June. He and Jackson set apart a week to press the case with Lords Halifax and Hillsborough and George Grenville. Franklin saw no reason "to doubt success" in persuading them to back the petition with their prestige and power.

Carefully laid plans fell apart early in July when Grenville's ministry fell, supplanted by a shaky coalition headed by Lord Rockingham. The shift in power made sudden waste of the months spent buttering up Grenville and his associates. Yet letters home exuded an unwarranted optimism. "Nothing yet appears that is discouraging," he told one friend; the change to royal government "must sooner or later take place, and I think it near at hand, whatever may be given out to the contrary," he wrote another; and to a third said, "I have very little doubt of a favorable progress and advantageous issue." He refused to admit that the bewildering state of British politics made it impossible to predict anything. He also refused to admit any uneasiness about the reception of the Stamp Act in America, news of which began filtering into London early in August.

3

The first reactions were mild. Philadelphia friends thought Parliament had stretched the cord "a little too tight," but gave no hint the act would be flouted. Then in August came news that the Stamp Act Congress—a startling act of defiance; never before had the colonies met to plan joint action except by royal invitation—would convene in October in New York to consult on a strategy of resistance. In a garbled news account Franklin read several rebellious-sounding resolves opposing the Stamp Act that had been introduced (but not passed as the news clipping said) in the Virginia House of Burgesses by a young man named Patrick Henry. Their rashness, said Franklin, "is amazing!" Pennsylvania must not follow Virginia's lead. She should "keep within the bounds of prudence and moderation; for that is the only way to lighten or get clear of our burthens," he wrote home. Eventually the people will become reconciled to the stamp duties. "In the meantime," he admonished, "a firm loyalty to the crown and faithful adherence to the government of this nation, which it is the safety as well as honor of the colonies to be connected with, will always be the wisest course for you and I to take, whatever may be the madness of the populace or their blind leaders, who can only bring themselves and country into trouble, and draw on great burthens by acts of rebellious tendency."

In mid-August he tried through the press to dispel an anti-American sentiment emerging in London. He published a letter Charles Thomson had written to him on the "very great uneasiness" the people of Pennsylvania felt from losing the right "of being governed by laws of their own making." A week later as "A Virginian" he praised his brethren "as loyal subjects as any the king has" who "do no more than what every good member in the British Parliament would do," if he thought his rights invaded. "If they are wrong, they want only to be convinced of it, to make them acquiesce." Early in September "A Virginian" reminded his English audience that "Americans are a reasonable people." Londoners were predicting "the Americans will shortly throw off their allegiance to the sovereign, and under that persuasion it is thought necessary to curb them." Tread carefully here, Franklin warned. "Can it be supposed that a people who have enjoyed the right of making laws among themselves for one hundred fifty years—but I will say no more, only that such a step would be big with the fate of Britain and her sons."

Franklin preached forebearance without sensing the depth of American feeling. Uneasiness about the Stamp Act's reception occupied only a corner of his mind. In September he shopped for furnishings for his house, sending his wife "a very handsome pair of tongs, and a pair of fire shovels," which he hoped "will come in time for your winter fires." While he shopped anger mounted back in Pennsylvania. "Philadelphia is cursed with a set of men who seem resolved to counteract all our efforts against the Stamp Act, and are daily endeavoring to suppress the spirit of liberty among us," a young Presbyterian remarked. "You know I mean the Quakers. They have openly spoke in favor of the act and declare it high treason to speak against the English Parliament." He pictured John Hughes as "a man so devoid of public spirit as to be willing to enslave his country if others will." The *"mobility"* must "extort a full and ample resignation from him." Franklin did not escape censure. "O, *Franklin, Franklin,* thou curse to Pennsylvania and America, may the most accumulated vengeance burst speedily on thy guilty head!"

In October unpleasant reports from home streamed into London steadily. Hall reported riots in New York and Boston. Thomas Hutchinson's house had been looted. Stamp officers everywhere had been hanged in effigy. The *Pennsylvania Gazette* had lost some five hundred customers because Hall refused to print essays attacking the Stamp Act. The dolorous report ended with a comment Hall knew would jolt Franklin. "I could wish you was on the spot, on many accounts," he said, "and yet I should be afraid of your safety, as the spirit of the people is so violent against everyone they think has the least concern with the stamp law, and they have imbibed the notion that you had a hand in framing it, which has occasioned you many enemies; but I make not the least doubt you would be able to clear yourself, if there was a necessity for it, of all the ill-natured things that have been laid to your charge."

Hall sent his letter on September 6. The "frenzy of madness" continued unabated, as Franklin learned from a log kept by John Hughes. "Our clamors run very high, and I am told my house shall be pulled down and the stamps burnt," Hughes reported on September 12. Hughes and Deborah Franklin lived in their houses for nine days under a state of siege. Deborah, her brother, and some friends made one of the downstairs rooms "into a magazine" and, she later told her husband, "I ordered some sort of defense upstairs such as I could manage myself." On September 16 a ship from London brought the news that Grenville's ministry had fallen. The city took this as a sign that the Stamp Act would soon be repealed. The story flew about town that Franklin had now lost all his influence in London, and William Allen proclaimed to every man he met in the London Coffee House that "the change of ministry was one of the most happy events in favor of America and that there was not the least fear of an alteration of our government; for that the proprietors had great weight and interest with the present ministers." As a leader of the opposition against the Stamp Act, Allen had reason to gloat.

That night bonfires flared throughout the city and in the midst of the joy men decided the time had come to pull down the Hughes and Franklin houses. "If I live till tomorrow morning I shall give you a farther account," Hughes wrote in his log, "but as it is now eight o'clock I am on my guard, and only write this between whiles, as every noise or bustle of the people calls me off." Across town Deborah Franklin patrolled her own battle station. William had urged her to come to Burlington. She let Sally go, but refused to leave herself. "I said when I was advised to remove that I was very sure that you had done nothing to hurt anybody, nor had I given any offense to any person at all, nor would I be made uneasy by anybody, nor would I stir or show the least uneasiness, but if anyone came to disturb me I would show proper resentment and I should be very much affronted with anybody." Those who had wondered what Franklin had seen in the carpenter's daughter he had brought into his house thirty-five years ago now knew.

Toward midnight several hundred friends surrounded the houses of Franklin and Hughes and the mobs that had been about to move dispersed. At five in the morning of September 17 Hughes reported: "We are all yet in the land of the living, and our property safe. Thank God."

4

Franklin's faction swept the annual October elections in Philadelphia, in spite of its equivocal stand on the Stamp Act. Galloway sent the results to London by the first boat. Franklin read the victory as a mandate to push ahead with the campaign to convert Pennsylvania into a royal colony, and on November 4 he presented the Assembly's petition to the Privy Council. He did so against the advice of Richard Jackson, who thought a government perplexed by an aroused America would be in no mood to decide another portentous matter. But Franklin knew better and assured colleagues back home he had "no reason to doubt of its success."

On November 22 the Privy Council, with unaccustomed promptness, said it would not consider the petition "for the present." The president of the council privately told Thomas Penn that the postponement was in fact "forever and ever." The ambiguous wording, Penn explained to his nephew in Pennsylvania, "is the most easy way of rejecting, and which they make use of when any considerable bodies of people petition; so that you may be assured we shall not have any further trouble about them." If the Privy Council had thought the petition had merit, it would have appointed a committee to study it. Instead, it concluded that the Pennsylvania Assembly had not given "any good reason for their request" and that it "prayed for a thing not in the king's power to grant nor in the least in his will."

Franklin knew enough about London politics to realize that the council's swift pronouncement dealt a staggering blow to his campaign. He said nothing in letters to friends at home about the decision. Instead, they learned of it from the newspapers, where Thomas Penn's remarks to his nephew were printed. This news "has struck our friends with the utmost consternation," Galloway said. "And indeed I am not a little alarmed at the consequences." Galloway, as leader of the faction in Franklin's absence, had been put in an embarrassing position. "I have been obliged to give many extracts of your letter to me," to convince colleagues they had not been misled about the petition's certain success, he told Franklin, adding peremptorily: "You will therefore be pleased to inform me in what state the petitions are before his Majesty's Council by the earliest opportunity, that I may be enabled to satisfy the people who rely on us, with certainty." When Franklin got around to it, he sent back a blithe reply: The petition had only temporarily been laid aside; it remained "ready to be proceeded on, as soon as these other affairs are out of hand."

5

The "other affairs" revolved around the Stamp Act. Repeal would calm the American storm, but Franklin saw little chance of the government backing a proposal that would "be deemed a tacit giving up the sovereignty of Parliament." The best to hope for was a three-year suspension of the act, which would give the government time to work out the constitutional problems with America. He thought representation of the colonies in Parliament would resolve the crisis. If the colonies refused to accept such a solution—"they are contented with their own little legislatures," he admitted—then he favored *"compelling* the Americans . . . to submit to an union [and] send representatives hither."

But before any solution could be proposed tempers had to be restored on both sides of the water. To be a useful plenipotentiary in this business, Franklin had first to ingratiate himself with the new ministry. He published a paragraph from one of his letters to America, the opening line of which—"Let us make as good a night of it as we can"—let the government know he had urged his countrymen to accept the Stamp Act. The scene set, he then visited the newly appointed president of the Board of Trade, Lord Dartmouth. He told Dartmouth that any attempt to enforce the Stamp Act would end "creating a deep-rooted aversion between the two countries, and laying the foundation of a future total separation." He predicted that the Stamp Act Congress would send a moderate and respectful address to the crown and urged that it be received with goodwill. Dartmouth grumbled that the Congress was "an irregular meeting, unauthorized by any American constitution." Franklin agreed but said he "hoped government here would not be too nice on that head; that the mode was indeed new, but to the people it seemed necessary, their separate petitions last year being rejected." Dartmouth listened attentively, and when Franklin rose to leave "he thanked me so politely for the visit, and desired to see me often." Four days later Franklin dined with Lord Rockingham, the new first lord of the Treasury, and doubtless after dinner while the port was being passed he repeated much of what Lord Dartmouth heard.

By mid-December London knew that November 1, the day set for the Stamp Act to go into operation, had come and gone without a single stamp or sheet of stamped paper being sold anywhere in America. "A stop is put to our commerce and our courts of justice is shut up," Franklin heard from home. "Our harbors are filled with vessels, but none of them . . . dare move, because neither the governor or collector will clear them out, and if they would the men of war threaten to seize them as forfeited for want of papers agreeable to the laws of trade." Pressure on the government to use troops to exact obedience from the "rebels" increased. Partly to inform the British public what the controversy was all about but more to defend his countrymen from slanderous attacks, Franklin now took to the press. In one month he published thirteen essays, several of them among the most heated he ever wrote. The attacks upon Americans simply because they were Americans infuriated him. "The gentle terms of *republican race, mixed rabble of Scotch, Irish, and foreign vagabonds, descendants of convicts, ungrateful rebels, etc.* are some of the sweet flowers of English rhetoric, with which our colonists have of late been regaled," he remarked angrily in an early piece. "Give me leave, Master JOHN BULL, to remind you that . . . you have mixed with your many virtues, a pride, a haughtiness, and an insolent contempt for all but yourself, that, I am afraid, will, if not abated, procure you one day or other a handsome drubbing. Besides your rudeness to foreigners, you are far from being civil even to your own family."

He warned those who called for stern repressive measures that a civil war lasting at least three years, costing millions of pounds, and tying up at least fifty thousand soldiers would result. In the end, with half the people killed and the rest driven over the mountains, the American colonies would be ruined as a market for British manufactures. The woolen industry was already suffering from the Americans' boycott, Franklin gloated with more hope than reason. "They resolved last spring to eat no more lamb; and not a joint of lamb has since been seen on any of their tables, throughout a country of 1500 miles extent, but the sweet little creatures are all alive to this day, with the prettiest fleeces on their backs imaginable."

Parliament was scheduled to convene on 14 January 1766. As members arrived in town early in the month Franklin went round to talk with them. "The assiduity of our friend Dr. Franklin is really astonishing,"

Strahan wrote Hall, hoping his praise would appear in the *Gazette* and help refurbish Franklin's reputation at home. "He is forever with one member of Parliament or another (most of whom by the bye seem to have been deplorably ignorant with regard to the nature and consequence of the colonies) endeavoring to impress them: first, with the importance of the present dispute; then to state the case clearly and fully, stripping it of everything foreign to the main point; and lastly, to answer objections arising either from a total ignorance, a partial knowledge, or a wrong conception of the matter. To enforce this repeatedly, and with propriety, in the manner he has done these last two months, I assure you is no easy task."

The day Parliament convened a man was hired to stand at the door of the House of Commons and pass out cards upon which was printed a cartoon devised by Franklin. It showed a distraught and dismembered Britannia leaning against a large globe. The reverse side explained the cartoon.

Great Britain is supposed to have been placed upon the globe; but the COLONIES (that is, her limbs) being severed from her, she is seen lifting her eyes and mangled stumps to heaven; her shield, which she is unable to wield, lies useless by her side; her lance has pierced New England; the laurel branch has fallen from the hand of Pennsylvania; the English oak has lost its head, and stands a bare trunk, with a few withered branches; briars and thorns are on the ground beneath it; the British ships have brooms at their topmasts' heads, denoting their being on sale; and BRITANNIA herself is seen sliding off the world (no longer able to hold its balance) her fragments overspread with the label, DATE OBOLUM BELLISARIO [Give a penny to Belisarius].

Though colonial agents were barred from the session Franklin in some way managed that day to get a seat in the gallery of the House, and there he heard William Pitt in a ringing speech excoriate the government for its treatment of the American colonies. "Mr. Pitt spoke some time before one could divine on which side of the question relating to America he would be; but beginning first to mention the Stamp Act by the soft term of that *unhappy* act, he went on, and every time he had occasion to mention it, it was by a term still stronger, as *unconstitutional, unjust, oppressive,* etc., till he finally declared in express terms that the British Parliament had in his opinion *no right* to raise internal taxes in America, tho' it had to regulate their commerce and even restrain their *manufactures.*" But even after listening to Pitt, Franklin still thought the Stamp Act stood little chance of outright repeal.

6

Franklin remained convinced through December and early January that the government needed a face-saving device before it would propose repeal of the Stamp Act to Parliament. To that end he urged on the Rockingham ministry the continental loan office he had offered Grenville. They "took a fancy to it," he said, "and a good deal of pains in considering it, had frequent conferences with me upon it, and really strengthened one another and their friends in the resolution of repealing the Stamp Act, on a supposition that by this plan of a loan office they could raise a greater sum with more satisfaction to the people." The ministry may have listened to the plan, but despite what Franklin said no evidence exists that they seriously considered it. A committee of "London Merchants trading to America"—formed by Barlow Trecothick, a Boston-reared merchant who now lived in London and specialized in American trade—first cracked open the door to repeal. The committee sent a circular letter to merchants throughout England asking them to flood Parliament with pro-repeal petitions. The letter, Edmund Burke said, was "the principal instrument in the happy repeal of the Stamp Act."

The petitions had piled up when the House of Commons on 28 January 1766 opened debate on the "American problem" behind closed doors. The majority of members agreed early on that Parliament had a "legal right" to pass binding laws on the colonies "in all cases whatsoever." They agreed, too, that the distinction supposedly raised in the colonies between internal and external taxes had no basis in fact. If we have the right to bind them by one kind of tax, said a ministerial spokesman, "we have a right to bind them in all." No one argued when Grenville held the stamp duty to be reasonable—"it is two or three times lower than in England"—nor when he wished it "had more faults than it had so that it might be repealed rather from the yielding to reason than to violence." Only when he insisted that the Stamp Act must be imposed on the colonies by force did heads shake. Charles Townshend had voted for the act but now spoke for repeal. He thought that given British military strength in America it would be impossible to make the colonies submit. "All colonies have their date of independence," warned Isaac Barré, an early and eloquent opponent of the act. "If we act injudiciously, this point may be reached in the life of many of the members of this House." He raised the specter of another international war if a military solution were attempted. Both the French and Spanish will think you "bold and wrongheaded."

A former officer in Grenville's ministry summed up the dilemma the Stamp Act presented Parliament. "If we do not repeal it, the disorder in America, the distress of our manufactures at home" will continue. "If we do repeal it, no minister will venture to tax them again. The Americans will never submit when they see resistance is the best argument for relief, and you will have the same argument urged not against this law alone but against every other which they do not perfectly approve of." To assert the right to tax then not to exercise it leaves Parliament "with no right at all." But Barré's warning forced him to end on a tentative note: "Whether this is a proper time for taxing America, supposing the right established, depends on the relative ability of this country and of America."

It was clear when debate ended at midnight on February 7 that the House would vote for repeal, but before voting members agreed to examine a panel of witness on the crisis. Barlow Trecothick testified on February 11 for four hours. Resistance to the Stamp Act, he said, had brought the whole of American trade—amounting to between two and three million pounds sterling—to a standstill, and meanwhile an equal if not larger amount of American debts to British merchants went unpaid. The next day the House heard from another witness about the situation in New York, then on February 13 it listened to two gentlemen from Virginia. All three emphasized that "the people to a man are against the act and think it unjust," that they distinguished between internal and external taxes, that it would require a large force to subdue them. Virginia alone had fifty-two thousand men in its militia who had "behaved very brave in action."

Franklin testified in the afternoon of the thirteenth. Over half the 174 questions thrown at him during his three hours before the bar came from the opposition led by Grenville. After several friendly questions had put Franklin at ease, Grenville rose:

Q: Do you think it right that America should be protected by this country and pay no part of the expense?

A: That is not the case. The colonies raised, clothed and paid, during the last war, near 25,000 men, and spent many millions.

Q: Were you not reimbursed by Parliament?

A: We were only reimbursed what, in your opinion, we had advanced beyond our proportion, or beyond what might reasonably be expected from us; and it was a very small part of what we spent. Pennsylvania, in particular, disbursed about 500,000 pounds, and the reimbursements, in the whole, did not exceed 60,000 pounds.

Q: You have said that you pay heavy taxes in Pennsylvania; what do they amount to in the pound?

A: The tax on all estates, real and personal, is eighteen pence in the pound, fully rated; and the tax on the profits of trades and professions, with other taxes, do, I suppose, make full half a crown in the pound.

All Franklin's figures were suspect, but Grenville chose not to question them. Later Grenville asked about the post office, a profit-making operation for the crown. He may have known that sometime earlier Americans had objected to it on the ground that "the Parliament could not levy any tax (for so they call the rates of postage) here without the consent of the General Assembly." But Franklin insisted that a postage stamp could not be a tax—"it is merely a quantum merit for a service done; no person is compellable to pay the money, if he does not choose to receive the service." When Grenville persisted that some people regarded the revised postal regulations of the previous year a tax, Franklin dodged a direct answer, saying only that the rates had been reduced and no one could "consider such an abatement as a tax."

A number of members pressed Franklin to distinguish between internal and external taxes. He elaborated on the point made about the post office—only what one is compelled to pay can be called a tax.

An external tax is a duty laid on commodities imported; that duty is added to the first cost and other charges on the commodity, and when it is offered to sale, makes a part of the price. If the people do not like it at that price, they refuse it; they are not obliged to pay it. But an internal tax is forced from the people without their consent, if not laid by their own representatives. The Stamp Act says, we shall have no commerce, make no exchange of property with each other, neither purchase nor grant, nor recover debts; we shall neither marry, nor make our wills, unless we pay such and such a sum, and thus it is intended to extort our money from us, or ruin us by the consequences of refusing to pay it.

When someone asked how Franklin would take an external tax "laid on the necessaries of life imported into your colony," the answer was: "I do not know a single article imported into the northern colonies, but what they can either do without or make themselves." What about wool to make cloth? America produces "very fine and good" wool in abundance, he said, though only a bit over a year ago he had confessed "as to clothing ourselves with our own wool, 'tis impossible." No one asked how the colonies would deal with a tax on tea.

Only occasionally did a member force Franklin to retract an exaggeration. When he said in regard to the need of British troops to protect the colonies from the Indians, "there is not the least occasion for it; they are very able to defend themselves," no one raised a doubt. But when he said only three hundred British regulars fought the French and Indians in Pennsylvania during the last war, Grenville stepped in. Only three hundred? Franklin qualified the statement and ended lamely with "I am not certain, but I think so." Charles Townshend toward the end of the interrogation forced him into an exchange he would later use to embarrass Franklin:

Q: Have you not seen the resolutions of the Massachusetts Bay Assembly?

A: I have.

Q: Do they not say, that neither external nor internal taxes can be laid on them by Parliament?

A: I don't know that they do; I believe not. [Townshend was right, Franklin wrong.]

Q: If the same colony should say neither tax nor imposition could be laid, does not that province hold the power of Parliament can hold neither?

A: I suppose that by the word imposition, they do not intend to express duties to be laid on goods imported, as regulations of commerce.

Franklin's missteps in the long examination should not obscure the overall adroitness of his performance, particularly when he dealt with the central issue—Parliament's right to legislate for the colonies in all matters. "I think the resolutions of right will give them very little concern, if they are never attempted to be carried into practice," he said at one point. "The colonies will probably consider themselves in the same situation, in that respect, with Ireland; they know you claim the same right with regard to Ireland, but you never exercise it. And they may believe you never will exercise it in the colonies, any more than in Ireland, unless on some very extraordinary occasion."

In the days that followed Franklin's examination the House continued its wordy debate, which one member summed up in a sentence— "We have only a choice of political evils, and the repeal of this act seems upon the whole liable to the least objection." On February 22, at 1:30 A.M. the House voted 275 to 167 to repeal the Stamp Act. (Earlier in secret

session the House had divided 274 to 134 in what could be taken as a test
vote on repeal of the Stamp Act. All but one of the thirty-four additional
members present for the final vote had joined the opposition to repeal,
indicating that none of the witnesses, including Franklin, had influenced
the final decision.) A few days later, after the House of Lords had approved repeal, the bill was sent to the king with another—the Declara-
tory Act—that declared Parliament had the right to make laws to bind
the people of America "in all cases whatsoever." The king signed both
bills into law on March 8.

7

Some of the sharpest questions aimed at Franklin during the examination had come from Robert Nugent. Two years later the two men met
again at court. "He gave me a great deal of flummery," Franklin recalled;
"saying that though at my examination I answered some of his questions
a little pertly, yet he liked me from that day, for the spirit I showed in
defense of my country." Franklin's testimony did not change the vote of
Nugent—he opposed repeal—nor for all the admiration it evoked apparently that of any member. But the examination had a lasting effect—it
refurbished Franklin's reputation at home.

The campaign to improve Franklin's image began even before he had
testified. Two weeks before his appearance, Professor Cecil Currey has
discovered, someone in London sent a dispatch to the *Gazette* to the effect
that "Our worthy friend Dr. Franklin, has gained immortal honor by his
behavior at the bar of the House. The answerer was always found equal
if not superior to the judgment of the questioner."

William Strahan served as a willing foil in promoting Franklin's
brilliance before the bar. "To this examination, more than to anything
else, you are indebted to the *speedy* and *total* repeal of this odious law,"
he wrote with pardonable exaggeration to David Hall, expecting his
remarks to appear in the *Gazette*, as they did. "The Marquis of Rockingham told a friend of mine a few days later, that he never knew truth make
so great a progress in so very short a time. From that very day, the *repeal*
was generally and absolutely determined, all that passed afterwards being
only mere formality. . . ." Before Franklin testified Strahan had arranged
with the clerk of the House for a transcription of the testimony, which
he sent to Hall in April to have published. Before the year was out it had
been translated into French and German and reprinted throughout
America as well as in London.

By the end of May the campaign had taken effect. "Your enemies at last began to be ashamed of their base insinuations and to acknowledge that the colonies are under obligations to you," Charles Thomson reported. The publication of the *Examination* had an even greater effect. It not only cleared the cloud from his reputation in Pennsylvania but changed him from being the spokesman for a single colony into spokesman for all America.

CHAPTER

22

"WE MUST USE PATIENCE"

DURING THE DEBATE over repeal of the Stamp Act, Parliament also talked about revising the cumbersome body of laws regulating American trade that had accumulated in the past century. Discussion continued after repeal and Franklin, though unwell all winter, took no holiday. At the end of March he drafted a bill that would repeal the Currency Act of 1764 and permit the colonies to issue paper money as legal tender. He doubted anything would come of his effort, "the ministry being inclined to consider the affair of paper money more extensively and therefore to leave it to another year."

Much of his time went to putting out brush fires. When the Admiralty announced a plan to tighten up its American operations and to ask Parliament for the right to impress American citizens into the royal navy, Franklin hastened to confer with Lord Egmont, head of the Admiralty Board. He told Egmont that it appeared "a terrible thing to establish such violence by a law, however necessary it may be in some cases; and I conceived it a power not fit to be given the officers of the navy, who might use it greatly to the oppression and injury of particular colonies." His lordship listened and when Franklin finished said "he was satisfied with my reasons, and the power of impressing should be omitted." Days later when Parliament proposed extending to Scotland the right to export felons to America, Franklin drafted a petition opposing this outrage. "Easing one part of the British dominions of their felons by burthening another part with the same felons, cannot increase the common happiness of his Majesty's subjects," he said. But if Parliament must have its way, then let "the said extension be carried farther, and the plantations be also by an equitable clause in the same bill permitted to transport their felons to Scotland."

Franklin deluded neither himself nor the Assembly at home that much would come of this busy work. "The frequent changes that have happened, and the general opinion even among the ministers themselves, that more will happen, disposes people generally to lie awhile upon their oars; till the ministry have so established themselves, as that they can afford attention to affairs, which not being of national concern they think may well be postponed. And indeed 'tis a kind of labor in vain to attempt making impressions on such moveable materials; 'tis like writing on the sands in a windy day."

Through the spring of 1766 Franklin moved about the city largely on nerve. Sometime after mid-May he became "very ill," but with what he did not specify. As always when unwell, he dreamed of a trip. In mid-June, though still "feeble," he and Dr. Pringle—now Sir John, for he had only a few days earlier been knighted—set out for Bad Pyrmont in Germany to take the waters there. ("Dr. Franklin needs very much" this trip, a worried Strahan reported, "as he has by no means recovered his late fatigue, which was very considerable indeed, both in body and mind.") Franklin preferred exercise to nostrums for mending a worn body, but out of deference to Pringle he "drank the waters" for two weeks, then the pair moved on to Hanover, an easy journey of thirty-five miles. Their fame traveled before them. Johann Friedrich Hartmann, head of the royal hospital in Hanover and an amateur electrician, greeted them as royal visitors. Hartmann's electrical experiments were hardly, as he put it, "worthy of the notice of so great and so learned a man" as Franklin, but his guest relieved embarrassment with queries about a gadget called a pulse-glass, a small tube half filled with water that boiled from the heat of any hand that held it. Hartmann gave it as a present to carry back to London. A few days later in Göttingen Franklin was inducted into the Royal Academy there—Pringle was already a member—and during the two-day visit he spent several hours being interrogated by a professor in the university. His remarks, later published in Germany, revealed the astonishing breadth and depth of Franklin's knowledge of America. Seemingly no detail had escaped him in travels up and down the coast. His information about New England included the fact that from "the membranes of the cod . . . a very good isinglass is made, for which formerly much money was paid to Russia." He described precisely the buffalo that roamed the back parts of Pennsylvania—"rather larger and stronger than ordinary cattle . . . and they have on back and shoulders a fine wool, which they shed yearly, about fifteen pounds from each buffalo"—and added apparently from firsthand experience that "their flesh is quite palatable." Though a city man, he judged oxen more useful than horses, "for they can be used for twelve years, and then slaughtered or sold." Hour after hour Franklin poured out facts and opinions about America, and though he spoke to an audience of one the performance equaled if not surpassed that before the House of Commons a few months earlier.

Word of Franklin's presence in Göttingen impelled the prince of Thuringia to send a messenger conveying a desire "to be granted the chance of a conversation with you." The prince of another state pleaded to learn how to install lightning rods on the buildings of his estate. But the travelers missed these emissaries, having moved on to Cassel, from there to Frankfort, Mainz, and Trier, and then down the Rhine to Cologne.

They arrived back in England in mid-August to find that the Rockingham ministry had fallen two weeks earlier. Pitt, now the Earl of Chatham, would direct the new ministry from the House of Lords. His chief lieutenants in the Commons, and the two most responsible for American affairs, would be the Earl of Shelburne, the new secretary of state for the southern department, and Charles Townshend, now chancellor of the Exchequer. Lord Hillsborough was the new president of the Board of Trade. Franklin regarded all three as generally friendly toward America and hoped "the farther points we would obtain relating to our commerce and currency may in the next session of Parliament meet with a favorable attention."

Hopes that seemed reasonable in August 1766 eroded during the ensuing year. "Here public affairs are in great disorder," Franklin remarked in April 1767. "We must use patience." In May he had "only time to say things continue here in the same uncertain state." In August "the confusion among our great men still continues as great as ever, and a melancholy thing it is to consider." A strong current of opposition against America, led by the still influential Grenville, forced the ministry to proceed cautiously. The absence of Chatham, "almost totally disabled by perpetual gout, and for some time past with fevers," contributed to the leaders' indecisiveness. "There is at present no access to him," Franklin said at the end of Chatham's first year in office; "he is said to be not capable of receiving any more than of giving advice. But still there is such a deference paid to him that much business is delayed on his account, that so when entered on it may have the strength of his concurrence or not be liable to his reprehension if he should recover his ability and activity." Through the year men shifted in and out of the ministry or from one post to another—"more changes talked of and daily expected," Franklin wrote one month but could have written at almost any time during the year— but three faces remained always present: those of Townshend, Hillsborough, and Shelburne.

Of the three Franklin knew only Shelburne well. They had met on Franklin's first trip to England, possibly through William, close to Shelburne in age and a friend of his. (Shelburne, then an ally of Bute, may have had a hand in winning the governorship of New Jersey for William.) Lord Shelburne at thirty was the youngest man in the new ministry. Contemporaries judged him brilliant and also difficult. "He was never satisfied with what anyone did, or even with what he did himself, but altered and changed without end," according to one; "sometimes passionate or unreasonable . . . and at other times offensively flattering," said another. "One of the most mystifying characters of the eighteenth century, a man of undoubtedly great talent in public affairs, he was also one of the most despised men of his time," a modern scholar has remarked. "There were reasons for this," another has added: "his personality—a mixture of hauteur and shyness; his self-conscious intellectuality; his claim to the confidence of the inscrutable Chatham; and, not the least of the reasons, his rapid swing in allegiance from Henry Fox, to the Earl of Bute, and then to William Pitt in the political melee of 1762–1763." Something of a father-son relationship may have existed between him and Franklin, who presented a genial contrast to the tyrannical father Shelburne had endured. In time such friends of Franklin as Joseph Priestley and Richard Price became his friends.

Franklin used the friendship relentlessly for his own interests and those of Pennsylvania and America. Shortly after the return from Germany he came round to talk about Pennsylvania's petition to the king. Shelburne, though married to the niece of Thomas Penn's wife, "was pleased to assure me," Franklin reported to the Assembly, "that he was of opinion Mr. Penn ought to part with the government voluntarily, and said he had often told him so." Indeed, a few weeks after the visit, Shelburne wrote Penn saying that the king, with an eye to purchasing the colony, wanted a full accounting of revenues and assets. (The Penns rendered accounts but refused to listen to any offers for their now profitable province.) In the months that followed Franklin used his goodwill with the minister to promote two other projects—one, the creation of western settlements in America under the aegis of the Illinois Company; the other, supplanting the Currency Act of 1764 with one that would allow the colonies to issue paper money as legal tender.

2

Toward the end of the interview with the professor at Göttingen, Franklin had remarked on whether the colonies would someday declare their independence. No, he said. "There are many disputes between them as to their borders, rivers, trade, etc. If the colonies were entirely independent, they would soon be at war with one another. Only the protection of the king and his authority prevent open outbreaks. This jealousy increases with the growth of the colonies."

Franklin believed what he said. But the realist within him constantly jarred with the visionary, and soon after returning from Germany he remarked: "America, an immense territory, favored by nature with all advantages of climate, soil, great navigable rivers and lakes, etc., must become a great country, populous and mighty; and will in a less time than is generally conceived be able to shake off any shackles that may be imposed on her, and perhaps place them on the imposers."

The certainty that America *must* become a great country hinged for Franklin on the creation of new colonies west of the Appalachian Mountains. He had preached the message for over a decade and when he intoned "what a glorious thing it would be," to George Whitefield it was one evangelist seeking to inspire another. The personal gains to be expected from America's spread westward went unmentioned in these sermons, but Franklin never lost sight of his golden rule—what benefited the empire would benefit him. Any promoter of western colonies could count on great profits from the sale of land to settlers. Then there would be the godlike satisfaction of creating a miniature nation out of a wilderness. What greater monument could a man erect to himself?

William Franklin rekindled his father's interest in western settlement during the debate over repeal of the Stamp Act. The Indian trader George Croghan, back from a tour of the country that lay between the Illinois and Mississippi rivers, had "obtained full permission from the several nations in that quarter for the English to enter their country," William reported. The land lay open to settlement. William sent over a plan he had drawn up—"Reasons and Proposals for Establishing a British Colony at the Illinois"—and said he had joined with Croghan, Sir William Johnson, and several Philadelphia friends to create the Illinois Company. Johnson, superintendent of Indian affairs, promised to use his considerable influence to promote the company with superiors in London. "It is proposed that the company shall consist of twelve now in

America, and if you like the proposals, you will be at liberty to add yourself, and such gentlemen of character and fortune in England, as you may think will be most likely to promote the undertaking," William wrote.

Franklin thought the plan "well drawn" and that "Sir William's approbation will go a great way in recommending it, as he is much relied on in all affairs that may have any relation to the Indians." But the scheme faced imposing obstacles. Western settlement had been closed off by the king's proclamation of 1763; that must be wiped from the books. A charter for the company must be obtained from the crown, no easy task when several of the ministers would surely voice opposition. Finally, the "continual changes here" discourage all applications to the ministry, Franklin warned. "I thought the last set well established, but they are broken and gone. The present set are hardly thought to stand very firm, and God only knows whom we are to have next."

But Franklin promised to promote the scheme and promptly visited Lord Shelburne, who laid out objections that could be expected from the ministry. First, the expense. The army had already run up "extraordinary charges" of over thirty thousand pounds just to take possession of the Illinois forts that had been occupied by the French. The Illinois Company would be financed by private individuals, answered Franklin, and thus of "very little expense to the crown." Second, continued Shelburne, the distance of the proposed settlement from the seacoast "would make it of little use to this country, as the expense on the carriage of goods would oblige the people to manufacture for themselves." Third, such a settlement "might lay the foundation of a power in the heart of America which in time might be troublesome to the other colonies, and prejudicial to our government over them." Fourth, "people were wanted both here and in the already settled colonies, so that none could be spared for a new colony."

All sound arguments. Franklin might have replied that nothing could prevent men from being drawn by the magnet of rich, cheap lands waiting to be carved into farms. Why resist the inevitable? Instead, he chose another line more appealing to an imperial officer—the settlement of America's heartland would give the crown a body of men "there which on occasion of a future war, might easily be poured down the Mississippi upon the lower country, and into the Bay of Mexico, to be used against Cuba, or Mexico itself." Franklin did not think small.

Nor did he play fair in this game of large stakes. He kept secret from Shelburne that a key adviser, Sir William Johnson, held shares in the Illinois Company. Shelburne must have known his friend Richard Jack-

son was also Franklin's friend. He could hardly expect a disinterested
opinion on the Illinois Company from Jackson, who now served as counsel for the Board of Trade, but he asked for one anyway. Jackson said, "I
have no doubt of its practicality," and that recommendation pleased
Franklin—"from him [it] appears less to be suspected of some American
bias." In the months ahead Shelburne acted as if he were Franklin's dupe.
In June 1767 he told Franklin he "highly approved" of the Illinois Company, in August that he saw "no obstacle" except the Board of Trade, and
in October he recommended to the board the creation of two western
colonies and, to cut down expenses, the return of Indian affairs to the
colonies. His plan—or Franklin's—offered a simplistic solution to complex problems. The Indians would not welcome the new settlements.
The colonies were no more capable now than earlier to deal wisely and
jointly with the Indians. But Franklin was a persuasive man. Just as
thirteen years ago he had cajoled his colleagues at Albany into approving
his Plan of Union, so he had with equal skill swung Lord Shelburne to
his side. Now only the Board of Trade stood between him and realization
of his dream.

3

In politics, Franklin once said, "chance has its share in many of the
determinations, so that the play is more like tric trac with a box of dice."
The campaign to wipe the Currency Act off the books verified the observation. He conducted it shrewdly and success seemed always to hover just
ahead. But in the end the dice rolled against him.

The Currency Act of 1764 forbade colonies to issue paper money as
legal tender. Hard money had always been in short supply in the colonies. Lack of an abundant legal currency stifled trade, and the Pennsylvania Assembly instructed Franklin after the Stamp Act repeal to make
the Currency Act his next target. Working with other colonial agents and
with the revived committee of merchants who specialized in American
trade, Franklin began again buttonholing members of the House of Commons. He drafted a speech against the act for the Duke of Grafton, the
indolent first lord of the Treasury, to deliver in the House of Lords.
Shelburne promised to promote repeal "to the utmost of his power," and
so, too, did Charles Townshend, but Townshend said the Board of Trade
must support the cause before he would ask the Commons to act.

There was the rub. The board had drafted the Currency Act when
Hillsborough headed it. It must confess it had erred before the ministry

would ask Parliament for repeal. Franklin drafted an impressive point-by-point refutation of the board's arguments for the act. The essay convinced the committee of merchants, up to then a divided body, that repeal was "absolutely necessary" and it petitioned the board to let the colonies issue paper money as legal tender. The arguments also impressed Lord Clare, current president of the board, and he agreed to push for repeal. Franklin admitted "the rest of the Board are still strong against it," but he still hoped for repeal before Parliament adjourned in July.

Suddenly storm clouds blanketed a blue sky. In March, London learned that the Massachusetts legislature had arrogantly pardoned, instead of punishing, all involved in the Stamp Act riots. Meanwhile New York had flouted the act that called for billeting troops in private houses, which Franklin had helped amend, and the merchants of that colony had sent Parliament a rude petition complaining of restraints imposed upon their trade. Instead of gratitude for repeal of the Stamp Act, Americans appeared surly as ever. Goodwill toward the colonies evaporated and a cloud of anti-American sentiment whipped up by Grenville "with much art and industry" filled the air. Grenville raised feeling "so high against America in general," Franklin reported home, "that our friends thought it not prudent to push the matter earlier than should be necessary to have a chance of getting it through this session." Shelburne reneged on his promise to pressure the Board of Trade for repeal.

Franklin again tried to calm the storm through the press, with one hand defending his countrymen in British journals, with the other warning Americans their obstreperousness would lead to repression. "The word *rebellion* was frequently used" he said of a recent parliamentary debate on American affairs. Friends and foes alike talk of measures "effectually to enforce the authority of Parliament, and to carry it into actual execution," he wrote. "It is also reported, and I fear the report is true, that a project is on foot, to render all the governors and magistrates in America independent of the annual support they receive of their several assemblies." The mysterious project was a set of "external" taxes devised by Charles Townshend, chancellor of the Exchequer.

4

Historians, at a safe distance from his wit and wrath, have called him "Champagne Charlie," because he gave one of his greatest speeches when supposedly half drunk on the wine. Contemporaries never dared to refer thus lightly to Charles Townshend, one of the most formidable politicians of his time, the only man William Pitt was jealous of because "his abilities were of the same kind, and so nearly equal to his own." Few could equal the brilliance of his conversation, yet he was a friendless man who showed affection for no one outside his family. "His abilities were deemed wonderful and he was said to have art enough to disguise anything except his prodigious vanity."

Few scholars have kind words for him. Even his friendly biographer Sir Lewis Namier judges his American policy as oppressive. "In the personalized terms in which the American problem was usually discussed, he, who had been the oppressed son, now became the heavy father. There was an interaction between his emotional life and his political ideas, and the confusion of the times enabled him to force his fantasies on to reality." Since 1753 he had steadfastly insisted Americans must be taxed to pay for running their part of the empire, but he wished neither to oppress nor punish the colonies. His schemes were moderate compared to those of Lord Shelburne, the supposed friend of America, who when he heard New York refused to let troops be billeted in private homes wanted to impose a military governorship and demanded an act that would make it "high treason to refuse to obey or execute any laws or statutes" passed by Parliament. Shelburne did not think Townshend's proposed duties either harsh or oppressive, only insufficient; he would have preferred to levy quitrents on American land.

During the interrogation before the House, Townshend had forced from Franklin a clarification between internal and external taxes. Early in 1767 before introducing his proposed duties Townshend told the House he thought the distinction between internal and external taxes "perfect nonsense," but he would accept it to please the colonies. All wings of American opinion agreed with Townshend—even Thomas Hutchinson and Samuel Adams united on this point—but Franklin held to the distinction. "The colonies submit to pay all external taxes laid on them by way of duty on merchandise imported into their country, and never disputed the authority of Parliament to lay such duties," he said in April 1767. But while the distinction exists it "seems to be immaterial," Franklin continued, speaking in the guise of an Englishman. If Americans "are willing to pay *external* though not *internal* taxes, and we say they are the same, 'tis then the same thing to us, provided we get the same money from them, as much as they ought or are able to pay, and we may let them please themselves with their futile distinction as long as they think proper." Townshend could not have put the thought better.

Townshend introduced his revenue measure to the Commons in mid-May, after the brilliant speech that won him the nickname "Champagne

Charlie" and in which he had warned "the House to beware lest the
provinces engage in a common cause," and that "should their disobedi-
ence return, the authority of Parliament had been weakened; and unless
supported with spirit and dignity, must be destroyed." He would levy
duties on glass, chinaware, paper, pasteboard, painters' colors, and tea.
(Earlier he obligingly removed salt from the list when pressured by the
colonial agents.) Few Americans would be able to follow Franklin's advice—"If I do not like it, at that price, I refuse it"—for most were necessi-
ties that had to be imported from England.

Grenville ridiculed the duties; they would bring in trifling amounts.
"I'll tell the honorable gentleman of a revenue that will produce something valuable in America," he told Townshend. "Make paper money for
the colonies, issue it upon loan there; take the interest and apply it as you
think proper." Franklin must have blanched to see resurrected the substitute he had advanced for the Stamp Act. He had heard from Galloway
that it would rouse "great clamors" and must have read by now the
doggerel on it in a New York newspaper:

> You'll find it another *Stamp Act* in disguise
> So I warn you to shun it, if freedom you prize.

Fortunately, Grenville sat down without revealing Franklin as the author of the scheme. Townshend, momentarily startled, recovered
quickly. Grenville had stolen the plan from him. He "had intended to
make it with the rest, but it had slipped his memory." He assured the
House that "a bill was prepared for the purpose and would soon be laid
before them." But on June 29 the Commons passed Townshend's list of
duties and a short while later adjourned without hearing any more from
Townshend about *his* currency scheme for America.

At no time did Franklin worry about the reception of the new duties.
He did not consider them taxes. His letters home spoke of the imposition
of taxes as a danger that lay in the future. "The idea of an American tax
is very pleasing to the landed men," he said in one letter written after
Parliament adjourned. "Every step is taking to render the taxing of
America a popular measure." He still held so strongly to the rightness
of his distinction between internal and external taxes that he had his
examination before the Commons republished and boasted that it "has
had a great run." He still failed to sense, even after the nearly disastrous
experience with the Stamp Act, how far he jogged behind American
opinion.

CHAPTER

23

"I AM OLD, HEAVY
AND GROW A LITTLE INDOLENT"

FROM 1766 ON Franklin talked often of returning home, then in a few weeks would change his mind, friends in England having persuaded him that for the good of America he ought to stay for one more session of Parliament. Confusion about where "home" lay contributed to his indecision. He thought about purchasing land in Northamptonshire that had been owned by his grandfather. "However, I shall not do it unless I determine to remain in England," he told his sister, "which I have not yet done."

Ties with America weakened with each passing month. In January 1767 the eighteen-year partnership with David Hall ended. Though Hall still professed affection for Franklin, he had since the Stamp Act not published "a single syllable either in approbation or disapprobation of the cause he was engaged in, or the part he took in it." Joseph Galloway and Thomas Wharton, with William Franklin's blessing, subsidized a new printer in town, William Goddard, who less than a month after the Franklin-Hall partnership ended put out the first issue of the competing *Pennsylvania Chronicle*. Franklin ceased to correspond with Hall but otherwise gave no sign of pique.

A more serious matter—the annual loss of between four and six hundred pounds' income from the partnership—for a time went unmentioned. Investments in lots and houses in Philadelphia together with the income from the post office were more than enough to keep his wife and family there in comfort. Investments in England plus the expense account from the Pennsylvania Assembly paid the bills in London. Though he said "my expenses amaze me," and that "I live here as frugally as possible not to be destitute of the comforts of life, making no dinners for anybody, and contenting myself with a single dish when I dine at home," he did little to economize. He continued to order best beer at thirty shillings a barrel, and the annual consumption of table beer at ten shillings a barrel amounted to about thirty-four barrels. When he heard from Deborah that "Billy don't like the blue room at all" in the new house, he sent detailed instructions how to redecorate the room.

The first time he worried aloud about money came as a reaction to a letter from Deborah received in June. "I am obliged to be father and mother," she remarked hesitantly, then told of Sally, aged twenty-four, being courted by a man of thirty named Richard Bache. "I hope I act to your satisfaction," she said. "I do according to my best judgment." From this momentous news she glided into other matters. Billy had been challenged to a duel by an affronted gentleman. Sally "was very much scared" and would not let him return to Burlington without her. "So you see this daughter of ours is a mere champion, and thinks she is to take care of us," said Deborah. "Her brother and she is very happy together indeed, but I long to see her back again, as I could not live above another day without her. . . . O, that you was at home." Franklin, who knew where the news lay in his wife's letter, ignored in his reply the challenge to his son, of which nothing came, and focused on Sally's impending marriage. "I would only advise that you do not make an expensive feasting wedding, but conduct everything with frugality and economy, which our circumstances really now require to be observed in all our expenses."

The more Franklin heard about the courtship the less he liked it. William reported Bache not "worth anything if all his debts were paid. In short, that he is a mere fortune hunter, who wants to better his circumstances [by] marrying into a family that will support him." Franklin opposed the marriage, but Sally, he remarked, "pleased herself and her mother" by marrying Bache on 20 October 1767. For months afterward he refused to answer Bache's letters, since "I could say nothing agreeable." Only after time "made me easier" did he welcome the gentleman into his family.

Deborah had always been strong-willed but now William, too, who almost never crossed his father, began to speak up. "I cannot entirely agree with you as to the expediency of joining the assemblies with the governors in granting the crown lands," he wrote in one letter, then went on to defend the prerogative of the executive, something his father had always fought against. Franklin let the heresy pass unnoticed in his reply.

Outwardly relations with his Philadelphia family remained unchanged. Deborah sent gifts by every ship—boxes of Indian and buckwheat meal, barrels of apples, crates of nuts. Her letters continued long and affectionate—addressed always to her "dear Pappy" or "dearest child"—though of late filled more and more with news about the death of friends. His replies got shorter and shorter, spaced farther and farther apart. He thanked her for the presents and sent some in return. He kept her posted on his health and, occasionally, on small but embarrassing changes, as when he reported, "I have got the clothes and have worn them, but find them too tight for me, and must have the waistcoat let out." (Or, as he put it more bluntly to an English friend, "I am old and heavy, and grow a little indolent.")

As a family man Franklin in 1767 concentrated on the one in Craven Street. He did not like it when Mrs. Stevenson took a long holiday from her housewife's chores. People "become tiresome guests at the end of three days at fartherest," he reprimanded when she extended a visit, not mentioning the plagiarism from Poor Richard. "My advice to you is, to return with the stage tomorrow." Don't, he hastened to add, think we here—Nanny and the cat—need you. "Everything goes smoothly, and the house is very quiet; and very clean, too, without my saying a word about it." Indeed, "I find such a satisfaction in being a little more my own master, going anywhere and doing anything just when and how I please without the advice or control of anybody's wisdom but my own," that I begin "to think I should be still happier if Nanny and the cat would follow their mistress, and leave me to the enjoyment of an empty house, in which I should never be disturbed by questions of whether I intend to dine at home, and what I would have for dinner; [or] by a mewing request to be let in or let out."

Mrs. Stevenson owned the house and Franklin paid room and board, but otherwise he ran the ménage. When close friends like the Strahans asked him out to dine, they included Mrs. Stevenson in the invitation. They inquired not about his health alone, but asked "if you and Mrs. Stevenson are well." When decisions had to be made and reprimands handed out, he handled them. "Your good mama and myself are both of opinion that the Christmas gambols at Bromley last a great deal too long," he wrote the absent Polly. "We expected you three days ago." His marching orders were firm and explicit. "On Monday between two and three you may expect me," he told Polly another time. "But then you will hold yourself ready to set out homewards at six, that we may be in town before night, and have time, after you have seen your mother, to go to Kensington; for you cannot conveniently lodge here, Sally being again ill with a fever."

Polly still lived in the suburbs with her elderly aunt. She turned

twenty-eight in June 1767 but refused to come to Craven Street to celebrate the day. She did not want to be reminded of her age. Franklin in
a string of verses sent as a present called this a foolish view held by those

> Who justly may suppose
> Their outward frame to be their better part
> And therefore grieve that time subjects it to decay.

Polly's place in the Craven Street household had been taken by Sally
Franklin, a niece on the English side of the family. She was thirteen when
her father "brought her to town to see me in the spring, and Mrs. Stevenson persuaded him to leave the child under her care for a little school-
ing and improvement." On school holidays she was joined by Temple
Franklin, the illegitimate son of William Franklin and now nearly six
years old. Strahan had been privy to the child's birth and arranged for
a foster home when William returned to America. When Franklin
learned about the boy on his return to London he took responsibility for
his upbringing. He sent him to a school in nearby Kensington in the
spring of 1767—carefully charging the cost to William—but all holidays
were spent with his grandfather.

Franklin's routine remained much as always, only now the days began
in a new way. "I rise early almost every morning, and sit in my chamber,
without any clothes whatever, half an hour or an hour, according to the
season, either reading or writing. This practice is not in the least painful,
but on the contrary, agreeable; and if I return to bed afterwards, before
I dress myself, as sometimes happens, I make a supplement to my night's
rest, of one or two hours of the most pleasing sleep that can be imagined.
I find no ill consequences whatever resulting from it, and that at least it
does not injure my health, if it does not in fact contribute much to its
preservation."

When well no man accomplished more in a day, but at least twice a
year, "tonic bath" or not, Franklin became seriously ill, usually once in
the winter and once in the summer. In August 1767 he began, on schedule,
"to find a little giddiness in my head, a token that I want the exercise I
have yearly been accustomed to." He planned a short trip to Bath, but
the French chargé d'affaires, abetted by Dr. Pringle, persuaded him to
make a longer one to Paris. The gentleman puzzled Franklin. "He is
extremely curious to inform himself in the affairs of America; pretends
to have a great esteem for me, on account of the abilities shown in my
examination; has desired to have all my political writings, invited me to
dine with him, was very inquisitive, treated me with great civility, makes
me visits, etc. I fancy that intriguing nation would like very well to

meddle on occasion and blow up the coals between Britain and her colonies; but I hope to give them no opportunity."

Nonetheless Franklin decided to vacation in Paris and to accept from the chargé a packet of "letters of recommendation to the Lord knows who." On August 28, with Dr. Pringle as a companion, Franklin set out for a six-week visit. "I am told I shall meet with great respect there."

2

The trip started badly. "All the way to Dover we were furnished with post chaises hung so as to lean forward, the top coming down over one's eyes, like a hood, as if to prevent one's seeing the country, which being one of my great pleasures, I was engaged in perpetual disputes with the innkeepers, hostlers and postillions about getting the straps taken up a hole or two before, and let down as much behind, they insisting that the chaise leaning forward was an ease to the horses, and that the contrary would kill them. I suppose the chaise leaning forward looks to them like a willingness to go forward; and that its hanging back shows a reluctance. They added other reasons that were no reasons at all, and made me, as upon a hundred other occasions, almost wish that mankind had never been endowed with a reasoning faculty, since they know so little how to make use of it, and so often mislead themselves by it; and that they had been furnished with a good sensible instinct instead of it."

The channel crossing offered a diversion. A number of innocent passengers ate a hearty breakfast before sailing. "Doubtless they thought that when they had paid for their breakfast, they had a right to it, and that when they had swallowed it they were sure of it. But they had scarce been out half an hour, before the sea laid claim to it, and they were obliged to deliver it up. So it seems there are uncertainties, even beyond those between the cup and the lip."

Franklin soaked up the sights of Paris with a mind and eye that recorded as precisely as a camera. When it occurred to him "we scarce ever hear of a fire," he "took particular notice of the construction of their houses"—walls of stone, roofs of slate, rooms lined with stucco—and later wrote a detailed account for his friend Samuel Rhoads, the builder of his Philadelphia home. He checked to find why the drinking water tasted better than London's, and found that "tho' from the river, they render [it] as pure as that of the best spring, by filtering it thro' cisterns filled with sand." The hand tremors of many of the people met puzzled him. Dr. Pringle said the excessive use of snuff was the cause—he had cured himself "of a tremor by leaving off snuff"—and Franklin, who "had never snuffed, chewed, or smoked," thought he was right. Another puzzle went unsolved. The crowded theaters stayed cool even on the hottest nights. "They must have some way of changing the air that we are not acquainted with. I shall inquire into it."

In England Franklin's renown among scientists did not carry over into the political world. In Paris all sides of society welcomed him as a great man. He and Pringle were invited to Versailles "and had the honor of being presented to the king; he spoke to both of us very graciously and cheerfully, is a handsome man, has a very lively look, and appears younger than he is." Franklin found Versailles, like much of Paris, "a prodigious mixture of magnificence and negligence, with every kind of elegance except that of cleanliness, and what we call *tidyness.*" Versailles's immense facade presented "shabby brick walls and broken windows not much better than the houses in Durham Yard."

The days passed "like a pleasing dream," spent "in the improving conversation and agreeable society of so many learned and ingenious men." The language, however, gave him trouble; Dr. Pringle had to interpret whenever they were with people who did not speak English. (Franklin never did master French, though he could read it and was eventually able to understand it with ease. He "acknowledged to me that he was wholly inattentive to the grammar," John Adams later said. "His pronunciation, too . . . which he seemed to think pretty well, I soon found was very inaccurate and some gentlemen of high rank afterwards candidly told me that it was so confused that it was scarcely possible to understand him.") Many of those he met became lifelong friends—Dalibard, who had been the first with "the courage to attempt drawing lightning from the clouds," as Franklin told him; Barbeu Dubourg, fluent in English and the future translator of Franklin's works; François Quesnay, the king's physician and leader of the physiocrats, a group of economists who held that the least government was the best. The electricians, most of whom called themselves *franklinistes*, queried him about the lightning rod, and Franklin took time to honor them with a short paper—"Of Lightning, and the Method (Now Used in America) of Securing Buildings and Persons from Its Mischievous Effects."

He also took time to send Polly Stevenson a long, gossipy account of the trip and its refreshing effect upon his mood. "Traveling is one way of lengthening life, at least in appearance. It is but about a fortnight since we left London, but the variety of scenes we have gone through makes it seem equal to six months living in one place. Perhaps I have suffered a greater change, too, in my own person, than I could have done in six years at home. I had not been here six days before my tailor and perrugier [wig maker] had transformed me into a Frenchman. Only think what a figure I make in a little bag-wig and naked ears. They told me I was become twenty years younger and looked very galante; so being in Paris where the mode is to be sacredly followed, I was once very near making love to my friend's wife.

"This letter shall cost you a shilling, and you may think it cheap when you consider that it has cost me at least fifty guineas to get into the situation that enables me to write it. Besides, I might, if I had stayed at home, have won perhaps two shillings of you at cribbage. By the way, now I mention cards, let me tell you that quadrille is quite out of fashion here, and English whisk [whist] all the mode, at Paris and the Court."

Franklin left Paris reluctantly and only because Dr. Pringle had to be back in London to supervise the birth of a new royal child. Plans went awry at Calais, where they were detained for a week "by contrary winds and stormy weather, which was the more mortifying to me," said Franklin, "when I reflected that I might have enjoyed Paris and my friends there all that time, and yet have been as soon at London."

3

"I returned last night from Paris," Franklin wrote his son on October 9, "and just now hear that the Illinois settlement is approved of in the cabinet council, so far as to be referred to the Board of Trade for their opinion, who are to consider it next week." Next week turned into next month, then into months, and still no decision came from the board. Meanwhile Sir William Johnson had negotiated a treaty with the Indians in which they agreed to let the white man settle west of the Appalachian Mountains. He sent the papers to the Board of Trade. When Franklin heard nothing from the board, he asked Shelburne why the treaty had not been confirmed. Shelburne said he had never heard of the treaty, that Franklin should query Lord Clare at the board. Lord Clare had never heard of the treaty. An assistant searched the files and could find nothing concerning such a treaty. Weeks later someone finally found the treaty, but by then Franklin's hopes for the Illinois Company had waned. "The purpose of settling the new colonies seems at present to be dropped," he sighed after a half year's runaround and without quite understanding why. "As to my own sentiments, I am weary of suggesting them to so many different inattentive heads, though I must continue to do it while I stay among them." ("We must use patience" would have been an apt refrain once again.)

Franklin tried not to let the frustrations of public affairs intrude upon the pleasures of private life. After arriving back from Paris he extended the holiday with a round of visits to the country estates of various friends —those of Thomas Pownall, of his old friend Peter Collinson, of Grey Cooper, the secretary of the Treasury. At Cooper's he wrote an essay on smuggling which, though it expressed views long held, obviously was meant to please his host. Franklin had often twitted Mrs. Stevenson's willingness to indulge the practice in small ways and one of his sentences —"Is any lady ashamed to request of a gentleman of her acquaintance, that when he returns from abroad, he would smuggle her home a piece of silk or lace from France or Flanders?"—seemed aimed at her. Though the piece had the tone of a sermon, Franklin could not resist at the end good-humoredly taking a dig at his English audience. "The Americans offend us grievously, when, contrary to our laws, they smuggle goods into their own country: and yet they had no hand in making those laws," he wrote. Such transgressions cannot be justified, "but I think the offense much greater in those who either directly or indirectly have been concerned in making the very laws they break."

American affairs occupied little of Franklin's thought after returning from Paris until near the end of the year. First reactions to the Townshend duties seemed good. Joseph Galloway thought the duties might help win Pennsylvania a royal government. "Must Pennsylvania and Maryland," the two proprietary colonies, he asked, "raise money for the support of all the royal governments, and by far the greatest share, and not have any part of it appropriated towards the support of their own officers?" Few rumbles came from the colonies until mid-November. New York, surprisingly, had been docile, but not Boston. "I wish the Boston people had been as quiet," Franklin said. Grenville in Parliament used Boston to cry up a rage against all America. "The resolutions of the Boston people concerning trade, make a great noise here," Franklin reported on December 29, two days before the Townshend duties were to go into effect. "Parliament has not yet taken notice of them, but the newspapers are in full cry against America." One evening when out in a large company Franklin argued that the Americans were "not quite so unreasonable as they appeared to be." Several of those present urged him "to make my sentiments public, not only for the sake of America, but as it would be some ease to our friends here, who are triumphed over a good deal by our adversaries on the occasion." To that end Franklin on 5 January 1768 published an essay entitled "Causes of the American Discontents before 1768."

The essay revealed again Franklin's marvelous political agility, his talent for masking errors of judgment that would have devoured the reputations of lesser men. When discussing the Townshend duties he abandoned reference to "external" taxes and said only they were designed for "the levying more money from America." He would not speak on the legitimacy of those duties ("It is not my intention to combat this opinion" of Parliament), but he would explain why Americans objected to them. The explanation summarized briefly, even eloquently, the American position, but for those who knew him to be the author of the essay it raised the puzzle why he had not comprehended that position when the duties were being considered by Parliament.

The Stamp Act had led Americans to think for the first time about their relations with England, and as they pondered a number of old grievances, "which from their respect and love for this country, they had long borne and seemed almost willing to forget," came fresh to mind. Americans could not make hats in one colony and sell them in another. They were forbidden to manufacture nails. Troops could be quartered in their homes. Felons—this "the most cruel insult"—could be imposed upon them against their will. "These are the wild ravings of the at present half distracted Americans," concluded Franklin. "To be sure, no reasonable man in England can approve of such sentiments, and, as I said before, I do not pretend to support or justify them. But I sincerely wish for the sake of the manufacturers and commerce of Great Britain, and for the sake of the strength which a firm union with our growing colonies would give us, that these people had never been thus needlessly driven out of their senses."

The editor of the *London Chronicle* "has drawn the teeth and pared the nails of my paper, so that it can neither scratch nor bite," Franklin complained two days after it appeared. "It seems only to paw and mumble." The changes amounted largely to striking out loaded adjectives and adverbs—a "frivolous complaint" became "slight"; duties "forced from the people" became "raised upon"; governors "frequently men of vicious characters" became only "sometimes" thus. Given Franklin's purpose "to palliate matters" the editing of the manuscript was judicious.

Shortly before the essay appeared Franklin received a stunning blow. Two of the seemingly pro-American members of the ministry—Henry Seymour Conway and Lord Shelburne—had been forced out, supplanted by two gentlemen who held little sympathy for the colonies. A new post designed specifically to deal with American affairs—secretary of state for the colonies—had gone to Lord Hillsborough. Franklin had yet to make up his mind about Hillsborough. Sometimes he seemed to be America's friend, sometimes her foe.

On the heels of these changes Franklin picked up a startling rumor that he immediately passed on to his son. "I am told there has been a talk of getting me appointed under secretary to Lord Hillsborough," he wrote 9 January 1768; "but with little likelihood, as it is a settled point here that I am too much of an American."

CHAPTER

24

"I SHOULD STAY
WITH PLEASURE"

WHEN FRANKLIN IN "Causes of the American Discontents" said he did "not undertake here to support these opinions of the Americans," he postured to lend objectivity to the essay, but only partly. The colonies had leaped ahead of him, and he played for time to absorb their arguments. Though no longer willing to "give myself the trouble to defend . . . my opinion," he still held rigidly to a distinction between external and internal taxes. "Only to you," he confided to his son, "I may say that not only the Parliament of Britain, but every state in Europe claims and exercises a right of laying duties on the exportation of its own commodities to foreign countries." (Did William think this an odd, inapt analogy, comparing America to a foreign country?) He read the "Letters from a Farmer in Pennsylvania" as they appeared in Philadelphia—in the *Chronicle* of all places, the supposed voice of moderation that Galloway had subsidized—and though unaware his enemy John Dickinson wrote them he disagreed with their main point—that Parliament had no power to levy taxes of any kind upon the colonies. "In my opinion the grievance is not that Britain puts duties upon her own manufactures exported to us, but that she forbids us to buy the like manufactures from any other country," he said. "This she does, however, in virtue of her allowed right to regulate the commerce of the whole empire, allowed I mean by the Farmer, though I think whoever would dispute that right might stand upon firmer ground and make much more of the argument."

Through the early months of 1768 Franklin used his son as a sounding board to clarify his thoughts. "I am not yet master of the idea these and the New England writers have of the relation between Britain and her colonies," he confessed in one letter. "I know not what the Boston people mean by the 'subordination' they acknowledge in their Assembly to Parliament, while they deny its power to make laws for them, nor what bounds the Farmer sets to the power he acknowledges in Parliament to 'regulate the trade of the colonies,' it being difficult to draw lines between duties for regulation and those for revenue, and if the Parliament is to be the judge, it seems to me that establishing such principles of distinction will amount to little. The more I have thought and read on the subject the more I find myself confirmed in opinion, that no middle doctrine can be well maintained, I mean not clearly with intelligible arguments. Something might be made of either extremes; that Parliament has a power to make *all laws* for us, or that it has a power to make *no laws* for us; and I think the arguments for the latter more numerous and weighty than those for the former." He would still like to see a union between the colonies and the mother country like that which existed between England and Scotland, "but such a union," he said, "is not likely to take place while the nature of our present relation is so little understood on both sides the water, and sentiments concerning it remain so widely different."

Through the first half of 1768 Franklin continued confused and uncertain about the nature of the colonies' relation with the mother country. "How far these sentiments are right or wrong I do not pretend at present to judge," he said in a preface to an English reprint of Dickinson's letters. While waiting for events to settle his mind, Franklin played a double game—on one side pleading through the English press, at dinner parties, in the offices of government officials for patience with America, on the other laying the groundwork among influential friends in France for a friendly attitude toward the colonies. "As our American disputes afford you some amusement, I sent you the Pennsylvania Farmer's letters," he wrote to one acquaintance in Paris. "They have been universally read in the colonies, and have had a prodigious effect in spiriting the people up against the late duties. No less than thirty editions were printed in the different provinces within six months." Barbeu Dubourg took the hint and translated the letters; they had a lively sale. Dickinson's pamphlet opened what soon became a stream of pro-American works flowing from Franklin's study in Craven Street to Paris. Seeding the ground there he hoped would excite English fears of a revived France allied with America and force concessions from Parliament; failing that, he could still have "the satisfaction in seeing that our part is taken everywhere."

In the role of "peace broker," Franklin dealt mainly with Lord Hillsborough, a man of strong opinions and considerable ability. He had helped frame the Currency Act of 1764 and opposed its repeal. He opposed settlement of the interior of North America, mainly, Franklin thought, because he feared the "dispeopling of Ireland," where he was one of the largest landholders. Opinions about the man varied. "I do not think this nobleman in general an enemy to America," Franklin said in January 1768. "I do not know a man of less judgment," George III would remark one day. A fuller, more balanced opinion came from one of Franklin's fellow agents who saw him often on business:

> Lord Hillsborough is esteemed a nobleman of good nature, abilities, and integrity; is a man of business, alert, lively, ready, but too fond of his own opinions and systems, and too apt to be inflexibly attached to them; by no means so gentle and easy to be entreated as [Shelburne] in that branch of business, but much more to be depended upon if he once adopts your ideas of any measure.

Hillsborough worked hard at his job as secretary of state for the colonies. When Franklin gave him some papers from the Pennsylvania Committee of Correspondence he "read them deliberately" and asked sensible questions about their contents. He could be gracious and appeared fair-minded. He studied Franklin's paper on the need for colonial paper currency as legal tender, and "was pleased to make me compliments upon [it], assuring me he had read it with great attention, that I had said much more in favor of such a currency than he had thought could be said." He still opposed the scheme but Franklin's arguments induced "him to leave the matter now to the judgment of others, and let it take its course, without opposing it as last year he had determined to have done." He seemed judicious. When Franklin spoke about Pennsylvania's petition to become a royal colony, "he was pleased to say he would inquire into the matter, and would talk with me farther upon it." Only on the matter of western colonies did he appear unreasonable. He flatly opposed them. Franklin accepted the judgment as law—"the purpose of settling the new colonies seems at present to be dropped," he said after a meeting with the secretary—but still thought he could serve comfortably as Hillsborough's assistant. But nothing would be done on that head until the elections to Parliament were over, which meant Franklin must be kept in suspense until mid-summer.

2

"The Parliament is up and the nation in a ferment with the new elections," Franklin remarked in March. He had said little about the elections in 1761, but since then either he or England had changed. "Great complaints are made that the natural interests of country gentlemen in their neighboring boroughs, is overborne by the monied interest of the new people who have got sudden fortunes in the Indies, or as contractors, etc. £4,000 is now the market price for a borough. In short, this whole venal nation is now at market, will be sold for about two millions; and might be bought out of the hands of the present bidders (if he would offer half a million more) by the very devil himself." Franklin's outburst puzzled his friend Strahan, for English electioneering had not changed in the past seven years. Except for "the unavoidable bustle occasioned by the elections, we are in a state of perfect tranquility," he said. "Much money will be expended, much riot will prevail; but there is no help for it. It is in some measure the unavoidable consequence of our liberty, which will every now and then run into licentiousness.— But still, take us for all in all, we are the happiest nation this world ever contained."

As the campaign wore on Franklin's disgust mounted, then turned to a rage that focused on one man—John Wilkes. He had lived in France since 1763 to escape prison for his libelous *North Briton No. 45*. Though the risk of prison remained, he had returned to stand for a seat in Parliament from the City of London. He lost that bid, but learning of an open seat from Middlesex county he now campaigned for that. " 'Tis really an extraordinary event, to see an outlaw and exile, of bad personal character, not worth a farthing, come over from France, set himself up as candidate for the capital of the kingdom, miss his election only by being too late in his application, and immediately carrying it for the principal county," Franklin wrote in mid-April, unaware or uncaring he again stepped out of tune with opinion in America, where Wilkes had become a continental hero. "The scenes have been horrible. London was illuminated two nights running at the command of the mob for the success of Wilkes in the Middlesex election; the second night exceeded anything of the kind ever seen here on the greatest occasion of rejoicing, as even the small cross streets, lanes, courts, and other out-of-the-way places were all in a blaze of lights, and the principal streets all night long, as the mobs went round again after two o'clock, and obliged people who had extinguished their candles to light them again. Those who refused had all their windows destroyed."

In letters home Franklin became obsessed with the adulation accorded Wilkes. On May 14 he and Sir John Pringle spent a pleasant afternoon with James Boswell chatting about such things as "whether infidels or Protestants had done most to pull down Popery." No one would have guessed this from the letters he wrote that day. "While I am writing, a great mob of coal porters fill the street, carrying a wretch of their business upon poles to be ducked, and otherwise punished at their pleasure for working at the old wages," he told one correspondent. "All respect to law and government seems to be lost among the common people, who are moreover continually enflamed by seditious scribblers to trample on authority and everything that used to keep them in order." And to another on the same day he said: "Even this capital, the residence of the king, is now a daily scene of lawless riot and confusion. Mobs are patrolling the streets at noonday, some knocking all down that will not roar for Wilkes and liberty."

He ended one letter with the announcement "I am preparing for my return" to Philadelphia.

3

But while he talked of returning he dreamed of staying on as Hillsborough's under secretary of state. By the spring of 1768 Hillsborough had become the dominant voice in the ministry on American affairs, as shown by his stern directives. In February the Massachusetts legislature had approved a circular letter to all the colonies urging, among other things, united resistance to the Townshend duties by refusing to import any goods from Great Britain. A majority of the ministry wished to reply with a "kind and lenient" circular letter of their own, but Hillsborough would have none of this. In April, after privately consulting with the king but not his colleagues in the ministry, who later denounced his action, he instructed Governor Bernard of Massachusetts to dissolve the legislature if it did not rescind the letter. He then sent out a circular letter of his own, ordering all governors to instruct their legislatures to ignore the Massachusetts letter and to dissolve them if they took notice of it. He also arranged for two regiments of troops to be sent to Boston. None of this perturbed Franklin. He still thought Hillsborough's "inclinations are rather favorable towards us (so far as he thinks consistent with what he supposes the unquestionable rights of Britain)."

On June 17 Hillsborough cemented control over American affairs by supplanting Lord Clare as president of the Board of Trade without relinquishing his job as secretary of state for America. At this point Franklin's "fast friend" Grey Cooper, secretary of the Treasury, in concert with the Duke of Grafton and Lord North, gave thought to bringing Franklin into the government as a meliorating influence on Hillsborough. Franklin learned about it on June 22 when Cooper asked him to stop by the office for a visit. Conversation opened on an unexpected and unpleasant note. Lord Sandwich, the new postmaster general and a friend of Grenville, had wondered about Franklin's absence from his office as deputy post-master general in America. Earlier, in an effort to reform the American bureaucracy, all absentee officeholders had been ordered to take up their posts in the colonies or abandon their commissions. Lord Sandwich, quite reasonably, thought the post office in America "suffered" by Franklin's absence, "and that it would be fit to appoint another, as I seemed constantly to reside in England." Now came the good news. Cooper said Lord Grafton, who headed the ministry during Chatham's prolonged absences, wanted Franklin to know that while taking up his post in America would satisfy Sandwich, "yet if I chose rather to reside in England, my merit was such in his opinion, as to entitle me to something better here, and it should not be his fault if I was not well provided for."

Franklin replied that Lord Sandwich's objection could easily be met, for he was "preparing to return home, and expected to be gone in a few weeks." He added, choosing words carefully, "that having lived long in England and contracted a friendship and affection for many persons here, it could not but be agreeable to me to remain among them some time longer, if not for the rest of my life; and that there was no nobleman to whom I could from sincere respect for his great abilities, and amiable qualities, so cordially attach myself, or to whom I should so willingly be obliged for the provision he mentioned, as to the Duke of Grafton, if his grace should think I could in any station where he might place me, be serviceable to him and to the public." These obsequious remarks referred to a nobleman who has been described as "youthful, indolent, and incompetent," but Cooper beamed as he listened, "as it so perfectly agreed with his inclinations to keep me here."

Cooper asked Franklin to call on the Duke of Grafton the next morning. The duke would be expecting him. Cooper asked Franklin to send him a copy of his essay on smuggling and another piece on the "laboring poor" in England. He wanted to pass them along to Lord North and the duke. (In the second essay Franklin praised England's treatment of the poor as "by far the best in Europe." He warned against raising their wages. They already got enough to spend "St. Monday" drinking in the alehouses.)

The meeting with Grafton did not work out, but Cooper carried him around to Lord North. The three chatted about American affairs, then North said:

"I am told by Mr. Cooper that you are not unwilling to stay with us. I hope we shall find some way of making it worth your while."

"I should stay with pleasure," Franklin replied, "if I could any ways be useful to government."

After the interview Cooper took Franklin to his country house for the night. During the following week Grafton twice broke appointments with Franklin, but Cooper "assures me the Duke has it at heart to do something handsome for me," Franklin reported to his son. "Sir John Pringle, who is anxious for my stay, says Mr. Cooper is the honestest man of a courtier he ever knew, and he is persuaded they are in earnest to keep me."

"So you see a turn of a die may make a great difference in our affairs," Franklin mused to his son. "We may be either promoted or discarded; one or the other seems likely soon to be the case, but 'tis hard to divine which. I am myself grown so old as to feel much less than formerly the spur of ambition, and if it were not for the flattering expectation, that by being fixed here I might more effectually serve my country, I should certainly determine for retirement, without a moment's hesitation."

He cared more than he dared admit. On July 2, the day he wrote to William, he also wrote to Galloway. He did not mention a possible post in the British government but did say: "Our friends wonder that I persist in my intention of returning this summer, alleging that I might be of much more service to my country here than I can be there, and wishing me by all means to stay the ensuing winter, as the presence of persons well acquainted with America, and of ability to represent these affairs in a proper light, will then be highly necessary."

Before the month ended Franklin made up his mind, though he had heard nothing more about the offer of a post. "I purpose remaining here another winter, and returning home to Pennsylvania in the spring," he said on July 25.

4

In mid-August Franklin had a long audience with Hillsborough. They talked about Pennsylvania's wish to become a royal colony. Later, in an abrupt note to Galloway, Franklin would say only that "the advice he gave us in order to obtain the change being such as I assured him we could not take. I shall therefore move the matter no farther during the administration of a minister that appears to have a stronger partiality for Mr. Penn than any of his predecessors."

More than Pennsylvania's petition was discussed in that long meeting with Hillsborough, for Franklin emerged from it enraged beyond reason. Hillsborough must have made it clear he would block any attempt made to appoint Franklin to a responsible post in the government. He may have salted his remarks with news that the coveted assignment of under secretary of state would go to John Pownall, the brother of Franklin's friend Thomas Pownall. John Pownall was a professional bureaucrat who for the past ten years had served as secretary to the Board of Trade, where Hillsborough had come to know and trust his judgment. Those who worked with Pownall judged him "to be a very good kind of a man and has a much better character than the governor [i.e., Thomas]," but Franklin despised his influence on the members of the board. "The Standing Secretary seems to have a strong bias against us," he said, "and to infect them one after another as they come to it." Pownall's appointment as under secretary came as a stunning blow.

Up to now he had written nothing for the press or in private letters to offend the ministry. At no time had he spoken ill of Hillsborough. He had explained American objections to the Townshend duties and stated other of their numerous grievances, but he had never warmly supported their opinions. Two of his essays, those on smuggling and on the laboring poor, could be considered propaganda pieces for the government.

Now, overnight, he swung about sharply. The Townshend duties became "offensive duties" and he promised to work assiduously for their repeal. They had been *forced* upon Americans by persons "not *chosen* for the purpose of imposing taxes upon them." They differed in no way from the obnoxious Stamp Act that Parliament had repealed. His first piece appeared on August 16, only a day or two after the meeting with Hillsborough. It ended insulting "a ministry, who, by this rage of heaping taxes on taxes, are only drawing into their own hands more and more wealth and power." A second essay, published August 25, talked about the civil war instigated by Hillsborough's ordering troops to Boston, a subject Franklin had avoided comment on up to now. He warned that English troops, "being ordered on this murdering service against their countrymen," would have trouble subduing Americans. He reckoned it would take five years to repress a single colony, "and this, by my computation, will amount to just seventy-five years," if one adds Canada and Florida to the other thirteen colonies. And all this for what?—"to convert millions of the king's loyal subjects into rebels, for the sake of establishing a new claimed power in P——— to tax a distant people. . . ."

Essays that followed on August 26, 27, and 31 attacked Hillsborough, "our new Haman." Franklin talked again of leaving for home—"I know not but I may still return this fall"—but this seemed unlikely until he had done what he could to topple Hillsborough from power.

CHAPTER

25

"AT PRESENT I ALMOST DESPAIR"

FRANKLIN CONTINUED HIS ATTACKS on the ministry while waiting for the new Parliament to convene in November 1768. One essay accused the government of taxing the colonies only to build a slush fund "for an American establishment, whereby they may be able to provide for friends and favorites." He no longer talked about American representation in Parliament. The colonies "are not presumptuous enough to ask an *union* with Britain," he said. They asked only to be left alone to enjoy their "native and dear-bought privileges." This blunt piece, signed "Francis Lynn," was reprinted throughout the colonies. "Everybody attributes it to you," William reported, "and some have had sagacity enough to discover that the signature is a pun on the real name of the author."

In one piece Franklin hinted that the colonies owed allegiance only to the crown, which in the past gave them "an internal legislative power, which no Parliament at that time found fault with, and which they have enjoyed ever since. . . ." But when Parliament assembled he carefully did not deny its power to tax the colonies, calling it only "an impracticable right." He still dodged the constitutional issue raised by America. Perhaps flouting the authority of Parliament challenged the honor of the nation, Franklin said, but let us be sensible. "Mankind have so far learned the wisdom of the serpent, as, I believe, to prefer interest to a point of honor, especially when, as in this case, the interest is very considerable."

He welcomed the new Parliament with hope—"a new being, not accountable for the actions of its predecessor, and may therefore more freely take them into consideration." The latest shift in power within the

ministry passed unmentioned. Chatham the previous month had at last
resigned from office. Shelburne left with him and now Lord North led
the government. North was lazy and indecisive—"Damn him, . . . nothing can goad him forward," a colleague once complained—and a man of
startling appearance. "Nothing could be more coarse or clumsy or ungra-
cious than his outside," Horace Walpole said. "Two large prominent eyes
that rolled about to no purpose (for he was utterly shortsighted), a wide
mouth, thick lips, and inflamed visage, gave him the air of a blind trum-
peter. A deep, untunable voice, which . . . he enforced with unnecessary
pomp, a total neglect of his person, and ignorance of every civil attention,
disgusted all who judge by appearance." Those who adjusted to the
exterior soon observed a witty, adept, and imperturbable politician hard
to deflect from his goal once goaded forward. As an ally of Grenville he
had voted against repeal of the Stamp Act. He did not question Parliament's right to tax America.

The colonies planned to put their nonimportation agreements into
operation early in 1769 if Parliament did not repeal the Townshend duties. Lord North unloaded a bundle of documents on American affairs
upon members to guide their debate. Few of the papers pictured the
colonies in a complimentary light. A riot in Boston the previous June
caused by the seizure of John Hancock's sloop *Liberty* received undue
attention in Franklin's view. "In a country so frequent in mischievous
mobs and murderous riots as this is, 'tis surprising to find such resentment of a trifling riot in Boston," he said; "and strange that it should be
thought just to punish all the colonies, by continuing an oppressive act
affecting the whole, for the offense only of one of them." Franklin saw
before Parliament had sat for a month that it would not repeal the
Townshend duties. "If any good may be done, I shall rejoice," he said;
"but at present I almost despair." A fear he sensed in Parliament "of
provoking the colonies too far, lest a rupture should become inevitable,
and the old enemies of the nation [France and Spain] take advantage of
it," kept him from total despair. So did the hope that nonimportation
would work. "The tide is yet strong against us," he told a friend in
Boston, "but it must turn; if your frugal and industrious resolutions
continue."

But the tide did not turn. The Townshend duties remained in force
when Parliament rose in May. "They flatter themselves that you cannot
long subsist without their manufactures," Franklin wrote to Boston;
"they believe that you have not virtue enough to persist in such agreements; they imagine the colonies will differ among themselves, deceive
and desert one another, and quietly one after the other submit to the yoke

and return to the use of British fineries; they think that tho' the men may
be contented with homespun stuffs, the women will never get the better
of their vanity and fondness for English modes and gewgaws. The ministerial people all talk in this strain, and many even of the merchants! I have
ventured to assert that they will all find themselves mistaken; and I rely
so much on the spirit of my country as to be confident I shall not be found
a false prophet, tho' at present not believed."

2

"Doctor Franklin looks heartier than ever I knew him in America,"
a friend from home reported in June, "and has a most surprising influence here, and is as much talked of as in America. He is now at the request
of the House of Commons forming some pipes, etc. to keep a proper
degree of warmth always in the House in winter, and is fixing [lightning
rod] wires on St. Paul's, the Royal Exchange, etc." The despair of the past
winter had vanished. Soon after Parliament rose, he learned from the
daily round of visits to ministry offices that "there is at present an appearance as if the Great Ones were about to change their conduct towards
us." He thought it "too much to expect that they will become thoroughly
wise at once. But a little time, with a prudent steady conduct on our side,
will, I hope, set all right." He had a further reason to be in good humor
during the summer of 1769. He and Samuel Wharton were building a
remarkable edifice which, if all went well, would bring to life an old
dream and at the same time destroy Hillsborough.

Wharton, the Quaker merchant who had been a force behind the
Illinois Company, had arrived from Philadelphia that spring. "You
would laugh to see him dressed," a friend said, "as he has not the least
sign of a Quaker about him and wears his sword, etc. with as much ease
as if he had always done it. On the [king's] birthday he and Doctor
Franklin went to Court together, dressed in rich silks, etc. and made a
very genteel appearance." Wharton had come to London to promote his
latest speculative scheme. The previous year he had traveled with Sir
William Johnson to Fort Stanwix to negotiate an Indian treaty that
would open land in the upper Ohio Valley to settlement by the Indiana
Company, which he had organized after giving up hope for the Illinois
Company. He expected prompt approval of the treaty in London but
Hillsborough blocked it. Johnson, a silent partner in the company, had
violated his instructions in opening up restricted territory to private
speculators. Wharton crossed the ocean to apply pressure in person—

"My *all* depends on the confirmation of the Indian grant"—but Hillsborough remained obdurate, saying flatly, "His Majesty does not think fit at present to confirm those grants." As Wharton traveled about in his finery he gathered that everyone in the ministry thought Hillsborough "mad" for objecting to the Fort Stanwix treaty but none ventured to cross him.

Franklin viewed the situation as a chess problem and saw in it a chance at last to checkmate an oppressive opponent. First, Johnson must be kept from buckling under Hillsborough's wrath, and through a friend he passed the word "that if Sir William did not suffer himself nor the Six Nations to be intimidated by the ministerial letters, but steadily supported his and their conduct, the whole transactions, as wisely settled by him at Fort Stanwix, would be undoubtedly ratified." Next, the Indiana Company must be abandoned; with only American backing it stood no chance of overriding Hillsborough's authority. Replace it with a new, enlarged company that included, along with the old group, a number of rich and powerful English gentlemen. By early June several of Franklin's friends had been enticed into the fold—Anthony Todd from the post office; Thomas Pownall, now a member of Parliament; John Sargent, a director of the Bank of England and also in Parliament; Grey Cooper, who had tried to find Franklin a post in the government; Francis Seymour Conway, who was close to the king; and finally Charles Pratt, once attorney general, now Lord Camden. The greatest catch was the Walpole brothers, Thomas and Richard, of such prestige and wealth that the group thereafter called itself the Walpole Associates, though it would officially be known as the Grand Ohio Company. When done, Franklin had constructed a mighty edifice, the most powerful land company in Anglo-American history. By June a petition had been prepared to present to the king.

Launching the joyous enterprise, surely as satisfying as any chess game Franklin had played, left Franklin exhausted and in mid-July he departed for a six-week visit to Paris, again with Dr. Pringle. He had little to say about the trip except to remark that "I found our dispute much attended to, several of our pamphlets being translated and printed there," not bothering to mention he had been the one to seed the ground with the propaganda. "In short, all Europe (except Britain) appears to be on our side the question. But Europe has its reasons. It fancies itself in some danger from the growth of British power, and would be glad to see it divided against itself. Our prudence will, I hope, long postpone the satisfaction our enemies expect from our dissensions."

3

Through the autumn of 1769 Franklin continued the round of pleasant dinners, the visits to clubs and country estates of friends, the chess games with Dr. Pringle. He appeared outwardly placid. Not even such friends as Strahan sensed he verged on a momentous decision. Before leaving for France he had told the merchants of Philadelphia to persist in the policy of buying no British goods; it offered the only "means, under GOD, of recovering and establishing the freedom of our country entire, and of handing it down complete to our posterity." He saw nonimportation as an economic weapon to use against Britain and also as a tool of reform by which "the country will be enriched by its industry and frugality, those virtues will become habitual, farms will be more improved, better stocked, and rendered more productive by the money that used to be spent in superfluities." William Allen, hitherto always a step ahead of Franklin in resistance to the measures of Parliament, saw the ominous implications in the exhortation. He warned friends in England that "many injudicious people among us are sanguine in their hopes that their present oppressions and distresses will, in the end, be useful to us, and will teach us the necessity of more industry and frugality. They say the good work is already begun; and that if things remain in their present state for a very few years, good will rise out of evil."

Still, as always, the visionary, Franklin had in his letter to the merchants launched himself and, he hoped, America, upon a crusade. But would the practical side of his nature let him persist in the cause if nonimportation won a partial victory from Parliament? He stood to lose the honor enjoyed among the great in England and the income from his position in the post office. Would he risk all this for a principle? After returning from France he found the ministry had not changed its mind about asking for only partial repeal of the Townshend duties. This would not do, he said, but as "peace broker" he still pretended to speak for the colonists, not himself. The colonists demanded repeal of *"all the laws* that have been made for raising a revenue in America by authority of Parliament. . . . It is not *the sum* paid in that duty on tea that is complained of as a burthen, but the principle of the act. . . ." He worried that partial repeal would "inflame matters still more" in America, that "rash measures there may create more resentments here," leading to fire feeding upon fire—"more troops may be sent over, which will create more uneasiness. . . . Mutual provocations will thus go on to complete the separation. . . ."

He spoke as he felt about the crisis only obliquely, as in an unsigned fable published in January 1770 and dedicated to Lord Hillsborough:

A lion's whelp was put on board a Guinea ship bound to America as a present to a friend in that country. It was tame and harmless as a kitten, and therefore not confined, but suffered to walk about the ship at pleasure. A stately, full-grown English mastiff, belonging to the captain, despising the weakness of the young lion, frequently took its *food* by force, and often turned it out of its lodging box, when he had a mind to repose therein himself. The young lion nevertheless grew daily in size and strength, and the voyage being long, he became at last a more equal match for the mastiff; who, continuing his insults, received a stunning blow from the lion's paw that fetched his skin over his ears, and deterred him from any future contest with such growing strength; regretting that he had not rather secured its friendship than provoked its enmity.

Through January and February Franklin published eleven essays restating the American position. Early in March as Parliament prepared to vote on the question of repeal, he sent to the press a long letter from Charles Thomson warning that "a partial redress will little avail to allay the heats and quiet the minds of the people." The ministry, after studying the reports from royal officials in America, decided to gamble that the rabble-rousers spoke for only a few discontented, that a land of farmers could not soon turn to manufacturing, that the fragile union would rip apart at the slightest pressure. Parliament accepted that judgment and in March repealed all the Townshend duties but that on tea.

Franklin responded without hesitation. In a long letter to Charles Thomson, which would be widely publicized in the colonies, he said: "There is no doubt that, if we are steady, and persevere in our resolutions," the English merchants "will soon begin a clamor, that much pains has hitherto been used to stifle." If Americans abandon nonimportation before "it has had its full effect, it can never again be used on any future occasion with the least prospect of success, and that if we do persist another year, we shall never afterwards have occasion to use it." The opposition here, he wrote Galloway a few days later with even more spirit, holds that "the different colonies were a rope of sand, and could not long hold together for any one purpose; and that a little firmness shown by the government here, would infallibly break us all to pieces. On this principle they have acted. If we give way, they and their friends will exult; their judgment and foresight will be admired; they will be extolled as able statesmen, worthy to hold the reins in governing America, and be established in their administration." Similar sermons went to friends in Boston. In one he dared say what only the boldest in America had hinted at—that Parliament lacked *all* authority over the colonies and that the king alone is "the sole legislator of his American subjects, and in that capacity is and ought to be free to exercise his own judgment unrestrained and unlimited by his Parliament here."

William Strahan listened to his friend of some forty years with astonishment. Strahan thought America ought to accept the tea duty, "which, laying aside the *principle* of the tax, is not worth mentioning, and to trust, with some degree of confidence, in the justice and wisdom of the Parliament for future relief. . . ." He thought Franklin had suddenly "by-passed his sound and perfect and manly understanding, upon which, on other occasions, I could securely depend. Nay, I will venture to tell you," he wrote an American friend, "that I really think him rather too partial to you, and perhaps too much hurt (tho' not altogether without cause) with the behavior of the mother country to her children." Franklin said Strahan had "grown a great courtier" and might have let the friendship cool. Strahan would not let this happen if he could help it. "Tho' we *differ* we do not *disagree*," he said; "and must ever be good friends, as I trust we aim at both the same end, tho' we differ in the means."

4

If Franklin had been capable of total despair, it would have come in the summer of 1770. The continuing ignorance about America appalled him. A respected counsellor-at-law one day approached Richard Jackson and gravely asked "whether Philadelphia was in the East or West Indies and said he had a notion it was upon the coast of Sumatra." Franklin's outspoken defense of the colonies and encouragement of nonimportation revived talk that he ought to be dismissed from the post office. His constant fear that the troops in Boston would eventually draw blood became a reality in March when several citizens were killed in what came to be called the Boston Massacre. He got the news in June and though knowing it would only harden the government's resolve to deal sternly with the colonies he insisted with unfounded optimism that "the next session will hardly pass over without repealing" the tea duty, "for the Parliament must finally comply with the sense of the nation."

If all this was not enough to dishearten, Franklin had to endure the sight of Hillsborough still eluding traps set for him, neatly blocking at every turn the Grand Ohio Company's request for a land grant. In late December 1769 he suddenly suggested the company ask for a larger grant.

Why request a mere two and a half million acres? Why not twenty million? He promised to urge the Treasury, which would set the purchase price, to expand the original grant. The company had planned to pay the modest sum of approximately £10,500 for the grant it had requested in its petition. If the grant were increased ten times, reasoned Hillsborough, then the Treasury would up the price proportionally, to something like one hundred thousand pounds, a price he doubted the company could afford. A clever move, but one Franklin could easily counter. Among those he had offered and who had accepted invitations to join the company were three of the gentlemen in the Treasury who would pass on the merits of the request for an enlarged grant. In January 1770, eight days after listening to the request, a government bureau that normally pondered the simplest decision for months handed down its approval. Checkmate? Not at all. Months passed before the revised petition had wormed its way from the Treasury past roadblocks erected by Hillsborough and back to the Privy Council and finally to the Board of Trade. By then enough opposition had been aroused against the Grand Ohio Company by such respected royal officials as Gen. Thomas Gage, by the Penn family, by the government of Virginia, by other groups of American speculators that Hillsborough could insist with reason that the petition called for further study before any action could be taken on it.

There matters stood in early August when Franklin received jolting news from America—the merchants of New York had lifted their ban on importing goods from Britain. "Thus the ice being now broke, the other colonies must soon follow their example," Strahan predicted. It was all for the good, he added, for "I have long thought the matter now in dispute between us a mere bagatelle."

CHAPTER

26

THE CRAVEN STREET GAZETTE

"I THINK OF LATE that my constitution rather mends," Franklin reported to Deborah at the end of 1768 as his sixty-third birthday approached. "I have had but one touch of the gout, and that a light one, since I left you; it was just after my arrival here, so that this is the fourth winter I have been free. Walking a great deal tires me less than it used to do. I feel stronger and more active. Yet I would not have you think I fancy I shall grow young again. I know that men of my bulk often fail suddenly. I know that according to the course of nature I cannot at most continue much longer, and that the living even of another day is uncertain. I therefore now form no scheme but such as are of immediate execution; indulging myself in no future prospect except one, that of returning to Philadelphia, there to spend the evening of life with my friends and family."

He enjoyed good health in 1769 but not in the following year. "As to myself," he reported to his wife in June 1770, "I had from Christmas till Easter a disagreeable giddiness hanging about me, which however did not hinder me from being about and doing business. In the Easter holidays, being at a friend's house in the country, I was taken with a sore throat, and came home half strangled. From Monday till Friday, I could swallow nothing but barley water and the like. I was bled largely, and purged two or three times. On Friday came on a fit of the gout, from which I had been free five years. Immediately the inflammation and swelling in my throat disappeared; my foot swelled greatly, and I was confined about three weeks; since which I am perfectly well, the giddiness and every other disagreeable symptom having quite left me." Deborah Franklin had tended her husband during earlier bouts with gout and knew the excruciating pain he suffered. "If your having the gout is of service to you, I won't say one word," she wrote, "only I wish I was near enough to rub it with a light hand." Later, when the gout returned, Franklin dared to quarrel openly with his tormentor.

FRANKLIN: Eh! Oh! Eh! What have I done to merit these cruel sufferings?

GOUT: Many things; you have ate and drank too freely, and too much indulged those legs of yours in their indolence.

FRANKLIN: Who is it that accuses me?

GOUT: It is I, even I, the Gout.

FRANKLIN: What! My enemy in person?

GOUT: No, not your enemy.

FRANKLIN: I repeat it; my enemy; for you would not only torment my body to death, but ruin my good name; you reproach me as a glutton and a tippler; now all the world, that knows me, will allow that I am neither the one nor the other.

GOUT: The world may think as it pleases; it is always very complaisant to itself, and sometimes to its friends; but I very well know that the quantity of meat and drink proper for a man, who takes a reasonable degree of exercise, would be too much for another, who never takes any.

FRANKLIN: I take—Eh! Oh!—as much exercise—Eh!—as I can, Madam Gout. You know my sedentary state, and on that account, it would seem, Madam Gout, as if you might spare me a little, seeing it is not altogether my own fault.

GOUT: Not a jot; your rhetoric and your politeness are thrown away; your apology avails nothing. If your situation in life is a sedentary one, your amusements, your recreations, at least, should be active. You ought to walk or ride; or, if the weather prevents that, play at billiards. But let us examine your courses of life. While the mornings are long, and you have leisure to go abroad, what do you do? Why, instead of gaining an appetite for breakfast, by salutary exercise, you amuse yourself with books, pamphlets, or newspapers, which commonly are not worth the reading. Yet you eat an inordinate breakfast, four dishes of tea, with cream, and one or two buttered toasts, with slices of hung beef, which I fancy are not things the most easily digested. Immediately afterward you sit down to write at your desk, or converse with persons who apply to you on business. Thus the time passes till one, without any kind of bodily exercise. But all this I could pardon, in regard, as you say, to your sedentary condition. But what is your practice after dinner? Walking in the beautiful gardens of those friends, with whom you have dined, would be the choice of men of sense; yours is to be fixed down to chess, where you are found engaged for two or three hours! This is your perpetual recreation, which is the least eligible of any for a sedentary man, because, instead of accelerating the motion of the fluids, the rigid attention it requires helps to retard the circulation and obstruct internal secretions. Wrapt in the speculations of this wretched game, you destroy your constitution. What can be expected from such a course of living, but a body replete with stagnant humors, ready to fall a prey to all kinds of dangerous maladies, if I, the Gout, did not occasionally bring you relief by agitating those humors, and so purifying or dissipating them? If it was in some nook or alley . . . deprived of walks, that you played awhile at chess after dinner, this might be excusable; but the same taste prevails with you . . . where there are the finest gardens and walks, a pure air, beautiful women, and most agreeable and instructive conversation; all which you might enjoy by frequenting the walks. But these are rejected for this abominable game of chess. Fie, then Mr. Franklin! But amidst my instructions, I had almost forgot to administer my wholesome corrections; so take that twinge—and that. . . .

FRANKLIN: Oh! Ehhh!—It is not fair to say I take no exercise, when I do very often, going out to dine and returning in my carriage.

GOUT: That, of all imaginable exercises, is the most slight and insignificant, if you allude to the motion of a carriage suspended on springs. . . .

FRANKLIN: What then would you have me do with my carriage?

GOUT: Burn it if you choose; you would at least get heat out of it once in this way. . . .

FRANKLIN: Ah! How tiresome you are!

GOUT: Well, then, to my office; it should not be forgotten that I am your physician. There.

FRANKLIN: Ohhh! What a devil for a physician.

GOUT: How ungrateful you are to say so! Is it not I who, in the character of your physician, have saved you from the palsy, dropsy, and apoplexy? one or the other of which would have done for you long ago, but for me.

FRANKLIN: I submit, and thank you for the past, but entreat the discontinuance of your visits for the future; for, in my mind, one had better die than be cured so dolefully. . . . Oh! Oh!—for Heaven's sake leave me! and I promise faithfully never more to play at chess, but to exercise daily, and live temperately.

GOUT: I know you too well. You promise fair; but, after a few months of good health, you will return to your old habits; your fine promises will be forgotten like the forms of last year's clouds. Let us then finish the account, and I will go. But I leave you with an assurance of visiting you again at a proper time and place; for my object is your good, and you are sensible now that I am your *real friend*.

2

Franklin spent a leisurely summer in the city, taking the usual week-ends in the country but no extended trip. Polly Stevenson, now aged thirty-one, became engaged to William Hewson, a surgeon, also thirty-one. She worried that her surrogate father did not approve of the match —he reassured her he did—and that lacking a fortune she would not be loved. "I should think you a fortune sufficient for me without a shilling," he told her. The couple was married on 10 July 1770 with Franklin present.

Though every ship from the colonies reported the nonimportation agreements were collapsing, and though his "political opinions" had forced him to fight for his job in the post office, he continued in a gay mood through the summer. In September Mrs. Stevenson and Sally Franklin went to visit a distant friend. Polly and her new husband came in to look after Franklin. He kept the absent landlady informed of events through

The Craven Street Gazette. No. 113

SATURDAY, 22 SEPTEMBER 1770

This morning Queen Margaret, accompanied by her first Maid of Honor, Miss Franklin, set out for Rochester. Immediately on their departure, the whole street was in tears—from a heavy shower of rain.

It is whispered that the new family administration which took place on her Majesty's departure, promises, like all other new administrations, to govern much better than the old one.

We hear that the *great* person (so called from his enormous size) of a certain family in a certain street, is grievously affected at the late changes, and could hardly be comforted this morning, tho' the new ministry promised him a roasted shoulder of mutton, and potatoes, for his dinner.

It is said that the same *great* person intended to pay his respects to another great personage this day, at St. James's, it being Coronation Day; hoping thereby to amuse his grief; but was prevented by an accident, Queen Margaret, or her Maid of Honor having carried off the key of the drawers, so that the Lady of the Bedchamber could not come at a laced shirt for his Highness. Great clamors were made on this occasion against her Majesty.

Other accounts say that the shirts were afterwards found, tho' too late, in another place. And some suspect that the wanting a shirt from those drawers was only a ministerial pretense to excuse picking the locks, that the new administration might have everything at command.

We hear that the Lady Chamberlain of the Household went to market this morning by her own self, gave the butcher whatever he asked for the mutton, and had no dispute with the potato woman—to their great amazement—at the change of times!

It is confidently asserted that this afternoon, the weather being wet, the great *person* a little chilly, and nobody at home to find fault with the expense of fuel, he was indulged with a fire in his chamber. It seems the design is to make him contented, by degrees, with the absence of the Queen.

A project has been under consideration of government, to take the opportunity of her Majesty's absence for doing a thing she was always averse to, viz. fixing a new lock on the street door, or getting a key made to the old one; it being found extremely inconvenient that one or other of the great officers of state should, whenever the maid goes out for a ha'pworth of sand or a pint of porter, be obliged to attend the door to let her in again. But opinion, being divided, which of the two expedients to adopt, the project is for the present laid aside.

We have good authority to assure our readers that a cabinet council was held this afternoon at tea; the subject of which was a proposal for the reformation of manners, and a more strict observation of the Lord's Day. The result was an unanimous resolution that no meat should be dressed tomorrow; whereby the cook and the first minister will both be at liberty to go to church, the one having nothing to do, and the other no roast to rule. It seems the cold shoulder of mutton and the apple pie were thought sufficient for Sunday's dinner. All pious people applaud this measure, and 'tis thought the new Ministry will soon become popular. . . .

SUNDAY, SEPTEMBER 23

It is now found by sad experience that good resolutions are easier made than executed. Notwithstanding yesterday's solemn Order of Council, nobody went to church today. It seems the *great* person's broad-built bulk lay so long abed that breakfast was not over 'till it was too late to dress. At least this is the excuse. In fine, it seems a vain thing to hope reformation from the example of our great folks. The cook and the minister, however, both took advantage of the order so far as to save themselves all trouble, and the clause of *cold dinner* was enforced, tho' the *going to church* was dispensed with; just as the common working people observe the commandment, *the seventh day thou shalt rest*, they think a sacred injunction; but the other *six days shalt thou labor* is deemed a mere piece of advice which they may practice when they want bread and are out of credit at the alehouse, and may neglect whenever they have money in their pockets. It must nevertheless be said in justice to our Court, that whatever inclination they had to gaming, no cards were brought out today. Lord and Lady Hewson walked after dinner to Kensington to pay their duty to the Dowager, and Dr. Fatsides made 469 turns in his dining room, as the exact distance of a visit to the lovely Lady Barwell, whom he did not find at home, so there was no struggle for and against a kiss, and he sat down to dream in the easy chair that he had it without any trouble.

MONDAY, SEPTEMBER 24

We are credibly informed that the *great* person dined this day with the Club at the Cat-and-Bagpipes in the City on cold round of boiled beef. This, it seems, he was under some necessity of doing (tho' he rather dislikes beef) because truly the ministers were to be all abroad somewhere to dine on hot roast venison. It is thought that if the Queen had been at home, he would not have been so slighted. And tho' he shows outwardly no marks of dissatisfaction, it is suspected that he begins to wish for her Majesty's return.

It is currently reported that poor Nanny had nothing for dinner in the kitchen for herself and puss, but the scrapings of the bones of Saturday's mutton.

This evening there was high play at the Groom Porter's in Craven Street house. The great person lost money. It is supposed the ministers, as is usually supposed of all ministers, shared the emoluments among them.

TUESDAY, SEPTEMBER 25

This morning the good Lord Hutton called at Craven Street house and inquired very respectfully and affectionately concerning the welfare of the absent Queen. He then imparted to the big man a piece of intelligence important to them both, which he had just received from Lady Hawkesworth, viz. that [the] amiable and excellent companion Miss Dorthea Blunt had made a vow to marry absolutely him of the two, whose wife should first depart this life. It is impossible to express with words the various agitations of mind appearing in both their faces on this occasion. *Vanity* at the preference given them to the rest of mankind; *affection* to their present wives; *fear* of losing them; *hope* (if they must lose them) to obtain the proposed comfort; *jealousy* of each other, in case both wives should die together; etc., etc., etc. All working at the same time, jumbled their features into inexplicable confusion. They parted at length with professions and outward appearances indeed of ever-enduring friendship; but it was shrewdly suspected that each of them sincerely wished health and long life to the other's wife; and that however long either of those friends might like to live himself, the other would be very well pleased to survive him.

It is remarked that the skies have wept every day in Craven Street the absence of the Queen.

The public may be assured that this morning a certain *great person* was asked very complaisantly by the Mistress of the Household if he would choose to have the blade bone of Saturday's mutton that had been kept for his dinner today, *broiled* or *cold?* He answered gravely, *if there is any flesh on it, it may be broiled; if not, it may as well be cold.* Orders were accordingly given for broiling it. But when it came to table there was indeed so very little flesh, or rather none at all (Puss having dined on it yesterday after Nanny) that if our new administration had been as good economists as they would be thought, the expense of broiling might well have been saved to the public, and carried to the Sinking Fund. But the nation is astonished at the insolent presumption that dares treat so much mildness in so cruel a manner.

A terrible accident had *like to have happened* this afternoon at tea. The boiler was set too near the end of the little square table. The first ministress was sitting at one end of the table to administer the tea; the great person was about to sit down at the other end where the boiler stood. By a sudden motion, the lady gave the table a tilt. Had it gone over, the great *person* must have been scalded; perhaps to death. Various are the surmises and observations on this occasion. The godly say it would have been a just judgment on him for preventing by his laziness the family's going to church last Sunday. The opposition do not stick to insinuate that there was a design to scald him prevented only by his quick catching the table. The Friends of the Ministry give out that he carelessly jogged the table himself, and would have been inevitably scalded had not the ministress saved him. It is hard for the public to come at the truth in these cases.

At six o'clock this afternoon news came by the post that her Majesty arrived safely at Rochester on Saturday night. The bells immediately rang—for candles to illuminate the parlor; the Court went into cribbage, and the evening concluded with every other demonstration of joy.

It is reported that all the principal officers of the state have received an invitation from the Dutchess Dowager of Rochester to go down thither on Saturday next. But it is not yet known whether the great affairs they have on their hands will permit them to make this excursion.

We hear that from the time of her Majesty's leaving Craven Street house to this day no care is taken to file the newspapers; but they lie about in every room, in every window, and on every chair, just where the Doctor lays them when he has read them. It is impossible government can long go on in such hands.

To the Publisher of the Craven Street Gazette

SIR:

I make no doubt of the truth of what the papers tell us, that a certain great *person* has been half-starved on the bare blade-bone *of a sheep* (I cannot call it *of mutton* because none was on it) by a set of the most careless, thoughtless, inconsiderate, corrupt, ignorant, blundering, foolish, crafty, and knavish ministers that ever got into a house and pretended to govern a family and provide a dinner. Alas, for the poor Old England of Craven Street! If these nefarious wretches continue in power another week, the nation will be ruined—undone!—totally undone, if the Queen does not return; or (which is better) turn them all out and appoint me and my friends to succeed them. I am a great admirer of your useful and impartial paper; and therefore request you will insert this without fail; from your humble servant

INDIGNATION

To the Publisher of the Craven Street Gazette

SIR:

Your correspondent *Indignation* has made a fine story in your paper against our excellent Craven Street Ministry, as if they meant to starve his Highness, giving him only a bare blade bone for his dinner, while they riot upon roast venison, etc. The wickedness of writers in this age is truly amazing! I believe we never had since the foundation of our state a more faithful, upright, worthy, careful, considerate, incorrupt, discreet, wise, prudent and beneficent Ministry than the present. But if even the Angel Gabriel would condescend to be our minister and provide our dinners, he could scarcely escape newspaper defamation from a gang of hungry, ever restless, discontented and malicious scribblers. It is, sir, a piece of justice you owe our righteous administration to undeceive the public on this [occasion], by assuring them [of] the fact, which is that there was provided and actually smoking on the table under his royal nose at the same instant, as fine a piece of ribs of beef, roasted, as ever knife was put into; with potatoes, horse radish, pickled walnuts, etc.; which beef his Highness might have eaten of, if so he had pleased to do; and which he forbore to do, merely from a whimsical opinion (with respect be it spoken) that beef doth not with him perspire well, but makes his back itch, to his no small vexation, now that he hath lost the little Chinese ivory hand [at] the end of the stick, commonly called a *scratchback*, presented to him by her Majesty. This is the truth; and if your boasted impartiality is real, you will not hesitate a moment to insert this letter in your next paper. I am, tho' a little angry with you at present, Yours as you behave

A HATER OF SCANDAL

JUNIUS *and* CINNA *came to hand too late for this day's paper, but shall have place in our next.*

Marriages. None since our last; but Puss begins to go a courting.
Deaths.   In the back closet, and elsewhere, many poor mice.

Stocks.   Biscuit very low.
         Buckwheat and Indian meal, both sour.
         Tea, lowering daily in the canister.

Postscript

WEDNESDAY, SEPTEMBER 26

Those in the secret of affairs do not scruple to assert soundly, that our present first ministress is very notable, having this day been at market, bought excellent mutton chops, and apples four a penny, made a very fine apple pie with her own hands, and mended two pair of breeches.

CHAPTER

27

DIALOGUE WITH
LORD HILLSBOROUGH

Franklin became the colonial agent for Georgia in 1768 and a year later for New Jersey. The royal governors in both colonies approved his appointment. In October 1770 the lower house of the Massachusetts legislature chose him as its agent, with Arthur Lee of Virginia as subagent. Gov. Thomas Hutchinson refused to approve either man, but both accepted the honor. On 16 January 1771 Franklin went to Lord Hillsborough's house to present his credentials.

THE PORTER AT FIRST denied his Lordship, on which I left my name and drove off. But before the coach got out of the square, the coachman heard a call, turned, and went back to the door, when the porter came and said, "His Lordship will see you, sir." I was shown into the levee room, where I found Governor Bernard, who, I understand, attends there constantly. Several other gentlemen were there attending, with whom I sat down a few minutes, when Secretary Pownall came out to us, and said his Lordship desired I would come in.

I was pleased with this ready admission and preference, having sometimes waited three or four hours for my turn, and, being pleased, I could more easily put on the open, cheerful countenance, that my friends advised me to wear. His Lordship came towards me and said, "I was dressing in order to go to court; but hearing that you were at the door, who are a man of business, I determined to see you immediately." I thanked his Lordship, and said that my business at present was not much; it was only to pay my respects to his Lordship, and to acquaint him with my appointment by the House of Representatives of Massachusetts Bay to be their agent here, in which station if I could be of any service— (I was going on to say —"to the public, I should be very happy"; but his Lordship, whose countenance changed at my naming that province, cut me short by saying with something between a smile and a sneer,)

L.H.: I must set you right there, Mr. Franklin, you are not agent.

B.F.: Why, my Lord?

L.H.: You are not appointed.

B.F.: I do not understand your Lordship; I have the appointment in my pocket.

L.H.: You are mistaken; I have later and better advices. I have a letter from Governor Hutchinson; he would not give his assent to the bill.

B.F.: There was no bill, my Lord; it was a vote of the House.

L.H.: There was a bill presented to the governor for the purpose of appointing you and another, one Dr. Lee, I think he is called, to which the governor refused his assent.

B.F.: I cannot understand this, my Lord; I think there must be some mistake in it. Is your Lordship quite sure that you have such a letter?

L.H.: I will convince you of it directly. *(Rings the bell.)* Mr. Pownall will come in and satisfy you.

B.F.: It is not necessary, that I should now detain your Lordship from dressing. You are going to court. I will wait on your Lordship another time.

L.H.: No, stay; he will come immediately. *(To the servant.)* Tell Mr. Pownall I want him.

(Mr. Pownall comes in.)

L.H.: Have not you at hand Governor Hutchinson's letter, mentioning his refusing his assent to the bill for appointing Dr. Franklin agent?

Sec. P.: My Lord?

L.H.: Is there not such a letter?

Sec. P.: No, my Lord; there is a letter relating to some bill for the payment of a salary to Mr. DeBerdt, and I think to some other agent, to which the governor had refused his assent.

L.H.: And is there nothing in the letter to the purpose I mention?

Sec. P.: No, my Lord.

B.F.: I thought it could not well be, my Lord; as my letters are by the last ships, and they mention no such thing. Here is the authentic copy of the vote of the House appointing me, in which there is no mention of any act intended. Will your Lordship please to look at it? *(With seeming unwillingness he takes it, but does not look into it.)*

L.H.: An information of this kind is not properly brought to me as Secretary of State. The Board of Trade is the proper place.

B.F.: I will leave the paper then with Mr. Pownall to be—

L.H. (Hastily): To what end would you leave it with him?

B.F.: To be entered on the minutes of that Board, as usual.

L.H. (Angrily): It shall not be entered there. No such paper shall be entered there, while I have any thing to do with the business of that Board. The House of Representatives has no right to appoint an agent. We shall take no notice of any agents, but such as are appointed by acts of Assembly, to which the governor gives his assent. We have had confusion enough already. Here is one agent appointed by the Council, another by the House of Representatives. Which of these is agent for the province? Who are we to hear on provincial affairs? An agent appointed by act of Assembly I can understand. No other will be attended to for the state, I can assure you.

B.F.: I cannot conceive, my Lord, why the consent of the governor should be thought necessary to the appointment of an agent for the people. It seems to me that—

L.H. (With a mixed look of anger and contempt): I will not enter into a dispute with YOU, sir, upon this subject.

B.F.: I beg your Lordship's pardon; I do not presume to dispute with your Lordship; I would only say, that it seems to me, that every body of men, who cannot appear in person, where business relating to them may be transacted, should have a right to appear by an agent. The concurrence of the governor does not seem to me necessary. It is the business of the people, that is to be done; he is not one of them; he is himself an agent.

L.H. (Hastily): Whose agent is he?

B.F.: The King's, my Lord.

L.H.: No such matter. He is one of the corporation by the province charter. No agent can be appointed but by an act, nor any act pass without his assent. Besides, this proceeding is directly contrary to express instructions.

B.F.: I did not know there had been such instructions. I am not concerned in any offense against them, and—

L.H.: Yes, your offering such a paper to be entered is an offense against them. *(Folding it up again without having read a word of it.)* No such appointment shall be entered. When I came into the administration of American affairs, I found them in great disorder. By *my firmness* they are now something mended; and, while I have the honor to hold the seals, I shall continue the same conduct, the same *firmness*. I think my duty to the master I serve, and to the government of this nation, requires it of me.

If that conduct is not approved, *they* may take my office from me when they please. I shall make them a bow, and thank them; I shall resign with pleasure. That gentleman knows it *(pointing to Mr. Pownall)* but while I continue in it, I shall resolutely persevere in the same FIRMNESS. *(Spoken with great warmth and turning pale in his discourse, as if he was angry at some thing or somebody besides the agent, and of more consequence to himself.)*

B.F. *(Reaching out his hand for the paper, which his Lordship returned to him):* I beg your Lordship's pardon for taking up so much of your time. It is, I believe, of no great importance whether the appointment is acknowledged or not, for I have not the least conception that an agent can *at present* be of any use to any of the colonies. I shall therefore give your Lordship no further trouble. *(Withdrew.)*

Epilogue:

I have since heard that his lordship took great offense at some of my last words, which he calls extremely rude and abusive. He assured a friend of mine that they were equivalent to telling him to his face that the colonies could expect neither favor nor justice during his administration. I find he did not mistake me.

CHAPTER

28

"THE CLOUD SEEMS TO BE BLOWN OVER"

FRANKLIN REFUSED TO ADMIT the interview with Hillsborough had depressed him. "One encouragement I have," he said, is "the knowledge that he is not a whit better liked by his colleagues in the ministry than he is by me, that he cannot probably continue where he is much longer, and that he can scarce be succeeded by anybody who will not like me the better for his having been at variance with me." An unreasonable optimism pervaded his letters. "At present the cloud that threatened our charter liberties seems to be blown over," he reassured a friend three weeks after meeting with Hillsborough. "The sentiments of a majority of the ministers are, I think, become more favorable towards us," he wrote to another.

Actually, the interview had stunned Franklin, and after it he grew "very reserved, which adds greatly to his *natural inactivity* and there is no getting him to take part in *anything.*" It hurt even more to find himself "not only on bad terms with Lord Hillsborough, but with the ministry in general." He saw his usefulness in London ended, and suggested that his name be stricken from the list of Walpole Associates, "as it might be of prejudice to the undertaking." There were rumors that "Dr. Franklin . . . is taking his measures to return to America in the squadron of Admiral Montague."

Four months after the interview Franklin at last admitted the situation looked hopeless. "I think one may clearly see, in the system of customs to be exacted in America by act of Parliament, the seeds sown of a total disunion of the two countries, though as yet that event may be at a considerable distance." He saw the malice of royal officers provoking further violence from the people, and this in turn pushing the ministry into further repressive measures. Soon "the British nation and government will become odious, the subjection to it will be deemed no longer tolerable; war ensues, and the bloody struggle will end in absolute slavery to America, or ruin to Britain by the loss of her colonies; the latter most probable, from America's growing strength and magnitude."

What could be done to prevent the depressing forecast from coming true? Franklin no longer offered bold proposals to stiffen American resistance. Now he wondered "whether it will not be better gradually to wear off the assumed authority of Parliament over America, . . . than by a general open denial and resistance to it," but he advanced the thought hesitantly. "I do not venture to advise in this case, because I see in this seemingly prudent course some danger of a diminishing attention to our rights, instead of a persevering endeavor to recover and establish them." Hope lay only in doing everything possible in delaying the outbreak of war as long as possible, for "the daily increasing strength and importance of [America] must give such weight in time to our just claims as no selfish spirit in this part of the empire will be able to resist."

Franklin had admitted that the cloud darkening imperial affairs had not blown away and that he saw nothing on the horizon about to disperse it. Confused and depressed, certain only of his uselessness, he sank deeper into lethargy. The lingering of "a severe and tedious winter"—late in April "a heavy storm of snow" hit the city—did not lighten his mood. When Wharton asked for help to push the Walpole Associates' petition through the bureaucracy, he refused "to stir in this business." Indeed, through most of 1771 he refused to stir in almost any business. In May he came to an extraordinary decision. He would do what he had never done before—turn his back on public affairs. He packed his bags and started out on the first of a series of journeys that would last over a half year.

2

On the first trip Franklin explored the English Midlands, the industrial heart of the nation. To make the break with politics complete, he chose for traveling companions two fellow scientists—John Canton and John Ingenhousz, both talented experimenters in electricity—and his nephew Jonathan Williams, then visiting him from Boston. The foursome inspected coal mines and canals near Manchester, the ironworks at Rotherham, clothing mills in Norwich, a china factory in Derby. Occasionally they paused to catch their breath, once for a pleasant morning

visit to Dr. Priestley's laboratory, later to sample the "good ale" in Bus-
ton. Williams kept a detailed journal of all they saw, for his uncle traveled
with a purpose. For months in letters home he had urged America to start
manufacturing. The colonies must be prepared to take care of themselves
if war broke out with the mother country. An accurate report of a canal
lock, of the machinery in a china factory, a weaving mill, or an iron
foundry could be useful to America in the years ahead.

Franklin ended the excursion abruptly at Manchester. He wanted to
be present at court to celebrate the king's birthday on June 4. "My
journey has been of use to my health," he wrote his wife from London,
"the air and exercise have given me fresh spirits, and I feel now exceeding
well." Not well enough, though, to face politics. Within a few days he
set off again, this time for the country house of Jonathan Shipley, Bishop
of St. Asaph, who lived in the village of Twyford, deep in the rolling
countryside of southern England. After a week's visit, Franklin left to
"breathe with reluctance the smoke of London" but promised to return
to Twyford when he had cleared up his mail.

With the thank-you note to the bishop and his family went a book and
a barrel of dried apples, just arrived from America. Franklin's thought-
fulness never ceased to astonish friends. On his desk in Craven Street he
found a letter from John Bartram, now seventy-two and worried that a
modest pension given by the king for his contributions to botany might
soon be cut off. Franklin checked and learned the pension would continue, regardless of the tension between Britain and her colonies. To that
favor he added another. "You take notice of the failing of your eyesight,"
he wrote Bartram. "Perhaps you have not spectacles that suit you, and
... therefore I send you a complete set, from number one to thirteen, that
you may try them at your ease; and, having pitched on such as suit you
best at present, reserve those of higher numbers for future use, as your
eyes grow still older; and with the lower numbers, which are for younger
people, you may oblige some other friends."

While he traveled about the city fulfilling requests from home, "a very
odd accident happened." A dealer in old books asked if he would like to
look at "a curious collection" of pamphlets. "On examining I found that
they contained all the principal pamphlets and papers on public affairs
that had been printed here from the Restoration down to 1715." A number
of the pieces had notes in the margins—all in the handwriting of his
father's brother, Uncle Benjamin. "I suppose he parted with them, when
he left England and came to Boston, . . . which was about the year 1716
or 1717, now more than fifty years since."

The incident put Franklin in a reminiscent mood, and when a few

days later he returned to Shipley's country home, this time for a visit of
two weeks, he escaped further from the troubled present by writing the
first and longest part of his autobiography. Franklin began it casually as
a letter to his son, whom he had not seen for seven years and might not
see again. At the start he planned to tell only about the Franklin family,
but by the time he had finished with his parents and Uncle Benjamin and
the house in Boston his interest was engaged. He paused to make an
outline and shifted from genealogy to autobiography. He wrote swiftly,
but keeping in mind that he was embarked on a large project made notes
along the way later to include documents then not at hand, such as the
journal of his voyage back to America in 1726 and the "Articles of Belief"
drawn up after nearly dying upon the return to Philadelphia. At the end
of the two weeks he had carried the story to 1731, the year the Library
Company was founded. "It was an engaging tale, and reliving it must
have been a satisfying experience," Paul Conner has remarked. "The
story was exhilarating but—written when it was—a bit incongruous. An
empire was about to rupture, and Franklin, whose position as colonial
agent now placed him astride the fissure, was beginning to sense his
inability to bridge the opening chasm. . . . It almost would seem that the
Autobiography was designed to bolster the spirits of its author, to reassure
him of his grip on affairs." Or, more likely, to let him escape from a
present he could not face into a reassuring and satisfying past that he
could shape to his pleasure.

Only for a moment, on the last page, did he mention the present.
When speaking of the subscription libraries that had spread throughout
the colonies, he said: "These libraries have improved the general conversation of the Americans, made the common tradesmen and farmers as
intelligent as most gentlemen from other countries, and perhaps have
contributed in some degree to the stand so generally made throughout the
colonies in defense of their privileges." Franklin returned to London in
a gay mood.

3

Franklin paused long enough in London to read his mail and pick up
fresh linen, then he and Richard Jackson set out for Ireland. The spirit
of Lord Hillsborough hovered over the trip like a portent. Just before
leaving London Strahan reported his lordship told him Franklin was "a
factious, turbulent fellow, always in mischief, a republican, enemy to the
king's service, and what not." The boat the tourists took across the Irish

Sea was named *Hillsborough*. Shortly after arriving in Dublin they met the gentleman in the flesh at a dinner party. "He was extremely civil," said the astonished Franklin. "He entered very frankly into conversation with us both, and invited us both to stop at his house in Hillsboro, as we should travel northward, and urged it in so polite a manner, that we could not avoid saying we would wait on him if we went that way." Jackson, as counsel to the Board of Trade that Hillsborough ruled over, knew he must accept the invitation, but Franklin "was determined not to go that way." (So he wrote his son, but in another letter "I concluded to comply with his invitation," he said, "as it might afford an opportunity of saying something on American affairs.")

Soon after issuing the invitation Hillsborough returned to his estate in northern Ireland. The skies cleared for Franklin and he steeped himself in the splendors of Dublin. A visit to the Irish Parliament provided an unexpected pleasure. A standing rule allowed members of the British Parliament to sit, but not vote, in the Irish legislature. Jackson, as a member of the House of Commons, was admitted to the floor while Franklin waited outside the bar. From there he heard the Speaker say, "he understood there was in town an American gentleman of . . . distinguished character and merit, a member or delegate of some of the parliaments of that country . . . and that he did suppose the House would consider the American assemblies as English parliaments." The House roared a unanimous "aye," and "two members came to me without the bar where I was standing, led me in, and placed me very honorably."

Franklin found Irish politicians "disposed to be friends of America," and he tried to link American grievances against British authority to those the Irish held. He hinted "that our growing weight might in time be thrown into their scale, and, by joining our interest with theirs might be obtained for them as well as for us, a more equitable treatment from this nation." Privately, though, he doubted that Ireland could throw much weight into the scale. The poverty he saw among the "lower people" amazed him. "They live in wretched hovels of mud and straw, are clothed in rags, and subsist chiefly on potatoes. Our New England farmers, of the poorest sort, . . . are princes when compared to them." An English gentleman, one of those absentee landlords "who lease their lands in gross to undertakers that rack the tenants and fleece them skin and all to make estates to themselves," asked Franklin why America "did not rival Ireland in the beef and butter trade to the West Indies, and share with it in its linen trade." "I supposed the reason might be," said Franklin, *"our people eat beef and butter every day, and wear shirts themselves."*

Franklin and Jackson traveled northward from Dublin together, planning to go their separate ways when they neared Lord Hillsborough's estate. But when the time came to part, no post chaise could be found at the inn for Franklin, "so I was obliged to go forward with Mr. Jackson." His lordship welcomed the travelers as if they were royalty. They spent four days in his great house. He paid "particular attention" to Franklin and "seemed attentive to everything that might make my stay in his house agreeable to me." When he sent Franklin out with his son as host to explore the countryside, he covered "me with his own great coat, lest I should take cold."

Not a cloud darkened the visit. His lordship appeared at every turn a genial, understanding friend of Franklin and America. He thought "America ought not to be restrained in manufacturing anything she could manufacture to advantage." He thought the production of wine should be encouraged there with a government subsidy. Would Mr. Franklin think about that; he would be pleased for his "opinion and advice." Newfoundland had grown populous enough to have a regular government, "but there were great difficulties in the forming such a kind of government as would be suitable to the particular circumstances of that country." Would Mr. Franklin consider the problem and sometime back in London "favor him with my sentiments"? Franklin ended the visit pondering a question of his own—why had Hillsborough been so "extremely solicitous to impress me, and the colonies thro' me, with a good opinion of him"?

From Hillsborough's estate Jackson returned to London while Franklin pushed on to Scotland. "Storms and floods" on the road to Edinburgh made the trip an ordeal. He arrived late at night and had to lodge "miserably at an inn." The next morning "that excellent Christian David Hume, agreeable to the precepts of the Gospel, . . . *received the* stranger" and in Hume's house he rested "most happily." After a fortnight there, he visited Lord Kames for a long weekend, moved on to Glasgow, spent two days at the Carron ironworks, then returned to Hume's. Continuing bad weather dampened his zest for sight-seeing, and the latter part of November he headed for London. "My last expedition convinced me that I grow too old for rambling," he admitted once back in the comfortable quarters on Craven Street, "and that 'twas probable I should never make such another journey."

4

Franklin began the year 1772 full of indecision. "I have of late great debates with myself whether or not I shall continue here any longer. I grow homesick, and, being now in my sixty-seventh year, I begin to apprehend some infirmity of age may attack me, and make my return impracticable," he wrote his son in January. "I have indeed so many good kind friends here, that I could spend the remainder of my life among them with great pleasure, if it were not for my American connections, and the indelible affection I retain for that dear country, from which I have so long been in a state of exile."

A lingering exhaustion from the trip to Scotland contributed to the low mood, and also the perplexing relationship with Hillsborough. "I have not met with Lord Hillsborough since my return from Ireland, seeing no use at present in attending his levees," Franklin told a friend. He said nothing untrue. He had not met with his lordship since arriving back in London, but if he meant to imply he had not tried to meet with him or that he thought a meeting worthless, he misled his correspondent. He spoke more openly to his son. "When I had been a little while re-turned to London, I waited on him to thank him for his civilities in Ireland, and to discourse with him on a Georgia affair. The porter told me he was not at home. I left my card, went another time, and received the same answer, though I knew he was at home, a friend of mine being with him. After intermissions of a week each, I made two more visits, and received the same answer. The last time was on a levee day, when a number of carriages were at his door. My coachman driving up, alighted, and was opening the coach door, when the porter, seeing me, came out, and surlily chid the coachman for opening the door before he had in-quired whether my Lord was at home; and then turning to me said, 'My Lord is not at home.' I have never since been nigh him, and we have only abused one another at a distance." (Hillsborough has never had the chance to tell his side of this episode or, indeed, of any part of his relations with Franklin. Until that happens, the historian must keep in mind that his lordship, one of the ablest ministers then serving his Majesty, may have had reason for what Franklin has pictured as most curious treatment of a well-meaning gentleman.)

The inexplicable brush-off from Hillsborough came as Samuel Whar-ton spread the word in letters to Philadelphia that Franklin should not be allowed "*any merit*" in promoting the Walpole Associates' petition for a land grant in the Ohio Valley. Franklin admitted he had not been "equally active" with Wharton, but since his advice had been "asked on every step" he assumed "I may have lent some weight to his negotia-tions." He said those in power listened to him because of "the greater confidence men are apt to place in one they know than in a stranger." The snide reference to Wharton as a "stranger" to the great in British affairs exposed the displeasure Franklin felt at his friend's ascendancy; Strahan a year earlier said Wharton had "acquired better connections here than any other American." While Hillsborough's animosity was swinging doors shut against Franklin, Wharton's cultivated acquaintances among the rich and powerful had reached the ear of the king. What, George III one day asked a friend of Hillsborough, had happened to the Walpole Associates' petition?

Through a deft use of the bureaucratic machinery Hillsborough had delayed an opinion on the petition for nearly a year. With the king's interest aroused, he dared delay no longer, and in April, speaking for the Board of Trade, he recommended that the government reject the petition. Normally the Privy Council accepted such judgments from the Board of Trade. But two of the council's most powerful members—Lord Gower, president, and Lord Rochford, secretary of state for the northern department—were shareholders in the Walpole Associates. They also detested Hillsborough and hoped through humiliating him to topple Lord North's ministry from power. In an unusual move, a committee of the council agreed to listen to the Associates' comments on Hillsborough's report. The shareholders chose Wharton to speak for them, but Franklin had a large hand in preparing the presentation. Wharton handled himself admirably. He replied "distinctly to each particular objection; and . . . fully convinced every lord present."

The hearing over, Franklin prepared for another holiday. But before leaving London he sent off to Strahan's newspaper a brief piece provoked by a decision just handed down by Lord Chief Justice Mansfield. James Somerset, a Jamaican slave brought to England by his master, had sued in court for his freedom. "The air of England has long been too pure for a slave," Lord Mansfield said in his judgment, "and every man is free who breathes it." Franklin thought the decision hypocritical. *"Pharisaical Britain!* to pride thyself in setting free a *single slave* that happens to land on thy coasts, while thy merchants in all thy ports are encouraged by thy laws to continue a commerce whereby so many *hundreds of thousands* are dragged into a slavery that can scarce be said to end with their lives, since it is entailed on their posterity!"

Over twenty years earlier Franklin had opposed slavery as a senseless institution that drained the economy more than it replenished it. But he continued to hold slaves. His wife, who cared for the slaves who helped her around the house as if they were her own children, helped to plant the seeds that made him uneasy about holding other humans in bondage. During his first trip to England she visited a school for Negroes in Philadelphia. "It gave me great pleasure, and I shall send Othello to the school," she wrote her husband. Franklin showed the letter to the Bray

Associates, a society for encouraging the education of blacks in America, and to his dismay they printed it, then chose him "one of the society, and I am at present chairman for the current year." He gave the society only desultory interest, but when he returned home he visited a Negro school, and "from what I then saw, have conceived a higher opinion of the natural capacities of the black race, than I had ever before entertained," he said. "Their apprehension seems as quick, their memory as strong, and their docility in every respect equal to that of white children. You will wonder perhaps that I should ever doubt it, and I will not undertake to justify all my prejudices, nor to account for them."

To conceive of blacks equal to whites in intelligence was a giant leap few Americans had made, but Franklin still refused to speak publicly against slavery. It could do him no good, and probably hurt him, politically. Few in America except a small band of Philadelphia Quakers led by the saintly Anthony Benezet, then favored abolition. Back in England Franklin kept silent until Granville Sharp, a dissenting clergyman, in 1770 ridiculed Americans for claiming the right to enjoy liberty when they kept hundreds of thousands of black men in chains. Franklin replied lamely that probably not one American family in a hundred held slaves, that Britain had imposed slavery on America, and, finally—*tu quoque*—Britons had no right to point a finger while they enslaved their own laboring poor. "All the wretches that dig coal for you, in those dark caverns under ground, unblessed by sunshine, are absolute slaves by your law, and their children after them, from the time they first carry a basket to the end of their days."

Franklin still would not condemn slavery as a moral obscenity. Then in the spring of 1772 Benezet wrote seeking to enlist Franklin as a "fellow traveler on a dangerous and heavy road." He told of the horrors blacks endured on the passage from Africa to America. The letter arrived as Mansfield handed down his decision. Letter and decision together sparked the brief, angry paragraphs Franklin sent to the *London Chronicle.* For the first time he attacked slavery as an outrage against humanity. "Can sweetening our tea, etc. with sugar, be a circumstance of such absolute necessity? Can the petty pleasure thence arising to the taste, compensate for so much misery produced among our fellow creatures, and such a constant butchery of the human species by this pestilential detestable traffic in the bodies and souls of men?" But nowhere in the short tract did Franklin commit himself to the antislavery movement. He used the misery of the blacks only to flail "pharisaical Britain." Yet at last he had publicly condemned slavery. His views changed with the speed of a snail, but unlike those of most men in their late sixties, they changed.

5

Franklin left for a month's holiday after sending his essay on Mansfield's decision to Strahan. He visited his wife's relations in Birmingham and his son-in-law's family in Preston. "In Cumberland," he told Deborah, "I ascended a very high mountain, where I had a prospect of a most beautiful country, of hills, fields, lakes, villas, etc., and at Whitehaven went down the coal mines till they told me I was eighty fathoms under the surface of the sea, which rolled over our heads; so that I have been nearer both the upper and lower regions than ever in my life before."

Back in London in mid-July he learned that the committee of the Privy Council had recommended approval of the Walpole Associates' petition for a grant of some twenty million acres of land in the Ohio Valley. Hillsborough said he would resign before implementing the judgment and on 1 August 1772 he did so. He believed Franklin had a large hand in his fall and called him "one of the most mischievous men in England." Franklin called him "as double and deceitful as any man I ever met with" and rejoiced "we have done with him, I hope, forever." But he took no credit for his removal. "His brother ministers disliked him extremely, and wished for a fair occasion of tripping up his heels," he said. "The king, too, was tired of him. . . ."

Earlier a friend at court had asked Franklin whether there was anyone then in the government who would be more acceptable to America if Lord Hillsborough happened to be removed? "Yes," he said, "there is Lord Dartmouth; we liked him very well when he was at the head of the Board [of Trade] formerly, and probably should like him again." Franklin did not know if his opinion "had any effect," but Lord Dartmouth replaced Hillsborough as secretary of state for American affairs and president of the Board of Trade. (Franklin's opinion probably had little effect. Dartmouth was the half-brother of Lord North and the obvious choice for a prime minister intent on shoring up control of his ministry.)

The cloud at last seemed to have blown over, and overnight Franklin became ebullient. "As to my situation here," he wrote the month Hillsborough left office, "nothing can be more agreeable, especially as I hope for less embarrassment from the new minister; a general respect paid me by the learned, a number of friends and acquaintance among them, with whom I have a pleasing intercourse; a character of so much weight, that it has protected me when some in power would have done me injury, and continued me in an office they would have deprived me of; my company

so much desired, that I seldom dine at home in winter, and could spend
the whole summer in the country houses of inviting friends, if I chose
it. Learned and ingenious foreigners, that come to England, almost all
make a point of visiting me; for my reputation is still higher abroad than
here. Several of the foreign ambassadors have assiduously cultivated my
acquaintance, treating me as one of their *corps,* partly I believe from the
desire they have, from time to time, of hearing something of American
affairs, an object become of importance in foreign courts, who begin to
hope Britain's alarming power will be diminished by the defection of her
colonies; and partly that they may have an opportunity of introducing me
to the gentlemen of their country who desire it. The king, too, has lately
been heard to speak of me with great regard." France chose this moment
to fill the cup further by electing him a member of its Royal Academy
of Sciences. "There are but eight of the *Assocités Etrangers* in all Europe,
and those of the most distinguished names of science," he boasted.

"These are flattering circumstances; but a violent longing for home
sometimes seizes me, which I can no otherwise subdue but by promising
myself a return next spring or next fall, and so forth. As to returning
hither, if I once go back, I have no thoughts of it. I am too far advanced
in life to propose three voyages more. I have some important affairs to
settle at home, and, considering my double expenses here and there, I
hardly think my salaries fully compensate the disadvantages. The late
change, however, being thrown into the balance, determines me to stay
another winter."

CHAPTER

29

"A MAN OF LETTERS"

GOV. THOMAS HUTCHINSON OF MASSACHUSETTS had considered Franklin a friend since they worked together in 1754 at the Albany Congress. After a Boston mob looted Hutchinson's house during the Stamp Act riots, he turned to Franklin for help in the name of "friendship in promoting compensation" from the crown for his losses. An amiable if desultory correspondence followed. Franklin in one letter asked for an "opinion upon an application . . . for representation" of the colonies in Parliament. Hutchinson replied that provincial leaders once in favor of the idea now found "the voice of the people against it"; Franklin soon after abandoned the proposal. As late as mid-1769 Hutchinson told Franklin he would "be much obliged to you if you will communicate any occurrences relative to the colonies which may be of use to me in my critical situation."

It is common to picture Hutchinson as stubborn, insecure, inflexible, a joyless man who found it hard to unbend, a worrier who talked himself into a nervous breakdown. Opposed to this frosty character stands the genial, imperturbable Franklin, who never confessed to a sleepless night, who seized each day with delight and adapted himself and his views gracefully to whatever surprises the day unfolded. Though Hutchinson was, as his biographer calls him, "the Puritan *manqué*"—an ascetic, humorless, hardworking man who found little to enjoy in life outside of home and office—he shared enough with Franklin to build what he thought was a friendship. They differed only five years in age, Hutchinson being the younger. Both had prospered in business. Neither blushed to fill political posts that came his way with friends and relatives. Hutchinson was a devout Congregationalist but like Franklin put little stress "upon modes and forms in religion" and refused to "love a good man the less because he and I are not just of the same way of thinking." He could be unbending when he saw a principle at stake but preferred to "strive to be more of a willow and less of an oak" in politics. "We don't live in Plato's commonwealth, and when we can't have perfection we ought to comply with the measure that is least remote from it." Both men were equally devoted to the mother country and to their beloved native "country," the colony of Massachusetts, but Hutchinson had a clearer understanding of the relationship between the two. Long before Franklin he opposed the Stamp Act vehemently, derided the distinction between internal and external taxes, and held that while Parliament had sovereign authority over the colonies common sense dictated it should not use that power to tax them.

Down to 1772 the two men's political views differed little. Hutchinson as a royal officer was forced to carry out instructions from London that jarred with his judgments while Franklin rode out the storm in London, letting the tide swing him from one position to another. Franklin never in his long life held an executive political post that forced him to deal day-by-day with an aggrieved body of people. The rioting in London upon John Wilkes's return in 1768 had appalled him; he said so frankly in letters that would have ruined him if they had been published in America, where Wilkes was a hero. He censured, too, the Stamp Act riots in Boston, but how would he have handled them as governor? He abhorred smuggling and aired his views in a lighthearted essay that pleased the ministry while Hutchinson in Boston had to deal with the crimes of that preeminent smuggler John Hancock. Franklin condemned the dumping of the East India Company's tea in Boston harbor, saying mobs must not be allowed to destroy private property, but it was Hutchinson who had to confront the event and its aftermath.

A year before the tea was dumped Franklin decided from his snug berth three thousand miles away from the uproar in Boston, as insulated from the raucous mobs that roamed the city's streets as the scholar who makes smug judgments from the safe distance of two centuries, that Thomas Hutchinson must go. In December 1772 he set out to wreck the governor's career.

2

Sometime in the fall of 1772 someone—John Temple, a friend of William Franklin, was later accused of the deed, but Bernard Bailyn has built a plausible case against Thomas Pownall, an old foe of Hutchinson and capable of duplicity—gave Franklin a packet of seventeen letters written several years earlier by five gentlemen from Massachusetts—one of whom was Gov. Thomas Hutchinson, another Andrew Oliver, the lieutenant governor—to Thomas Whately, a London bureaucrat who had recently died. Hutchinson's letters revealed little he had not said publicly in Massachusetts, but Franklin thought the contents heinous. The cautious governor, who rarely risked his reputation on paper, only once let down his guard. "There must be an abridgement of what are called English liberties," he wrote in one letter. "I wish the good of the colony, when I wish to see some further restraint of liberty rather than the connection with the parent state should be broken, for I am sure such a breach must prove the ruin of the colony." If Franklin had paused to consider the tumults Boston had endured when Hutchinson wrote, if he had recalled his own momentary disenchantment with "English liberty" during the Wilkes riots, he might have seen the letters for what they were —occasionally indiscreet, hardly heinous.

Franklin sent the packet of letters to Speaker Cushing in Boston. "I thought it my duty to give some principal people there a sight of them," he said later, "very much with this view—that when they saw the measures they complained of took their rise in a great degree from the representations and recommendations of their own countrymen, their resentment against Britain on account of those measures might abate, as mine had done, and a reconciliation be more easily obtained." Cushing could show the letters to friends and foes of Hutchinson but they must not be copied or published. The gentleman who had purloined them insisted on this. But view this as an advantage, said Franklin, for "possibly, as distant objects, seen only through a mist, appear larger, the same may happen from the mystery in this case."

The decision to send the letters to Cushing was the most momentous in Franklin's long life as a public figure. Anyone who pondered what manner of man Franklin was had to wonder why he acted as he did. Bernard Bailyn has accepted Franklin's explanation—the letters were sent "simply and solely to clear the ministry, and with them the English nation. . . ." This seems too neat. Franklin's character was one of the most elusive produced by eighteenth-century America. He was, as has been said of another, "the most approachable and the most impenetrable of men, easy and delightful of acquaintance, impossible of knowledge." Surely other ingredients helped shape his decision.

Revenge, perhaps. Hutchinson had refused to approve Franklin's election as the House of Representatives' agent in London and vetoed every bill sent up authorizing the agent's salary. Franklin had not received a pence in the two years he had served the House.

Then, he may have wished to improve his standing with Samuel Adams and his coterie in Massachusetts. Franklin admitted that in England he was thought "too much of an American," but "I have in America been deemed too much of an Englishman." Adams had preferred Arthur Lee of Virginia, a sometime physician and lawyer then living in London, for the House's agent but could only manage Lee's election as Franklin's subagent and replacement if the old man died or returned to America. Lee and Franklin did not rub along well, and in mid-1772 the Virginian wrote Adams that Franklin was little more than a hireling of the British ministry. The packet of purloined letters would do much to mend Franklin's reputation with Samuel Adams.

Ambition for power may also have been an ingredient that contributed to Franklin's decision. Earlier, when Governor Bernard had been removed from office—his reputation also ruined by stolen letters— Franklin had heard from Boston that "we want a governor and almost everybody wishes Doctor Franklin might come." His son William confirmed the rumor. "Many of the principal people there wish you to be the man, and say that you would meet with no opposition from any party, but would soon be able to conciliate all differences." If Hutchinson's letters toppled him from office, as Bernard's had, who better than Franklin could fill the vacancy? Enemies in England thought this his real reason for sending the letters. "It was not easy before this to give credit to such surmises," one man said, "but nothing surely but a too eager attention to an ambition of this sort, could have betrayed a wise man into such conduct as we have now seen."

About the time Franklin got his first glimpse of the stolen letters he had written: "Several of the foreign ambassadors have assiduously cultivated my acquaintance, treating me as one of their *corps.*" The flattery may have led Franklin to reconceive his role as agent, transmuting himself into an ambassador for America. At least one member of the British government thought this one reason for sending the letters. Ambassadors, said Alexander Wedderburn, the solicitor general, in an excoriating attack on Franklin, "may bribe a villain to steal or betray any state papers; he is under the command of another state, and is not amenable to the laws of the country where he resides; and the secure exemption from punishment may induce a laxer morality. But Dr. Franklin, whatever he may teach the people at Boston, while he is *here* at least is a subject; and if a subject injure a subject, he is answerable to the law. And the Court of

Chancery will not much attend to his new self-created importance."

All this is not to say that Franklin was not appalled by what he read in Hutchinson's letters. His son thought the contents innocuous. "Being of that country myself," meaning Massachusetts, Franklin replied, "I think those letters more heinous than you seem to think them." But even if he had read the letters as his son had, Franklin would have still sacrificed Hutchinson in order, as he put it, to bring the dispute between America and England "to a crisis." That dispute had boiled on for eight years. The time seemed right to force all contested issues to a decision now that the genial Lord Dartmouth, known to be friendly to the colonies, commanded American affairs. The "Psalmsinger," as colleagues called him because of his attachment to George Whitefield and Methodism, had virtues Lord Hillsborough saw as defects—"too much humanity—too much religion." His step-brother Lord North and the king were deeply attached to him. He favored the creation of a western colony. What better man to have at the helm if revelation of Hutchinson's letters forced Anglo-American relations to a crisis?

A flaw marred Franklin's reasoning. He judged his lordship knowing little about him. Dartmouth was weak and indecisive. He equivocated on sensitive issues; if pressed for an opinion he would only promise to recommend to the king "all such measures, as with propriety he could," without revealing what he thought proper. He cared little for power. While Dartmouth relaxed on his country estate, the ministry and bureaucracy made crucial decisions concerning America without consulting him. "My Lord Dartmouth is a quiet man," a colleague remarked. "He did not complain." Hillsborough had demanded and got an authoritative voice in all decisions regarding the colonies. Within months after his fall most of the power over American affairs accumulated during his tenure had slipped into other hands. "Our business has hitherto been as light as you could wish," an aide complained less than a year after Dartmouth took over, "and I think it is likely to continue so, for what can Lord Dartmouth have to do" while others in the government "will not let us have anything to say . . . ?"

In letters home Franklin appeared well informed on the ministry's thinking about America when in fact he was not. The fall of Hillsborough had not swung open closed doors. He hardly knew Lord North, who had firm control of the government, and was intimate with no one involved with making policy. His isolation from the men in power led to a stupendous miscalculation—that the benign Lord Dartmouth would be able to settle the dispute with America.

3

Franklin, as agent for Massachusetts, officially met his lordship in October 1772. "He received me very obligingly, made no objection to my acting as agent without an appointment assented to by the governor, as his predecessor had done, so that I hope business is getting into a better train." Franklin presented a petition from the Massachusetts legislature that complained against a proposal to pay the local judiciary out of revenue from customs duties. A few days later Dartmouth asked him to drop by to discuss the petition. "The king would be exceedingly offended" by it, his lordship said, and if laid before Parliament, "the censure of both houses would be drawn upon" Massachusetts. He wished Franklin would withdraw the petition and "consult [his] constituents, who might possibly on reconsideration think fit to order its being deferred." After further talk, Franklin officially withdrew the petition, impressed by Lord Dartmouth's "good disposition towards us." Franklin left the meeting certain his lordship intended to put American affairs on a new tact. On December 2 he sent the Hutchinson-Oliver letters to Speaker Cushing.

A second interview a week later reinforced first impressions. Dartmouth said he had "the best disposition" toward the colonies, that "he wished sincerely for their welfare, though possibly he might not always think with them, as to the means of obtaining that end." Massachusetts's list of grievances to be redressed required "much consideration, and therefore it could scarce be expected that a sudden change should be made in so many measures," he went on, but "if the Americans continued quiet, and gave no fresh offense to government, those measures would be reconsidered, and such relief given as upon consideration should be thought reasonable." Beyond these general remarks—"I could then obtain nothing more particular," said Franklin—Dartmouth refused to go, but Franklin left the meeting full of optimism.

The optimism continued into 1773. Franklin heard in January that after deducting all expenses the customs office in America the previous year had netted only eighty-five pounds. That revelation came with other good news—the mammoth East India Company verged on bankruptcy. "The continued refusal of North America to take tea from hence has brought infinite distress on the company," Franklin reported home. "They imported great quantities in the faith that that agreement could not hold; and now they can neither pay their debts nor dividends; their stock has sunk to the annihilating near three millions of their property, and government will lose its £400,000 a year; while their teas lie upon hand." The catastrophe had forced the company to petition Parliament to lift the duty on tea imported in America. Continued resistance on America's part should soon bring "a total change of measures with regard to us," said Franklin. "In confidence of this coming change in our favor, I think our prudence is meanwhile to be quiet, only holding up our rights and claims on all occasions in resolutions, memorials, and remonstrances; but bearing patiently the little present notice that is taken of them. They will all have their weight in time, and that time is at no great distance."

While Franklin counseled patience and restraint, London learned in March that Governor Hutchinson had sought in an ill-timed speech to the legislature to clarify the constitutional relationship of Massachusetts to the mother country. The people who settled the colony knew they must "remain subject to the supreme authority of Parliament," he said, and that their local legislature had only "subordinate power" to exercise. "I know of no line that can be drawn between the supreme authority of Parliament and the total independence of the colonies." The legislature answered that it was *not* subject to Parliament's supreme authority. When Franklin next talked with Dartmouth the conversation turned on Hutchinson's speech and the legislature's blunt reply.

"What difficulties that gentleman has brought us all into by his imprudence!" said Dartmouth, "tho' I suppose he meant well; yet what can now be done? It is impossible that Parliament can suffer such a declaration of the General Assembly asserting its independency, to pass unnoticed."

"In my opinion," said Franklin, "it would be better and more prudent to take no notice of it. It is *words* only. Acts of Parliament are still submitted to there. No force is used to obstruct their execution. And while that is the case, Parliament would do well to turn a deaf ear, and seem not to know that such declarations had ever been made. Violent measures against the province will not change the opinion of the people. Force could do no good."

"I do not know that force would be thought of," said Dartmouth, then added ominously, "but perhaps an act may pass to lay them under some inconveniences, till they rescind that declaration. Can they not withdraw it? I wish they could be persuaded to reconsider the matter, and do it of themselves voluntarily, and thus leave things between us on the old footing, the points undiscussed. Don't you think such a thing possible?"

"No, my lord," said Franklin, "I think it impossible. If they were even to wish matters back in the situation before the governor's speech, and the dispute obliterated, they cannot withdraw their answers till he first withdraws his speech, which methinks would be an awkward operation, that perhaps he will hardly be directed to perform. As to an act of Parliament laying that country under inconveniences, it is likely that it will only put them as heretofore upon inventing some method of incommoding this country till the act is repealed; and so we shall go on injuring and provoking each other, instead of cultivating that good will and harmony so necessary to the general welfare."

"But what," said Dartmouth, "if you were in my place, would or could you do? Would you hazard the being called to account in some future session by Parliament for keeping back the communicating of dispatches of such importance?"

"I," said Franklin, "only give my poor opinion with regard to Parliament, that, supposing the dispatches laid before them, they would act most prudently in ordering them to lie on the table, and take no farther notice of them. For were I as much an Englishman as I am an American, and ever so desirous of establishing the authority of Parliament, I protest to his lordship I cannot conceive of a single step the Parliament can take to increase it, that will not tend to diminish it, and after abundance of mischief they must finally lose it. The loss in itself perhaps would not be of much consequence because it is an authority they can never well exercise for want of due information and knowledge, and therefore it is not worth hazarding the mischief to preserve it."

Franklin had asked for the interview in order to resubmit the Massachusetts petition withdrawn in November 1772 and to present a second petition detailing further grievances. This time Dartmouth accepted both petitions. The royal reply came in June. In commenting upon it, Franklin remarked that the king had shown "a great share of what his friends call *firmness,*" underscoring a word that had been a favorite of Hillsborough's when talking about how to deal with the colonies. "His Majesty," said Franklin, continuing his explication of the reply, "as he will ever attend to the *humble* petitions of his subjects and be forward to redress every *real* grievance, so he is determined to support *the constitution* and resist with firmness every attempt to derogate from the authority of the *supreme legislature.*"

The curt dismissal of the petitions was unsettling, for the king had become the centerpiece in Franklin's conception of the constitutional relationship of the colonies to the mother country. "From a long and thorough consideration of the subject, I am indeed of opinion that the Parliament has no right to make any law whatever, binding on the colonies," he told his son; "that the king, and not the king, Lords, and Commons collectively, is their sovereign; and that the king, with their respective parliaments, is their only legislator." But the theory meant nothing if the king rejected it, indeed, was a dangerous theory if the king acted with the same *"firmness"* shown by Hillsborough. In the thirteen years George III had been on the throne Franklin had honored him with reverent respect. Now, suddenly, the king revealed himself no more tolerant toward the colonies than the obnoxious Hillsborough. From the day of the royal reply to the petitions Franklin's reverence turned slowly to hate. "He often and indeed always appeared to me to have a personal animosity and very severe resentment against the king," John Adams once remarked. "In all his conversations and in all his writings, when he could naturally and sometimes when he could not, he mentioned the king with great asperity."

Normally Franklin glowed with the approach of the English summer. Parliament had adjourned and left him free to wander. He no longer journeyed to distant places but did accept every chance to spend long weekends, sometimes weeks, on the country estates of friends. The visits continued through the summer of 1773, and though Franklin continued to be a genial, witty, entertaining guest, the king's reply in June to the Massachusetts petitions set the tone for what turned out to be his season of discontent. He learned that Lord North had decided to bail out the East India Company by making "tea cheaper in America than foreigners can supply us, and to confine the duty there to keep up the exercise of the right." He had second thoughts about Dartmouth. "He is truly a good man, and wishes sincerely a good understanding with the colonies," he now saw, "but does not seem to have strength equal to his wishes." Then early in July came a personal snub that cut deep. Lord North and his wife visited a country house where Franklin was a guest. His lordship "seemed studiously to avoid speaking to me. . . . They stayed the night, so that we dined, supped, and breakfasted together, without exchanging three sentences."

The day Franklin returned to London, with Lord North's snub a fresh memory, he wrote a long letter to Speaker Cushing, burying within it some startling advice:

> Perhaps it would be best and fairest for the colonies, in a general congress now in peace to be assembled, or by means of the correspondence lately proposed, after a full and solemn assertion and declaration of their rights, to engage firmly with each other, that they will never grant aids to the crown in any general war, till those rights are recognized by the king and both houses of Parliament; communicating at the same time to the crown this their resolution. Such a step I imagine will bring the dispute to a crisis; and whether our demands

are immediately complied with, or compulsory measures thought of
to make us rescind them, our ends will finally be obtained; for even
the odium accompanying such compulsory attempts will contribute
to unite and strengthen us, and in the meantime all the world will
allow that our proceeding has been honorable.

By the time these lines reached Boston the Hutchinson-Oliver letters
sent a half year earlier had been published, despite Franklin's request
they not be. The wounded Hutchinson, though unaware Franklin had
caused his misery, meanwhile came upon a copy of the letter to Cushing
advising a call for a general congress of the colonies. Hutchinson thought
the suggestion treasonable. In his eyes Franklin, a royal official like himself, was urging the colonies in effect to blackmail the mother country
into redressing their grievances. The governor sent a copy of the letter
to Lord Dartmouth. After pondering the contents, his lordship ordered
a search made for attested copies or originals of Franklin's letters to
Cushing to use in an indictment for treason. When Franklin heard what
was afoot, he insisted he had written nothing treasonable. "I know not
what letters of mine Governor H. could mean, as advising the people to
insist on their independency," he wrote his son. "I shall, however, be able
at any time to justify everything I have written; the purport being uni-
formly this, that they should carefully avoid all tumults and every violent
measure, and content themselves with verbally keeping up their claims,
and holding forth their rights whenever occasion requires; secure, that,
from the growing importance of America, those claims will ere long be
attended to and acknowledged."

Franklin reacted calmly to the news that Hutchinson's letters had
been published. No one in England but the man who had stolen them
knew who had sent them. Reports from Boston indicated the published
letters were doing what Franklin wanted. The people, "having lately
discovered, as they think, the authors of their grievances to be some of
their own people, their resentment against Britain is thence much
abated." These remarks were made to Dartmouth in August in a note
enclosing a new petition from Massachusetts, this one calling for the
removal of the governor and the lieutenant governor.

4

Dartmouth sent a cordial reply to Franklin's note. He promised to lay
the Massachusetts petition before the king "the next time I shall have the

honor to be admitted into his presence." It pleased his lordship to hear "that a sincere disposition prevails in the people of that province to be on good terms with the mother country. . . ." Franklin reacted to that genial note in a strange way for one seeking to reconcile differences between America and the mother country. In mid-September, hardly two weeks after Dartmouth's reply, he swung from rage to wit in two essays that were to become among the most famous he wrote in England. The first, *Rules by Which a Great Empire May be Reduced to a Small One*, was an insulting attack directed "to all ministers who have the management of extensive dominions, which from their very greatness are become troublesome to govern, because the multiplicity of their affairs leaves no time for *fiddling*." Those determined to demolish the empire should:

> I. In the first place, gentlemen, you are to consider that a great empire, like a great cake, is most easily diminished at the edges. Turn your attention, therefore, first to your remotest provinces; that, as you get rid of them, the next may follow in order.
>
> II. That the possibility of this separation may always exist, take special care the provinces are never incorporated with the mother country; that they do not enjoy the same common rights, the same privileges in commerce; and that they are governed by severer laws, all of your enacting, without allowing them any share in the choice of legislators.

Eighteen more "rules" followed. Rule IV called upon the ministry "to *suppose*" the colonists "always inclined to revolt, and treat them accordingly. Quarter troops among them, who by their insolence may *provoke* the rising of mobs, and by their bullets and bayonets *suppress* them." Franklin further advised that for customs collectors send "the most *indiscreet, ill-bred,* and *insolent* you can find," and for governors and judges only the "ignorant, wrong-headed, and insolent." Parliament must flout all the colonists' claims, "reject their petitions, refuse even to suffer the reading of them, and treat the petitioners with utmost contempt. Nothing can have a better effect in producing the alienation proposed; for though many can forgive injuries, *none ever forgave contempt.*" Also, make sure you tell them your power to tax "has *no limits.*" Only in number XVI did Franklin touch obliquely on Thomas Hutchinson, whose letters the London press was then wondering who had stolen.

> Take all your informations of the state of the colonies from your governors and officers in enmity with them. Encourage and reward these *leasing-makers;* secrete their lying accusations, lest they should be

confuted; but act upon them as the clearest evidence; and believe nothing you hear from the friends of the people: suppose all *their* complaints to be invented and promoted by a few factious dema- gogues, whom if you could catch and hang, all would be quiet. Catch and hang a few of them accordingly; and the *blood of the martyrs* shall *work miracles* in favor of your purpose.

No one in England or America had ever before so ably censured imperial policy as Franklin did here. Yet he chose a curious time to do so. If, as he said, he had sent Hutchinson's letters to Boston in order to shift blame for past policies from the ministry to the governor, why should he suddenly feel the need to excoriate the ministry? Particularly now when exposure of the malevolent Hutchinson appeared to have achieved the end sought. Perhaps the rankling snub from Lord North— "though many can forgive injuries, *none ever forgave contempt*"—prompted the essay. Regardless of why he wrote it, he did so, clearly, in an unforgiv- ing mood, placing all blame for the troubles with America upon the ministry—he dared not yet attack the king—and not upon Hutchinson. If he hoped the vitriol poured upon those who ran the empire would lead to understanding, he erred again. If he hoped it would lead to a stiffening of resistance to British policy in America, he calculated correctly but in the process demolished his argument for sending the Hutchinson letters to Boston.

Franklin liked the essay—"for the quantity and variety of the matter contained, and a kind of spirited ending of each paragraph," he said. "But I find that others here generally prefer the second," he added, meaning *An Edict by the King of Prussia*, an elegant hoax published eleven days after *Rules*. Frederick the Great's "edict" proclaimed the British isles to be colonies of Prussia, settled by "our renowned ducal ancestors." And whereas these colonies had yielded no profits to Prussia, Frederick was hereby imposing a 4 1/2 percent duty on all goods moving in and out of "the said colonies in Britain." Hereafter no hats could be made, no wool woven, no iron smelted in those colonies.

And lastly, being willing farther to favor our said colonies in Britain, we do hereby also ordain and command that all the thieves, highway and street robbers, housebreakers, forgers, murderers, s–d——tes, and villains of every denomination, who have forfeited their lives to the law in Prussia, but whom we in our great clemency do not think fit here to hang, shall be emptied out of our goals into the said island of Great Britain, for the better peopling of that country.

Franklin asked the editor of the *Public Advertiser* "to take care that the compositor observe strictly the italicking, capitalling, and pointing" to give the hoax authenticity. The editor followed orders, then, fearing the piece would have been lost if buried among other foreign news, put it on the front page capped by a headline.

For the Public Advertiser
THE SUBJECT of the following Article of
FOREIGN INTELLIGENCE
being exceedingly EXTRAORDINARY, is the
Reason of its being separated from the usual
Articles of *Foreign News*

Franklin was in the country when the piece appeared. While he was chatting over breakfast with his host, another guest came rushing in with a copy of the *Advertiser* in his hand.

"Here!" says he, "here's news for ye! *Here's the King of Prussia, claiming a right to this kingdom!*"

Everyone stared as the piece was read aloud. *"Damn his impudence,"* said another guest after listening to several paragraphs, *"I dare say, we shall hear by the next post that he is upon his march with one hundred thousand men to back this."*

Soon, however, one of the gentlemen "began to smoke it," and looking Franklin in the face, said: *"I'll be hanged if this is not some of your American jokes upon us."* The reading continued and, said Franklin, "ended with abundance of laughing and a general verdict that it was a fair hit."

5

Franklin returned to London with time on his hands. The expected reply to the Massachusetts petition had not come forth. Ships loaded with the cut-rate tea for America were setting out for the chief ports there. "I much want to hear how that tea is received," Franklin said, then went on to spread false optimism among his countrymen. "The Parliament is not to meet till the middle of January. It is said there is a disposition to compose all differences with America before the next general election, as the trading and manufacturing part of the nation are generally our well-wishers, think we have been hardly used, and apprehend ill consequences from a continuance of the measures that we complain of." This was a just assessment of those among whom Franklin moved; it did not reflect the views of those who counted—Lord North and his ministry.

Though he knew the Anglo-American dispute approached a crisis, Franklin, with that incredible ability to seize whatever joy each day had to offer, put politics largely out of mind through the autumn of 1773. He collaborated with his friend Lord Le Despencer, a "seasoned old sinner" who headed the post office, on an abridgment of the *Book of Common Prayer*. Earlier Franklin had revised the Lord's Prayer into "more concise, equally expressive, and better modern English":

Our Father which art in Heaven.	Heavenly Father.
Hallowed be thy Name.	May all revere thee.
Thy Kingdom come.	And become thy dutiful Children and faithful Subjects.
Thy Will be done on Earth as it is in Heaven.	May thy Laws be obeyed on Earth as perfectly as they are in Heaven.
Give us this Day our daily Bread.	Provide for us this Day as thou has hitherto done.
Forgive us our Debts as we forgive our Debtors.	Forgive us our Treaspasses, and enable us likewise to forgive those that offend us.
And lead us not into Temptation, but deliver us from Evil.	Keep us out of Temptation, and deliver us from Evil.

In his new venture into religious reformation, Franklin cut the Anglican catechism to two questions—"What is your duty to God?" and "What is your duty to your neighbor?"—with appropriately brief responses. The new version, he said, was better "adapted to the capacities of children." The abbreviated liturgy, largely the work of Le Despencer, had a number of virtues. The traditional liturgy, said Franklin, is "so long and filled with so many repetitions, that the continued attention suitable to so serious a duty becomes impracticable, the mind wanders, and the fervency of devotion is slackened." Moreover, it burdens "many pious and devout persons, whose age or infirmities will not suffer them to remain for hours in a cold church, especially in the winter season. . . . These, by shortening the time, would be relieved, and the younger sort . . . would probably more frequently, as well as cheerfully, attend divine service, if they were not detained so long at any one time." Copies of the published *Abridgement* attracted little attention. "Some were given away, very few sold, and I suppose the bulk became waste paper."

While Franklin indulged in religious reform, the London press wondered who had stolen and sent to Boston the Hutchinson-Oliver letters. Franklin continued about his business outwardly serene, showing little interest in political matters. Instead, he occupied himself with a scientific experiment. He had long been fascinated by "the wonderful quietness of oil on agitated water." In reading an account of Captain Cook's voyages through the South Pacific, he had been struck how often the "violent surf breaking on the shore" had prevented landing on some fertile island. "My idea was, that possibly by sailing to and fro at some distance from such lee-shore, continually pouring oil into the sea, the waves might be so much depressed, and lessened before they reached the shore, as to abate the height and violence of the surf, and permit a landing. . . ." In mid-October Franklin and three friends from the Royal Society went to Portsmouth to test the idea. "The experiment had not, in the main point, the success we wished, for no material difference was observed in the height or force of the surf upon the shore; but those who were in the longboat could observe a tract of smoothed water the whole distance in which the barge poured the oil, and gradually spreading in breadth toward the longboat. I call it smoothed; not that it was laid level but because, though the swell continued, its surface was not roughened . . . and none or very few whitecaps (or waves whose tops turn over in foam) appeared in that whole space, though to windward and leeward of it there were plenty; and a wherry that came round the point under sail, in her way to Portsmouth, seemed to turn into that tract of choice and use it from end to end as a piece of turnpike road."

Early in November Franklin wrote up the experiment, introducing it with an essay of thoughts and observations he had been accumulating since as a boy he had "read and smiled at Pliny's account of a practice among the seamen of his time to still the waves in a storm by pouring oil into the sea." The report had the sharpness and polish of the sixty-eight-year-old gentleman's best scientific writing, and the Royal Society later published it, though he had by then been humiliated by the government. No hint of private uneasiness mars the stately and vivid paragraphs, though Franklin knew as he wrote that a private disaster lay just ahead. William Whately, brother of Thomas, whose letters had been stolen, had insinuated in the press that John Temple was the thief. The two men fought a duel on December 11. Though Temple pinked his opponent in the shoulder, the outcome satisfied neither gentleman. A rematch seemed inevitable. To "prevent further mischief" Franklin sent William Strahan a note which was published in the *Chronicle* on Christmas Day.

Finding that two gentlemen have been unfortunately engaged in a duel about a transaction and its circumstances of which both of them are totally ignorant and innocent, I think it incumbent upon me to declare (for the prevention of further mischief, as far as such a declaration may contribute to prevent it) that I alone am the person who obtained and transmitted to Boston the letters in question. . . .

A few days later Franklin told his son: "I am now seriously preparing for my departure to America."

CHAPTER

30

THE COCKPIT

IN HIS NOTE to the press exculpating Temple, Franklin insisted that the Hutchinson-Oliver letters "were not of the nature of *private* letters between friends." Franklin was wrong. Whately held no public office at the time of the correspondence. The letters expressed private views on political issues that men feel free to reveal among friends. To steal, and worse, to publish them violated the code of a gentleman. This revulsion against the invasion of privacy helps explain the raging attack that would be made against Franklin in the Cockpit by the solicitor general, Alexander Wedderburn, who for years had shared bachelor quarters with Whately. "My lords," said Wedderburn, "the late Mr. Whately was most scrupulously cautious about his letters. We lived for many years in the strictest intimacy; and in all those years I never saw a single letter written to him. These letters, I believe, were in his custody at his death. . . . Nothing, then, will acquit Dr. Franklin of the charge of obtaining them by fraudulent or corrupt means for the most malignant purposes, unless he stole them from the person who stole them. This argument is irrefragable."

The theft gave the ministry an excuse to assail Franklin. But lacking that excuse, another would have been found. The ministry saw Franklin as "the great director" of resistance in Massachusetts. To undercut his supposed power he must be publicly humiliated. The campaign began early in January when Franklin was told on three days' notice that the Massachusetts petition for removal of Hutchinson and Oliver would receive a formal hearing before the Privy Council's committee for plantation affairs. The announcement came as a surprise. Normally after receiving a petition the king consulted privately with his advisers, then handed

down a written reply. Then came another surprise—Hutchinson and
Oliver would be represented by counsel, namely Wedderburn. Franklin
learned this the day before the hearing "very late in the afternoon." He
had no time to find counsel to speak for the Massachusetts legislature's
petition.

The hearing was held 11 January 1774 at Whitehall in a room known
since the days of Henry VIII, when cockfights were held there, as the
Cockpit. A fire in the huge fireplace relieved the dankness of the wintry
London day; otherwise Franklin saw little to cheer him. The solemn
councillors sat at a long table in the sparsely furnished room. All others
had to stand. Lord Gower, whom Franklin knew as a member of the
Walpole Associates and the man chiefly responsible for easing Hillsborough out of office, presided at the head of the table, his back to the
fireplace. Franklin stood with William Bollan, agent for the Massachusetts council or upper house. Bollan in one capacity or another had been
a spokesman for Massachusetts for nearly thirty years, and Franklin had
asked him to put the case for the petition today. Alongside Wedderburn
stood Israel Mauduit, the agent for Hutchinson and Oliver in London.

When Bollan stepped forward to speak several of the councillors
grumbled that he was not a party to the petition. Bollan pushed on,
despite the objections, "but without effect; they would scarce hear out a
sentence, and finally set him aside." The Massachusetts petition was read;
Franklin then offered attested copies of the Hutchinson-Oliver letters to
substantiate the charges in it. Lord Chief Justice De Grey glanced at the
copies and noticed none was addressed. He raised a substantial point—
were these private letters expressing personal views or official letters
proposing policy? Franklin said lightly that "though it did not appear to
whom they were directed, it appeared who had written them." Wedderburn said he would not quibble over the copies' authenticity. He only
wished to reserve "the right of inquiring how they were obtained."

"Certainly," said Lord De Grey coldly, "and to whom they were
directed; for the perfect understanding of the passages may depend on
that and other such circumstances. We can receive no charge against a
man founded on letters directed to nobody, and perhaps received by
nobody. The laws of this country have no such practices."

Franklin now turned to the presence of Wedderburn. "I did not
expect that counsel would have been employed on this occasion," he said.

"Had you not notice sent you of Mr. Mauduit's having petitioned to
be heard by counsel on behalf of the governor and lieutenant governor?"

"I did receive such notice; but I thought that this had been a matter
of politics and not of law, and I have not brought any counsel."

"Where a charge is brought, the parties have a right to be heard by counsel or not, as they choose."

"My lords," said Israel Mauduit at this point, offering Franklin a graceful back-handed compliment, "I know well Dr. Franklin's abilities, and wish to put the defense of my friends more upon a parity with the attack. He will not therefore wonder that I choose to appear before your lordships with the assistance of counsel. . . ."

"Dr. Franklin," said Lord Gower, "may have the assistance of counsel, or go on without it, as he shall choose."

"I desire to have counsel."

"What time shall you want?"

"Three weeks."

With that exchange the hearing ended. As Franklin gathered up his papers, Lord Gower, near whom he was standing, asked if he intended to reveal how he had obtained the letters. "In that," said Franklin, "I shall take counsel."

2

Lord Gower may have said something more to Franklin after the hearing adjourned. The charter for the Grand Ohio Company had yet to be approved by the crown, one reason being, the attorney general let it be known, that Franklin was "unworthy the favors of the crown." Gower, as one of the partners in the company, could have suggested that to speed the charter's approval Franklin should resign as a shareholder.

On the premise that the best defense was an offense, Franklin the day after the hearing wrote Thomas Walpole: "I never considered the agreement with the Treasury for these lands as a matter of *favor*, unless it was such from us to government, by showing them that the lands they used to give away might produce something to the public treasury." Nor did he consider the agreement "a great bargain to the purchasers: —I do therefore desire that you will strike my name out of the list of your Associates, and hereafter not look upon me as one of them." As usual, Franklin chose his words with care. He did not resign from the company; he only desired to. Privately, Walpole agreed to keep him on the list and allow another member to vote his shares. Four years later, in the midst of the Revolution, Franklin admitted, "I am still to be considered as an Associate, and was called upon for my payments as before."

If Franklin had any pleasant recollections of the three weeks between hearings, he failed to record them. "I was called an incendiary, and the papers were filled with invectives against me. Hints were given me, that there was some thoughts of apprehending me, seizing my papers, and sending me to Newgate." While rounding up a team of lawyers to present his case, he was "harassed with a subpoena from the Chancellor to attend his court the next day, at the suit of Mr. William Whately concerning the letters."

Franklin's lawyers had some good news and some bad news for him. They said emphatically he "was not and could not be obliged" to explain how he had obtained the letters. They also said the letters did *not* substantiate the charges in the Massachusetts petition against Hutchinson and Oliver. The personal opinions they contained could not be used as evidence of malfeasance in office. "The counsel therefore thought it . . . more advisable to state as facts the general discontent of the people, that the governors had lost all credit with them, and were become odious, etc." —in short, base the case for the petition on the petition.

The discouraging string of events was topped off on January 22, a week before the second hearing, by the news that on 16 December 1773 over three hundred chests of tea had been dumped into Boston harbor by a band of citizens disguised as Indians. The "act of violent injustice on our part" appalled Franklin. "I am truly concerned," he said, "that there should seem to any a necessity for carrying matters to such extremity, as, in a dispute about public rights, to destroy private property." Stockholders of the East India Company "are not our adversaries," he added. "I cannot but wish and hope that before any compulsive measures are thought of here, our General Court will have shown a disposition to repair the damage and make compensation to the Company."

Against that backdrop, Franklin on January 29 prepared for his second visit to the Cockpit.

3

It was as if the room had reverted to its original use. The scene had the gaiety of an audience gathered for a cockfight. "All the courtiers were invited, as to an entertainment," said Franklin, "and there never was such an appearance of privy councillors on any occasion, not less than thirty-five, besides an immense crowd of other auditors." (In counting the councillors seated at the long table, Franklin missed Lord North, who arrived late and was forced to stand through the long hearing.) The Archbishop of Canterbury was there, along with the Bishop of London, who directed affairs of the Anglican Church in America. Lord Dartmouth was there. Lord Hillsborough, too, had arrived for the show. Scattered through the crowd were a few of Franklin's English friends— Edmund Burke, Joseph Priestley, Lord Shelburne—but only a few.

As the hearing opened Franklin found a place near one end of the fireplace, only a few feet behind Lord Gower. He stood "conspicuously erect, without the slightest movement of any part of his body. The muscles of his face had been previously composed, so as to afford a placid, tranquil expression." The hearing began quietly with a second reading of the Massachusetts petition and then of the Hutchinson-Oliver letters. Franklin's lawyers spoke first. They ignored the letters in their arguments, resting their case on the petition, saying it sufficed as proof that the people of Massachusetts were discontented. They urged the king and his councillors out of their wisdom and goodness to remove Hutchinson and Oliver in order to restore peace in Massachusetts.

Now Alexander Wedderburn stepped up to the table. Eight years earlier, as a loyal follower of Grenville, he had voted against repeal of the Stamp Act. After Grenville died Lord North silenced his vituperative opposition in Parliament by offering Wedderburn, who, said North, had the "invaluable gift of an accommodating conscience," the post of solicitor general. Wedderburn accepted the offer. "I have no opinion of his heart," a fellow Scot said of him, "tho' he is a very clever lawyer."

In his opening remarks Wedderburn told the gentlemen assembled at the long table they had gathered this day to decide a momentous question —"whether the crown shall ever have in its power to employ a faithful and steady servant in the administration of a colony." He then reviewed, as Franklin put it, "what he called a history of the province for the last ten years, and bestowed plenty of abuse upon it, mingled with encomium on the governors." A friendly biographer of Franklin has called Wedderburn's opening statement "a cogent defense of his client's conduct, and his violated correspondence."

For years "Dr. Franklin's constituents" have sought "some ground" from which to attack Governor Hutchinson, Wedderburn continued. The stolen letters provided it. "Dr. Franklin therefore stands in the light of the first mover and prime conductor"—surely the audience smiled at that allusion to a phrase that Franklin the electrician had given to the language—"of the whole contrivance against his Majesty's two governors; and having by the help of his own special confidants and party leaders, first made the Assembly his agents in carrying on his own secret designs, he now appears before your lordships to give the finishing stroke to the work of his own hands."

Franklin later insisted that when Wedderburn mentioned the stolen letters he wandered "from the question before their lordships"—the Massachusetts petition. He forgot that it was he who had introduced the letters at the first hearing as evidence to substantiate charges in the petition. His lawyers later convinced him the letters were useless as evidence, but the advice came too late. A door had been opened, and Wedderburn, enraged at the invasion of his friend Whately's privacy, strode through it.

"I hope, my lords," he went on, "you will mark and *brand* the man, for the honor of this country, of Europe, and of mankind. Private correspondence has hitherto been held sacred in times of the greatest party rage, not only in politics but religion. He has forfeited all the respect of societies and of men. Into what companies will he hereafter go with an unembarrassed face, or the honest intrepidity of virtue? Men will watch him with a jealous eye; they will hide their papers from him, and lock up their escritoires. He will henceforth esteem it a libel to be called a man of letters; this man of *three* letters." This must have been one of the spots where Franklin recalled the audience "burst out in loud applauses." The spectators knew that the three letters referred to a Roman play in which a thief (*fur* in Latin) was called a "trium litterarum homo."

Wedderburn had not finished with his literary allusions. Drawing on a contemporary drama in which the villain was a Negro named Zanga, he said: "My lords, what poetic fiction only had penned for the heart of a cruel African, Dr. Franklin has realized, and transcribed from his own. His, too, is the language of a Zanga.

> Know then 'twas—I
> I forged the letter—I disposed the picture
> I hated, I despised, and I destroyed."

Wedderburn seemed at times beside himself with fury as he continued to pour abuse on Franklin. Several times he slammed his fist into a cushion on the table near Lord Gower. "I would, not for double the greatest fee the orator could on that occasion have received, been in the place of that cushion," said a spectator. "The ear was stunned at every blow. . . . The table groaned under the assault."

After exhausting invective on Franklin, Wedderburn turned in his closing remarks back to Hutchinson and Oliver. "They are convinced that the people, though misled, are innocent," he said. They "love the soil, the constitution, the people of New England; they look with reverence to this country and with affection to that. For the sake of the people they wish some faults corrected, anarchy abolished, and government re-established. But these salutary ends they wish to promote by the gentlest means and the abridging of no liberties which a people can use to its own advantage. A restraint from self-destruction is the only restraint they desire to be imposed upon New England."

Through all of this Franklin stood "the whole time like a rock, in the same posture, his head resting on his left hand, and in that attitude abiding the pelting of the pitiless storm."

After Wedderburn finished, one of Franklin's lawyers stepped forward to make a final statement. He, like everyone in the room, was exhausted—both from the torrent of abuse heaped upon the impassive Franklin and from standing so long. His voice was "so feeble, as to be scarce audible," said Franklin. "What little I heard was very well said, but appeared to have little effect."

Nine years later Strahan's *London Chronicle* reported that as Franklin left the Cockpit he whispered to Wedderburn, "I will make your master a LITTLE KING for this." Only those certain they comprehend the manner of the man know whether Franklin could have made such a remark.

4

After the Cockpit had been cleared the councillors conferred. They quickly concluded that the Massachusetts petition was founded on "groundless, vexatious, and scandalous" allegations, and that they had heard nothing during the hearing "which does or can . . . in any manner or in any degree impeach the honor, integrity, or conduct of the said governor or lieutenant governor, and their lordships are humbly of opinion that the said petition ought to be dismissed."

The next day, Sunday, January 30, Franklin's friend Lord Le Despencer told him his Majesty *"found it necessary"* to dismiss him from the post office.

Franklin lingered a few days in the house on Craven Street, then suddenly vanished from sight. It was said that he had left for a "month or two's ramble" through Ireland and Scotland. Actually, he was hiding out in London—in the house of a friend named David Williams. Dr. Franklin, Williams later revealed, "apprehensive that his papers would be seized, took a trunk under his arm, and unknown to the family where he lodged conveyed it by a boat from Hungerford Stairs to my house at Chelsea, where he remained several weeks in perfect privacy and concealed . . . until the public pulse was felt, his important papers were out of danger, and himself in a condition to prepare for his departure."

CHAPTER

31

"LET ALL THE MALES THERE BE C–ST——ED"

FOR THOSE WHO SOUGHT to know the man, Franklin's last months in England offered one more puzzle. He told everyone, "I only await the arrival of the April packet with the [post office] accounts, that I may settle here before I go," yet he lingered for over a year—with no certainty that the government might not any day decide to arrest him.

In the early weeks after his humiliation he occasionally ventured on visits to tested friends in the country, but for the most part stayed holed up in David Williams's house. He spent the days defending himself in letters to America and in writing a long vindicating essay which he planned to publish immediately but never did, on the advice of friends "who represented the falsehoods in question as meriting contempt, rather than a public refutation." Instead, Franklin "held a cool, sullen silence, reserving myself to some future opportunity."

To judge by the letters he seemed calm and confident. "Be assured, my good friend," he wrote a friend on the Continent, "that I have done nothing unjustifiable, nothing but what is consistent with the man of honor and with my duty to my king and country; and this will soon be apparent to the public as it is now to all here who know me." But the bitterness buried beneath an outward serenity emerged in a note to William; he wished to see his son "well settled in your farm," a clear hint that to honor his father he should resign the governorship. Common sense quickly led Franklin to reverse himself; he knew, as a mutual friend put it, William had "little or no corn in the crib." "Let them take your place if they want it," he wrote in a follow-up note; "one may make something of an injury, nothing of a resignation."

After a test of the air indicated the government had no immediate plans to pursue him further, Franklin moved back to Craven Street. "I do not find that I have lost a single friend on the occasion," he said with pride. "All have visited me repeatedly with affectionate assurances of their unaltered respect and affection, and many of distinction, with whom I had before but slight acquaintance." Friends visited, but he did little visiting in return. He dined mostly at home. For the next nine months he saw no member of the ministry.

"Where is Dr. Franklin, my lord?" the king several months later asked Lord Dartmouth.

"I believe, sir, he is in town. He was going to America, but I fancy he is not gone."

"I heard he was going to Switzerland," the king said, "or to some part of the Continent."

"I think, sir, there has been such a report."

2

The government's real or pretended indifference to Franklin did not carry over to the people of Boston, who still refused to pay for the dumped tea. Franklin tried to warn his "countrymen" of the danger ahead. "I suppose we never had since we were a people so few friends in Britain," he wrote Speaker Cushing. "The violent destruction of the tea seems to have united all parties here against our province, so that the bill now brought into Parliament for shutting up Boston as a port till satisfaction is made, meets with no opposition." If Boston refused to bend, worse lay in store for all Massachusetts. "An alteration in our charter relating to the choice of the council is also talked of, but it is not certain that it will be proposed at present. I cannot but hope that the affair of the tea will have been considered in the Assembly before this time, and satisfaction proposed if not made; for such a step will remove much of the prejudice now entertained against us, and put us again on a fair footing in contending for our old privileges as occasion may require."

The Boston Port Act aimed at starving that city into docile contrition. The port would be closed to all traffic by water, by which the city received most of its food and supplies, until the price of the tea and the tax upon it had been paid in full. The act came to Parliament in mid-March and passed with little opposition in either house. It would go into effect on 1 June 1774. By then the government would sense it had made a stupendous blunder. Previously, Boston's act of violence had received slight approval among colonial leaders outside Massachusetts. They, like Franklin, deplored the destruction of private property. When news of the Port Act reached America, sentiment swung overnight in Boston's favor.

The inanity of the ministerial decision to punish a city for the act of a mob astonished Franklin. Here in England, he said in a pseudonymous piece published soon after the act passed, "mobs of English sawyers can burn sawmills; mobs of English laborers destroy or plunder magazines of corn; mobs of English coal heavers attack houses with firearms; English smugglers can fight regularly the king's cruising vessels, drive them ashore, and burn them, as lately on the coast of Wales, and on the coast of Cornwall; but upon these accounts we hear no talk of England's being in *rebellion*, no threats of taking away its Magna Charta, or repealing its Bill of Rights; for we well know, that the operations of a mob are often unexpected, sudden, and soon over, so that the civil power can seldom prevent or suppress them, not being able to come in before they have dispersed themselves; and therefore it is not always accountable for their mischiefs."

On the heels of the Port Act, the ministry recalled Governor Hutchinson and sent in his place Gen. Thomas Gage with the clear implication that he impose military rule upon Massachusetts. That decision led to one of the most corrosive pieces of sarcasm Franklin ever published. In it he offered a more "feasible method of humbling our rebellious vassals of North America." Orders should be sent immediately to General Gage "that all the males there be c–st——ed." This can easily be done:

> Let a company of sow gelders, consisting of one hundred men, accompany the army. On their arrival at any town or village, let orders be given that on the blowing of the horn all the males, be assembled in the market place. If the corps are men of skill and ability in their profession, they will make great dispatch, and retard but very little the progress of the army. . . . The most notorious offenders, such as Hancock, Adams, etc., who have been the ringleaders in the rebellion of our servants, should be shaved quite close. . . . It is true blood will be shed, but probably not many lives lost. Bleeding to a certain degree is salutary. The English, whose humanity is celebrated by all the world, but particularly by themselves, do not desire the death of the delinquent, but his reformation. The advantages arising from this scheme being carried into execution are obvious. In the course of fifty years it is probable we shall not have one rebellious subject in North America. This will be laying the axe to the root of the tree. In the

meantime a considerable expense may be saved to the managers of the opera, and our nobility and gentry be entertained at a cheaper rate by the fine voices of our own c–st———i, and the specie remain in the kingdom, which now, to an enormous amount, is carried every year to Italy. It might likewise be of service to our Levant trade, as we could supply the Grand Signor's seraglio, and the harems of the grandees of the Turkish dominions with cargoes of eunuchs, as also with handsome women, for which America is as famous as Circassia. I could enumerate many other advantages. I shall mention but one: It would effectually put a stop to the emigrations from this country now grown so very fashionable.

With General Gage on his way to Boston, the North ministry now handed Parliament a series of bills to tighten control over the Massachusetts government. The council would hereafter be appointed by the crown; the governor's salary would be paid by London; town meetings throughout the province would be carefully regulated. Franklin saw "little hope that they will not pass, we having very few friends in Parliament at present." Edmund Burke spoke at length against them in the Commons and Lord Chatham broke several years of silence on imperial affairs to oppose them in the House of Lords. He "blamed us for destroying the tea, and our declaration of independence of Parliament," Franklin reported home; "but condemned strongly the measures taken here in consequence, and spoke honorably of our province and people, and of their conduct in the late war."

Soon after the Coercive or Regulating Acts, as they were known in England—Americans called them the Intolerable Acts—passed Parliament, Arthur Lee chose for some reason to make a Grand Tour of the Continent. He "probably will be absent near a year," Franklin wrote Speaker Cushing. "I had resigned your agency to him, expecting to leave England about the end of this month; but on his departure he has returned me all the papers, and I feel myself now under a kind of necessity of continuing till you can be acquainted with this circumstance, and have time to give further orders." If he had doubts about lingering longer in London, the next news from America erased them. A congress of the colonies was scheduled to meet in Philadelphia early in September. "I have been advised by our friends to stay till the result of your Congress should arrive," he now said.

The decision took some courage, and it only slightly tarnishes the act that he felt the need to boast about it in letters home. "My situation here is thought by many to be a little hazardous," he wrote; "for that if by some accident, the troops and the people of New England should come to blows, I should probably be taken up; the ministerial people affecting everywhere to represent me as the cause of all the misunderstanding; and I have been frequently cautioned to secure my papers, and by some advised to withdraw. But I venture to stay, in compliance with the wish of others, till the result of Congress arrives, since they suppose my being here might on that occasion be of use, and I confide in my innocence, that the worst which can happen to me will be an imprisonment on suspicion, tho' that is a thing I should much desire to avoid, as it may be expensive and vexatious, as well as dangerous to my health."

3

"I am told by gentlemen who are of the Royal Society," Thomas Hutchinson, who arrived in London in July, wrote in his diary of Franklin, "and who used to be a philosophical club with him, that he has never shown his head among them, nor in any other company that they could hear of, for a twelve-month past. . . ." Hutchinson erred slightly. Franklin still paid no visits to public offices nor saw any of the ministry, but by August he was again leading a full social life, though he took care to circulate only among those he knew to be friendly toward America. His and Hutchinson's paths never crossed, though they eyed one another from a distance. Once, in the gallery of the House of Commons, Hutchinson saw Franklin "staring with his spectacles," listening to a member say of Americans: "We must pinch them; they must be compelled to submit without delay." "No doubt," Hutchinson mused in his diary, "before this time the relation of this speech is on its way to America."

What the Americans would call a revolution and the British a rebellion Franklin and Hutchinson saw as something else—a civil war, one that split families and severed friendships. The tragedy was intensified for Hutchinson, the war's first notable victim; he had been sacrificed to the cause by a friend with whom he shared a vision of America's future greatness.

"Pray, Mr. Hutchinson," the king had asked at one point in a long interview, "does population greatly increase in your province?"

"Very rapidly, sir," the governor replied, then dared to hint to the king what Franklin had long been saying—that the future lay with America. "I used to think that Doctor Franklin, who has taken much pains in his calculations, carried it too far when he supposed the inhabitants of America, from their natural increase doubled their number in twenty-five years; but I rather think now that he did not; and I believe it will appear from the last return I made to the Secretary of State, that the Massachusetts has increased in that proportion. And the increase is supposed, including the importation of foreigners, to be upon the whole greater in most of the southern colonies than in the Massachusetts. We import no settlers from Europe, so as to make any sensible increase."

Franklin, no more than Hutchinson, wished to wrench America from the empire. It is "for the common welfare of the British empire, I most ardently wish," he said. Both men were appalled by the corruption of British society—Hutchinson even more than Franklin—and feared the mother country might soon inoculate America with the disease. Both wished fervently to avoid the horror of civil war. "I am," said Franklin in the fall of 1774, "in perpetual anxiety lest the mad measure of mixing soldiers among a people whose minds are in such a state of irritation, may be attended with some sudden mischief; for an accidental quarrel, a personal insult, an imprudent order, an insolent execution of even a prudent one, or twenty other things, may produce a tumult, unforseen, and therefore impossible to be prevented, in which such a carnage may ensue as to make a breach that can never afterwards be healed." If Franklin had yearned for independence, as Hutchinson and others thought he did, he would have returned home to work for the cause. Instead, he risked his freedom by staying in London to work for peace—but it had to be peace on his terms: America would acknowledge allegiance only to the king. On that point Franklin broke with Hutchinson and with his son, who held that the colonies must accept the supreme authority of Parliament.

Franklin rarely in his long life apologized or showed regret for anything he had done. If he felt remorse for sharing in the wrecking of Hutchinson's career, he never revealed it. Nor did he ever comment on a more personal tragedy the civil war was bringing to a head—the split between him and William. After twelve years in office, William was in point of service the oldest royal governor in America, yet his father continued to advise him, and to expect the advice to be followed, as though he were still a youngster. When William dared to suggest that Boston deserved the Port Act for refusing to pay for the tea, the father ended a defense of his native town with, "But you, who are a thorough courtier, see everything with government eyes," the harshest slap he had ever handed his son. The anger owed something to a letter William had written to Strahan censuring his father's role in the stolen letters affair. To Franklin's embarrassment, Strahan showed the letter so widely about London that even Hutchinson learned of it. Perhaps, too, Franklin had learned of a letter William had written to Lord Dartmouth after the Port Act passed. "His Majesty may be assured that I shall omit nothing in my power to keep this province quiet and that," said William, with a pointed reference to his father, "let the event be what it may, no attachments or connections shall ever make me swerve from the duty of my station."

Father and son did all they could to postpone a final break. Their letters continued affectionate, and they avoided talk of politics. "If there was any prospect of your being able to bring the people in power to your way of thinking, or of those of your way of thinking being brought into power," then stay in London, William wrote in one note, daring, for a change, to give advice. "But as you have had by this time pretty strong proofs that neither can be reasonably expected, and that you are looked upon with an evil eye in that country, and are in no small danger of being brought into trouble for your political conduct, you had certainly better return, while you are able to bear the fatigues of the voyage to a country where the people revere you."

4

William Franklin, like Thomas Hutchinson, thought the colonies could be coerced into respect for imperial authority. Benjamin Franklin thought the mother country could be coerced into respect for colonial rights. In the enormous chess match he had engaged in—the stakes were the future of a continent—his strategy hinged on a single move—economic coercion. He had favored the same move to get the Townshend duties repealed. Then it had failed. The colonies had wavered, then abandoned their nonconsumption policy just when victory seemed certain to Franklin. The strategy must be tried again, and to that end on 25 July 1774 he wrote a momentous letter. (So the government regarded it. "There are various opinions" on what delegates to the First Continental Congress will do, a sub-minister remarked after reading a stolen copy of the letter, "but I esteem Dr. Franklin's the best because they will probably do what he bids them to do. . . .") Franklin timed the letter to arrive in Philadelphia as Congress convened. It was addressed to Thomas Cushing but meant to be read by all the delegates.

"The spirit which has appeared in all America, has given much uneasiness to our wicked ministers," he wrote, "and I conjecture they will by their emissaries try every expedient to bring about a disunion among you, when the Congress meets; therefore with much circumspection you should watch their motions, and take all possible precaution to defeat their attempts. It appears to me the greatest stake that was ever played for, no less than whether Americans, and their endless generations shall enjoy the common rights of mankind, or be worse than eastern slaves.''

Congress must draw up a bill of rights that lists "every oppressive act of Parliament" during the past decade, "and if this is done with decency and manly firmness, I think Lord Chatham and his friends will support it, though it is by no means prudent to rely over much on any support on this side the water; your chief confidence must be in your own virtue, unanimity and steadiness; temper and resolution must be joined." But that bill of rights "or petition, will not be in the least regarded, unless you compel the merchants, manufacturers, and people of England to join you. For this end I know no possible means, but immediately to stop all commerce with this country, both exports and imports, which plan must be steadily and with the strictest faith adhered to, until you have obtained redress."

The government allowed the message to go through, to its later regret. "We were flattered with hopes by the merchants that the General Congress would come to no resolutions respecting trade," another sub-minister said after Congress adjourned. The delegates from "New York, Jersey, some of New Hampshire and Pennsylvania were said to be against all violent proceedings; a letter from Dr. Franklin advising such measures brought over the Pennsylvania delegates, so the resolutions were taken."

Franklin had convinced himself that "if the non-consumption agreement should become general, and be firmly adhered to, this ministry must be ruined, and our friends succeed them. . . ." He could not have been more wrong, but among the many reasons the prediction failed to come true were two Franklin could not cope with—one a delusion that obsessed British leaders, the other Lord North.

The power of the delusion was impressed on Franklin late in August when, returning from a weekend in the country, the great Lord Chatham asked him to stop by for a talk on American affairs. During the long conversation Chatham said that the strong opposition to America in Parliament owed much to a conviction that the colonies were determined on independence. Franklin assured his lordship that during all his travels in America "I never had heard in any conversation, from any persons drunk or sober, the least expression of a wish for a separation or hint that such a thing would be advantageous to America." Chatham was reassured but Franklin was not. A few weeks later Franklin recalled a remark his good friend Lord Camden had made sixteen years earlier: "For all what you Americans say of your loyalty and all that, I know you will one day throw off your dependence upon this country, and notwithstanding your

boasted affection to this country, you will set up for independence."
Franklin told the story many times the rest of his life, as if to say that
American independence sprang first from the deluded minds of British
leaders and having convinced themselves they convinced America.

Lord North upset Franklin's calculations by an unexpected and ingenious move in October. Parliament still had a year to run before the
ministry was forced to call a general election. Franklin counted on that
year for American nonconsumption to exert enough pressure, as he had
written home, "to convince the candidates . . . of the necessity there is
to do you justice by repealing all the late wicked acts." North shattered
this strategy by calling a general election for October 1774. It would be
held before the results of the First Congress reached England, before any
economic boycott could take place. If the new Parliament had a large
anti-American majority, and there was good reason to expect it would,
North and his ministry would have seven years to bend the colonies to
Parliament's will without having to listen to the voice of the people.

Until North made his move Franklin had been certain all would soon
be well for America. "I have reason to think a strong push will be made
at the very beginning of the session to have all the late acts reversed," he
said, "and a solemn assurance given America that no future attempts shall
be made to tax us without our consent." North's announcement blotted
out that optimism. He began to rail against the corruption of British
elections. Most members of Parliament win their seats by "bribing or
purchasing to get in," he said, and once in "there is little doubt of selling
their votes to the minister for the time being, to reimburse themselves."

The election gave the North ministry an overwhelming majority in
Parliament. Hereafter "Parliament would not—could not—concede,"
Lord North told Hutchinson soon after the results were in. "For aught
he could see it must come to violence. He had the kingdom with him.
There was no danger of a change in Parliament. There was no danger of
a change in administration." The king, too, felt the time had come for
stern measures. "The dye is now cast, the colonies must either submit or
triumph," he wrote North. "I do not wish to come to severer measures,
but we must not retreat" in the face of American threats. "I have no
objection afterwards to their seeing that there is no inclination for the
present to lay fresh taxes on them, but I am clear there must always be
one tax to keep up the right."

CHAPTER

32

"THIS OLD ROTTEN STATE"

FRANKLIN HAD HOPED for time to make an economic boycott felt in England. North had checked that strategy, and every man close to government sensed after the general election that the ministry now had the power to force a showdown with America. Some, however, thought war might yet be avoided if negotiations were opened with Franklin, generally accepted as America's unofficial ambassador in London. From December until he left for home in March, few days passed when Franklin did not hold secret talks with leaders in and out of government. He carried an enormous burden—negotiating for a continent, a nation yet unborn, alone, without advice from home. A misstep and he would be accused by Americans of either imposing a dishonorable peace upon them or plunging them into a bloody civil war. As weeks passed into months and the talks continued, the tension led to sleepless nights, and "whatever robs an old man of his sleep," he told a friend, "soon demolishes him." Once, when he thought reconciliation close at hand, he broke down and wept, and at the end when he saw all was lost his ragged nerves led to a blunder that might have landed him in jail but for the intervention of friends.

December 1—"Mr. David Barclay [a Quaker merchant and old friend] called on me to have some discourse concerning the meeting of merchants to petition Parliament. When that was over, he spoke of the dangerous situation of American affairs, that a civil war might be brought on by the present measures, and the great merit that person would have, who could contrive some means of preventing so terrible a calamity, and bring about

337

a reconciliation. He was then pleased to add, that . . . no man had it so much in his power as myself."

Franklin said he "thought an accommodation impracticable, unless both sides wished it; and, by what I could judge from the proceedings of the ministry, I did not believe they had the least disposition towards it."

"Mr. Barclay apprehended I judged too hardly of the ministers; he was persuaded they were not all of that temper, and he fancied they would be very glad to get out of their present embarrassment on any terms, only saving the honor and dignity of government. He wished there that I would think of the matter, and he would call again and converse with me farther upon it. I said I would do so, as he requested it, but I had no opinion of its answering any purpose. We parted upon this."

December 2—Miss Howe, "fancying she could beat me," invited Franklin for an afternoon of chess. She was the sister of Lord Richard Howe, an admiral in the navy, and Sir William Howe, a general rumored to be sent soon to America with an army. "I went, . . . played a few games with the lady, whom I found of very sensible conversation and pleasing behavior, which induced me to agree most readily to an appointment for another meeting a few days later."

December 4—Met again with the "agreeable" Miss Howe. "After playing as long as we liked, we fell into a little chat, partly on a mathematical problem, and partly about the new Parliament then just met, when she said:

'And what is to be done with this dispute between Great Britain and the colonies? I hope we are not to have a civil war.'

'They should kiss and be friends. What can they do better? Quarreling can be of service to neither, but is ruin to both.'

'I have often said, that I wished government would employ you to settle the dispute for 'em. I am sure nobody could do it so well. Don't you think that the thing is practicable?'

'Undoubtedly, madam, if the parties are disposed to reconciliation; for the two countries have really no clashing interests to differ about. It is rather a matter of punctillio, which two or three reasonable people might settle in half an hour. I thank you for the good opinion you are pleased to express of me. But the ministers will never think of employing me in that good work; they choose rather to abuse me.'

'Aye, they behaved shamefully to you. And indeed some of them are now ashamed of it themselves.' "

5 p.m., same day—Goes to meet Barclay at home of Dr. John Fothergill, the Quaker physician who seventeen years earlier had helped Franklin in the negotiations with Thomas Penn. Fothergill said "he hoped I had put pen to paper, and formed some plan for consideration, and brought it with me. I answered that I had formed no plan; as, the more I thought of the proceedings against the colonies, the more satisfied I was, that there did not exist the least disposition in the ministry to an accommodation; that therefore all plans must be useless. He said I might be mistaken; that whatever was the violence of some he had reason, *good reason,* to believe others were differently disposed; and that if I would draw a plan, which we three upon considering should judge reasonable, it might be made use of, and answer some good purpose, since he believed that either himself or D. Barclay could get it communicated to some of the most moderate among the ministers, who would consider it with attention; and what appeared reasonable to us, two of us being Englishmen, might appear so to them." Franklin thought it improper to offer any plan until Congress had been heard from. Both gentlemen said "the least delay might be dangerous." Franklin promised to draw up a plan.

December 6, evening—Came to Fothergill's house with a paper entitled "HINTS FOR CONVERSATION *upon the Subject of Terms that might probably produce Union between Britain and the Colonies.*" The "hints" opened on a generous note—"The tea destroyed to be paid for"—but the remaining sixteen points in effect asked the government to repeal all imperial regulations laid down during the past decade, and in several instances to abandon powers the mother country had exercised since the founding of the colonies. Point 14, for example, asked Britain to "give up its monopoly of the American commerce," and number 17 that "all powers of internal legislation in the colonies to be disclaimed by Parliament."

Fothergill and Barclay thought several of the points either "totally inadmissable" or "could hardly be obtained," but Fothergill promised to show the paper to Lord Dartmouth, whose physician he was, and Barclay to Lord Hyde, a powerful noble whose views were "a good deal attended to" by the ministry.

December 11–24—The proceedings of the First Continental Congress arrived. They were addressed to all the colonial agents in London but sent in the care of Franklin. The days were taken up "in meetings with the other agents to consult about presenting the petition, in waiting three different days with them on Lord Dartmouth, in consulting upon and writing letters to the speakers of assemblies, and other business." This was the first time Franklin had spoken to Dartmouth since the humiliation at the Cockpit nearly a year ago. At the third meeting, Dartmouth said "he had presented the petition to his Majesty, who had been pleased to receive it very graciously, and to command him to tell us it contained matters of such importance, that as soon as they met, he would lay it before his two houses of Parliament."

December 25, evening—Visited Miss Howe. "She told me as soon as I came in, that her brother, Lord Howe, wished to be acquainted with me; that he was a very good man, and she was sure we should like each other. I said I had always heard a good character of Lord Howe, and should be proud of the honor of being known to him."

"He is but just by; will you give me leave to send for him?"

"By all means, madam, if you think proper."

Lord Howe soon after came in and after "some extremely polite compliments" to Franklin said he "did conceive that if I would indulge him with my ideas of the means proper to bring about a reconciliation, it might be of some use." Franklin doubted an "accommodation could be expected" from the present ministry. His lordship thought "some of the ministry were extremely well disposed to any reasonable accommodation, preserving only the dignity of government." Would Franklin draw up a paper containing the terms that would lead to a reconciliation? Franklin agreed to, and when ready would bring the paper to Miss Howe's house, where a meeting with Lord Howe would arouse no suspicion, "as it was known we played together at chess."

December 26—Arrived at Lord Chatham's country estate early in the afternoon. "He received me with an affectionate kind of respect, that from so great a man was extremely engaging." Chatham praised the "temper, moderation, and wisdom" of Congress. "He inquired much and particularly concerning the state of America, the probability of their perseverance, the difficulties they must meet with in adhering for any long time to their resolutions, the resources they might have to supply the deficiency of commerce; to all which I gave him answers with which he seemed well satisfied." Franklin said "that no accommodation could properly be proposed and entered into by the Americans while the bayonet was at their breasts; that to have any agreement binding all force should be withdrawn. His lordship seemed to think these sentiments had something in them that was reasonable."

Franklin spent the night at the nearby estate of John Sargent, his banker, friend, and a fellow shareholder in the Grand Ohio Company.

December 27—"It being in my way to town," called on Lord Camden. "We had that afternoon and evening a great deal of conversation on

American affairs, concerning which he was very inquisitive, and I gave him the best information in my power. I was charmed with his generous and noble sentiments; and had the great pleasure of hearing his full approbation of the proceedings of the Congress. . . ." Camden thought that if America continued cool "he did not doubt they would succeed in establishing their rights and obtain a solid and durable agreement with the mother country."

December 28—Returned to town "in time to meet, at the hour appointed, Lord Howe." His lordship asked what Franklin thought of sending someone over to America to work out a settlement. Excellent, said Franklin, "a person of rank and dignity, who had a character of candor, integrity, and wisdom, might . . . be of great use."

"I wish, brother, you were to be sent thither on such a service," Miss Howe said. "I should like that much better than General Howe's going to command the army there."

"I think, madam," said Franklin, "they ought to provide for General Howe some more honorable employment."

Howe took out a copy of the "Hints" written for Barclay and Fothergill. Franklin acknowledged he had written it. Howe was "rather sorry" to hear this, "since he had reason to think there was no likelihood of the admission of those propositions." Could Franklin draw up a more acceptable plan? his lordship asked, adding "that he should not think of influencing me by any selfish motive, but certainly I might with reason expect any reward in the power of government to bestow." ("This to me," Franklin said later of this delicate bribe, "was what the French call *spitting in the soup.*") Franklin doubted he could draw up a plan preferable to the "Hints" but he would try.

December 30—A revised proposal sent to Howe through his sister. Redress the grievances listed in the petition to the king, said Franklin, and all will be well. Congress has promised "that when the causes of their apprehensions are removed, their future conduct will prove them not unworthy of the regard they have been accustomed in their happier days to enjoy." Accept that promise as sincerely made, said Franklin. "If Britain can have any reliance on these declarations (and perhaps none to be extorted by force can be more relied on than these which are thus freely made) she may, without hazard to herself, try the expedient proposed, since, if it fails, she has it in her power at any time to resume her present measures."

December 31—Called on Miss Howe, "who informed me she had transcribed and sent the paper to Lord Howe in the country."

January 8–14—Negotiations with Lord Howe continue, though his lordship confesses he sees little hope of an accommodation.

Confers with David Barclay on merchants' petition to Parliament on American affairs.

Dr. Fothergill stops by to say he has given the "Hints" to Lord Dartmouth, "who, after consideration, had told him, some of them appeared reasonable, but others were inadmissable or impracticable." Fothergill had talked to the speaker of the House of Commons, who said "it would be very humiliating to Britain to be obliged to submit to such terms." Fothergill had replied "that the pill might be bitter, but it would be salutary, and must be swallowed."

January 17—Mrs. Stevenson gives a party for Franklin, "with a number of American gentlemen and British ladies in celebration of Dr. Franklin's birthday, who made one of the festive company, though he this day enters the [seventieth] year of his age."

January 19—The petition from Congress is laid before Parliament. "We flattered ourselves from the answer given by Lord Dartmouth that the king would have been pleased to recommend it to the consideration of Parliament by some message, but we were mistaken. It came down among a great heap of letters of intelligence from governors and officers in America, newspapers, pamphlets, handbills, etc., from that country, the last in the list, and was laid upon the table with them, undistinguished by any particular recommendation of it to the notice of either House."

January 20—At 2 P.M. Lord Chatham met Franklin in the lobby of the House of Lords. "This is Dr. Franklin," Chatham said in a loud voice to a doorkeeper, "whom I would have admitted into the House." From the floor his lordship moved his Majesty dispatch orders for General Gage to remove British troops from Boston. The motion was rejected.

January 27—Visited Chatham at his country estate. They talked over a plan for reconciliation Chatham would soon propose to the House of Lords. "I dined with him, his family only present, and returned to town in the evening."

January 29, Sunday morning—Chatham "came to town, and called upon me in Craven Street. He brought with him his plan transcribed, in the form of an Act of Parliament, which he put into my hands, requesting me to consider it carefully, and communicate to him such remarks upon it as should occur to me." Franklin promised to bring his comments out to the country Tuesday morning.

"He stayed with me near two hours, his equipage waiting at the door, and being there while people were coming from church, it was much taken notice of, and talked of, as at that time was every little circumstance that men thought might possibly any way affect American affairs. Such a visit from so great a man, on so important a business flattered not a little my vanity; and the honor of it gave me the more pleasure, as it happened on the very day twelve month that the ministry had taken so much pains to disgrace me before the Privy Council."

The plan Chatham left behind, though it reasserted Parliament's authority over the colonies, had much in it to please Franklin. All obnoxious acts objected to by the colonies were to be temporarily suspended; the Continental Congress would be recognized by the crown; Americans would be allowed to tax themselves. Franklin jotted down two pages of points he wanted to raise with his lordship when they conferred.

January 31—Spent nearly four hours with Chatham at his country house. They got through less than half the points Franklin wanted to raise about the plan, for his lordship "is not easily interrupted." No matter, said his lordship, "if it was not so perfect as might be wished, it would at least serve as a basis for treaty, and in the meantime prevent mischiefs."

February 1—To the House of Lords to hear Chatham present his plan. Lord Dartmouth said he thought the plan ought to be considered by the House. Lord Sandwich, "in a petulant, vehement speech, opposed its being received at all, and gave his opinion that it ought to be immediately *rejected* with the contempt it deserved." He also said "it appeared to him rather the work of some American; and turning his face towards me, who was leaning on the bar, said he fancied he had in his eye the person who drew it up, one of the bitterest and most mischievous enemies this country had ever known." Lord Dartmouth near the end of the debate reversed himself and said the plan should be rejected immediately. It was so done, by a vote of two to one. The House had treated Chatham and his plan "with as much contempt as they could have shown to a ballad offered by a drunken porter."

February 4—Met with Fothergill and Barclay in the evening. Told that the ministry had accepted five of the points in the "Hints," accepted nine others with qualifications, and rejected three outright. When it was mentioned during the discussion that the British had the power to burn every American seaport, Franklin lost his temper. He said "they might make bonfires of them whenever they pleased; that the fear of losing them would never alter my resolution to resist to the last that claim of Parliament; and that it behooved this country to take care what mischief it did us; for that sooner or later it would certainly be obliged to make good all damages with interest!"

February 5–11—A week in which "my time was much taken up among the members of Parliament."

Learned that his wife Deborah had died in mid-December. William in the letter reporting the news said that Deborah's "disappointment" in Franklin's postponement of his return had "preyed a good deal on her spirits." He also said: "However mad you may think the measures of the ministry are, yet I trust you have candor enough to acknowledge that we are noways behindhand with them in madness on this side of the water." All Franklin had to say about his wife's death was that because he "had left the care of my affairs" in her hands, "it was become necessary for me to return thither as soon as conveniently might be."

February 14—Franklin wrote home that "both houses have addressed the king declaring a rebellion to be in Massachusetts Bay, in consequence whereof more troops are about to be sent thither, and administration seems determined on reducing the colonies by force to a solemn acknowledgment of the power claimed by Parliament of making laws to bind the colonies in all cases whatsoever. A bill is preparing to deprive the four New England colonies of their fishery and other severities are threatened. Yet many here are confident that if the non-consumption of British manufactures in America is soberly and steadily adhered to another year, those measures will all be reversed and our rights acknowledged."

February 16—Met with Fothergill and Barclay, who offered a draft of fifteen points "conformable chiefly to what had been proposed and conceded on both sides." Discussion focused on the first point—"the tea destroyed to be paid for." Payment for the tea would give the ministry "some ground on which to found the commencement of conciliating measures." Franklin then made an astonishing proposal. He would risk both his reputation in Massachusetts and his private fortune by personally guaranteeing payment of the tea—if the ministry would promise repeal of the acts against Massachusetts. He made this offer because he wanted to put America and Britain on the road to reconciliation before "such a carnage may ensue as to make a breach that can never afterwards be healed." None of the three men thought the ministry would accept the offer.

February 17—Spent morning drawing up petitions to the king and to Lord Dartmouth urging a commissioner with power to negotiate a settlement be sent at once to America.

Note received from Miss Howe saying her brother wished to meet with Franklin tomorrow morning.

Met with Fothergill and Barclay in the evening. They doubted that the ministry would heed the petitions but would forward them along. Franklin said he would gladly meet directly with the ministry if that would hasten negotiations.

February 18—Met with Lord Howe at 11 A.M. His lordship "seemed very cheerful," having heard "I had consented to petition and engage payment for the tea." He said he might be sent as a commissioner to America. Would Franklin accompany him? Yes, if he first knew "what propositions were intended for America." Howe then said that to show "their good disposition towards yourself," the ministry would be pleased to pay all the "arrears of your salary, as agent for New England, which I understand they have stopped for some time past." Franklin said such favors "would be considered as so many bribes to betray the interest of my country." No more was said on the subject.

February 20—Lord North offered a vaguely worded "olive branch" resolution to Parliament: If the colonies, through legislation that must be approved by Parliament, agreed to tax themselves for their common defense and for the support of their governments, then Parliament would not tax them. Franklin thought the proposal sounded like that from a highwayman who, with a pistol in his victim's face, says: "Give me your purse, and then I will not put my hands into your pocket. But give me all your money, or I will shoot you through the head."

February 25—Wrote letters. In one he said: "The eyes of all Christendom are now upon us, and our honor as a people is become a matter of the utmost consequence to be taken care of. If we tamely give up our rights in this contest, a century to come will not restore us in the opinion of the world; we shall be stamped with the character of dastards, poltroons, and fools; and be despised and trampled upon, not by this haughty, insolent nation only, but by all mankind."

In another he condemned any plan that called for closer ties with the mother country. "When I consider the extreme corruption prevalent among all orders of men in this old rotten state, and the glorious public virtue so predominant in our rising country, I cannot but apprehend more mischief than benefit from a closer union. I fear they will drag us after them in all the plunder wars, which their desperate circumstances, injustice, and rapacity, may prompt them to undertake; and their wide-wasting prodigality and profusion is a gulf that will swallow up every aid we may distress ourselves to afford them."

February 28—At Franklin's request, met Lord Howe shortly after noon. Franklin said he planned to return to America but would linger if his lordship thought there were a chance he might be useful. Howe asked him to talk to Lord Hyde before abandoning hope.

March 1—Met with Lord Hyde shortly after 8 A.M. His lordship asked many questions. "I answered all, but with little effect; for though his lordship seemed civilly to hear what I said, I had reason to believe he attended very little to the purport of it, his mind being employed the while in thinking on what he himself purposed to say next."

Hyde at one point said "I might be assured I should never obtain better terms than what were now offered by Lord North." He also said that if Franklin brought about a reconciliation that pleased the government he would "be honored and rewarded perhaps, beyond my expectations." Nettled that after two months of exhausting negotiations the government still did not trust him, still thought he could be bought off, Franklin wearily reminded his lordship that to give the government an opening wedge he had pledged his fortune to pay for the tea. He also said: "That in truth private resentments had no weight with me in public business; that I was not the reserved man imagined, having really no secret instructions to act upon; that I was certainly willing to do everything that could reasonably be expected of me. But if any supposed I could prevail with my countrymen to take black for white, and wrong for right, it was not knowing either them or me; they were not capable of being so imposed on, nor was I capable of attempting it."

After leaving Lord Hyde, Franklin still had energy enough to take a young visiting American out for a tour of the British Museum. They arrived to find the place closed, the day being Ash Wednesday. The two returned to Craven Street and talked of American affairs. The visitor said that everyone friendly to the colonies to whom he had talked thought "a civil war is inevitable." Absolutely not, said Franklin. If the union can be preserved and violence avoided, the economic boycott will take effect. "By no means take any step of great consequence (unless on a sudden emergency) without advice of the Continental Congress," he warned. He also said that New England alone "could hold for ages against this country, and if they were firm and united in seven years would conquer them," and that "he had the best intelligence that the manufacturers were bitterly feeling and loudly complaining of the loss of the American trade. Let your adherence be to the non-importation agreement, a year from next September, or to the next sessions of Parliament, and the day is won."

March 7—Met Lord Howe at 11 A.M. His lordship was sorry that "at present there was no appearance of things going into the train he had wished, but that possibly they might yet take a more favorable turn."

"I assured him of my readiness at all times of cooperating with him, in so good a work; and so, taking my leave and receiving his good wishes, ended the negotiation with Lord Howe."

March 14—Met with Barclay and Fothergill. They, too, agreed negotiations had reached a dead end, and said that "the salvation of English liberty depended now on the perseverance and virtue of America."

March 15—Heard in the House of Lords "many base reflections on American courage, religion, understanding, etc., in which we were treated with the utmost contempt, as the lowest of mankind, and almost of a different species from the English of Britain. . . . I went home somewhat irritated and heated; and partly to retort upon this nation . . . drew up a memorial to present to Lord Dartmouth, before my departure."

The Memorial said in part: "I give notice, that satisfaction will probably one day be demanded for the injury" the people of Massachusetts have suffered by the oppressive acts of Parliament, "and that the injustice of the proceeding is likely to give such umbrage to *all the colonies*, that in no future war, wherein other conquests be meditated, either a man or a shilling will probably be obtained from any of them to aid such conquests, till full satisfaction be made as aforesaid."

Franklin showed the paper to his friend Thomas Walpole, with whom he had worked so long to make the Grand Ohio Company a reality. Walpole "looked at it and at me several times alternately, as if he apprehended me a little out of my senses. As I was in the hurry of packing up, I requested him to take the trouble of showing it to his neighbor, Lord Camden, and ask his advice upon it, which he kindly undertook to do."

March 16—Walpole says in a note that if the Memorial is sent to Lord Dartmouth "it is thought [it] might be attended with dangerous consequences to your person, and contribute to exasperate the nation."

March 17—"Mr. Walpole called at my house . . . and hearing I was gone to the House of Lords, came there to me, and repeated more fully what was in his note; adding, that it was thought my having no instructions directing me to deliver such a protest, would make it appear still more unjustifiable, and be deemed a national affront. I had no desire to make matters worse, and being grown cooler took the advice so kindly given me."

March 19—Spent several hours with Edmund Burke "opening his mind without reserve." (Three days later Burke would deliver his speech *On Conciliation with the American Colonies.*)

Sent a note to Arthur Lee, saying "I leave directions with Mrs. Stevenson to deliver you all the Massachusetts papers when you please to call for them."

March 20—Spent the day packing. He had told a friend he would return to London in October and thus was leaving behind most of the things he had accumulated during the last ten years in England.

Joseph Priestley spent the day with his friend. Priestley reported Franklin was "deeply stirred by the prospect of civil war, which he thought he had done all he could to prevent." While reading through a batch of newspapers from America, he told Priestley what to have reprinted in the English press. "Now and then he could not read for the tears that filled his eyes and ran down his cheeks. If there should be a war, he was sure America would win, but it would take ten years, and he would never live to see the end."

March 21—Departed from Portsmouth for America.

Also on this day Thomas Penn died. Eighteen years earlier Franklin had come to England to wrest Pennsylvania from Penn. Penn had outmaneuvered him and died with the colony still firmly in his family's hands.

CHAPTER

33

"YOU ARE NOW MY ENEMY,
AND I AM YOURS"

FRANKLIN REACHED PHILADELPHIA on Friday evening, May 5. His return was announced "by ringing of bells, to the great joy of the city." Not until two days later did William Franklin hear of his arrival, "which is quite unexpected news to me."

Soon after stepping ashore Franklin learned that what he had long feared had happened two weeks earlier—the outbreak of fighting between British regulars and American militiamen at Lexington and Concord. He sent a note to Mrs. Stevenson asking "all his furniture etc. to be sent to America, which indicates his despair of ever being able to return to England." He also sent a cool note to his son:

> I don't understand it as any favor to me or to you, the being continued in an office by which, with all your prudence, you cannot avoid running behindhand, if you live suitably to your station. While you are in it I know you will execute it with fidelity to your master, but I think independence more honorable than any service, and that in the state of American affairs which, from the present arbitrary measures is likely soon to take place, you will find yourself in no comfortable situation, and perhaps wish you had soon disengaged yourself.

He signed the note, not as in the past, "your affectionate father," but simply "B. Franklin."

On Saturday morning the Pennsylvania Assembly added Franklin's name to the colony's delegation to the Second Continental Congress, which would convene in four days. Franklin accepted the honor, which Joseph Galloway had refused earlier. "I am concerned at your resolution of quitting public life at a time when your abilities are so much wanted," Franklin wrote Galloway. As soon as possible he wanted to talk with him and William. He signed the note "With unalterable esteem and affection."

William came over from New Jersey for a hurried reunion. His colony, like all the colonies, was in an uproar. Every "day alarms are spread, which have a tendency to keep the minds of the people in a continual ferment," he said, "and prevent their paying any attention to the dictates of sober reason and common sense." He also said, "I am convinced that matters are now carried so far that the Americans in general are disposed to run the risk of total ruin rather than suffer a taxation by any but their own immediate representatives, and that there is not the least reason to expect they will ever, in this instance, consent to acknowledge the right, even if they should be obliged to submit to the power of Parliament."

Franklin and his son "avoided any conversation" at this first meeting in eleven years that might widen the gulf between them, but William could not resist saying before he left that he hoped that if his father "designed to set the colonies in a flame, he would take care to run away by the light of it."

The reunion with Galloway went no better. Galloway "opened his mind" and said he "hoped he was come to promote reconciliation." Franklin was reserved and "kept upon his guard." They met again the next morning. Franklin said: "Well, Mr. Galloway, you are really of the mind that I ought to promote reconciliation."

"Yes," said Galloway, and no more on the matter passed between them. They agreed to meet again with William when mutually convenient and talk through the subject.

2

Shortly before Congress convened on May 10 the delegates from New England rode into town as a body. Philadelphia showed its sympathy for beleaguered Boston, now under the military rule of General Gage, with "every mark of respect." Thousands of citizens watched silently from the curbs as several miles of carriages and horsemen and soldiers with swords at salute position moved at a solemn pace through the streets accompanied by the tolling of muffled church bells.

Congress convened in a chamber on the first floor of the State House where the Pennsylvania Assembly normally met. Franklin felt at home in a room where for so many years he had sat first as a clerk, then as a deputy. But now most of the faces he saw were those of strangers. He knew George Washington, whom he had met as Braddock's aide twenty years ago. A majority of the some fifty gentlemen present had been youngsters when Franklin retired from business. His only contemporary was Stephen Hopkins of Rhode Island, with whom he had attended the Albany Congress twenty-one years earlier. The dominant voice in the Pennsylvania delegation was his old enemy John Dickinson, who still refused to put a lightning rod on his house.

The delegates to the Second Congress were not to be envied. "When fifty or sixty men have a constitution to form for a great empire," said one, "at the same time they have a country of fifteen hundred miles extent to fortify, millions to arm and train, a naval power to begin, an extensive commerce to regulate, numerous tribes of Indians to negotiate with, a standing army of twenty-seven thousand men to raise, pay, victual, and officer, I shall really pity those fifty or sixty men." Congress had slim powers to work with while doing all this. It could request but not order; it could advise but not demand. It did not legislate; it recommended. Its power and authority over the "great, unwieldy body" called America depended on the goodwill granted it by the people. The thirteen colonies resembled "a large fleet sailing under convoy," said John Adams. "The fleetest sailers must wait for the dullest and slowest."

The rub came when someone like Ethan Allen dashed out ahead of the convoy and forced decisions Congress did not want to make. Seven days after it convened Allen, accompanied by Benedict Arnold, captured Fort Ticonderoga. Congress had planned to tell the world America was fighting a defensive war against Britain. Allen and Arnold's offensive move against Ticonderoga—and their later capture of Crown Point and St. John's, which gave the Champlain Valley to the Americans—put the delegates in an awkward position. Should Congress accept the gift handed it?

During the debate over the question Franklin sat napping, or pretending to nap, in his chair. When awake he listened but said nothing. At the end of each day's session he went directly home. He dined there and accepted no invitations to dine with others. "People seemed at a loss what party he would take," said Galloway. No man dared to ask the great man to declare himself, and Franklin used his fame to play for time. He would pay for his silence; the story persisted the rest of his life that he had returned to Philadelphia "strongly opposed to independence." There is no evidence for this. If the obdurate ministry had not convinced him independence was inevitable, Lexington and Concord had. He wanted time not to settle his own mind but to persuade his son and Galloway, whom he regarded as all but his son, to side with him in the war against Britain.

Franklin met with them both early in June as the delegates in Congress began "to entertain a great suspicion that Dr. Franklin came rather as a spy than as a friend." He read aloud from a long account of his negotiations during the last four months in London which he had written as a letter to his son during the six-week voyage from England. He had got through three-fourths of the account when the arrival of company cut short the reading and discussion had to be postponed.

Through the rest of June Franklin continued to sit silently in Congress as rumors about him proliferated. He accepted every assignment handed him, and when not attending Congress was busy setting up a new postal system, seeking ways to promote the manufacture of saltpeter for gunpowder, arranging for the printing of a continental currency. (Congress carefully avoided placing him on committees that called for policy decisions.) When the Pennsylvania Assembly chose him for the Committee of Safety, which would direct the colony's war effort, he accepted the added burden. The work kept the old man constantly on the move. "In the morning at six, I am at the Committee of Safety," he told a friend, "which committee holds till near nine, when I am at the Congress, and that sits till after four in the afternoon." Evenings went to one or another of the congressional committees he sat on.

On June 23 Congress listened to a report of the battle at Bunker Hill, the first full-scale fight between Americans and British soldiers. The British gained the hill but lost over a thousand men doing it. During the battle shots from warships in the harbor started a string of fires that destroyed some three hundred houses.

The news enraged Franklin. He returned home to cut his last ties with England, first settling his financial affairs with his banker in London, then his accounts with his "dear, dear friend" Mrs. Stevenson. "You will be in possession of a complete £1,000 which as a friend I would not advise you to trust in your stocks," he advised Mrs. Stevenson; "for Britain having begun a war with us, which I apprehend is not likely soon to be ended, and may possibly draw on one with some European power, there is great probability of those stocks falling headlong, as you remember the India did. You had better, therefore, I think, put your money out on a good mortgage of land."

Next, he met with his son and Galloway, and for the first time in over a decade the three had a convivial evening. "And the glass having gone about freely," Galloway said later, "the doctor, at a late hour, opened himself, and declared in favor of measures for attaining independence—exclaimed against the corruption and dissipation of the kingdom and signified his opinion, that from the strength of opposition, the want of union in the ministry, the great resources in the colonies, they would finally prevail." He urged Galloway to return to public life.

Franklin stressed British weaknesses. "America would be united, and always able to draw her powers into exertion, while the British nation, and its public councils, were and would be yet more, divided and distracted," he said. Moreover, "the friends to the American cause in Britain, would incessantly maintain and increase that division and distraction, by opposing the measures of government." Galloway replied that the war would still political quarrels in Britain and a united nation would quickly suppress the rebellion. Remember, he said, trespassing on Poor Richard's territory, remember the "fable of the two bulldogs tearing each other to pieces, yet on the appearance of their common enemy, their enmity instantly ceased, and their whole powers became united, and exerted to reduce him."

The evening ended with the three men parting "as they met, unconverted to the principles of each other."

In Congress Franklin continued silent. On July 5, driven by the eloquence of John Dickinson, the delegates approved a new petition to the king—the so-called Olive Branch petition. It begged the king in suppliant phrases to intercede for the colonies against his designing Parliament. After it passed, Franklin wrote a short note to his old friend in London:

Mr. Strahan:
    You are a member of Parliament, and one of that majority which has doomed my country to destruction.—You have begun to burn our towns, and murder our people.—Look upon your hands! They are stained with the blood of your relations!—You and I were long friends:—You are now my enemy,—and I am
                                        Yours, B. Franklin

3

The letter to Strahan became one of the most famous Franklin ever penned. It was widely published in America and Europe and people continued to remark on it long after the Revolution.

Little Franklin wrote reveals more of the man and yet clouds an answer to the question—what manner of man? The traditional picture of the imperturbable man of reason vanishes here. The tone is cool, cold even, yet who after reading it can say Franklin lacks "fire in his belly"?

Those who hated or distrusted him found his failings in these few terse lines. They revealed him to be

Cruel—Franklin had sacrificed Hutchinson to a cause. Now he singled out "dear Straney."

Vengeful—Strahan as a member of Parliament had voted to send troops to Boston, and thus deserved to be publicly humiliated for his act.

Deceitful—The letter was a hoax, a publicity stunt. Franklin never sent it. He did not break with Strahan. A few days after releasing it to the press, he sent a friendly letter to his old friend and the two continued to correspond until death.

Vain—While others in Congress worked behind closed doors to prod America toward independence Franklin performed in public. With a few dramatic lines of prose he made himself the first continental hero of the Revolution. "The people of England have thought that the opposition in America was wholly owing to Dr. Franklin," John Adams said a few days after the letter was published; "and I suppose their scribblers will attribute the temper and proceedings of this Congress to him; but there cannot be a greater mistake. He has had but little share farther than to cooperate and assist."

Those who loved or admired Franklin found his virtues in the letter. It revealed him to be

Generous—Possibly Strahan's printing business and political standing might suffer from the long and close friendship with the now notorious Franklin. What better way to protect him than to sever the tie publicly? (The ministry, as Franklin may have suspected, was reading Strahan's mail to America. Two centuries later copies of his letters to Franklin were found among Lord Dartmouth's papers.)

Compassionate—The man who had wept as a child when laughed at for paying too much for the whistle and learned early to hide his feelings was here masking deep sorrow as he reminded the world America and Britain were now engaged in a doubly painful civil war—one between Englishmen and, as Franklin knew from the split within his own family, between Americans.

Courageous—Exactly one year minus a day before Congress approved Thomas Jefferson's majestic paper, Franklin dared to make his personal declaration of independence before the world. Long before others he publicly pledged his life, his fortune, and his honor to the American cause.

Regardless of how men felt about the letter all had to admire its effectiveness as propaganda for the cause and for Franklin's reputation. "The suspicions against Dr. Franklin have died away," a Philadelphian remarked after reading it. "Whatever his design at coming over here, I believe he has now chosen his side, and favors our cause." In Congress he now spoke his thoughts. "He does not hesitate at our boldest measures," John Adams said, "but rather seems to think us too irresolute and backward. He thinks us at present in an odd state, neither in peace nor war, neither dependent nor independent. But he thinks that we shall soon assume a character more decisive." The old man's faith in America impressed Adams. "He thinks that we have the power of preserving ourselves, and that even if we should be driven to the disagreeable necessity of assuming a total independency, and set up a separate state, we could maintain it."

The violent feelings Franklin had kept bottled up startled the delegates when they burst out. A few days after the letter to Strahan he submitted to Congress a paper that accused the British nation of being so impatient to seize all America that they have

> proceeded to open robbery, declaring by a solemn act of Parliament, that all our estates are theirs, and all our property found upon the seas divisible among such of their armed plunderers as shall take the same; and have even dared in the same act to declare, that all the spoilings, thefts, burnings of houses and towns, and murders of innocent people, perpetrated by their wicked and inhuman corsairs on our coasts, previous to any war declared against us, were just actions, and shall be so deemed, contrary to several commandments of God (by which this act they presume to repeal), and to all the principles of right, and all the ideas of justice, entertained heretofore by every other nation, savage as well as civilized.

The passionate language embarrassed Congress and the paper went unmentioned in its journal. But Franklin continued to press for decisions that would carry the colonies toward independence. He submitted a draft of a constitution for the united colonies. It was ignored. He moved that the ports of America be opened to the world. The motion was rejected. He urged that foreign nations be approached for aid. A decision was postponed. For a decade Franklin had trailed behind American opinion. Now he had moved out ahead of it and must pause until it caught up with him.

4

The twelve months that followed his personal declaration of independence were among the most painful and also selfless in Franklin's life. Though constantly "under the fatigue of more business than is suitable to my age and inclination," he accepted every assignment given him. When Congress adjourned for the month of August to escape the dreadful heat of Philadelphia, Franklin continued regularly to attend the meetings of the Committee of Safety. At the end of the month he visited William at Perth Amboy, making one last attempt to persuade him to join the cause. He failed and soon had to endure the humiliation of seeing his son publicly condemned as an enemy of America.

When Congress reassembled in September, it asked him to travel with two other delegates to Boston to confer with General Washington. He went. He returned in November and resumed his heavy schedule. "Mr. Franklin I find to be a daring, artful, insinuating incendiary," a British spy in Philadelphia reported to the ministry. Such was Franklin's reputation that when Thomas Paine published *Common Sense* in January 1776, Franklin was "generally allowed to be the author, though he denies it," said the spy. "This pamphlet," he went on, "has debauched many of the people, and I'm sorry to be obliged to add that the perfidious traitor Franklin exerts himself to alienate the affection of the people from the best of kings; in short, I know not a worse nor a more dangerous man."

In February the old man began to weaken. "My eyes will now hardly serve me to write by night," he said, "and these short days have been all taken up by such a variety of business, that I seldom can sit down ten minutes without interruption." But a few weeks later when Congress asked him to make an excruciating trip to Canada he agreed to go, though the snow had not cleared the ground. The trip nearly killed him. He arrived back in Philadelphia at the end of May exhausted and suffering from an attack of the gout. He spent the early part of June recuperating on a friend's farm outside the city.

He heard from friends in Congress that on June 7 a resolution had been presented to the delegates calling for a declaration of independence. Four days later he heard that he had been chosen as one of a committee of five, headed by Thomas Jefferson, to draw up a paper explaining to the world why the colonies were taking this momentous step. On Friday morning, June 21, Thomas Jefferson sent a message out to the farm:

The inclosed paper has been read and with some small alterations approved of by the committee. Will Doctor Franklin be so good as to peruse it and suggest such alterations as his more enlarged view of the subject will dictate? The paper having been returned to me to change a particular sentiment or two, I propose laying it again before the committee tomorrow morning, if Doctor Franklin can think of it before that time.

Franklin read the paper and made only a few changes, all minor. One dealt with style. In an early draft Jefferson had complained that Great Britain was sending over "Scotch & foreign mercenaries to invade & destroy us." The last two words seemed too mild. He crossed them out and substituted "deluge us with blood." Franklin, unaware of the original wording, crossed out the florid substitution and replaced it, curiously, with the identical phrase Jefferson had rejected. Another of his changes seemed equally insignificant. Where Jefferson had written "When in the course of human events it becomes necessary for a people to . . ." Franklin altered "a people" to "one people." His intent was clear. The Declaration must appear as the voice of a united people, and this slight change tended to increase that illusion. Unfortunately, Franklin lacked the energy to trace down the nine other uses of "a people" in the paper. The oversight helped to encourage a debate that would rage for three-quarters of a century whether the Declaration spoke for a single people or for thirteen separate and independent peoples. Only a long and bloody war would eventually silence discussion on the point.

Franklin was well enough to attend Congress on July 2 and cast his vote for independence. He was present the next two days when Congress edited Jefferson's paper. The delegates were severer critics than Franklin, cutting the paper's length by something like a quarter. The editing was particularly harsh toward the end of the document. Sixteen lines were cut from the next to last paragraph. Some of Jefferson's happiest phrases —"the road to happiness and glory is open to us too; we will climb it apart from them"—went by the board. The loss nettled Jefferson and it was probably at this point that Franklin, "who perceived that I was not insensible to these mutilations," leaned over from his seat next to Jefferson and tried to divert him with a story.

"I have made it a rule," Franklin said, "whenever in my power, to avoid becoming a draughtsman of papers to be reviewed by a public body. I took my lesson from an incident which I will relate to you. When I was a journeyman printer one of my companions, an apprentice hatter, having served out his time, was about to open shop for himself. His first concern was to have a handsome signboard, with a proper inscription. He composed it in these words:

John Thompson, Hatter

makes and sells hats for ready money

with a figure of a hat subjoined. But he thought he would submit it to his friends for their amendments. The first he showed it to thought the word 'hatter' tautologous, because followed by the words 'makes hats' which show he was a hatter. It was struck out. The next observed that the word 'makes' might as well be omitted, because the customers would not care who made the hats. If good and to their mind, they would buy, by whomever made. He struck it out. A third said he thought the words 'for ready money' were useless, as it was not the custom of the place to sell on credit. Everyone who purchased expected to pay. They were parted with, and the inscription now stood:

John Thompson

sells hats

'*Sells* hats' says his next friend. 'Why nobody will expect you to give them away. What then is the use of that word?' It was stricken out, and 'hats' followed it, the rather, as there was one painted on the board. So his inscription was reduced ultimately to

John Thompson

with the figure of a hat subjoined."

On 2 August 1776 Congress paused in the business of the day in order that all those present might sign the engrossed copy of the Declaration of Independence. Facts about the signing are few; anecdotes abound. Hancock, after centering his name below the text, is supposed to have said: "There! John Bull can read my name without spectacles, and may now double his reward of £500 for my head. *That* is my defiance." He is also supposed to have said: "We must be unanimous. There must be no pulling different ways; we must all hang together." To that remark Benjamin Franklin is supposed to have replied: "Yes, we must all hang together, or most assuredly we shall all hang separately."

NOTES

I. "A SHORT, FAT, TRUNCHED OLD MAN"

1   "announced by ringing of bells": quoted in Hawke, *In the Midst*, p. 87.
"a short, fat, trunched old man": Cutler, *Life*, vol. 1, pp. 267–268.
"Didst thee ever know": quoted in Hawke, *In the Midst*, p. 88.

2   Congress "begin to entertain": ibid., p. 89.
"By every intelligence I can get": Seed, "A British Spy in Philadelphia," 30 May 1775, p. 8.
"among those who are for moderation": ibid., 19 June 1775, p. 12.
"He has not assumed anything": John Adams to his wife, 23 July 1775, Butterfield, *Adams Family Correspondence*, vol. 1, p. 253.
"passion for reputation and fame": John Adams in his diary, 10 May 1779, Butterfield, *Adams Diary and Auto.*, vol. 2, p. 367.
Wilson anecdote: Corner, *Autobiography of Benjamin Rush*, p. 188.
"Punctual and indefatigable": ibid., p. 148.

3   "a great part of the time fast asleep": John Adams quoted in Van Doren, *BF*, p. 530.
His indolence "will prevent": John Adams in his diary, 9 February 1779, Butterfield, *Adams Diary and Auto.*, vol. 2, p. 346.
"Oh! don't shut the window": ibid., vol. 3, p. 418.
Adams's tales about Franklin: John Adams to Mercy Warren, 3 August 1807 (microfilm reel 118 in Adams Papers), quoted in Evans, "John Adams's Opinion of Franklin," pp. 221–222.

4   "His understanding is good enough for common uses": Thomas Jefferson to James Monroe, 5 July 1785, Boyd, *Jefferson Papers*, vol. 8, p. 262.
"He has very moderate abilities": Adams in his diary, 10 May 1779, Butterfield, *Adams Diary and Auto.*, vol. 2, p. 367.
"I always knew him to be a very factious man": David Hume to Adam Smith, 13 February 1774, quoted in Eliot, "Adam Smith and BF," p. 79.
"I am afraid that B. F.": Richard Peters to Thomas Penn, quoted in *Auto.*, p. 294.

The most "hypocritical old rascal": quoted in Warren, "A Young American's Adventures in England and France," p. 252.

"I have a very high opinion of B. F.'s virtue": Richard Peters to Thomas Penn, quoted in *Auto.*, p. 294.

"I never really was much of an admirer": Maclay, *Journal*, p. 232.

"a very artful, insinuating fellow": William Allen to John Ferdinand Paris, 18 March 1758, vol. 7, p. 363n.

Dickinson and lightning rod: Chastellux, *Travels*, vol. 1, p. 294.

BF motto on coat of arms: vol. 13, p. 245n. See also vol. 2, facing p. 250.

2. GROWING UP IN BOSTON

5   "lived to grow up": BF to Jane Mecom, 9 January 1760, vol. 9, p. 18.

"laughed at me": to Madame Brillon, 10 November 1779, Smyth, *Writings*, vol. 7, p. 415.

"don't give": ibid.

"Tho' I flatter myself": William Smith to Thomas Penn, September 1755, vol. 6, p. 211.

"rather deliberate": Thomas Collinson to his uncle, 12 September 1760, vol. 9, p. 211.

"a lowly building": Van Doren, *Jane Mecom*, p. 3.

6   "You have never mentioned": to John Franklin, 2 January 1753, vol. 4, p. 409.

"I feel some affection": ibid.

without "a line from any relation": to Sarah Davenport, [June? 1730], vol. 1, p. 171.

"Our father, who was a very wise man": Van Doren, *Jane Mecom*, p. 9.

"Fish and visitors": *Poor Richard* (1736), vol. 2, p. 137.

"telling me verse makers were generally beggars": *Auto.*, p. 60.

"fell far short in elegance": ibid., p. 61.

"saw the justice of his remarks": ibid., p. 61.

"sound understanding": ibid. pp. 54–55.

7   "Honored Father": to Josiah and Abiah Franklin, 6 September 1744, vol. 2, p. 413.

"I think, father": quoted in Parton, *BF*, vol. 1, p. 50.

"Seest thou a man": *Auto*, p. 144.

"at his table he liked to have": ibid., p. 55

"a clear pleasing voice": ibid. p. 54.

"In his travels he went upon liking to a tailor": from Josiah Franklin, 26 May 1739, vol. 2, p. 230.

"there was nine children": ibid., p. 231.

The walls of the parlor: Parton, *BF*, vol. 1, p. 18.

8   "By the way, is our relationship": to Jane Mecom, 3 August 1789, Smyth, *Writings*, vol. 10, p. 33.

"A mad philosopher": Aldridge, *BF*, p. 7.

9   *"called a woodchuck"*: to Peter Collinson, 26 June 1755, vol. 6, p. 85.

"it is what we here call a *groundhog*": ibid.

Long Wharf: Bridenbaugh, *Cities in the Wilderness*, p. 172.

females who "by throwing their heads": Silence Dogood, No. 13 (24 September 1722), vol. 1, p. 42.

"In the concerns of civil life": Bridenbaugh, *Cities in the Wilderness*, p. 253.

10   "I was generally a leader": *Auto.*, p. 54.

"Believe me, Ben": Parton, *BF*, vol. 1, p. 34.

"had a strong inclination for the sea": *Auto.*, p. 53.

"the mean living": ibid.

11 Harvard students "dunces and blockheads": Silence Dogood, No. 4 (14 May 1722), vol. 1, pp. 15, 17.

"hankering for the sea": *Auto.*, p. 58.

"I stood out some time": ibid., pp. 58–59.

"James Franklin remains eternally transfixed": Miller, *The New England Mind*, p. 336.

12 "one newspaper being . . . enough": *Auto.*, p. 67.

"short pieces, serious, sarcastic": Miller, *The New England Mind*, p. 335, quoting from 14 August 1720 issue of *Courant*.

Matthew Adams, "who had a pretty collection of books": *Auto.*, p. 59.

"Maister, ye ken vary weel": Miller, *The New England Mind*, p. 358.

"began to drink too much brandy": BF: Observations on North America, 1766, vol. 13, p. 348.

"reflecting on the clergy": Miller, *The New England Mind*, p. 335.

"a pious and charitable design": Blake, "Inoculation Controversy," p. 493.

"houses in this town": Bridenbaugh, *Cities in the Wilderness*, p. 226.

"novel and dubious practice": William Douglass to Cadwallader Colden, 1 May 1722, New-York Historical Society *Collections*, 1 (1912), 143–144.

13 Boston "a town which Satan has taken": Miller, *The New England Mind*, p. 336.

"reform the present declining age": ibid., quoting from 20 November 1721 issue of *Courant*.

Mather aspires to "reign Detractor General": ibid., p. 337.

"I cannot but pity poor Franklin": ibid., pp. 337–338.

"was extremely ambitious": *Auto.*, p. 62.

his brother "thinking it might turn to account": *ibid.*, p. 59.

14 "sat up in my room reading": ibid.

"human freedom": Ketcham, *BF*, p. 25.

"Neighbors! you stand related": Miller, *The American Puritans*, p. 216.

Mather's essays "perhaps gave me a turn of thinking": *Auto.*, p. 58.

"a thorough deist": ibid., p. 114.

15 speak to "men in a very easy and familiar manner": Horner, BF's *Dogood Papers*, p. 508.

Perry Miller has said: *From Colony to Province*, p. 342.

Mrs. Dogood's vernacular phrases: vol. 1, pp. 16, 19, 40.

"the exquisite pleasure": *Auto.*, p. 68.

"that though I wrote": Silence Dogood, No. 13 (24 September 1722), vol. 1, pp. 41–42.

"monstrous topsy-turvy *mortar pieces*": Silence Dogood, No. 6 (11 June 1722), vol. 1, p. 22.

"a little religion": Silence Dogood, No. 9 (23 July 1722), vol. 1, p. 30.

16 "I am naturally very jealous": Silence Dogood, No. 2 (16 April 1722), vol. 1, p. 13.

"when the civil government": Miller, *From Colony to Province*, p. 337.

folly "in affronting the government": Duniway, *Freedom of the Press in Massachusetts*, p. 99.

"and I made bold to give our rulers": *Auto.*, p. 69.

"Better men than myself": Van Doren, *BF*, p. 27, quoting from *Courant*, 16 July 1722.

hypocrites, who *"dissemble* and *lie"*: Miller, *From Colony to Province*, p. 339.

to avoid "malicious scribbles": The Printer to the Reader, 11 February 1722, vol. 1, p. 49.

17 indenture contract "with a full discharge": *Auto.*, p. 69.
"he wrote good sense": Miller, *The New England Mind*, p. 341, quoting from *Courant*, 1726.
"passion too often urged him": *Auto.*, p. 70.

18 "I had already made myself a little obnoxious": *Auto.*, p. 71.
"The Boston manner": to John Lathrop, 31 May 1788, Smyth, *Writings*, vol. 9, p. 649.
"a citizen of Boston": Oliver Wendell Holmes, quoted in Rossiter, *Six Characters in Search of a Republic*, p. 207.
bill "was framed in imitation of a law": to Isaac Norris, 9 June 1759, vol. 8, p. 399.
"my education in New England": *Auto.*, p. 184.
"A NEW ENGLANDMAN": To the Printer of the CHRONICLE, 9 May 1759, vol. 8, p. 356.
"my country": to Samuel Cooper, 30 December 1770, vol. 17, p. 311.
"our charter rights": to Thomas Cushing, 24 December 1770, vol. 17, p. 308.
"And now that I am writing": to Jonathan Williams, 16 February 1786, Smyth, *Writings*, vol. 9, p. 484.

3. "A CONFUSED VARIETY OF DIFFERENT SCENES"

19 "I have been the more particular in this description": *Auto.*, p. 75.
"he *actually creates himself as a character*": Levin, "Auto. of BF," p. 259.
"His confessed *errata*": Sanford, "American Pilgrim's Progress," p. 309. See also Sayre, *The Examined Self* for excellent comments on the *Auto.*

20 "oppressors and bigots": Bradford quoted in DeArmond, "Andrew Bradford," p. 469.
"I say, give me a wooden one": Dr. Solomon Drowne, quoted in Hawke, *In the Midst*, p. 38.

21 Quakers "remarkably grave and reserved": *Fithian Journal*, quoted in ibid., p. 39.
"which made me then think": *Auto.*, p. 124.
"Families who had lived well": quoted in Nash, *Quakers and Politics*, p. 332.
Philadelphia port traffic: Lydon, "Philadelphia's Expansion," p. 402.

22 to teach "male Negroes to read": quoted in Bloore, "Samuel Keimer," p. 265.
"It is neither the great": Wendel, "Keith-Lloyd Alliance," p. 296.
"the new, vile people": ibid., p. 299.
"with a condescension": *Auto.*, p. 80.
"a genteel new suit": ibid., p. 81.

23 a man "of small discretion": ibid., p. 82.
"had been so industrious": ibid., p. 83.
"In truth, he was an odd fish": ibid., pp. 112–113.
"I used to work him so with my Socratic method": ibid., p. 88.
The governor continued "to like my company": ibid., p. 92.
"as I was about to take a long voyage": ibid., p. 89.

24 "ingenious, genteel in his manners": ibid., p. 90.
"It is not amiss": to Deborah Franklin, 13 December 1766, vol. 13, p. 519.
"It was a habit he had": *Auto.*, p. 95.
Defoe's classification: quoted in Rudé, *Hanoverian London*, p. 37.

25 "a good deal of my earnings": *Auto.*, p. 96.
Ralph "let me know he thought": ibid., p. 99.

A Dissertation on Liberty and Necessity, 1725, vol. 1, pp. 57–71.
"By some means": *Auto.*, p. 97.
26 "began to think" ibid., p. 99.
"fits of indigestion": quoted in Aldridge, *BF*, 21.
"The thing pleased me": *Auto.*, p. 105.
come "to see me": *Auto.*, p. 97; *Papers*, vol. 1, p. 54.
27 "Let me, therefore, make some resolutions": vol. 1, pp. 99–100.
"despairing with reason": *Auto.*, p. 107.
Keimer "had got a better house": ibid.
modesty "makes the most homely virgin amiable": to Jane Mecom, 6 January 1727, vol. 1, p. 100.
Denham's death: incorrectly given in *Auto.*, p. 107. Correct date given in Roach, "BF Slept Here," p. 135, which also mentions Denham's ten-pound Christmas gift to BF.
"was rather disappointed": *Auto.*, p. 107.
28 "without virtue man can have no happiness": Articles of Belief, 20 November 1728, vol. 1, p. 103.
"I grew convinced": *Auto.*, p. 114.
"He is not above caring for us": Articles of Belief, 20 November 1728, vol. 1, p. 103.
"he counselled me as a father": *Auto.*, p. 107.
"I was . . . remote from the eye and advice of my father": ibid., p. 115.
BF's religious service: Articles of Belief, 20 November 1728, vol. 1, pp. 101–109.
Keimer tempted "with an offer": *Auto.*, p. 108.
"I made the ink": ibid., p. 110.
29 "I went on, however, very cheerfully": ibid., p. 108.
"I am about courting a girl": Miscellaneous Observations, vol. 1, p. 270.
"hard-to-be governed passion of youth": *Auto.*, p. 128.
"F———N, tho' plagued": quoted in Newcomb, *Franklin and Galloway*, p. 93.
"I have marked him particularly": Thomas Jefferson to James Madison, 14 February 1783, quoted in Conner, *Poor Richard's Politics*, p. 253.
Possible extramarital affairs: Butterfield, *Adams Diary and Auto.*, vol. iv, p. 134.
30 "formed most of my ingenious acquaintances": *Auto.*, p. 116.
"The Junto fainted last summer": from Philip Syng, 1 March 1766, vol. 13, p. 190.
Junto members: Meredith, *Auto.*, p. 108; Potts, to Hugh Roberts, 16 September 1758, vol. 8, p. 159; Webb, *Auto.*, p. 108; Coleman, *ibid.*, p. 118; Parsons, to Hugh Roberts, 16 September 1758, vol. 8, p. 159; Maugridge, *Auto.*, p. 117; Scull, ibid., p. 117; Godfrey, ibid., p. 117; Grace, ibid., pp. 117–118.
"Your walls are thick": James, *Memorial of Thomas Potts*, p. 388.
She refused "to marry": ibid., p. 386.
"unmistakable": Ketcham, *BF*, p. 30.
31 "hum'd in consort": Proposals and Queries, 1732, vol. 1, p. 259.
"Three queries in philosophy were first": Wainwright, "Scull's 'Junto' Verses," p. 82.
Junto topics for discussion: Proposals and Queries, 1732, vol. 1, pp. 257–258, 260, 262, 263.
32 "fill and drink a glass of wine": ibid., p. 259.
"the witty bards inspire": Wainwright, "Scull's 'Junto' Verses," p. 83.
"You are all my intimate pot companions": On the Providence of God, 1732, vol. 1, p. 264.
"For my own part": to Hugh Roberts, 26 February 1761, vol. 9, p. 280.
services "became every day of less importance": *Auto.*, p. 110.

4 . MAKING IT

33 "to abstain long from dram-drinking": *Auto.*, p. 111.
"want of candor": McMaster, *Man of Letters,* quoted in Bloore, "Samuel Keimer," p. 281.
worked "exceeding hard": *Auto.*, p. 118.

34 "the freezing of our river": Busy-Body, 4 February 1729, vol. 1, p. 115.
"We have little news of consequence": DeArmond, *Bradford,* p. 119.
"if he proceed farther": Martha Careful, 28 January 1729, vol. 1, p. 112.
"run about and do petty mischief": Busy-Body, 25 February 1729, vol. 1, p. 123.
A Modest Enquiry: vol. 1, pp. 139–157.

35 "highly ingenious and effective": Fetter, "Early History of Political Economy," p. 51.
"been of some service": *Auto.*, p. 124.
"Shipped by the Grace of God": Thomas, *History of Printing,* p. 370n.
"many things abstruse . . . to us": The Printer to the Reader, 2 October 1729, vol. 1, p. 158.
a "paltry thing": *Auto.*, p. 119.
"the typography of the *Mercury*": Thomas, *History of Printing,* p. 433.

36 "guardian of his country's reputation": to Francis Hopkinson, 24 December 1782, quoted in Levy, *Freedom of Speech,* p. 187n.
"a wicked and seditious libel": quoted in DeArmond, "Andrew Bradford," p. 471.
"fixed and honorable salary": 9 October 1729, vol. 1., pp. 159n, 161.
These "spirited remarks": *Auto.*, p. 121.
excerpts from *Gazette:* "And sometime last week," 16 October 1720, vol. 1, p. 165; "From New York," 19 June 1732, vol. 1, p. 274; "The same day," 10 February 1730, vol. 1, p. 184.

37 "When Mr. Bradford": 19 March 1730, vol. 1, p. 185.
"Thursday last, a certain p____r": 23 September 1731, vol. 1, p. 219.
"At present I am much hurried": to Sarah Davenport, June 1730, vol. 1, p. 171.
"was often seen drunk": *Auto.*, p. 122.

38 "leave the whole in your hands": ibid., p. 123.
"a serious courtship on my part ensued": *ibid.,* p. 127.
" 'Tis generally known here": George Roberts to Robert Grafton, 9 October 1763, quoted in Mariboe, *William Franklin,* p. 24.
"a fat, jolly dame": Aldridge, *BF,* p. 32.

39 "calling in as she passes by": to Abiah Franklin, 7 September 1749, vol. 3, p. 388.
"I was not fit to be seen": from Deborah Franklin, 16 May 1767, vol. 14, p. 158.
"I have to tell you sum thing": from ibid., 20–27 November 1769, vol. 16, p. 231.
"we had the best buckwheat cakes": from ibid., 3 November 1765, vol. 12, p. 351.
"Women of that character": A Scolding Wife, 5 July 1733, vol. 1, p. 325.
"D. Read came into the house": Jordan, "BF as Genealogist," p. 22.
"always knew what I did not": Aldridge, *BF,* p. 34.

"read over and over again": from Deborah Franklin, 8 October 1765, vol. 12, p. 300.

"my dame being from home": to Richard Peters, [30? April 1754], vol. 5, p. 269.

40 "Oh, my child": from Deborah Franklin, 6–13 October, 1765, vol. 12, p. 298.

"That you may not be offended": quoted without date in Bruce, *BF Self-Revealed*, vol. 1, pp. 213–214.

"Mr. Fisher": Fisher, "Diary," p. 276.

41 "apprehensive of a powerful rival": *Auto.*, p. 126.

"were all carried on and ended amicably": ibid., p. 181.

"a game played according to settled and known rules": Conner, *Poor Richard's Politics*, p. 12.

"The Morals of Chess": Sparks, *Works*, vol. 2, pp. 187–192.

43 "too much to bear": to William Strahan, 27 July 1756, vol. 6, p. 476.

"continually employed in serving all parties": Apology for Printers, 10 June 1731, vol. 1, p. 195.

"He's a fool": *Poor Richard* (1745), vol. 3, p. 5.

"Let his air, his manner": On Conversation, 15 October 1730, vol. 1, p. 181.

"She assisted me cheerfully": *Auto.*, p. 144.

items for sale: vol. 1, pp. 186, 219, 276, 277, 334, 348, 379; vol. 2, 133, 134.

Bradford and Harry described: *Auto*, p. 126.

44 BF joins Masons: vol. 1, pp. 202–204.

"We kept no idle servants": *Auto.*, p. 145.

Philadelphische Zeitung: vol. 1, pp. 230–231, 233–234.

45 *Rhode-Island Almanack*: Brigham, "James Franklin," pp. 536–544.

Poor Richard (1733): vol. 1, pp. 287–318.

Poor Richard on Leeds: (1733), vol. 1, p. 311; (1734), p. 350; (1735), vol. 2, pp. 3–4.

46 "Forewarned, forearmed": (1736), vol. 2, p. 141.

"Alas! 'tis as easy": (1739), vol. 2, p. 217.

"He that lives upon hope": (1736), vol. 2, p. 138.

"Force shits": (1736), vol. 2, p. 141.

"Study Poor Richard a little": to Sarah Bache, 6 April 1773, Smyth, *Writings*, vol. 6, p. 32.

47 "Our former differences were forgotten": *Auto.*, pp. 169–170.

5. "IMPROVING THE TASTE OF THE TOWN"

48 "the dirty fingers": to Lord Kames, 28 February 1768, vol. 15, p. 61.

"filthy, unmannerly custom": Pennsylvania Fireplaces, 1744, vol. 2, p. 439.

"round hand": Lingelbach, "BF's *American Instructor*," p. 379.

"*Spell* is a vulgar English word": to Jacques Barbeu Dubourg, 26 December 1772, quoted in MacLaurin, *BF's Vocabulary*, p. 33.

"The *unshakeable*, too": to David Hume, 27 September 1760, vol. 9, p. 229–230.

"NOTICE has been turned into a verb": quoted in MacLaurin, *BF's Vocabulary*, p. 31.

"I rise in the morning and read": Journal of a Voyage, 1726, vol. 1, p. 86.

49 "I have not the propensity to sitting still": to William Strahan, 8 August 1761, vol. 10, p. 320.

"Man is a sociable being": Journal of a Voyage, 1726, vol. 1, p. 85.

"in some degree the loss of the learned education": *Auto.*, p. 143.

"a pleasant air": to Mary Hewson, 25 November 1771, vol. 18.

"in the bosom of my family": to John Jay, 21 September 1785, Smyth, *Writings*, vol. 9, p. 467.

"Understanding 'tis a current report": 30 December 1736, vol. 2, p. 154.

"The DELIGHT of all that knew him": vol. 2, p. 154n.

"evade going to meeting": to Jane Mecom, [June? 1748], vol. 3, p. 302.

50 "spent no time in taverns": *Auto.*, p. 143.

"We hear that on Monday night last": 16 June 1737, vol. 2, p. 187.

Masonic hoax: A Defense of Conduct, 15 February 1738, vol. 2, pp. 198–202.

51 "I assure you": Richard Peters to Thomas Penn, November 1743, quoted in Cummings, *Peters*, p. 86.

Shipping statistics: Lydon, "Philadelphia's Expansion," p. 403.

"have the advantage of good looks": "Busy-Body," 4 February 1728, vol. 1, pp. 115–116.

"improving the taste of the town": "Busy-Body," 25 February 1729, vol. 1, p. 122.

"all libelling and personal abuse": *Auto.*, p. 165.

"I shall venture to lay it down": On Literary Style, 2 August 1733, vol. 1, p. 331.

"corrupt the morals": Petition on Fairs, [1731], vol. 1, p. 212.

52 Library Company: *Auto.*, p. 130; Korty, "BF and 18th-Century Libraries," pp. 5–15.

"So few were the readers": *Auto.*, p. 142.

"the mother of all . . . subscription libraries": ibid., p. 130.

BF on night watch: ibid., p. 173.

on fire protection: 4 February 1735, vol. 2, pp. 12–15.

53 "A useful piece": *Auto.*, p. 174.

"obliged every member": ibid., p. 174.

"whether there is a city in the world better provided": ibid., p. 175.

confessed "with some emotion": Williams, "More Light on BF's Religious Ideas," p. 810.

54 Puritanism, "that firm tradition": Levin, "Auto. of BF," p. 261.

"I was generally thought proud": *Auto.*, p. 158.

gardener who "works on one of the beds at a time": ibid., p. 152.

"All his experience indicated": Levin, "Auto. of BF," p. 271.

"explications of the peculiar doctrines": headnote to "Dialogue between Two Presbyterians," 1735, vol. 2, p. 27.

"a vile heretic": Observations on the Proceedings against Mr. Hemphill, 1735, vol. 2, p. 39.

"But surely *morality* can do us no harm": "Dialogue between Two Presbyterians," 10 April 1735, vol. 2, p. 31.

55 "since 'tis an uncertainty": ibid., p. 33.

Observations on the Proceedings: ibid., vol. 2, pp. 37–65

"their pretending to be the directors of men's consciences": Preface to A Letter to a Friend in the Country, 1735, vol. 2, p. 66.

"Nothing, in all probability": ibid., p. 67.

"The generality of the clergy": ibid., p. 66.

A Defense: 1735, vol. 2, pp. 90–126.

56 "On our defeat he left us": *Auto.*, p. 168.

"gown and wig white with powder and bushy": Bell, "Watson Addenda," p. 159.

"On Thursday last": 15 November 1739, vol. 2, p. 242.

"The multitudes of all sects": *Auto.*, p. 175.

57 "copies of his journals and sermons": 15 November 1739, vol. 2, p. 242.

"The alteration in the face of religion": 12 June 1740, vol. 2, pp. 287–288.

"rejected my counsel": *Auto.*, p. 177.

"I emptied my pocket wholly": ibid., p. 177.

"every accent, every emphasis": ibid., p. 180.

58 "Dear sir, adieu": from George Whitefield, 26 November 1740, vol. 2, p. 270.

"a merely civil friendship": *Auto.*, p. 178.

accepted the post "readily": ibid., p. 172.

"besides the pay for immediate service as clerk": ibid., p. 171.

he who "loves money most shall lose": Journal of a Voyage, 1726, vol. 1, p. 75.

59 "Your Uncle Benjamin made inquiry": from Josiah Franklin, 26 May 1739, vol. 2, p. 229–230.

BF rents Grace's house: Roach, "BF Slept Here," p. 146.

"B. Franklin, typographer": from Robert Grace, Lease, 30 December 1745, vol. 3, p. 51.

"clothed from head to foot": to Deborah Franklin, 6 April 1766, vol. 13, p. 233.

"thought *her* husband": *Auto.*, p. 145.

"at least twenty pair of old breeches": to Deborah Franklin, 6 April 1766, vol. 13, p. 233.

"coat lined with silk": 22 February 1739, vol. 2, p. 236.

"wealth is not his that has it": *Poor Richard* (1736), vol. 2, p. 138.

6. "LET THE EXPERIMENT BE MADE"

(The clarity and accuracy of this and succeeding chapters that deal with Franklin's electrical experiments have been much improved by the careful reading given by Dean George Wheeler, Lehman College, C.U.N.Y. My gratitude to him is great.)

60 "How exact and regular": *A Dissertation, on Liberty and Necessity*, 1725, vol. 1, p. 62.

61 "Whence comes the dew": Proposals and Queries, 1732, vol. 1, p. 260.

Godfrey's "excellent natural genius": quoted in Bridenbaugh, *Rebels and Gentlemen*, p. 307.

quadrant "not only made, but used at sea": ibid., p. 308.

62 BF on fireplaces and stoves: ibid., vol. 2, pp. 425, 428.

Greenwood's *"course of philosophical lectures"*: June, 1740, vol. 2, p. 286.

63 "various experiments concerning electrical attraction"; quoted in Lemay, *Kinnersley*, pp. 48–49.

"truth . . . supported by mathematics": quoted in Cohen, *BF and Newton*, p. 245.

"many of the truths of Newtonian science": quoted in ibid., p. 241.

"A Proposal": 14 May 1743, vol. 2, pp. 378–383.

"We have seldom any news": to William Strahan, 4 July 1744, vol. 2, p. 411.

64 Bartram's society of "ingenious and curious men": headnote, vol. 2, p. 379.

Colden as "Summus Perfectus": quoted in Hindle, *Pursuit of Science*, p. 41.

"the cause of gravitation": quoted in ibid., p. 43.

"I accidentally . . . fell into company with a printer": Cadwallader Colden to William Strahan, 3 December 1743, vol. 2, p. 386n.

65 "imperfectly performed": *Auto.*, p. 240.

"very brisk and surprising motions": John Smith, a Philadelphia Quaker,

who witnessed Spencer's experiments, quoted in Cohen, introduction to
BF's Experiments and Observations, p. 51. Evidence that Smith copied his remarks from Hauksbee in Heathcote, "BF's Introduction to Electricity,"
pp. 29–35.
"the true character of the experiments he had seen": Heathcote, ibid., p. 35.
"long absence . . . put my business so much behind-hand": to Cadwallader
Colden, 4 November 1743, vol. 2, p. 387–388.

66   "We have been together all day": to Cadwallader Colden, 13 September 1744,
vol. 2, p. 415.
"Thus, tho' you should get no praise among us": to Cadwallader Colden,
16 October 1746, vol. 3, pp. 89–90.
"The members are very idle gentlemen": to Cadwallader Colden, 15 August
1745, vol. 3, p. 36.
"if we could but exchange the time": quoted in Hindle, *Pursuit of Science*,
p. 72.
essay in *Gentleman's Magazine* reprinted in Lemay, *Kinnersley*, pp. 54–58.

67   "eagerly seized the opportunity": *Auto.*, p. 241.
"My house was continually full": ibid., p. 241.
"Yesterday was the first time": from James Logan, 23 February 1747, vol. 3,
p. 110.
"For my own part": to Peter Collinson, 28 March 1747, vol. 3, pp. 118–119.

68   Hopkinson "a gentleman possessed of many virtues": obituary of, 14
November 1771, vol. 4, p. 208.
"the power of points to *throw off*": to Peter Collinson, 25 May 1747, vol. 3,
p. 128.
"even tho' the candle is at a foot distance": ibid., pp. 128–129.
"This difference": *ibid.*, p. 129.
"electrical fire is a common element": *ibid.*, p. 131.
a "Species of matter": to Cadwallader Colden, 5 June 1747, vol. 3, p. 143.
"In this discovery, they were beforehand with us": *ibid.*, p. 143.

69   B thereupon becomes "electrised *positively*": to Peter Collinson, 25 May 1747,
vol. 3, p. 131.
"not *created* by friction": to Cadwallader Colden, 5 June 1747, vol. 3, p. 143.
"This is probably the first clear expression": Rollers, *Development of Concept
of Electric Charge*, p. 59.
"As a broad generalization": Cohen, *BF and Newton*, p. 303.
"progress . . . half discourages me": to Peter Collinson, 28 July 1747, vol. 3,
p. 157.

70   "On some further experiments since": to Peter Collinson, 14 August 1747,
vol. 3, p. 171.

7. WAR AND THOSE "DAMNED QUAKERS"

71   "There never was a good war, nor a bad peace": quoted in Van Doren, *BF*,
p. 698.
"On Monday our governor": 17 April 1740, vol. 2, p. 283.
"As a design against": ibid., pp. 283–284.
two hundred and fifty servants enlist: Thayer, *Pennsylvania Politics*, p. 13.

72   they "are all embarked": 8 September 1740, vol. 2, p. 289.
"If you do not part with them": George Thomas to John Penn, 25 March
1741, quoted in Osgood, *American Colonies in 18th Century*, vol. 4, p. 61.
Weiser and Logan letters: Tolles, *James Logan*, pp. 154–156.

election of 1741: Thayer, *Pennsylvania Politics*, p. 17.

73   election of 1742: Cohen, "Philadelphia Election Riot of 1742," pp. 306–319. Sailors' comments appear on p. 318.

sailors were "mostly strangers": 7 October 1742, vol. 2, p. 363.

baptized "eight adult persons": 11 June 1741, vol. 2, p. 325.

74   commending "the undertaking publicly": Notes on Assembly Debates, 26–28 February 1745, vol. 3, p. 16.

"I think they ought to be open and honest": ibid., p. 17.

"I told them these people were as much obliged to them": ibid.

"Our people are extremely impatient": to John Franklin, May? 1745, vol. 3, p. 26.

a cruiser "took four sail in a few days": 6 June 1745, vol. 3, p. 56.

" 'Twas near nine o'clock": 18 July 1745, vol. 3, p. 57.

75   voted for "the King's use": vol. 3, p. 195n.

"I shall take the money": *Auto.*, p. 189.

William "left my house": to Jane Mecom, June 1748, vol. 3, p. 303.

"No one imagined it was hard usage at home": ibid.

"Billy is so fond of a military life": to John Franklin, 2 April 1747, vol. 3, p. 119.

"assist him with your advice or countenance": to Cadwallader Colden, 5 June 1747, vol. 3, p. 142.

"that the French know our bay": Richard Peters to proprietors, 29 November 1747, vol. 3, p. 214. For further details on the privateers' incursions see Balch, *Provincial History of Pennsylvania*, pp. 7–15, and DeArmond, *Bradford*, pp. 22–24.

76   "we hope there is no danger": headnote to *Plain Truth*, vol. 3, p. 183.

"apprehensive of a visit from the French": Richard Peters to proprietors, 29 November 1747, vol. 3, p. 215.

"declared that more mischief was hatched": Election Paper, 1764, vol. 11, pp. 375–376.

"Should we tell them": *Plain Truth*, vol. 3, p. 200.

"A scheme was formed": Richard Peters to proprietors, 29 November 1747, vol. 3, p. 215.

Plain Truth: vol. 3, pp. 188–204: "when your persons, fortunes," p. 198; "we, the middling people," p. 199; "All we want is order," p. 202; "At present we are like the separate filaments of flax," p. 202; "the writer of it will," pp. 203–204.

77   tradesmen were "the first movers in every useful undertaking": Richard Peters to proprietors, 29 November 1747, vol. 3, p. 216.

"with a good firelock": Form of Association, 29 November 1747, vol. 3, p. 206.

This "is intended to prevent": ibid., p. 209.

"No, let us not sign yet": Richard Peters to proprietors, 29 November 1747, vol. 3, p. 216.

78   "The house was pretty full": *Auto.*, p. 183.

"near eight hundred have signed": to James Logan, 7 December 1747, vol. 3, p. 225.

"proceedings were not disapproved": 3 December 1747, vol. 3, p. 239.

ministers exhorted to "take this province": Proclamation for a General Fast, 9 December 1747, vol. 3, p. 228.

"He at first refused us premptorily": *Auto.*, p. 184.

"I have expected to see thee here": from James Logan, 3 December 1747, vol. 3, pp. 219–220.

79   "had nothing in view": Richard Peters to proprietors, 29 November 1747, vol. 3, p. 217.
     "This Association is founded on contempt": Thomas Penn to Richard Peters, 30 March 1748, vol. 3, pp. 186–187.
     "His voice was low": Cutler, *Life*, vol. 1, P. 268.
     "unless he has some diverting story to tell": quoted in Bruce, *BF Self-Revealed*, vol. 2, p. 9.
     "a natural and good-humored . . . wit": Logan, *Memoirs of Dr. Logan*, p. 39n.
     "I was a bad speaker": quoted in Parton, *BF*, vol. 1, p. 328.
80   "We are well pleased": Thomas Penn to Richard Peters, 31 August 1748, vol. 3, p. 188.
     "In Europe the encouragements to learning": Proposals, 1749, vol. 3, p. 400n.
     "By this time twelve-month": to William Strahan, 19 October 1748, vol. 3, p. 323.

8. "PASS MY TIME AGREEABLY ENOUGH"

81   "having all the materials ready": to William Strahan, 10 July 1743, vol. 2, p. 384.
     partnership with Hall: to William Strahan, 1 June 1747, vol. 3, p. 140. Articles of Agreement, 1 January 1748, pp. 263–267.
     "to a more quiet part of the town": to Cadwallader Colden, 29 September 1748, vol. 3, p. 318.
     "For my own part": to Abiah Franklin, 12 April 1750, vol. 3, pp. 474–475.
82   Strahan enrolls William at Middle Temple: Bedwell, "American Middle Templars," p. 683.
     stolen items: 1 November 1750, vol. 4, pp. 72–73.
83   "Send 50 reams largest demi": to Deborah Franklin [1754?], vol. 5, p. 463.
     "but possibly may resume": to Peter Collinson, 18 October 1748, vol. 3, p. 320.
     letters to Collinson and John Mitchell: 29 April 1748, vol. 3, pp. 352–376.
     on Kinnersley, see Lemay, *Kinnersley*.
84   "Lightning rends some bodies": to John Mitchell, 29 April 1748, vol. 3, p. 376.
     "very curious pieces": from Peter Collinson, 3 February 1750, vol. 3, p. 460.
     friends "of whom the Junto furnished a good part": *Auto.*, pp. 192–193.
     "Numbers of our inhabitants": On the Need for an Academy, 24 August 1749, vol. 3, p. 386.
     "And this is the more necessary now": Paper on the Academy, 31 July 1750, vol. 4, p. 36.
85   *Proposals:* 1749, vol. 3, pp. 397–421: "For us, who are now to make a beginning," p. 399n; must be "frequently exercised," p. 402; "things . . . likely to be *most useful,*" p. 404; to write and speak "properly, distinctly," p. 407; "yet none that have an ardent desire," p. 415; "that *benignity of mind,*" pp. 418–419.
     People "think we go too fast": Thomas Penn to James Hamilton, 12 February 1750, vol. 4, p. 5n.
     "The first instance of partiality": "Observations relative to the Academy in Philadelphia" (1789), quoted in vol. 3, p. 425n.
86   "the scholars will be freed": from Cadwallader Colden, November 1749, vol. 3, p. 431.
     "instruction of poor children gratis": Paper on the Academy, 31 July 1750, vol. 4, p. 35.
     "The care and trouble of agreeing with the workmen": *Auto.*, p. 195.

"I asked Mr. Franklin": Richard Peters to Thomas Penn, 17 February 1750, vol. 4, p. 35.

"They go on much slower . . . at home": to Cadwallader Colden, 13 February 1750, vol. 3, p. 463.

"Electrical fluid agrees with lightning": to John Lining, 18 March 1755, vol. 5, pp. 523–524.

87   "For the doctrine of *points*": to Peter Collinson, 2 March 1750, vol. 3, pp. 472–473.

"Opinions and Conjectures . . .": to Peter Collinson, 29 July 1750, vol. 4, pp. 9–34: "The electrical matter consists of," p. 10; metal objects "have a property," p. 16; "Nor is it of much importance," p. 17; "On top of some high tower," pp. 19–20; *"that we cannot . . . force the electrical fluid thro' glass,"* p. 25; "But I shall never have done," p. 34.

88   "the fullest on the nature and operations of the electrical matter": to Cadwallader Colden, 11 October 1750, vol. 4, p. 69.

89   "our experiments on animals": to Peter Collinson, 27 July 1750, vol. 4, p. 8.

"I have lately made an experiment": to John Franklin, 25 December 1750, vol. 4, pp. 82–83.

9. "HE AIMS AT GREAT MATTERS"

91   flourished "beyond expectation": to Jared Eliot, 12 September 1751, vol. 4, p. 194.

"being crowded and our air taken away": to Samuel Johnson, 11 July 1751, vol. 4, p. 146.

"but we have reason to think": ibid., p. 147.

Pennsylvania Hospital: "Some Account of . . ." (1754), vol. 5, pp. 283–330; *Auto.*, pp. 199–203.

92   "I believe Mr. Franklin": Thomas Penn to Richard Peters, 9 January 1753, vol. 5, p. 291n.

"I find you grow more and more famous": from George Whitefield, 17 August 1752, vol. 4, p. 343.

93   The office would "be suitable to me": to Peter Collinson, 21 May 1751, vol. 4, p. 135.

Allen's "considerable sum": ibid., p. 134.

"his namesake": "An Answer to Mr. Franklin's Remarks," Walker, *Burd Papers,* p. 120.

"that such laws are against the public utility": Felons and Rattlesnakes, 9 May 1751, vol. 4, pp. 131–133.

94   "people increase faster": *Poor Richard* (1749), vol. 3, p. 441.

"Observations concerning the Increase of Mankind": vol. 4, pp. 225–234: acturial tables, p. 227; marriages "are more general," p. 228; "This million doubling," p. 233; "The labor of slaves," p. 229; "the number of purely white people," p. 234.

95   "This will in a few years become a German colony": to James Parker, 20 March 1751, vol. 4, pp. 120–121.

"Why should the Palatine boors be suffered": "Increase of Mankind," vol. 4, p. 234.

"a majority of Dutch lived in those countries": Election Paper, 1764, vol. 11, p. 382.

"estimate that population in America": Conner, *Poor Richard's Politics,* pp. 69–70. See also Aldridge, "BF as Demographer," pp. 25–44.

96   "against my inclination": "Remarks on a Late Protest, 1764," vol. II, p. 433.
     "more agreeable to me": *Auto.*, pp. 196–197.
     "Should we address that wealthy and powerful body of people": *Plain Truth*,
     1747, vol. 3, p. 199.
     "finding that more knowledge of the common law": *Auto.*, p. 197.
97   "by me entirely unsolicited: ibid., p. 197.
     BF "being returned": quoted in Van Doren, *BF*, p. 201.
99   "we could wish our proprietaries had rather thought fit": Reply to the
     Governor, 21 August 1751, vol. 4, p. 183.
     "an appearance of impartiality": to Peter Collinson, 29 December 1754, vol.
     5, p. 453.
     it "gives a man sometimes much more weight": ibid.
100 Assembly would "bounce violently": James Hamilton to Thomas Penn, 18
     March 1752, quoted in Hutson, *Pennsylvania Politics*, p. 11.
     "the moment this instruction should be known": quoted in ibid., pp. 11–12.
     "your quit rents are shamefully in arrears": Richard Peters to Thomas
     Penn, quoted in Hanna, *BF and Pennsylvania Politics*, p. 48.
     Logan's death: 7 November 1751, vol. 4, p. 207.
     Hopkinson's death: 14 November 1751, vol. 4, p. 208.
     Godfrey "continually muddled with drink": to Cadwallader Colden, 13 Feb-
     ruary 1750, vol. 4, pp. 462–463.
101 chess book order canceled: to William Strahan, 20 June 1752, vol. 4, p. 323.
     "that this *new year*": *Poor Richard* (1752), vol. 4, p. 247.

10. THE KITE

102 "or to have anything to do with the government": to Samuel Johnson, 2 July
     1752, vol. 4, p. 325.
     Philadelphia Contributionship: Deed of, 25 March 1752, vol. 4, pp. 281–295.
     a "vessell is actually fitting": to Jared Eliot, 19 December 1752, vol. 4, p. 389.
103 "She has lived a good life": to Edward and Jane Mecom, 21 May 1752, vol.
     4, p. 318.
     silk "fitter to bear the wet wind": BF's statement, 19 October 1752, vol. 4,
     p. 367.
     "the episode of the kite": Van Doren *BF*, p. 164.
     "I will not swell this narrative": *Auto.*, p. 244.
     "The Doctor . . . having published": Priestley's account, vol. 4, pp. 368–369.
105 clouds "are electrified negatively": to Cadwallader Colden, 12 April 1753, vol.
     4, pp. 463–464.
     How to Secure Houses: Poor Richard (1753), vol. 4, pp. 408–409.
106 "I think there would be none": "Opinions and Conjectures," 29 July 1750,
     vol. 4, p. 20.
     Dalibard "as being the first": to Thomas-François Dalibard, 31 January 1768,
     vol. 15, p. 35.
     "Every simple explanation of the kite mystery": Van Doren, *BF*, p. 167.
     "The *Tatler* tells us": to Jared Eliot, 12 April 1753, vol. 4, pp. 466–467.
107 "If both bottles were electrified": to Peter Collinson, September 1753, vol.
     5, p. 69.
     "I beheld with great surprise": ibid., p. 70.
     BF writes Colden: 12 April 1753, vol. 4, pp. 463–465.
     "Yet notwithstanding so many experiments": to Peter Collinson, Septem-
     ber 1753, vol. 5, p. 70.

108   "These thoughts, my dear friend": ibid., p. 70.
       "I know not whether any of your learned body": to Royal Society, 29 May
       1754, vol. 5, p. 334.
       "author of a considerable part of those discoveries": William Smith quoted,
       vol. 8, p. 189.
109   "I was very much surprised": Ebenezer Kinnersley, 30 November 1758, vol.
       8, pp. 189–190.

                         11. ''JOIN OR DIE''

111   "I think I have never been more hurried": to Jared Eliot, 3 May 1753, vol.
       4, p. 472.
       visits Lancaster: Memorandum, 14 June 1753, vol. 4, pp. 506–507.
       read "with great approbation": to William Smith, 19 April 1753, vol. 4.,
       p. 469.
       "For my part": to William Smith, 3 May 1753, vol. 4, p. 475.
112   letter of introduction to Peter Collinson: 26 June 1753, vol. 4, pp. 511–512.
       "Mr. Smith's a very ingenious man": from Peter Collinson, 12 August 1753,
       26 January 1754, vol. 5, pp. 20, 193.
       Harvard degree: 25 July 1753, vol. 5, pp. 16–17.
       "jolly conversation": to Samuel Danforth, 25 July 1773, Smyth, *Writings*, vol.
       6, p. 106.
       Carlisle Indian conference: vol. 5, pp. 64–66, 84–107: "could not proceed to
       business," p. 85; "we jointly . . . dig a grave," p. 92; "I desire you would hear,"
       p. 96; "If only honest and sober men were to deal with us," p. 97; "the rum
       ruins us," p. 97.
113   "If you can procure and send me": to James Bowdoin, 18 October 1753, vol.
       5, p. 80.
114   postmaster general appointment: *Auto.*, p. 208; *Papers*, 10 August 1753, vol. 5,
       p. 18.
       Mitchell "was really bamboozelled": from Peter Collinson, 26 January 1754,
       vol. 5, p. 192.
       "Mr. Hunter has found security": William Allen to Barclay and Sons, 5
       November 1753, Walker, *Burd Papers*, p. 11.
       "be paid out of the money arising from the postage": from Post Office, 10
       August 1753, vol. 5, p. 18.
       "I think if the post riders were regulated": from John Franklin, 26 Novem-
       ber 1753, vol. 5, pp. 118–119.
       instructions to postmasters (1753): vol. 5, pp. 162–177. See also Butler, *BF*,
       Postmaster General.
       "a freak of the minister's": *Auto.*, p. 208.
115   "Secretary . . . I would move that": quoted in Hare, "Electro Vitrifrico,"
       62–66.
116   against all "propositions for an union": headnote, vol. 5, p. 277.
       "The confidence of the French in this undertaking": 9 May 1754, vol. 5,
       pp. 274–275.
117   "as it may give notice to the French": to Thomas Clap, 20 August 1753, vol.
       5, p. 22.
       "the dreaded junction of the French settlements": "A Plan for Settling Two
       Western Colonies," 1754, vol. 5, p. 458; "as there already in the old colonies,"
       p. 462; "a great sum of money might be raised", p. 460; "they might easily,
       by their joint force," p. 459.

"It would be a very strange thing": to James Parker, 20 March 1751, vol. 4, pp. 118–119.

118 "For reasonable, sensible men": ibid., p. 118.

"Short Hints": vol. 5, pp. 337–338.

"a pipe of the oldest and best Madeira wine": Richard Peters to William Alexander, 23 May 1754, Boyd, *Susquehannah Company Papers*, vol. 1, p. 92.

"Look about your country and see": quoted in Van Doren, *BF*, p. 222.

119 "Nothing of much importance was transacted": to Peter Collinson, 14, 29 July 1754, vol. 5, pp. 393, 394.

"whenever the lands . . . should be settled": quoted in Wallace, *Weiser*, p. 359.

Plan of Union: vol. 5, headnote, pp. 374–387; text, pp. 387–392.

union "absolutely necessary": Proceedings of Albany Congress, 24 July 1754, vol. 5, p. 347.

"It is not altogether to my mind": to Cadwallader Colden, 21 July 1754, vol. 5, p. 394.

120 "sought to take a leap": Gipson, "Hutchinson and Albany Plan," p. 26.

"The governor of Pennsylvania": *Auto.*, p. 212.

"Our Assembly were not inclined": to Cadwallader Colden, 30 August 1754, vol. 5, p. 427.

hoped "to be at home in the winter": ibid., pp. 426–427.

121 "Poor Mr. Hunter": to William Franklin, 14 October 1754, vol. 5, p. 438.

BF and Shirley on colonial union: *Auto.*, p. 211; to William Shirley, 3, 4, 22 December 1754, vol. 5, pp. 441–446, 449–451: "I apprehend, that excluding the *people*": to William Shirley, 3 December 1754, vol. 5, p. 443; Americans "are likely to better judges": to William Shirley, 4 December 1754, vol. 5, p. 444; "it is supposed an undoubted right": 4 Dec., p. 444; "provided they had a reasonable number of representatives": 22 December 1754, vol. 5, p. 449; "I should hope, too": ibid., pp. 449–450.

none of the colonies "will act upon it": to Peter Collinson, 29 December 1754, vol. 5, p. 454.

122 The "obstinate disorder": to Anthony Todd, 10 June 1763, vol. 10, p. 283.

"Your favors come mixed with the snowy fleeces": to Catharine Ray, 4 March 1754, vol. 5, p. 503.

"But he never did it": to John Franklin, 16 March 1755, vol. 5, pp. 520–521.

"I left New England slowly": to Catharine Ray, 4 March 1754, vol. 5, p. 503.

123 "The crown disapproved it": Remarks on Albany Plan, 9 February 1789, vol. 5, p. 417.

"ill consequence to be apprehended": Speaker of House of Commons, quoted in Olson, "British Government and Colonial Union, 1754," p. 31.

"For the colonies, if so united": Remarks on Albany Plan, 9 February 1789, vol. 5, p. 417.

12. "THE RASHEST GOVERNOR I HAVE KNOWN"

124 BF-Morris meeting in New York: *Auto.*, p. 212. On Morris, see also McAnear, "An American in London," pp. 164–217.

"a kind, amicable, sensible man": Richard Peters quoted in Wallace, *Weiser*, p. 408.

"even a veteran scrawler": to Richard Peters, 17 September 1754, vol. 5, pp. 431–432.

125 "I know not why he should imagine": to Peter Collinson, 29 December 1754, vol. 5, p. 453.

"I much fear from a letter Mr. Franklin showed": William Smith to Thomas Penn, September 1755, vol. 6, p. 214.

"ill-judged and ill-timed": to Peter Collinson, 26 June 1755, vol. 6, p. 86.

"pusillanimous and improper behavior": Braddock to Isaac Norris, 28 February 1755, vol. 6, p. 13n.

126 "advised Mr. Quincy": to William Shirley [July 1756], vol. 6, p. 478.

BF's way out of impasse: *Auto.*, pp. 214–215.

Quakers' "readiness to comply": Israel Pemberton to John Fothergill, 19 May 1755, vol. 6, p. 53.

governor and friends "are angry with me": to Peter Collinson, 27 August 1755, vol. 6, p. 171.

"the mode of conducting . . . dispatches": *Auto.*, p. 216.

whirlwind anecdote: to Peter Collinson, 25 August 1755, vol. 6, pp. 167–168.

127 "Such is the infatuation": Morris to St. Clair and Braddock, January 1755, in Root, *Relations of Pennsylvania*, pp. 302–303.

on trafficking with enemy: Morris to Braddock, 12 March 1755, quoted in Johnson, "Fair Traders," p. 128.

Braddock's appearance: McCardell, *Ill-Starred General, passim.*

"After taking Fort Dusquesne": *Auto.*, p. 223.

"To be sure, sir": ibid., p. 224.

"These savages may indeed be a formidable enemy": Ibid., p. 224.

128 the general "presumed too much": to Peter Collinson, 27 August 1755, vol. 6, p. 170.

what a pity the army "had not been landed rather in Pennsylvania": *Auto.*, p. 217.

BF broadside to backcountry farmers: vol. 6, pp. 19–22.

"I cannot but honor Franklin": William Shirley quoted in McCardell, *Ill-Starred General*, p. 178.

130 The governor's message animated "Franklin so effectually": Israel Pemberton to John Fothergill, 19 May 1755, vol. 6, p. 55.

"I am heartily sick of our present situation": to Peter Collinson, 26 June 1755, vol. 6, p. 86.

gift packages for officers: *Auto.*, p. 222.

"not well enough to go about the town": to Richard Peters, 5 June 1755, vol. 6, p. 68.

131 "Did you never hear this old catch?": to Peter Collinson, 26 June 1755, p. 6, pp. 86–87.

"Franklin," the governor said: *Auto.* pp. 213–214.

to like "neither the governor's conduct nor the Assembly's": to Collinson, 26 June 1755, vol. 6, p. 86.

BF "has very out of the way notions": Morris to Penn, 16 June 1755, Hutson, "BF and Pennsylvania Politics," p. 311n.

"all the world claimed": Fisher, "Diary," p. 272.

Braddock letter of praise for BF: to Morris, 24 May 1755, vol. 7, p. 74n.

Masonic parade: Fisher, "Diary," p. 273.

132 Morris's embargo: Johnson, "Fair Traders," p. 130.

Morris election to Royal Society: Stearns, *Science in British Colonies*, p. 710.

"the governor sent in haste for me": *Auto.* p. 240.

"in great numbers": Fisher, "Diary," p. 274.

"His proposed amendment": *Auto.*, p. 229.

133 "tart, and sometimes indecently abusive": ibid., p. 213.

"How odious it be to sensible manly people": Assembly Reply to Governor, 8 August 1755, vol. 6, p. 138.

lacking that *"spirit of government"*: Assembly Reply to Governor, 19 August 1755, vol. 6, p. 150.

"though a subject like ourselves": ibid., pp. 161–162.

"The substance of these late inflammatory messages": William Smith to Thomas Penn, September 1755, vol. 6, p. 211.

Their claims "amounted to near £20,000": *Auto.*, p. 228.

134 "He promised me": ibid., p. 227.

"A number of falsehoods": to Peter Collinson, 27 August 1755, vol. 6, p. 171.

"He is . . . the rashest . . . governor that I have known": ibid., p. 169.

the "very abusive messages": William Morris to Secretary of State Sir Thomas Robinson, 28 August 1755, quoted in Hutson, "BF and Pennsylvania Politics," p. 352.

"I abhor these altercations": to Peter Collinson, 27 August 1755, vol. 6, p. 171.

"many more people love me now": to Peter Collinson, 11 September 1775, vol. 6, p. 182.

"and shall use those means in due time": ibid., p. 172.

"what that scheme is": William Smith to Thomas Penn, September, 1755, vol. 6, p. 211.

king petition "to interpose your royal authority": vol. 6, pp. 231n–232n.

13. "THE PEOPLE HAPPEN TO LOVE ME"

136 "when I hope to be home again": to William Shirley, 23 October 1755, vol. 6, p. 228.

"Just now arrived in town": to Peter Collinson, 25 October 1755, vol. 6, p. 229.

"to supply such as are without and unable to buy": to Richard Partridge, 25 October 1755, vol. 6, p. 231.

"confined to my room and bed": to James Read, 2 November 1755, vol. 6, p. 234.

"not waste your time offering me such bills": Isaac Morris to Assembly, 3 November 1755, vol. 6, p. 238.

137 Scaroyady visit to Assembly: vol. 6, pp. 244n, 254.

Assembly "had reason to believe": Assembly to Governor, 11 November 1755, vol. 6, p. 242.

"We being as desirous as the governor": ibid., pp. 239–240.

dispute must "be determined by his Majesty": Isaac Morris to Assembly, 17 November 1755, vol. 6, pp. 249, 252.

"As we are most of us natives of the country": Assembly to Governor, 18 November 1755, vol. 6, p. 253.

Militia Act: vol. 6, pp. 266–273.

138 act "of a very extraordinary nature": vol. 6, p. 267.

"with no other view but that I should refuse it": Isaac Morris to Horatio Sharpe, 26 November 1755, vol. 6, p. 268n.

"the militia act violated fundamentals": Ketcham, "Politics in Pennsylvania," p. 422.

Penn's "free gift": vol. 6, p. 257n.

frontiersmen "did not know that their liberties were invaded": Isaac Morris to John Penn, 28 November 1755, vol. 6, p. 281.

"mean selfish claim of a right": to Richard Partridge, 27 November 1755, vol. 6, p. 274.

"If we cannot have a governor of some discretion": ibid., p. 273.

139   "We meet every day": to William Parsons, 5 December 1755, vol. 6, p. 290.
"was to carry the war": Commissioners to Morris, 13 June 1756, vol. 6, p. 455.
"In case of meeting": to James Read, 2 November 1755, vol. 6, p. 235.
"that by a chain of forts": Commissioners to Morris, 13 June 1756, vol. 6, p. 455.
"Think of suitable officers": to William Parsons, 15 December 1755, vol. 6, p. 293.

140   "if people are but well disposed": to William Parsons, 5 December 1755, vol. 6, p. 290.
"A Dialogue between X, Y, and Z": 18 December 1755, vol. 6, pp. 296–306.
"Half an hour afterwards"; to Deborah Franklin, 25 January 1756, vol. 6, p. 365.
Bethlehem "in so good a posture": *Auto.*, p. 231.

141   "It seems they were either deceived": ibid., p. 232.
"All business is at an end": to _____, 25 December 1755, vol. 6, p. 311.
"regularly enlisted to serve": to Peter Collinson, 19 December 1756, vol. 7, p. 52.
"immediately to raise": to _____, 29 December 1755, vol. 6, p. 313.
"much more tender": to Deborah Franklin, 19 February 1758, vol. 7, p. 380.
Morris "fearful that the whole country will fall": vol. 6, p. 342.
"We found this place filled with refugees": to Isaac Morris, 4 January 1756, vol. 6, p. 357.

142   "wagons loaded with bread and some axes": ibid., p. 358.
threatening "to disband or remove": ibid., p. 358.
"Here all round appears nothing": Thomas Lloyd to _____, 30 January 1756, vol. 6, p. 381.
got "up some shelter": to _____, 20 January 1756, vol. 6, p. 362.
Monday "it rained": ibid., pp. 362–363.
"The Reverend Mr. Beatty is with us": ibid., p. 363.
"This day we hoisted your flag": to _____, 25 January 1756, vol. 6, p. 367.

143   "We have enjoyed your roast beef": to Deborah Franklin, 25 January 1756, vol. 6, pp. 364–365.
"Here are ten Lehigh people buzzing me": to Timothy Horsefield, 28 January 1756, vol. 6, p. 374.
"I thought to have wrote you a long letter": to Deborah Franklin, 30 January 1756, vol. 6, p. 378.
"Mr. Franklin will at least deserve a statue": Thomas Lloyd to _____, 30 January 1756, vol. 6, pp. 381–382.
"a letter from the governor": *Auto.*, pp. 235–236.
"The first night being in a good bed": ibid., p. 236.
"When I was on the frontier last winter": to Peter Collinson, 5 November 1756, vol. 7, p. 13.

144   "a pain and giddiness in my head": to Deborah Franklin, 18 March 1760, vol. 9, p. 35.
"As our number grows less": to Jane Mecom, 12 February 1756, vol. 6, p. 400.
the people "are afraid of going to their plantations": from Bishop Spangenberg, 25 February 1756, vol. 6, p. 412.
"If they have no regard to it": to Bishop Spangenberg, 1 March 1756, vol. 6, p. 414.
"turn and twist as he pleases": Richard Peters to Thomas Penn, 25, 29 April 1756, vol. 6, p. 410.

145   "against all reason and without advice": Richard Peters to Thomas Penn, 18 February 1756, vol. 6, p. 410.
governor would "lose all character": ibid., p. 410.

"whether between six and seven hundred men": *Pennsylvania Journal*, 11 March 1756, vol. 6, p. 411n.
BF takes regiment to Academy: vol. 6, p. 416.
second review: vol. 6, pp. 411n, 416.
regiment "accompanied me": *Auto.*, p. 238.
"twenty officers of my regiment": to Peter Collinson, 5 November 1756, vol. 7, pp. 13–14.

146 Anglicans "are gone off . . . in favor of him": Richard Peters to Thomas Penn, 29 April 1756, vol. 7, p. 2.
Peter's illness: to Deborah Franklin, 21 March 1756, vol. 6, p. 425.
in Virginia: to Deborah Franklin, 25? March 1756, vol. 6, pp. 427–28.
"I do not find that England anywhere produces cider": to Isaac Norris, 16 September 1758, vol. 8, pp. 155–156.
"I have been well": to Deborah Franklin, 30 March 1756, vol. 6, p. 429.

147 "We have almost finished our business": to Deborah Franklin, 5 April 1756, vol. 6, pp. 431–432.
"The trustees had reaped the full advantage": to Ebenezer Kinnersley, 28 July 1759, vol. 8, p. 416.
"the church by soft and easy means": Smith quoted in Ketcham, "BF and Smith," p. 154.
"I sometimes wish": to George Whitefield, 2 July 1756, vol. 6, p. 468–469.

148 "all the stiff rumps": to Peter Collinson, 15 June 1756, vol. 6, p. 456.
"They are mere Franklinists": Richard Peters to Thomas Penn, 26 June 1756, vol. 6, p. 457.
Letter from Pownall: BF to Sir Everard Fawkener, 22 July 1756, vol. 6, p. 472.
BF's aversion "ceased": Richard Peters to Thomas Penn, 26 June 1756, vol. 6, p. 486n.

149 Morris hopes Loudoun would not "countenance in any shape": Morris to William Shirley, 22 July 1756, vol. 6, p. 470n.
"He seems to me very well fitted": to Sir Everard Fawkener, 27 July 1756, vol. 6, p. 472.

14. OLD TROUBLES WITH A NEW GOVERNOR

150 On Denny see Wainwright, "Gov. Denny," pp. 170–198.
reception of Denny: vol. 6, pp. 489–490.
"After dinner . . . he took me aside": *Auto.*, p. 246.
"when with men he ought to fear": Morris to Thomas Penn (undated), quoted in Wainwright, "Gov. Denny," p. 175.

151 Quakers "were never more assiduous": Richard Peters to Thomas Penn, 2 October 1756, quoted in Newcomb, *BF and Galloway*, p. 34
BF "sabotaged the compromise": Newcomb, ibid., p. 34n.
"Tho' at present": to Peter Collinson, 5 November 1756, vol. 7, pp. 14–15.

152 "I know not what to say about the governor": Richard Peters to Thomas Penn, 2 October 1756, quoted in Wainwright, "Gov. Denny," pp. 174–175.
"He is extremely slow and formal": Morris to John Penn, no date, quoted in ibid., p. 175.
"*what they please*": Richard Peters to Thomas Penn, 11 December 1756, vol. 7, p. 50n.
frontier "in a deplorable condition": Denny to his council, vol., 7, p. 9n.
militia act "in every respect the most improper": vol. 6, p. 269n.

153 "with colors flying": quoted in Wallace, *Weiser*, p. 459.

"the charge has never died": Wainwright, "Gov. Denny," p. 176.
"As we are now met": quoted in Wallace, *Weiser,* p. 461.
question "was a very absurd one": ibid., p. 461.
"This very ground": Teedyuscung quoted in vol. 7, p. 18.
154   "Tell me what will satisfy you:" Denny speech to Indians, 15 November 1756, vol. 7, pp. 20–21.
we shall never "have a firm peace with the Indians": to Thomas Pownall, 19 August 1756, vol. 6, p. 487.
"the Delawares were grossly abused": to Peter Collinson, 22 November 1756, vol. 7, p. 23.
This "ill-humor spreading itself everywhere": Richard Peters to Thomas Penn, 26 December 1756, vol. 7, p. 41n.
"exactly conformable": Assembly to Governor, 19 December 1756, vol. 7, p. 41.
155   "a very deep snow fell": vol. 7, p. 43n.
"that the whole town would soon become a hospital": vol. 7, p. 47n.
Assembly "into a ferment": vol. 7, p. 48n.
"large professions of the good disposition": vol. 7, p. 53.
"indecent, frivolous, and evasive": ibid., p. 53.
"that the House could only prepare laws": Pennsylvania Assembly Committee: Report on a Conference about Quartering, 20 December 1756, vol. 7, p. 54.
"since there was room enough in the public houses": ibid., p. 57.
"Upon the whole": vol. 7, p. 53.
"behaved with great rudeness": Richard Peters to Thomas Penn, 26 December 1756, vol. 7, p. 57n.
156   "if the law were properly executed": Pennsylvania Assembly Committee Report on Governor's Message, 24 December 1756, vol. 7, p. 59.
"if the number of troops": vol. 7, p. 62n.
"expressing his sentiments": Richard Peters to Thomas Penn, 26 December 1756, vol. 7, p. 62n.
troops would "be quartered in town": to Henry Bouquet, 26 December 1756, vol. 7, pp. 64–65.
"that had he applied directly to B.F.": Richard Peters to Thomas Penn, 10 January 1757, vol. 7, p. 64n.
"to alarm everybody": Richard Peters to Thomas Penn, 27 January 1757, vol. 7, p. 107.
157   "to solicit a removal of the grievances": Pennsylvania Assembly Resolutions, 28 January 1757, vol. 7, p. 109.
"to deprive the Assembly and people of their rights": Assembly Committee Report, 22 February 1757, vol. 7, p. 138.
"as I know your presence": from Lord Loudoun, 20 February 1757, vol. 7, p. 133.
Loudoun "talked over the situation": Loudoun diary, quoted in vol. 7, p. 147.
neither man "agreed in the facts": ibid., p. 148.
"always had the disposal of all presents": to Lord Loudoun, 21 March 1757, vol. 7, p. 151.
"treat him with *contempt*": Richard Peters to Thomas Penn, 26 December 1756, quoted in Zimmerman, "Gov. Denny and Quartering Act," p. 272.
"refused to do duty": quoted in Hutson, *Pennsylvania Politics,* p. 33.
Denny "should for this time": Lord Loudoun to William Pitt, 25 April 1757, vol. 7, p. 152n.
158   "Mr. Franklin's reflections": Penn to ?, 13 August 1757, vol. 7, p. 153n.

"look out sharp": to William Strahan, 31 January 1757, vol. 7, p. 116.

"a red line over all such accounts": Ledger A and B, vol. 1, p. 173.

"trusty and loving friend": Power of Attorney to Deborah Franklin, 4 April 1757, vol. 7, pp. 169–170.

Dunlap "should have a little book": to William Dunlap, 4 April 1757, vol. 7, p. 169.

"be capable of removing some difficulties": Israel Pemberton to John Fothergill, 1 July 1757, vol. 7, p. 173n.

"I leave some enemies": to Joseph Galloway, 11 April 1757, vol. 7, p. 179.

"overcast, threatening a wrecking storm": William Franklin to Elizabeth Graeme, 17 April 1757, pp. 177–178.

159   "As *having their own way*": to Jane Mecom, 19 April 1757, vol. 7, p. 190.

A stream of orders: to Deborah Franklin, 28 April and 27 May 1757, pp. 206, 219.

Loudoun's accustomed splendor: Pargellis, *Loudoun*, p. 167.

"His lordship has on all occasions": to Isaac Norris, 30 May 1757, vol. 7, p. 228.

Loudoun on BF not to be trusted: diary for June, Hanna, *BF and Pennsylvania Politics*, p. 123.

160   " 'Tis an uneasy situation": to Joseph Galloway, 25 April 1757, vol. 7, p. 198.

BF will of 1757: vol. 7, pp. 199–205.

161   "I have been very low-spirited all day": to Deborah Franklin, 27 May 1757, vol. 7, p. 219.

"got drunk": quoted in Aldridge, *BF*, p. 129.

15. "A CORDIAL AND THOROUGH CONTEMPT"

162   "In general, we were highly favored with winds": William Franklin to Elizabeth Graeme, 17 July 1757, vol. 7, p. 244.

"About nine o'clock the fog began to rise": *Auto.*, p. 259.

"The bell ringing for church": to Deborah Franklin, 17 July 1757, vol. 7, p. 243.

Father Abraham's speech: vol. 7, pp. 340–350.

163   "in such a way as to lay up": quoted in Namier and Brooke, *History of Parliament*, vol. 3, p. 490.

"we have four rooms furnished": to Deborah Franklin, January ? 1758, vol. 7, p. 369.

164   expenses in August: Eddy, "Account Book," p. 102.

"Those instructions": to Isaac Norris, 19 March 1759, vol. 8, p. 293.

"I told his lordship this was new doctrine": *Auto.*, pp. 261–262.

neither man "had been aware": Kaplan, *Colonies into Nation*, p. 18.

165   Paris "a proud angry man": *Auto.*, p. 263.

Paris "had a peculiar talent": quoted in vol. 7, p. 247n.

"had an uncanny ability to expedite business": Kammen, *Rope of Sand*, p. 12.

"He is a sensible artful man": Isaac Morris to Ferdinand John Paris, 4 July 1757, vol. 7, p. 247n.

"Certain it is that B.F.'s view is": Richard Peters to Thomas Penn, 31 January 1757, vol. 7, p. 110n–111n.

"I think I wrote you before": Thomas Penn to Richard Peters, 14 May 1757, vol. 7, p. 111n.

166 on Thomas Penn see Pound, *Penns of Pennsylvania and England,* pp. 282, 284.
     On Penn's purchase at BF's shop, vol. 1, p. 371.
     "we spoke of things generally": Thomas Penn to Richard Peters, 5 September 1757, vol. 7, p. 250.
     "Heads of Complaint": 20 August 1757, vol. 7, pp. 251–252.
     "This they would endeavor to obtain": to Isaac Norris, 19 January 1759, vol. 8, p. 233.
     Paris asked could the proprietors "lawfully restrain": quoted in Hutson, *Pennsylvania Politics,* 43n.
167 "a violent cold": to Deborah Franklin, 22 November 1757, vol. 7, p. 273.
     "I had another severe cold": ibid.
     Dr. Fothergill "grew very angry": ibid.
     "I was seized one morning:" ibid., p. 274.
     Penn sent "peremptory orders": Thomas Penn to William Denny, 14 November 1757, vol. 7, p. 279.
     proprietors pleased "to use their utmost endeavors": from Ferdinand John Paris, 23 November 1757, vol. 7, p. 280.
     they "always treated him with great civility": William Franklin to Elizabeth Graeme, 9 December 1757, vol. 7, p. 291.
168 "that we were only a kind of corporation": to Isaac Norris, 14 January 1758, vol. 7, p. 361.
     Penn's "position was logical and soundly based": Hanna, *BF and Pennsylvania Politics,* p. 127.
     "Your father's charter": to Isaac Norris, 14 January 1758, vol. 7, pp. 361–362.
169 done nothing "in any manner": Thomas Penn to Richard Peters, 5 July 1758, vol. 7, pp. 363n–364n.
     "I begin to think": to Deborah Franklin, 21 January 1758, vol. 7, p. 364.
     "the proprietors will be gibbetted": to Joseph Galloway, 17 February 1757, vol. 7, p. 374.
     that "inveterate scribbler": from Isaac Norris, 21 February 1758, vol. 7, p. 385.
     "deprived of the common modes of defense": quoted in Thayer, *Pennsylvania Politics,* p. 69.
     "looked upon . . . as an open declaration of war": to Joseph Galloway, 16 September 1758, vol. 8, p. 150.
     "the Assembly of Pennsylvania was not a Parliament": Ferdinand John Paris to William Allen, 13 May 1758, vol. 8, p. 63n.
170 counsel held "all representative bodies": to Thomas Leech, 13 May 1758, vol. 8, p. 61.
     board members "are but young in office": Ferdinand John Paris to William Allen, 13 May 1758, vol. 8, p. 63n.
     electrical purchases: Eddy, "Account Book," p. 110.
     To Cambridge they "went accordingly": to Deborah Franklin, 6 September 1758, vol. 8, p. 134.
     Mary Fisher, "five years older than Sister Douse": to Deborah Franklin, 6 September 1758, vol. 8, pp. 134–135.
     "carried us out into the church yard": ibid., p. 137.
     Mrs. Salt "is a jolly lively dame": ibid., p. 144.
     traveling "continually on the foot": ibid., p. 144.
171 "twenty miles on foot to see us": ibid., p. 146.
     traveling as a way "partly to recover my health": to Joseph Galloway, 6 September 1758, vol. 8, p. 146.
     "from this time I will not have any conversation with him": Thomas Penn to Richard Peters, 5 July 1758, vol. 7, p. 364n.

"His reputation as a man": John Fothergill to Israel Pemberton, 12 June 1758, vol. 8, pp. 100n–101n.

172 "The agreeable conversation I meet with": to Deborah Franklin, 22 November 1757, vol. 7, p. 279.

cloak of "the newest fashion": to Deborah Franklin, 22 November 1757, ibid., p. 278.

Common Prayer book in large-size print: to Deborah Franklin, 10 June 1758, vol. 8, p. 94

"a newest fashioned white hat and cloak": ibid., p. 91.

such paintings "never look well": ibid., p. 91.

"some pippins for myself": ibid., p. 93.

"Goodies I now and then get a few": to Deborah Franklin, January 1758, vol. 7, p. 369.

"my shirts are always well aired": to Deborah Franklin, 19 February 1758, vol. 7, p. 380.

"your kind advice about getting a chariot": ibid.

"Peter behaves very well to me": ibid.

"the best . . . of hers": ibid., p. 384.

173 This news "was to have been kept a secret": to Deborah Franklin, 10 June 1758, vol. 8, p. 95.

"However, to take off all pretense of clamor": Paris's Answer to Heads of Complaint, 27 November 1758, vol. 8, p. 182.

BF's request for clarification: to Thomas and Richard Penn, 28 November 1758, vol. 8, pp. 186–188.

BF's "disrespect": Proprietors to Assembly, 28 November 1758, vol. 8, pp. 184, 185.

BF "answered not a word": Thomas Penn to William Allen, 9 December 1758, vol. 8, p. 187n.

"had not endured such a string": Hutson, *Pennsylvania Politics*, p. 47.

16. "I AM A BRITON"

174 "esteemed the best acquainted": to Thomas Leech and Assembly Committee of Correspondence, 10 June 1758, vol. 8, p. 88.

Jackson's report to BF: [24 April 1758?] vol. 8, pp. 22–27.

"offered an opportunity to visit Old Testament vengeance": Hutson, *Pennsylvania Politics*, pp. 54–55.

"I believe it will in time be clearly seen": to Israel Pemberton, 19 March 1759, vol. 8, p. 299.

175 "the royal crown cures": *Poor Richard* (1757), vol. 7, p. 84.

"The prevailing opinion": to Isaac Norris, 19 March 1759, vol. 8, p. 293.

"the Parliament would establish more liberty": ibid., p. 296.

"our best chance . . . is": ibid., p. 295.

"for tho' there are many members": ibid.

"I am too old to think of changing countries": to Joseph Galloway, 7 April 1759, vol. 8, p. 310.

"petition the crown to take": to Joseph Galloway, 16 September 1758, vol. 8, p. 150.

"*removing the prejudices*": to Thomas Leech and Assembly Committee of Correspondence, 10 June 1758, vol. 8, p. 89.

"Appealing to the public will displease": Thomas Penn to Richard Peters, 13 May 1758, vol. 8, p. 89n.

176 "a notorious lie": quoted in Wallace, *Weiser*, p. 360.

"engage the attention": to Thomas Leech and Assembly Committee of Correspondence, 10 June 1758, vol. 8, p. 89.

"was not permitted to alter": to Isaac Norris, 9 June 1759, vol. 8, p. 402.

to give "Parliament and ministry a clearer knowledge": ibid., p. 402.

"and I flatter myself": to Isaac Norris, 19 March 1759, vol. 8, p. 292.

"customary New Year's gifts": to Isaac Norris, 21 February 1763, vol. 10, p. 196.

"collected many materials": to David Hall, 8 April 1759, vol. 8, p. 319.

177 "If I do not correspond so fully": ibid., p. 317.

Smith "dancing attendance": to Joseph Galloway, 7 April 1759, vol. 8, p. 311.

Board of Trade report: 1 June 1763, vol. 8, pp. 379–389.

Privy Council censure of Assembly: 26 June 1763, vol. 8, p. 403n. "for a contempt to any former Assembly," p. 403n; Pennsylvania "must not be compared," p. 403n.

178 if the Privy Council "censure anything": to Joseph Galloway, 7 April 1759, vol. 8, p. 311.

"Peter continues with me": to Deborah Franklin, 27 June 1760, vol. 9, p. 174.

summer trip: "among the gentry there": to Deborah Franklin, 29 August 1759, vol. 8, p. 431; "The journey agrees extremely well with me": ibid.; saucepans "which instead of being tinned within": to Deborah Franklin, 21 February 1760, vol. 9, p. 25.

William "open and communicative": *Autobiography of the Rev. Dr. Alexander Carlyle* (1860), pp. 394–395, quoted in Eliot, "Adam Smith and BF" p. 76.

"six weeks of the *densest* happiness": to Lord Kames, 3 January 1760, vol. 9, p. 9.

179 "No one can rejoice more sincerely than I do": ibid., pp. 6–7.

"that to keep Canada": to John Hughes, 7 January 1760, vol. 9, pp. 13–14.

"an epidemical cold": to Deborah Franklin, 21 February 1760, vol. 9, p. 25.

"which was of great service": ibid., p. 25.

"grown a little thin": to Deborah Franklin, 18 March 1760, vol. 9, p. 36.

180 chapter title for BF pamphlet: Conner, *Poor Richard's Politics*, p. 89.

"in which the interest of the whole nation": quoted in Kaplan, *Colonies into Nation*, p. 14.

"a more grandiose vision": Stourzh, *Benjamin Franklin and American Foreign Policy*, p. 78.

Interest of Great Britain Considered: vol. 9, pp. 59–100: "surpass the number that can subsist," p. 73; "must take some centuries to fulfill," p. 78; "they have never been able," p. 90; "When I say such an union is impossible," pp. 90–91.

"it might induce him": William Franklin to Joseph Galloway, 16 June 1760, vol. 9, pp. 123–124.

"as much distinguished by his great capacity": *Interest*, vol. 9, p. 71.

181 "as I think our affairs here will now soon": to David Hall, 28 March 1760, vol. 9, p. 40.

"I gave him, however, two reasons": to Deborah Franklin, 5 March 1760, vol. 9, p. 33.

"I have not all the confidence I could wish": to Joseph Galloway, 9 January 1760, vol. 9, pp. 16–17.

"almost rebellious declarations": vol. 9, p. 128.

"that the assessors were honest and discreet men": *Auto.*, p. 265.

182 Board of Trade report: 24 June 1760, vol. 9, pp. 131–173: "one of the most

inviolable prerogatives," p. 143; Pennsylvania should be paid "with as few delays as possible," p. 167.
BF-Mansfield conference: *Auto.*, pp. 265–266.

17. ''WE HAVE NOT KEPT HIM''

184   "a very sensible knowing gentleman": Thomas Collinson to his uncle, 12 September 1760, vol. 9, p. 211.
"being contrary to their rules": to Isaac Norris, 19 November 1760, vol. 9, p. 245. A full account of BF's handling of this grant is found in Eddy, "Account Book," pp. 127–132 *passim.*
stocks "which will certainly at a peace produce a profit": to Isaac Norris, 19 November 1760, vol. 9, p. 245.

185   "in philosophical and . . . electrical matters": Thomas Penn to Gov. James Hamilton, 13 April 1761, vol. 10, p. 119n.
"judged . . . to be nine inches": to Joseph Priestley, 4 May 1772, Smyth, *Writings,* vol. 5, pp. 394–395.
"in honor of your musical language": to Giambatista Beccaria, 13 July 1762, vol. 10, p. 130.
"The instrument is played": ibid.
"As to Benjamin Franklin": William Logan to William Smith, 20 February 1761, quoted in Hanna, *BF and Pennsylvania Politics,* pp. 145–146.

186   visit to Continent: William Franklin to Sally Franklin, 10 October 1760, vol. 9, pp. 365–368.

187   "The commission I have had the honor . . . to receive": to Earl of Bessborough, October 1761, vol. 9, p. 379.

188   BF stock troubles: vol. 10, *passim;* Hutson, "BF and the Parliamentary Grant of 1758," pp. 575–595; Eddy, "Account Book," pp. 127–132 *passim.*
"without accepting any security": from Sargent Aufrere and Co., 15 January 1762, vol. 10, p. 11.
"preparing to return": to Edward Pennington, 9 January 1762, vol. 10, p. 6.
BF and Smith: Hutson, "BF and William Smith," pp. 109–113.

189   in a "great Dudgeon": William Smith to Richard Peters, 14 August 1762, vol. 10, 78n.
it "contained many particulars": William Strahan to John Kelly, [Feb, 1763], vol. 10, p. 78n.
"An eminent Dissenter called on me": Smith, *Life of Smith,* vol. 1, p. 336, quoting undated letter of Smith, but which Hutson, "BF and Smith," p. 111, identifies as Smith to Peters, 14 September 1762.

190   BF and Springett Penn: Hutson, *Pennsylvania Politics,* pp. 55–59.
"mind and heart": Ayling, *George III,* p. 41.
"The precise nature": Hutson, *Pennsylvania Politics,* p. 144.
"that your seas afforded none of any value": from John Pringle, [May? 1763], vol. 10, p. 268.

191   BF and N.J. governorship: vol. 10, pp. 146n–147n, 155n.
"the whole of this business has been transacted": John Penn to William Alexander, 3 September 1762, vol. 10, p. 147n.
"I cannot find that": James Hamilton to Jared Ingersoll, 8 July 1762, vol. 10, p. 113.

192   "I value myself much": to William Strahan, 23 July 1762, vol. 10, p. 137.
"I know not where to find his equal": William Strahan to David Hall, 10 August 1762, vol. 10, p. 141.

"I am very sorry": from David Hume, 10 May 1762, vol. 10, pp. 81–82.

"I am going from the old world to the new": to Lord Kames, 17 August 1762, vol. 10, p. 147.

"Of all the enviable things England has": to Mary Stevenson, 25 March 1763, vol. 10, p. 232.

193   "determined . . . to return to England": from John Pringle, [May? 1763], vol. 10, p. 268.

Smith's reaction to William's appointment: Hutson, "BF and Smith," pp. 111–113.

18. "I COULD NOT WISH FOR A MORE HEARTY WELCOME"

194   "a little touch of the gout": to Jane Mecom, 11 November 1762, vol. 10, p. 153.

"I . . . had the pleasure": to Richard Jackson, 2 December 1762, vol. 10, p. 160.

"my fellow citizens": to William Strahan, 2 December 1762, vol. 10, pp. 161–162.

"my friends as cordial": to Peter Collinson, 7 December 1762, vol. 10, p. 165.

"I could not wish for a more hearty welcome": to William Strahan, 7 December 1762, vol. 10, p. 166.

Deborah had moved: Roach, "BF Slept Here," p. 167.

195   armonica concert: vol. 10, p. 423.

Lord Bute's picture hung: Hutson, *Pennsylvania Politics*, p. 145.

"occasioned a universal astonishment": Hamilton to Thomas Penn, 21 November 1762, vol. 10, p. 155n.

BF's expense account: to Isaac Norris, 9 and 15 February 1763, vol. 10, pp. 193–197.

"This I mention to you: to Richard Jackson, 8 March 1763, vol. 10, p. 210.

cost of living had "greatly advanced": ibid., p. 209.

"our tradesmen are grown as idle": ibid.

"the streets seem thinner of people": ibid.

"you have an opportunity of hearing them all": to William Strahan, 7 December 1762, vol. 10, p. 168.

Havana would "contribute a due share of weight": to Caleb Whiteford, 9 December 1762, vol. 10, p. 172.

196   "I congratulate you on the glorious peace: to Philip Ludwell, 22 February 1763, vol. 10, p. 199.

"God bless you": to William Strahan, 7 December 1762, vol. 10, p. 169.

wished even the "devil": William Franklin to William Strahan, 25 April 1763, Hart, "William Franklin Letters," pp. 424–425.

"If any *gentleman* had been appointed": John Penn to William Alexander, Lord Sterling, 3 September 1762, Duer, *Life of William Alexander*, pp. 70–71.

197   Trip through New Jersey: Mariboe, "Life of William Franklin," pp. 120–121; *Papers*, vol. 10, pp. 200n–201n.

"a solidity of judgment": William Strahan to Deborah Franklin, 13 December 1757, vol. 7, p. 297.

"I could wish to hear": to Richard Jackson, 8 March 1764, vol. 11, p. 97.

198   "It is impossible for you": from William Franklin, 30 April 1766, vol. 13, p. 256.

"my father will never be induced": William Franklin to William Strahan, 25 April 1763, Hart, "William Franklin Letters," p. 426.

"crystallized in Franklin's mind": Roach, "BF Slept Here," p. 169

BF hires Smith and Rhoads: ibid., p. 170.

199 BF instructions to Deborah Franklin: in letters dated 14 February, 4 June and August 1765, vol. 12, pp. 62, 167, 250–251.

"I suppose the blue room is too blue": to Deborah Franklin, 22 June 1767, vol. 14, pp. 194–195.

"You tell me only of a fault": to Deborah Franklin, 13 July 1765, vol. 12, p. 211.

200 "there are already several schemes on foot": to Richard Jackson, 17 April 1763, vol. 10, p. 255.

"the proper constitution of government": to Richard Jackson, 8 March 1763, vol. 10, p. 214.

"Since all the country is now ceded to us": ibid., p. 208.

"I trust I shall see you": to William Strahan, 28 March 1763, vol. 10, p. 237.

201 "rendering correspondence in the vast empire": to Anthony Todd, 14 April 1763, vol. 10, p. 254.

"The advantage of the office of a postmaster": to Anthony Todd, 10 June 1763, vol. 10, pp. 281–282.

"I am sensible that the care of": to Benjamin Walker, 1 August 1763, vol. 10, p. 317.

"the Indians on the Ohio have broke out again": to Richard Jackson, 6 June 1763, vol. 10, pp. 273–274.

202 The Indians must be "prudently prepared": to Richard Jackson, 10 June 1763, vol. 10, p. 286.

"But others here say the Indians": to Richard Jackson, 27 June 1763, vol. 10, pp. 295–296.

trip from New York to Boston: chronology, vol. 10, pp. 277–278.

"a harpsichord": to Jane Mecom, 19 June 1763, vol. 10, p. 292.

"the soreness in my breast": to Catharine Ray Greene, 19 July 1763, vol. 10, p. 312.

203 "I am now so used to it" to Deborah Franklin, 16 June 1763, vol. 10, p. 291.

"I am almost ashamed to tell you": to Catharine Ray Greene, 5 September 1763, vol. 10, p. 338.

"before they had heard of the peace": to William Strahan, 22 September 1763, vol. 10., p. 343.

"Not an hour have I spent on cribbage": from William Strahan, 18 August 1763, vol. 10, p. 330.

"No friend can wish me more in England": to William Strahan, 8 August 1763, vol. 10, p. 320.

milk punch recipe: to James Bowdoin, 11 October 1763, vol. 10, pp. 351–352.

204 "I perceive the artifice of your eloquence": to Joshua Babcock, 5 September 1763, vol. 10, p. 337.

Connecticut's "excessively strict observation of Sunday": to Jared Ingersoll, 11 December 1762, vol. 10, p. 175.

"That I have not the propensity to sitting still": to William Strahan, 8 August 1763, vol. 10, p. 320.

19. "RUNNING FAST INTO ANARCHY AND CONFUSION"

205 "because the authorities are taking": Muhlenburg Journals, vol. 1, p. 709, quoted in vol. 11, p. 27.

"I am allowed to know": to Jane Mecom, 15 December 1763, vol. 10, p. 393.

"I could have been of use": to Richard Jackson, 19 December 1763, vol. 10, p. 404.

"I am not coming over": to Peter Collinson, 19 December 1763, vol. 10, p. 401.
"Now I am returned": to William Strahan, 19 December 1763, vol. 10, pp. 406–407.

206 Penn met "in various places at dinner": to Peter Collinson, 19 December 1763, vol. 10, p. 401.
"I had but an indifferent opinion": William Allen to Benjamin Chew, 7 October 1763, Kimball and Quinn, "Allen-Chew Correspondence," p. 212.
"give no occasion": to Peter Collinson, 19 December 1763, vol. 10, p. 401.
"I only fear we shall conclude a new peace": to Richard Jackson, 19 December 1763, vol. 10, p. 405.
Pennsylvania alone "complied fully": to Richard Jackson, 24 December 1763, vol. 10, p. 409.
Indians "who have lived peaceably": *Narrative of the Late Massacres*, vol. 11, p. 51.

207 "barbarous men . . . in defiance of government": ibid., p. 53.

208 "the spirit of killing all Indians": to Richard Jackson, 11 February 1764, vol. 11, p. 77.
Narrative of the Late Massacres: vol. 11, pp. 47–69: "THE BLOOD OF THE INNOCENT," p. 53; "O ye unhappy perpetrators," pp. 66–67.
"from all parts of our frontier": to Richard Jackson, 11 February 1764, vol. 11, p. 77.
"up the different roads": vol. 11, p. 72.

209 The governor "did me the honor": to John Fothergill, 14 March 1764, vol. 11, p. 103.
"frankly confessed . . . they had set out": Jenkins, "Foulke Journal," 7 February 1764, p. 70.

210 "At present we are pretty quiet": to Richard Jackson, 11 February 1764, vol. 11, p. 77.
"The back people have a right": William Allen to Benjamin Chew, 13 April 1764, Kimball and Quinn, "Allen-Chew Correspondence," pp. 222–223.
"And within twenty-four hours": to John Fothergill, 14 March 1764, vol. 11, pp. 103–104.
"The Assembly's proposal": to Richard Jackson, 14 March 1764, vol. 11, p. 107.

211 dropped "all inquiry": to John Fothergill, 14 March 1764, vol. 11, p. 104.
"Would you believe it": ibid., pp. 101–102.
"The mobs strike a general terror": to Richard Jackson, 14 March 1764, vol. 11, p. 107.
another "of the same tenor": Hutson, "White Oaks," p. 17.
legislature "was truly desirous": quoted in vol. 11, p. 8.
"that the best of the proprietor's located uncultivated lands": to Richard Jackson, 8 March 1764, vol. 11, pp. 95–96.

212 "near £7 tax": to Richard Jackson, 14 March 1764, vol. 11, p. 106.
Provisions contradicted "common justice and common sense": ibid., p. 106.
"with an absolute refusal": ibid., p. 105.
"than that the House have, by inserting the officer's name": John Penn to Assembly, 12 March 1764, vol. 11, p. 104n.
"by the governor's party, to awe the Assembly": to Richard Jackson, 14 March 1764, vol. 11, p. 107.
"a sincere desire to continue on good terms": ibid., p. 106.
"Do you please yourself with the fancy": to John Fothergill, 14 March 1764, vol. 11, pp. 101, 105.

213 House "complied to the best of their understanding": Message to the Governor, 22 March 1764, vol. 11, p. 113.

concluded "that the powers of government, ought . . . be separated": Assembly Resolves Upon the Present Circumstances, 24 March 1764, vol. II, p. 132.
"necklace of resolves": to William Strahan, 30 March 1764, vol. II, p. 149.
"in order to consult their constituents": Assembly Resolves, 24 March 1764, vol. II, p. 132.

20. ''MR. FRANKLIN DIED LIKE A PHILOSOPHER''

214   *"change of government"*: Cool Thoughts, April 1764, vol. II, p. 171.
"the way from proprietary slavery": quoted in Newcomb, *BF and Galloway*, p. 83.
215   "You will endear yourself to us": to Richard Jackson, 29 March 1764, vol. II, p. 148.
"prepare the minds of those in power": to William Strahan, 30 March 1764, vol. II, p. 149.
"We continue in great disorder here": to Richard Jackson, 1 May 1764, vol. II, p. 185.
"We are now in the utmost confusion": to Richard Jackson, 31 March 1764, vol. II, p. 150.
"many talk of quitting the province": to Peter Collinson, 30 April 1764, vol. II, p. 181.
Cool Thoughts: vol. II, pp. 153–173: "there are *faults on both sides*"; p. 159.
"Dear Mr. Strahan": to William Strahan, 24 September 1764, vol. II, pp. 353–355.
216   "Isaac's rage": William Allen to Thomas Penn, 25 March 1761, quoted in Hutson, *Pennsylvania Politics*, p. 156.
Assembly voted "by a great majority": vol. II, p. 193.
Dickinson's speech: Ford, *Writings of Dickinson*, vol. I, pp. 21–49. Quotations come from pp. 110, 22, 43, 34, 30, 33.
217   "it was observed that the speaker was so ill": ibid., vol. I, p. 139.
218   "the long sitting of yesterday": vol. II, p. 196.
waived its "important parliamentary rights": vol. II, p. 206.
secrecy of petition of "no great importance": Preface to Galloway's Speech, 1764, vol. II, p. 300.
"They would fain have sent me home": to Richard Jackson, 1 June 1764, vol. II, p. 219.
"I believe (but you best not mention it)": William Franklin to William Strahan, 1 May 1764, Hart, "William Franklin Letters," p. 436.
"My father seems to be preparing in earnest": William Franklin to William Strahan, 18 June 1764, ibid., p. 438.
"I bore the personal abuse": to Richard Jackson, 1 September 1764, vol. II, p. 329.
219   "to congratulate him on his arrival": ibid., p. 328.
"Parliament will oblige us": ibid., pp. 327–328.
"I can scarcely conceive": ibid., p. 328.
petition "will . . . meet with success": from Richard Jackson, 11 August 1764, vol. II, p. 312.
"I think, therefore, that for the present": ibid., p. 313.
"the present ministry are desirous": Ford, *Writings of Dickinson*, vol. I, p. 89.
Halifax called resolves *"rebellion!"*: to Richard Jackson, 1 September 1764, vol. II, p. 328.
"Now is your time to make a good bargain": ibid.
Lord Hyde warned "all the officers of the crown": *ibid.*, p. 318n.

220 "was not to be *Hyde-bound*": John Penn to Thomas Penn, 22 September 1764, quoted in Currey, *Road to Revolution*, p. 58.
"My enemies . . . are now representing": to Henry Bouquet, 16 August 1764, vol. II, pp. 318, 319.
"Piss-brute-tarians": quoted in Newcomb, *BF and Galloway*, p. 96.
"Why should the Palatine boors": *Increase of Mankind* (1751), vol. 4, p. 234.
"boors" rendered "bauerntolpels": Newcomb, *BF and Galloway*, p. 94.
"but as far as I can perceive": to Richard Jackson, 20 September 1764, vol. II, pp. 339–340.
"the king's little finger we should find": *Remarks on a Late Protest*, vol. II, p. 432.
"very gloomy and thoughtful": William Allen to Thomas Penn, 25 September 1764, vol. II, p. 492n.

221 "they keep them back in hopes": to Peter Collinson, 24 September 1764, vol. II, p. 352.
"I am not much alarmed": to Richard Jackson, 16 January 1764, vol. II, pp. 19–20.
"Undoubtedly the illicit trade ought to be stopped": to Richard Jackson, 16 June 1764, vol. II, p. 215.
"my political faith is": *Poor Richard* (1765), vol. 12, pp. 4, 5.
"Your objection to internal taxes": to Richard Jackson, 1 May 1764, vol. II, p. 186.
"When any tax for America is proposed": ibid.
"If you choose to tax us": ibid.
"had not WILLIAM ALLEN": *Pennsylvania Gazette*, 7 June 1764, quoted in Kimball and Quinn, "Allen-Chew Correspondence," p. 204.

222 "Our people are very unjust to Mr. Penn": William Allen to Benjamin Chew, 9 December 1763, Kimball and Quinn "Allen-Chew Correspondence," p. 217.
"we are to be their grand milch cow": Allen to Chew, 13 April 1764, ibid., p. 225.
"The cat can yield but her skin": to Peter Collinson, 30 April 1764, vol. II, pp. 181–182.
"I begin, as I grow old": to Richard Jackson, 25 June 1764, vol. II, p. 237.
"Nothing is now talked of all over America but frugality": to Richard Jackson, 25 September 1764, vol. II, p. 359.
supplying "ourselves": *Poor Richard* (1765), vol. 12, p. 5.
"the very tails of the American sheep": "A Traveller," 20 May 1765, vol. 12, p. 134.

223 William "to keep open house at Germantown": John Penn to Thomas Penn, 9 October 1764, quoted in Newcomb, *BF and Galloway*, p. 97.
"both sides seem confident of success": William Allen to Barclay and Sons, 25 September 1764, Walker, *Burd Papers*, pp. 56–57.
Polls "so crowded": Read, *Life of Reed*, vol. I, pp. 36–37.

224 election results: vol. II, pp. 390–394.
Galloway-BF reactions to results: Read, *Life of Reed*, vol. I, p. 37.
"quite a laughing matter": to Richard Jackson, 11 October 1764, vol. II, p. 397.
"numberless falsehoods": *Remarks on a Late Protest*, vol. II, p. 434.
"A day or two after the governor left": Benjamin Chew to Thomas Penn, 5 November 1764, quoted in Konkle, *Chew*, pp. 103–104.
BF's "fixed enmity to the proprietors": Ford, *Writings of Dickinson*, vol. I, p. 151.

225 "I am afraid the frenzy has seized him": John Watts to General Monckton, 10 Nov. 1764, *Letter Books of Watts*, p. 310.
Allen's invectives: "An Answer to Mr. Franklin's Remarks on a Late Protest," Walker, *Burd Papers*, pp. 109, 117, 119, 120.
"And what comfort can it afford you": *Remarks on a Late Protest*, vol. 11, p. 434.
"as a rod to hang over you": William Allen to Thomas Penn, 11 March 1765, quoted in Hutson, *Pennsylvania Politics*, p. 180.
"If the Ministry was ready": Hanna, *BF and Pennsylvania Politics*, pp. 174–175.
226 BF's departure: vol. 11, pp. 447–448; Gleason, "Scurrilous Election," pp. 83–84.
"In short, the respect that was paid": ibid.

21. "O, FRANKLIN, FRANKLIN, THOU CURSE"

227 "occasioned . . . great and general joy": from Cadwallader Evans, 15 March 1765, vol. 12, p. 82
Quakers "ran about like mad men": John Penn to Thomas Penn, 16 March 1765, vol. 12, p. 82n.
"and the maid could not tell": to Mary Stevenson, [12–16 December 1764], vol. 11, p. 521.
"a most violent cold": to Deborah Franklin, 27 December 1764, vol. 11, p. 534.
228 "the mind of a clerk": quoted in Ayling, *George III*, p. 107.
"He had nothing seducing in his manners": Thomas Pitt, Jr., quoted in Namier and Brooke, *History of Parliament*, vol. 2, p. 539.
"alone among the British statesmen": Ritcheson, *British Politics*, pp. 9, 11.
Loan Office plan: 11–12 February 1765, vol. 12, pp. 47–60.
229 "by the interest of these loans": "Observations on America, 1766," vol. 13, p. 373.
"It will operate as a general tax": Loan Office plan, vol. 12, p. 55.
"in the present temper of Americans": Joseph Galloway to William Franklin, 21 December 1766, quoted in Ernst, "Currency Act Repeal," p. 189.
"I think it will affect the printers more than anybody": to David Hall, 14 February 1765, vol. 12, pp. 65–66.
"stood entirely neuter": Dennys DeBerdt, quoted in Kaplan, *Colonies into Nation*, p. 35.
"was his first consideration": Hanna, *Pennsylvania Politics.*, pp. 176–177.
230 "We might as well have hindered the sun's setting": to Charles Thomson, 11 July 1765, vol. 12, pp. 207–208.
"Mr. Grenville was desirous": to Josiah Tucker, 26 February 1774, Smyth, *Writings*, vol. 6, pp. 200–201.
"to hire vacant buildings": vol. 12, p. 106.
231 "Our petition . . . becalmed": to John Ross, 8 June 1765, vol. 12, p. 173.
"Nothing yet appears": to Hugh Roberts, 7 July 1765, vol. 12, p. 202.
"must sooner or later take place": to Samuel Rhoads, 8 July 1765, vol. 12, p. 205.
"I have very little doubt": to John Hughes, 9 August 1765, vol. 12, pp. 235–236.
"a little too tight": from Thomas Wharton, 27 April 1765, vol. 12, p. 114.
Their rashness "is amazing!": to John Hughes, 9 August 1765, vol. 12, p. 234.
232 "keep within the bounds of prudence": ibid., pp. 234–235.
Thomson letter: entitled "A Merchant in Philadelphia," vol. 12, pp. 183–188.

"as loyal subjects as any the king has": "A Virginian," 23 August 1765, vol. 12, p. 246.

"Americans are a reasonable people": "A Virginian," 5 September 1765, vol. 12, p. 254.

"a very handsome pair of tongs": to Deborah Franklin, 2 October 1765, vol. 12, p. 290.

"Philadelphia is cursed": Benjamin Rush to Ebenezer Hazard, 8 November 1765, Butterfield, *Letters of Rush,* vol. 1, p. 18.

"mobility" must "extort": Benjamin Rush to Ebenezer Hazard, 18 November 1765, ibid., p. 20.

"O, *Franklin, Franklin":* ibid., p. 18.

233   "I could wish you was on the spot": from David Hall, 6 September 1765, vol. 12, p. 259. *Gazette's* loss of customers: from David Hall, 14 October 1765, p. 320.

"Our clamors run very high": from John Hughes, 12 September 1765, vol. 12, p. 266.

downstairs "into a magazine": from Deborah Franklin, 22 September 1765, vol. 12, p. 271.

"the change of ministry": from [Samuel Wharton], 13 October 1765, vol. 12, p. 315.

"If I live till tomorrow": from John Hughes, 12 September 1765, vol. 12, p. 266.

"I said when I was advised": from Deborah Franklin, 22 September 1765, vol. 12, pp. 271–272.

234   "We are all yet in the land of the living": from John Hughes, 17 September 1765, vol. 12, p. 266.

"no reason to doubt of its success": quoted in Hutson, *Pennsylvania Politics,* p. 204.

"for the present": vol. 12, p. 420n.

"forever and ever": Thomas Penn to John Penn, 30 November 1765, vol. 12, p. 421n.

"is the most easy way of rejecting": Thomas Penn to John Penn, 30 November 1765, vol. 13, p. 180n.

"any good reason for their request": ibid.

"has struck our friends with the utmost consternation": from Joseph Galloway, 27 February 1766, vol. 13, p. 180.

235   "I have been obliged": ibid., p. 181.

"You will therefore be pleased": ibid., p. 182.

"ready to be proceeded on": to Pennsylvania Assembly Committee of Correspondence, 12 April 1766, vol. 13, p. 240.

"be deemed a tacit giving up": to William Franklin, 9 November 1765, vol. 12, p. 364.

"they are contented with their own little legislatures": "N.N.," 29 January 1766, vol. 13, p. 65.

"compelling the Americans": ibid., pp. 65–66.

interview with Lord Dartmouth: to William Franklin, 9 November 1765, vol. 12, pp. 362–364.

236   "A stop is put to our commerce": from Joseph Galloway, 16–28 November 1765, vol. 12, pp. 376–377.

"The gentle terms of *republican race":* "N.N." 28 December 1765, vol. 12, p. 414.

"Give me leave, Master JOHN BULL": "Homespun," 15 January 1766, vol. 13, p. 47.

"They resolved last spring": "Homespun," 2 January 1766, vol. 13, p. 8.
"The assiduity of our friend Dr. Franklin": William Strahan to David Hall, 11 January 1766, "Strahan-Hall Correspondence," p. 92.

237 "Great Britain is supposed": vol. 13, pp. 70–71.
"Mr. Pitt spoke some time": to William Strahan, 14 January 1766, vol. 13, p. 41.

238 "took a fancy to it": to Joseph Galloway, 11 October 1766, vol. 13, p. 449.
"the principal instrument in the happy repeal": Edmund Burke to James West, 11 February 1766, quoted in Namier and Brooke, *History of Parliament*, vol. 3, p. 558.

239 All quotations from the House of Commons Debates are drawn from Gipson, "The Great Debate . . . as Reported by Nathaniel Ryder," pp. 10–41.
BF's Examination before the House: vol., 13, pp. 129–162. The first exchange with Grenville appears on pp. 133–134, the second concerning the post office, on p. 144.

240 "the Parliament could not levy any tax": Butler, *BF, Postmaster General*, p. 27.
"An external tax is a duty": vol. 13, p. 139; "I do not know a single article": vol. 13, p. 140; "very fine and good" wool: ibid.; "as to clothing ourselves": to Richard Jackson, 25 September 1764, vol. 11, p. 359; "there is not the least occasion for it": vol. 13, p. 152; "I am not certain, but I think so": ibid.; exchange with Townshend: vol. 13, p. 157; "I think the resolutions of right": p. 141.

241 "We have only a choice of political evils": Gipson, "The Great Debate . . . as Reported by Nathaniel Ryder," p. 38.

242 "He gave me a great deal of flummery": to William Franklin, 2 July 1768, vol. 15, p. 163.
"Our worthy friend Dr. Franklin": *Pennsylvania Gazette*, 27 February 1766, quoted in Cecil B. Currey, *Road to Revolution*, p. 191.
"To this examination, more than to anything else": William Strahan to David Hall, 10 May 1766, "Strahan-Hall Correspondence," pp. 220–221.

243 "Your enemies at last began to be ashamed": from Charles Thomson, vol. 13 p. 278.

22. "WE MUST USE PATIENCE"

244 "the ministry being inclined": to Pennsylvania Assembly Committee of Correspondence, 12 April 1766, vol. 13, p. 238.
"a terrible thing to establish such violence by a law": ibid., p. 239.
"Easing one part of the British dominions": Petition to the House of Commons, 12–15 April 1766, vol. 13, p. 242.

245 "The frequent changes that have happened": to Pennsylvania Assembly Committee of Correspondence, 10 June 1766, vol. 13, pp. 298–299.
"very ill": to Deborah Franklin, 13 June 1766, vol. 13, p. 315.
"Dr. Franklin needs very much": William Strahan to David Hall, 14 June 1766, "Strahan-Hall Correspondence," p. 228.
trip to Germany: vol. 13, pp. 299, 314–316, 383–384, 407–408: "Drank the waters," to Pennsylvania Assembly Committee of Correspondence, 22 August 1766, p. 383; "worthy of the notice of so great . . . a man," from Johann Friedrich Hartmann, 1 October 1767, vol. 14, p. 264; pulse glass, Van Doren, *BF*, p. 357.
BF's "Observations on America": vol. 13, pp. 348–377: "the membranes of the cod," p. 364; buffalo "rather larger and stranger," p. 365; "for they can be used for twelve years," p. 366.

246 "to be granted the chance of conversation": from Johann Friedrich Hartmann, 1 October 1767, vol. 14, p. 265.
"the farther points we would obtain": to Pennsylvania Assembly Committee of Correspondence, 22 August 1766, vol. 13, p. 384.
"Here public affairs are in great disorder": to John Ross, 11 April 1767, vol. 14, pp. 116–117.
"only time to say things continue here in the same uncertain state": to Joseph Galloway, 23 May 1767, vol. 14, p. 167.
"the confusion among our great men": to Joseph Galloway, 8 August 1767, vol. 14, p. 228.
Chatham "almost totally disabled": to Joseph Galloway, 14 April 1767, vol. 14, pp. 124–125.
"There is at present no access to him": to Cadwallader Evans, 5 August 1767, vol. 14, p. 223.

247 "more changes talked of and daily expected": to Joseph Galloway, 14 April 1767, vol. 14, p. 125.
"He was never satisfied with what anyone did": quoted in Namier and Brooke, *History of Parliament*, vol. 3, p. 272.
"One of the most mystifying characters": Ritcheson, *British Politics*, p. 86.
"There were reasons for this": Shy, *Toward Lexington*, p. 239.
"was pleased to assure me": to Joseph Galloway, 11 October 1766, vol. 13, p. 448.

248 proposed purchase of Pennsylvania: Lord Shelburne to John Penn, 11 December 1766, paraphrased in Shepherd, *History of Proprietary Government*, p. 569.
"There are many disputes between them": "Observations on America," vol. 13, p. 376.
"America, an immense territory, favored by nature": to Lord Kames, 25 February 1767, vol. 14, pp. 69–70.
"what a glorious thing it would be": to George Whitefield, 2 July 1756, vol. 6, p. 468.
"obtained full permission from the several nations": from William Franklin, 17 December 1765, vol. 12, p. 403.
"It is proposed": from William Franklin, 30 April 1766, vol. 13, p. 257.

249 plan "well drawn": to William Franklin, 12 September 1766, vol. 13, p. 415.
"continual changes here": ibid., p. 415.
"extraordinary charges" of army: to William Franklin, 11 October 1766, vol. 13, p. 447.
"very little expense to the crown": to William Franklin, 28 August 1767, vol. 14, p. 243.
"would make it of little use to this country": to William Franklin, 27 September 1766, vol. 13, pp. 424–425.
"there which on occasion of a future war": to William Franklin, 28 August 1767, vol. 14, p. 243.

250 Jackson: "I have no doubt of its practicality": quoted in vol. 13, p. 486n.
"from him [it] appears": to William Franklin, 8 November 1766, vol. 13, p. 486.
Shelburne "highly approved": to William Franklin, 13 June 1767, vol. 14, p. 180.
saw "no obstacle": to William Franklin, 28 August 1767, vol. 14, p. 243.
weaknesses of plan for western settlement: Sosin, *Whitehall and the Wilderness*, p. 158.
"chance has its share": quoted in Conner, *Poor Richard's Politics*, p. 12.

Shelburne "to the utmost of his power": quoted in Ernst, "Currency Act Repeal," p. 194.

251   repeal "absolutely necessary": quoted in Greene and Jellison, "Currency Act of 1764," p. 497.

"the rest of the Board are still strong against it": to Joseph Galloway, 14 April 1767, vol. 14, p. 123.

Grenville "with much art and industry": ibid., p. 124.

"The word *rebellion*": Report on Debate in House of Lords, 11 April 1767, vol. 14, p. 108.

"It is also reported": ibid., p. 109.

252   Pitt's "abilities were of the same kind": quoted in Namier and Brooke, *Townshend,* p. 1.

"His abilities were deemed wonderful": ibid., p. 185.

"In the personalized terms": ibid., p. 147.

Shelburne's plan to punish New York: Chaffin, "Townshend Acts," p. 103.

external taxes "perfect nonsense": quoted in Currey, *Road to Revolution,* p. 222.

"The colonies submit to pay all external taxes": "Benevolus": "On the Propriety of Taxing America," 11 April 1767, vol. 14, pp. 114–115.

253   warned "the House to beware": report on May 13 speech quoted in Namier and Brooke, *Townshend,* p. 179.

"If I do not like it": "Benevolus": "On the Propriety of Taxing America," 11 April 1767, vol. 14, p. 115.

"I'll tell the honorable gentleman": to Joseph Galloway, 13 June 1767, vol. 14, p. 181.

"You'll find it another *Stamp Act* in disguise": quoted in Ernst, "Currency Act Repeal," p. 189n.

He "had intended": to Joseph Galloway, 13 June 1767, vol. 14, p. 181.

"The idea of an American tax": to Joseph Galloway, 8 August 1767, vol. 14, p. 229.

"Every step is taking to render the taxing of America a popular measure": ibid., p. 229.

"has had a great run": ibid., p. 230.

23. ''I AM OLD AND HEAVY AND GROW A LITTLE INDOLENT''

254   "However, I shall not do it": to Jane Mecom, 1 March 1766, vol. 13, p. 188.

"a single syllable either in approbation or disapprobation": William Strahan to David Hall, 11 April 1767, "Strahan-Hall Correspondence," vol. 10, p. 231.

"I live here as frugally as possible": to Deborah Franklin, 22 June 1767, vol. 14, p. 193.

255   "Billy don't like the blue room at all": from Deborah Franklin, 20–25 April 1767, vol. 14, p. 138.

"I am obliged to be father and mother": ibid., p. 136.

Sally "was very much scared": from Deborah Franklin, 16 May 1767, vol. 14, p. 157.

"I would only advise": to Deborah Franklin, 22 June 1767, vol. 14, p. 193.

Bache not "worth anything": from William Franklin, May 1767, vol. 14, p. 174.

Sally "pleased herself and her mother": to Jane Mecom, 21 February 1768, vol. 15, p. 57.

"I could say nothing agreeable": to Richard Bache, 13 August 1768, vol. 15, p. 186.

"I cannot entirely agree with you": from William Franklin, 22 August 1767, vol. 14, p. 236.

256 "I have got the clothes and have worn them": to Deborah Franklin, 6 February 1767, vol. 14, p. 23–24.

"I am old and heavy": to John Alleyne, 9 August 1768, vol. 15, p. 184.

People "become tiresome guests": to Margaret Stevenson, 3 November 1767, vol. 14, pp. 299–300.

"if you and Mrs. Stevenson are well": from Anthony Tissington, 13 June 1769, vol. 16, p. 158.

"Your good mama and myself": to Mary Stevenson, 9 January 1765, vol. 12, p. 16.

"On Monday between two and three you may expect me": to Mary Stevenson, 16 May 1767, vol. 14, p. 154.

"Who justly may suppose": to Mary Stevenson, 15 June 1767, vol. 14, p. 188.

257 her father "brought her to town": to Deborah Franklin, 11 October 1766, vol. 13, p. 446.

"I rise early almost every morning": to Barbeu Dubourg, 28 July 1768, vol. 15, pp. 180–181.

"to find a little giddiness in my head": to Deborah Franklin, 5 August 1767, vol. 14, pp. 224–225.

"He is extremely curious": to William Franklin, 28 August 1767, vol. 14, p. 244.

258 trip to Paris: fullest account to Mary Stevenson, 14 September, 1767, vol. 14, pp. 250–255, from which most of the quotations in this section come. Exceptions are: "we scarce ever hear of a fire," to Samuel Rhoads, 26 June 1770, vol. 17, p. 182; hand tremors of Parisians, "Excerpts from the Papers of Dr. Rush," p. 24; BF "had never snuffed," ibid., p. 24; "like a pleasing dream," to Thomas-François Dalibard, 31 January 1768, vol. 15, p. 35; "His pronunciation, too": Butterfield, *The Adams . . . Diary and Autobiography*, vol. iv, pp. 59–60; "the courage to attempt," to Dalibard, 31 January 1768, vol. 15, p. 35; "Of Lightning and the Method . . . ," vol. 14, pp. 260–264; "by contrary winds and stormy weather," to Thomas-François Dalibard, 31 January 1768, vol. 15, p. 35.

260 "I returned last night from Paris": to William Franklin, 9 October 1767, vol. 14, p. 275.

"The purpose of settling the new colonies": to William Franklin, 13 March 1768, vol. 15, p. 74.

261 "Is any lady ashamed to request": "F.B.": "On Smuggling," 24 November 1767, vol. 14, 317.

"The Americans offend us grievously": ibid., p. 319.

"Must Pennsylvania and Maryland": from Joseph Galloway, 9 October 1767, vol. 14, p. 277.

"I wish the Boston people had been as quiet": to William Franklin, 25 November 1767, vol. 14, p. 323.

"The resolutions of the Boston people": to William Franklin, 29 December 1767, vol. 14, p. 349.

"Parliament has not yet taken notice of them": ibid., p. 349.

Americans were "not quite so unreasonable as they appeared": to Joseph Galloway, 13 January 1768, vol. 15, p. 17.

"Causes of the American Discontents before 1768": vol. 15, pp. 3–13: "the levying more money from America," p. 17; "which from their respect and love for this country," p. 9; this "the most cruel insult," p. 11; "To be sure, no reasonable man in England," p. 13.

262   "has drawn the teeth and pared the nails": to William Franklin, 9 January 1768, vol. 15, p. 16.

changes in "Causes" essay: "frivolous complaint," p. 10; "forced from the people," p. 9; "frequently men of vicious characters," p. 8.

263   "I am told": to William Franklin, 9 January 1768, vol. 15, p. 16.

24. "I SHOULD STAY WITH PLEASURE"

264   "not undertake here to support these opinions": "Causes of American Discontents," 5–7 January 1768, vol. 15, p. 5.

"give myself the trouble to defend": to William Franklin, 13 March 1768, vol. 15, p. 76.

"Only to you": ibid., p. 76.

"In my opinion the grievance is not": ibid., pp. 76–77.

"I am not yet master of the idea": ibid., pp. 75–76.

265   "How far these sentiments are right or wrong": Preface to Letters, 8 May 1768, vol. 15, p. 112.

"As our American disputes afford you some amusement": to Jean-Baptiste LeRoy, 21 September 1768, vol. 15, p. 206.

"the satisfaction in seeing that our part is taken everywhere": quoted in Kaplan, Colonies into Nation, p. 61.

266   "dispeopling of Ireland": to William Franklin, 12 September 1766, vol. 13, p. 414.

"I do not think this nobleman in general an enemy to America": to Joseph Galloway, 9 January 1768, vol. 15, p. 16.

"I do not know a man of less judgment": quoted in Namier and Brooke, History of Parliament, vol. 2, p. 627.

"Lord Hillsborough is esteemed a nobleman of good nature": William Samuel Johnson of Connecticut, quoted in Shy, Toward Lexington, p. 293.

he "read them deliberately": to Joseph Galloway, 13 March 1768, vol. 15, p. 79.

"was pleased to make me compliments": to Joseph Galloway, 17 February 1768, vol. 15, p. 49.

induced "him to leave the matter now": ibid., p. 49.

"he was pleased to say": ibid.

"the purpose of settling the new colonies": to William Franklin, 13 March 1768, vol. 15, p. 74.

"The Parliament is up and the nation in a ferment": ibid., pp. 77–78.

267   "Great complaints are made": ibid., p. 78.

"the unavoidable bustle": William Strahan to David Hall, 12 March 1768, "Strahan-Hall Letters," pp. 332–333.

" 'Tis really an extraordinary event": to William Franklin, 16 April 1768, vol. 15, pp. 98–99.

"whether infidels or Protestants": Brady and Pottle, Boswell, p. 167.

"While I am writing, a great mob of coal porters fill the street": to Joseph Galloway, 14 May 1768, vol. 15, p. 127.

268   "Even this capital": to John Ross, 14 May 1768, vol. 15, p. 129.

"I am preparing for my return": to Joseph Galloway, 14 May 1768, vol. 15, p. 128.

Hillsborough's "inclinations are rather favorable towards us": to Joseph Galloway, 2 July 1768, vol. 15, p. 164.

269   negotiations for post in government: to William Franklin, 2 July 1768, vol. 15, pp. 159–164.

"youthful, indolent, and incompetent": Chaffin, "Townshend Acts," p. 91.

270   "Our friends wonder": to Joseph Galloway, 2 July 1768, vol. 15, p. 165.

"I purpose remaining here another winter": to Charles-Guillaume-Frédéric Dumas, 25 July 1768, vol. 15, p. 180.

mid-August meeting with Hillsborough: to Joseph Galloway, 20 August 1768, vol. 15, pp. 189–190.

271   "to be a very good kind of a man": quoted in Kammen, *Rope of Sand*, p. 65.

"The Standing Secretary seems to have a strong bias against us": quoted in ibid., p. 260.

BF's letters to the press: (1) Queries, 16 August 1768, vol. 15, pp. 187–189; (2) On Civil War, 25 August 1768, pp. 191–193; (3) On Absentee Governors, 26 and 27 August 1768, pp. 193–195; (4) To Dennys De Berdt, 31 August 1768, pp. 196–199.

"I know not but I may still return this fall": to Joseph Galloway, 20 August 1768, vol. 15, p. 190.

25. "AT PRESENT I ALMOST DESPAIR"

272   "for an American establishment": "On Sinecures," 28 September 1768, vol. 15, p. 222.

colonies "are not presumptuous enough": "Reply to Thomas Crowley," 21 October 1768, vol. 15, p. 241.

"Everybody attributes it to you": from William Franklin, 2 March 1769, vol. 16, pp. 59–60.

"an internal legislative power": Arguments Pro and Con, 18–20 October 1768, vol. 15, p. 234.

"an impracticable right": The State of the Trade with the Northern Colonies, 1–3 November 1768, vol. 15, p. 251.

"Mankind have so far learned the wisdom of the serpent": Arguments Pro and Con, 27–29 October 1768, vol. 15, p. 243.

Parliament "a new being": The State of the Trade with the Northern Colonies, 1–3 November 1768, vol. 15, p. 252.

273   Lord North: descriptions drawn from Namier and Brooke, *History of Parliament*, vol. 3, 204–205.

"In a country so frequent in mischievous mobs": to Joseph Galloway, 9 January 1769, vol. 16, p. 12.

"If any good may be done": to _____, 28 November 1768, vol. 15, p. 273.

"The tide is yet strong against us": to Samuel Cooper, 24 February 1769, vol. 16, p. 52.

"They flatter themselves that you cannot long subsist": to Samuel Cooper, 27 April 1769, vol. 16, p. 118.

274   "Doctor Franklin looks heartier": William Trent, 10 June 1769, Lingelbach, "Trent Calls on BF," p. 49.

"there is at present an appearance": to Humphry Marshall, 9 July 1769, vol. 16, p. 174.

"You would laugh to see him dressed": William Trent, 10 June 1769, Lingelbach, "Trent Calls on BF," p. 49.

275   "My *all* depends on the confirmation": quoted in Sosin, *Whitehall*, p. 184.

"his Majesty does not think fit at present": Hillsborough to Sir William Johnson, 13 May 1769, quoted in Currey, *Road to Revolution,* p. 241.

Hillsborough "mad": quoted in Sosin, *Whitehall,* p. 184.

"that if Sir William did not suffer himself": William Trent, 10 June 1769, Lingelbach, "Trent Calls on BF," p. 48.

"I found our dispute much attended to": to Samuel Cooper, 30 September 1769, vol. 16, p. 211.

276 "means, under GOD": To the Philadelphia Merchants, 9 July 1769, vol. 16, p. 174–175.

"many injudicious people among us": William Allen to David and John Barclay, 7 November 1769, Walker, *Burd Papers,* p. 177.

repeal of *"all the laws"*: to William Strahan, 29 November 1769, vol. 16, p. 243.

"It is not *the sum* paid": ibid., pp. 244–245.

"inflame matters still more": ibid., p. 248.

277 "A lion's whelp": New Fables, 2 January 1770, vol. 17, pp. 3–4.

"a Partial redress will little avail": from Charles Thomson, 26 November 1769, vol. 16, p. 237.

"there is no doubt": to Charles Thomson, 18 March 1770, vol. 17, p. 113.

"the different colonies were a rope of sand": to Joseph Galloway, 21 March 1770, vol. 17, p. 117.

278 king "the sole legislator of his American subjects": to Samuel Cooper, 8 June 1770, vol. 17, p. 163.

"which, laying aside the *principle* of the tax": William Strahan to David Hall, 7 April 1770, quoted in Cochrane, *Strahan,* p. 188.

Strahan "grown a great courtier": quoted in Kammen, *Rope of Sand,* p. 210.

"Tho' we *differ"*: Strahan to Hall, 7 November 1770, "Strahan-Hall Letters," p. 357.

gravely asked "whether Philadelphia was in the East or West Indies": quoted in Kammen, *Rope of Sand,* p. 224.

"the next session will hardly pass over": to Samuel Cooper, 8 June 1770, vol. 17, p. 162.

"Thus the ice being now broke": William Strahan to David Hall, 24 August 1770, "Strahan-Hall Letters," p. 351.

26. THE CRAVEN STREET GAZETTE

280 "I think of late that my constitution rather mends": to Deborah Franklin, 21 December 1768–26 January 1769, vol. 15, pp. 292–293.

"As to myself": to Deborah Franklin, 10 June 1770, vol. 17, pp. 167–168.

281 "If your having the gout is of service to you": from Deborah Franklin, 16 August 1770, vol. 17, p. 205.

Dialogue with the Gout: 22 October 1780, Smyth, *Writings,* vol. 8, pp. 312–320.

283 "I should think you a fortune": to Mary Stevenson, 31 May 1770, vol. 17, pp. 152–153.

The Craven Street Gazette: vol. 17, pp. 220–226.

27. DIALOGUE WITH LORD HILLSBOROUGH

290 interview with Hillsborough: to Samuel Cooper, 5 February 1771, "Minutes of the Conference mentioned in the preceding letter," dated 16 January 1771, Smyth, *Writings,* vol. 5, pp. 300–304.

293 Epilogue: to Samuel Cooper, 5 February 1771, quoted in Van Doren, *BF,* p. 387.

28. "THE CLOUD SEEMS TO BE BLOWN OVER"

294 "One encouragement I have": to Samuel Cooper, 5 February 1771, Smyth, *Writings*, vol. 5, p. 299.

"At present the cloud that threatened": to James Bowdoin, 5 February 1771, ibid., vol. 5, p. 297.

"The sentiments of a majority": to Thomas Cushing, 5 February 1771, ibid., vol. 5, p. 293.

"very reserved": Strahan to William Franklin, 3 April 1771, *Papers*, vol. 18, p. 65.

"as it might be of prejudice": William Strahan to William Franklin, 3 April 1771, *ibid.*

"Dr. Franklin . . . is taking his measures": Edward Hughes to Joshua Sharpe, 28 April 1771, quoted in Currey, *Road to Revolution*, p. 277.

"I think one may clearly see": to the Committee of Correspondence in Massachusetts, 15 May 1771, Smyth, *Writings*, vol. 5, p. 317.

295 "the British nation . . . will become odious": ibid., p. 318.

"whether it will not be better gradually to wear off": to Thomas Cushing, 10 June 1771, ibid., pp. 323–324.

"a severe and tedious winter": to William Franklin, 20 April 1771, ibid., vol. 5, p. 313.

refused "to stir": William Strahan to William Franklin, 3 April 1771, quoted in Currey, *Road to Revolution*, p. 274.

trip through English Midlands: summarized in Sachse, *Colonial American in Britain*, p. 38 from Williams's journal, which is in the Yale Library.

296 "My journey has been of use": to Deborah Franklin, 5 June 1771, Smyth, *Writings*, vol. 5, p. 321.

"breathe with reluctance": to Jonathan Shipley, 24 June 1771, ibid., vol. 5, p. 329.

"You take notice of the failing of your eyesight": to John Bartram, 17 July 1771, ibid., vol. 5, p. 335.

"a very odd accident happened": to Samuel Franklin, 12 July 1771, ibid., vol. 5, pp. 333–334.

297 "It was an engaging tale": Conner, *Poor Richard's Politics*, pp. 10–11.

"These libraries have improved": *Auto.*, pp. 130–131.

"a factious, turbulent fellow": to William Franklin, 30 January 1772, Smyth, *Writings*, vol. 5, p. 378.

298 "He was extremely civil": ibid., p. 378.

"was determined": to William Franklin, ibid., vol. 5, p. 378.

"I concluded": to Thomas Cushing, 13 January 1772, ibid., vol. 5, p. 364.

"he understood there was in town": ibid., p. 367.

"disposed to be friends": ibid.

"They live in wretched hovels": ibid., p. 368.

299 "so I was obliged": to William Franklin, 30 January 1772, ibid., vol. 5, p. 379.

He paid "particular attention": to Thomas Cushing, 13 January 1772, ibid., vol. 5, pp. 365, 366.

"America ought not to be restrained": ibid., pp. 365–366.

"Storms and floods": to William Strahan, 27 October 1771, ibid., vol. 5, p. 344.

"My last expedition convinced me": to Sir Alexander Dick, 11 January 1772, ibid., vol. 5, p. 347.

"I have of late great debates": to William Franklin, 30 January 1772, ibid. vol. 5, pp. 381–382.

300   "I have not met with Lord Hillsborough": to Thomas Cushing, 13 April 1772, ibid., vol. 5, p. 392.
      "When I had been a little while returned to London": 19 August 1772, ibid., vol. 5, p. 413.
      "*any merit*": to John Foxcroft, 4 February 1772, ibid., vol. 5, p. 382.
      "equally active": ibid., p. 383.

301   Wharton has "acquired better connections": William Strahan to William Franklin, 3 April 1771, quoted in Currey, *Road to Revolution*, pp. 274–275.
      replied "distinctly to each . . . objection": quoted in ibid., p. 290.
      "The air of England": quoted in Conner, *Poor Richard's Politics*, p. 83.
      "*Pharisaical Britain!*": "The Somerset Case and the Slave Trade," *London Chronicle* 20 June 1772, in Crane, *BF's Letters to the Press*, p. 223.
      "It gave me great pleasure": from Deborah Franklin, 9 August 1759, vol. 8, p. 425.

302   chose him "one of the society": to Deborah Franklin, 27 June 1760, vol. 9, p. 174.
      "from what I then saw": to John Waring, 17 December 1763, vol. 10, p. 396.
      "All the wretches that dig coal for you": "Conversation on Slavery," *Public Advertiser*, 30 January 1770, in Crane, *BF's Letters to the Press*, p. 190.
      "fellow traveler on a dangerous and heavy road": from Benezet, 27 April 1772, quoted in Conner, *Poor Richard's Politics*, p. 83.
      "Can sweetening our tea": "The Somerset Case and the Slave Trade," *London Chronicle*, 20 June 1772, in Crane, *BF's Letters to the Press*, pp. 222–223.

303   "In Cumberland I ascended": to Deborah Franklin, 14 July 1772, Smyth, *Writings*, vol. 5, p. 409.
      "one of the most mischievous men": quoted in Van Doren, *BF*, p. 398.
      "as double and deceitful": to William Franklin, 19 August 1772, Smyth, *Writings*, vol. 5, p. 413.
      "His brother ministers disliked him": to William Franklin, 17 August 1772, ibid., vol. 5, p. 410.
      "Yes, there is Lord Dartmouth": to William Franklin, 19 August 1772, ibid., vol. 5, p. 414.
      "As to my situation here": ibid., p. 414.

304   "These are flattering circumstances": ibid., pp. 414–415.

29. "A MAN OF LETTERS"

305   "friendship in promoting compensation": from Thomas Hutchinson, 27 October 1765, vol. 12, p. 340.
      "opinion upon an application": from Thomas Hutchinson, 1 January 1766, vol. 13, p. 3.
      "the voice of the people": ibid., p. 3.
      "be much obliged": from Thomas Hutchinson, 29 July 1769, vol. 16, p. 182.
      "the Puritan *manqué*": Bailyn, *Hutchinson*, p. 26.

306   "upon modes and forms in religion": ibid., p. 22.
      to "strive to be more of a willow": ibid., p. 17.

307   "There must be an abridgement": Butterfield, *Adams Diary and Auto.*, vol. 2, p. 80n.
      "I thought it my duty": to William Franklin, 1 September 1773, Smyth, *Writings*, vol. 6, p. 117.
      "possibly, as distant objects, seen only through a mist": to Samuel Cooper, 7 July 1773, as quoted in Hutchinson, *Diary and Letters*, vol. 2, pp. 337–338n.

"simply and solely to clear the ministry": Bailyn, *Hutchinson*, p. 236.

"the most approachable and the most impenetrable of men": Albert J. Nock, *Jefferson* (1926), p. 33.

308   "I have in America": "Tract Relative to . . . Hutchinson's Letters," Smyth, *Writings*, vol. 6, p. 261.

"we want a governor": from Jonathan Williams, Sr., 27 August 1770, vol. 17, p. 213.

"Many of the principal people there": from William Franklin, 11 May 1769, vol. 16, p. 130.

"It was not easy before this to give credit to such surmises": Wedderburn, quoted in Fleming, *The Man Who Dared Lightning*, p. 249.

"several of the foreign ambassadors": to William Franklin, 19 August 1772, Smyth, *Writings*, vol. 5, p. 414.

"may bribe a villain": quoted in Fleming, *The Man Who Dared Lightning*, p. 248; Van Doren, *BF*, p. 471.

309   "Being of that country myself": to William Franklin, 1 September 1773, Smyth, *Writings*, vol. 6, p. 117.

"too much humanity—too much religion": quoted in Bailyn, *Hutchinson*, p. 326.

"all such measures": quoted in Kammen, *Rope of Sand*, p. 259.

"My Lord Dartmouth is a quiet man": quoted in Shy, *Road to Lexington*, p. 405.

"Our business has hitherto been as light as you could wish": ibid., p. 406.

310   "He received me very obligingly": to Thomas Cushing, 4 November 1772, Smyth, *Writings*, vol. 5, p. 448.

"The king would be exceedingly offended": to Thomas Cushing, 2 December 1772, ibid., p. 449.

"the best disposition": to Thomas Cushing, 5 January 1773, ibid., vol. 6, p. 2.

"The continued refusal of North America to take tea": to William Franklin, 14 February 1773, ibid., pp. 12–13.

311   "In confidence of this coming change": to Thomas Cushing, 5 January 1773, ibid., p. 4.

"I know of no line that can be drawn between the supreme authority of Parliament and the total independence of the colonies": quoted in Richard D. Brown, *Revolutionary Politics in Massachusetts* (1970), p. 88.

"What difficulties that gentleman has brought us all into": to Thomas Cushing, 6 May 1773, Smyth, *Writings*, vol. 6, p. 49.

312   "a great share of what his friends call *firmness*": to William Franklin, 14 July 1773, ibid., p. 98.

"His Majesty, as he will ever attend to the *humble* petitions": to Thomas Cushing, 7 July 1773, ibid., p. 74.

"From a long and thorough consideration": to William Franklin, 6 October 1773, ibid., p. 144.

313   "He often and indeed always appeared to me to have a personal animosity": Butterfield, *Adams Diary and Auto.*, vol. 4, p. 150.

"tea cheaper in America": to Thomas Cushing, 2 June 1773, Smyth, *Writings*, vol. 6, p. 57.

"He is truly a good man": to William Franklin, 14 July 1773, ibid., p. 98.

His lordship "seemed studiously to avoid speaking to me": ibid., p. 97.

"Perhaps it would be best": to Thomas Cushing, 7 July 1773, ibid., p. 77.

314   "I know not what letters of mine Governor H. could mean": to William Franklin, 6 October 1773, ibid., p. 144.

The people "having lately discovered": to Lord Dartmouth, 21 August 1773, ibid., p. 281n.

"the next time I shall have the honor": ibid.

315 *Rules by Which a Great Empire:* ibid., pp. 127–137.

316 "for the quantity and variety of the matter": to William Franklin, 6 October 1773, ibid., p. 145.

An Edict of the King of Prussia: ibid., pp. 118–124.

317 "to take care that the compositor": quoted in Crane, *BF's Letters to the Press,* p. 237, which also reproduces the original headline for the essay.

"Here! . . . here's news for ye!": to William Franklin, 6 October 1773, Smyth, *Writings,* vol. 6, p. 146.

"I much want to hear how that tea is received": to Joseph Galloway, 3 November 1773, ibid., pp. 152, 151.

318 a "seasoned old sinner": Van Doren, *BF,* p. 438.

Lord's Prayer revised: vol. 15, p. 301.

"so long and filled with so many repetitions": Preface to *An Abridgement of the Book of Common Prayer,* Smyth, *Writings,* vol. 6, pp. 165–171.

"Some were given away": ibid., vol. 9, p. 111.

319 scientific experiment: to William Brownrigg, 7 November 1773, ibid., pp. 153–165.

To "prevent further mischief": to William Franklin, 5 January 1774, ibid., p. 174.

320 "Finding that two gentlemen": ibid., p. 284n.

"I am now seriously preparing for my departure to America": to William Franklin, 5 January 1774, ibid., p. 174.

30. THE COCKPIT

321 "were not of the nature of *private* letters": to Printer of *Public Advertiser,* 25 December 1773, Smyth, *Writings,* vol. 6, p. 284n.

"My lords, . . . the late Mr. Whately": quoted in Fleming, *The Man Who Dared Lightning,* p. 247.

322 "very late in the afternoon": to Thomas Cushing, 15 February 1774, Smyth, *Writings,* vol. 6, p. 183.

"but without effect": ibid.

De Grey–BF exchange: ibid., pp. 184, 185.

"I did not expect that counsel would have been employed": this and rest of the dialogue quoted in Van Doren, *BF,* pp. 462–463.

"In that I shall take counsel": to Thomas Cushing, 15 February 1774, Smyth, *Writings,* vol. 6, pp. 185–186.

323 "unworthy the favors of the crown": BF memorandum, 14 July 1778, quoted in Currey, *Road to Revolution,* p. 335.

"I never considered the agreement": to Thomas Walpole, 12 January 1774, quoted in ibid., pp. 333–334.

"I am still to be considered as an Associate": BF memorandum, 14 July 1778, quoted in ibid., p. 335.

"I was called an incendiary": to Thomas Cushing, 15 February 1774, Smyth, *Writings,* vol. 6, pp. 186, 187.

324 he "was not and could not be obliged": ibid., p. 186.

"The counsel therefore thought": ibid., p. 188.

"act of violent injustice. . . . I am truly concerned": to Thomas Cushing, 2 February 1774, ibid., p. 179.

"All the courtiers were invited": to Thomas Cushing, 15 February 1774, ibid., pp. 188–189.

325 He stood "conspicuously erect": quoted in Fleming, *The Man Who Dared Lightning*, p. 246.

"invaluable gift of an accommodating conscience": Alan Valentine, *Lord North* (2 vols., 1967), vol. 1, p. 222, as quoted in *ibid.*, p. 240. For another sketch of Wedderburn, see Namier and Brooke, *History of Parliament*, vol. 3, pp. 618–620.

"I have no opinion of his heart": William Strahan to David Hall, 22 May 1769, Strahan, "Correspondence," p. 105.

"a cogent defense": Crane, *BF and a Rising People*, p. 146.

Wedderburn's speech: lengthy and judicious selections drawn from the two extent versions—one edited by Israel Mauduit in 1774, the other by Franklin's friend Benjamin Vaughan, published in 1779—are found in Fleming, *The Man Who Dared Lightning*, pp. 246–249, and in Van Doren, *BF*, pp. 468–473.

326 wandered "from the question": to Thomas Cushing, 15 February 1774, Smyth, *Writings*, vol. 6, p. 188.

327 Franklin stood "the whole time like a rock": quoted in Fleming, *The Man Who Dared Lightning*, p. 249.

His voice was "so feeble": to Thomas Cushing, 15 February 1774, Smyth, *Writings*, vol. 6, p. 190.

"I will make your master a LITTLE KING": *London Chronicle*, 8 May 1783, quoted in Aldridge, *BF*, p. 237.

"groundless, vexatious, and scandalous" allegations: quoted in Bailyn, *Hutchinson*, p. 256.

"found it necessary": to Thomas Cushing 15 February 1774, Smyth, *Writings*, vol. 6, p. 191.

left for a "month or two's ramble": Michael Collinson to Cadwallader Colden, 11 March 1774, quoted in Sosin, *Agents and Merchants*, p. 169.

"apprehensive that his papers would be seized": Williams, "More Light on BF's Religious Ideas," p. 811.

31. "LET ALL THE MALES THERE BE C–ST——ED"

328 "I only await the arrival of the April packet": to John Foxcroft, 18 February 1774, Smyth, *Writings*, vol. 6, p. 198.

"who represented the falsehoods in question": Edward Bancroft, quoted in Crane, *BF's Letters to the Press*, p. 254.

"held a cool, sullen silence": quoted in Van Doren, *BF*, p. 488.

"Be assured, my good friend": to Jan Ingenhousz, 18 March 1774, Smyth, *Writings*, vol. 6, p. 219.

"well settled in your farm": to William Franklin, 2 February 1774, ibid., p. 176.

"little or no corn in the crib": Thomas Wharton, 3 May 1774, quoted in Mariboe, *William Franklin*, p. 400.

"Let them take your place if they want it": to William Franklin, 18 February 1774, Smyth, *Writings*, vol. 6, p. 197.

329 "I do not find that I have lost a single friend": to Jan Ingenhouze, 18 March 1774, *ibid.*, p. 219.

"Where is Dr. Franklin, my lord?": Hutchinson, *Diary*, vol. 1, p. 163.

"I suppose we never had since we were a people so few friends": to Thomas Cushing, 21 March 1774, Smyth, *Writings*, vol. 6, p. 223.

330 "mobs of English sawyers can burn sawmills": ibid., p. 218.
"Let a company of sow gelders": 21 May 1774, in Crane, *BF's Letters to the Press*, pp. 263–264.

331 "little hope that they will not pass": to Thomas Cushing, 16 April 1774, Smyth, *Writings*, vol. 6, p. 229.
He "blamed us for destroying the tea": to Thomas Cushing, 1 June 1774, ibid., p. 232.
He "probably will be absent near a year": ibid., p. 232.
"I have been advised by our friends to stay": to Thomas Cushing, 3 September 1774, ibid., p. 238.
"My situation here is thought by many to be a little hazardous": to Joseph Galloway, 12 October 1774, ibid., p. 254.

332 "I am told by gentlemen": Hutchinson, *Diary*, vol. 1, p. 356.
"staring with his spectacles": ibid., vol. 1, p. 404.
"Pray, Mr. Hutchinson": ibid., vol. 1, p. 170.

333 "for the common welfare of the British empire": to Thomas Cushing, 6 October 1774, Smyth, *Writings*, vol. 6, p. 250.
"I am in perpetual anxiety": ibid., pp. 250–251.
"But you, who are a thorough courtier": to William Franklin, 7 September 1774, ibid., p. 241.
William's letter to Strahan: referred to in Mariboe, *William Franklin*, pp. 414–415, and in Hutchinson, *Diary*, vol. 1, p. 119.

334 "His Majesty may be assured": to Lord Dartmouth, 31 May 1774, quoted in Mariboe, *William Franklin*, p. 402.
"If there was any prospect": from William Franklin, 21 December 1774, quoted in ibid., p. 418.
"There are various opinions": John Pownall to William Knox, 31 August 1774, quoted in Currey, *Road to Revolution*, p. 367.
"The spirit which has appeared in all America": to [Cushing], 25 July 1774, in Crane, *BF's Letters to the Press*, pp. 265–267.

335 "We were flattered with hopes": memorandum of William Knox, quoted in ibid., p. 267n.
"if the non-consumption agreement should become general": to Thomas Cushing, 3 September 1774, Smyth, *Writings*, vol. 6, p. 239.
"I never had heard in any conversation": "An Account of Negotiations in London," ibid., p. 323.
"For all what you Americans say of your loyalty": "Journal of Josiah Quincy, Jun."; 14 December 1774, p. 448.

336 "to convince the candidates": to Thomas Cushing, 25 July 1774, in Crane, *BF's Letters to the Press*, p. 267.
"I have reason to think": to Thomas Cushing, 15 September 1774, Smyth, *Writings*, vol. 6, p. 245.
"bribing or purchasing to get in": to Thomas Cushing, 10 October 1774, ibid., p. 251.
"For aught he could see": Hutchinson, *Diary*, vol. 1, p. 293.
"The dye is now cast": quoted in Currey, *Road to Revolution*, p. 361.

32. "THIS OLD ROTTEN STATE"

337 "Whatever robs an old man of his sleep": quoted in Aldridge, *BF*, p. 247.
All quotations in the December 1774–March 1775 "log" unless other-

wise noted below come from BF's "An Account of Negotiations in London . . . ," Smyth, *Writings*, vol. 6, pp. 318–399.

339 *December 11–24:* Dartmouth said "he had presented the petition to his Majesty": to Charles Thomson, 5 February 1775, ibid., p. 304.

342 *January 17:* birthday party mentioned in "Journal of Josiah Quincy, Jun.," p. 456.
January 19: "We flattered ourselves": to Charles Thomson, 5 February 1775, Smyth, *Writings*, vol. 6, p. 304.

343 *February 4:* For discussion of ministry reception of the "Hints," see Bargar, *Dartmouth*, pp. 134–138.

344 *February 5–11:* on Deborah Franklin's death, from William Franklin, 21 December 1774, quoted in Mariboe, *William Franklin*, p. 417.
February 14: "both houses have addressed the king": to Samuel Tucker and others, 14 February 1775, Smyth, *Writings*, vol. 6, p. 308.

345 *February 20:* "Give me your purse": to Joseph Galloway, 25 February 1775, ibid., p. 314.
February 25: letters to Joseph Galloway and James Bowdoin, ibid., pp. 309–314.

346 *March 1:* visit to British Museum and conversation afterward recounted in "Journal of Josiah Quincy, Jun.," pp. 468–469.

348 *March 19:* "opening his mind without reserve": quoted in Wecter, "Burke," p. 318. Letter to Lee quoted in Currey, *Road to Revolution*, p. 385.
March 20: Priestley's recollections drawn from Van Doren, *BF,* p. 521.

33. ''YOU ARE NOW MY ENEMY, AND I AM YOURS''

349 "by ringing of bells": quoted in Hawke, *In the Midst*, p. 87.
"which is quite unexpected news": William Franklin to William Strahan, 7 May 1775, "Strahan-Franklin Letters," p. 454.
"all his furniture etc.": Thomas Hutchinson to Earl of Harwicke, 7 July 1775, quoted in Currey, *Road to Revolution*, p. 383.
"I don't understand": to William Franklin, 7 May, 1775, Smyth, *Writings*, vol. 6, pp. 399–400.
"I am concerned at your resolution": to Joseph Galloway, 8 May 1775, quoted in Newcombe, *BF and Galloway*, p. 281. The affectionate ending is quoted in Fleming, *The Man Who Dared Lightning*, p. 292.

350 Every "day alarms are spread": quoted in Mariboe, *William Franklin*, pp. 428, 429, 430.
"designed to set the colonies in a flame": Hutchinson, *Diary and Letters*, vol. 1 p. 237. All quotations in the Franklin-Galloway meetings come from this source, pp. 237–238.
"every mark of respect": quoted in Hawke, *In the Midst*, p. 87.

351 "When fifty or sixty men": John Adams, quoted in Hawke, *A Transaction*, p. 6.
"People seemed at a loss": Hutchinson, *Diary and Letters*, vol. 1, p. 237.
"strongly opposed to independence": Corner, *Autobiography of Benjamin Rush*, p. 188.

352 "to entertain a great suspicion": quoted in Hawke, *In the Midst*, p. 89.
"In the morning at six": to Joseph Priestley, 7 July 1775, Smyth, *Writings*, vol. 6, p. 409.
"dear, dear friend": to Margaret Stevenson, 17 July 1775, ibid., p. 411.
Galloway-Franklin talk: Hutchinson, *Diary and Letters*, vol. 1, pp. 237–238,

and Galloway, *Letters from Cicero to Catiline the Second,* quoted in Newcombe, *BF and Galloway,* p. 284n.

353   "Mr. Strahan": to William Strahan, 5 July 1775, *ibid.,* p. 407.

354   "The people of England have thought": John Adams to his wife, 23 July 1775, Butterfield, *Adams Family Correspondence,* vol. 1, p. 253.

355   "The suspicions against Dr. Franklin": quoted in Hawke, *In the Midst,* p. 89.
"He does not hesitate at our boldest measures": John Adams to his wife, 23 July 1775, Butterfield, *Adams Family Correspondence,* vol. 1, p. 253.
"proceeded to open robbery": Smyth, *Writings,* vol. 6, pp. 419–420n.

356   "under the fatigue of more business": to Margaret Stevenson, 17 July 1775, Smyth, *Writings,* vol. 6, p. 411.
"Mr. Franklin I find to be a daring": Seed, "A British Spy in Philadelphia," 11 September 1775, p. 20.
"generally allowed to be the author": ibid., 16 March 1776, p. 32.
"My eyes will now hardly serve": to Charles Lee, 11 February 1776, Smyth, *Writings,* vol. 6, p. 439.

357   "The inclosed paper": Thomas Jefferson to BF, 21 June, 1776, quoted in Hawke, *A Transaction,* p. 163.
"I have made it a rule": quoted in ibid., pp. 197–198.

358   "anecdotes about the Signing": quoted in Alexander Graydon, *Memoirs of His Own Time* (1846), p. 131n. Graydon attributes Franklin's remark to Richard Penn.

BIBLIOGRAPHY

Abbot, George Maurice. *A Short History of the Library Company of Philadelphia; Compiled from the Minutes, together with some personal reminiscences* (1913).

Abernathy, Thomas P. "The Origin of the Franklin-Lee Imbroglio," *North Carolina Historical Review*, vol. 15 (1938), pp. 41–52.

Aldridge, Alfred Owen. *Benjamin Franklin, Philosopher and Man* (1965).

––––––. "Benjamin Franklin and Jonathan Edwards on Lightning and Earthquakes," *Isis*, vol. 41 (1959), pp. 162–164.

––––––. "Benjamin Franklin and the *Pennsylvania Gazette*," American Philosophical Society *Proceedings*, vol. 106 (1962), pp. 77–81.

––––––. "Benjamin Franklin as Georgia Agent," *Georgia Review*, vol. 6 (1952), pp. 164–173.

––––––. "Franklin as Demographer," *Journal of Economic History*, vol. 9 (1949), pp. 25–44.

––––––. "Franklin's Deistical Indians," American Philosophical Society *Proceedings*, vol. 94 (1950), pp. 398–410.

––––––. "Franklin's 'Shaftesburyian' Dialogues not Franklin's," *American Literature*, vol. 21 (1949), pp. 151–159.

––––––. "A Religious Hoax by Benjamin Franklin," *ibid.*, vol. 36 (1964), pp. 204–209.

Asimov, Isaac. *Understanding Physics*, vol. 2, *Light, Magnetism, and Electricity* (1966).

Ayling, Stanley. *George the Third* (1972).

Bailyn, Bernard. *The Ordeal of Thomas Hutchinson* (1974).

Balch, Thomas, ed. *Letters and Papers Relating Chiefly to the Provincial History of Pennsylvania* (1855).

Barck, Dorothy C. *Letter Book of John Watts, Merchant and Councillor of New York, January 1, 1762–December 22, 1765*, New-York Historical Society *Collections*, vol. 61 (1928).

Bargar, B. D. *Lord Dartmouth and the American Revolution* (1965).

Becker, Carl. "Benjamin Franklin," *Dictionary of American Biography*, reprinted separately (1946).

Bedwell, C. E. A. "American Middle Templars," *American Historical Review*, vol. 25 (1920), pp. 680–689.

Bell, Whitfield J., Jr. "All Clear Sunshine, New Letters of Franklin and Mary Stevenson Hewson," American Philosophical Society *Proceedings*, vol. 100 (1956), pp. 521–536.

———. "Addenda to Watson's Annals of Philadelphia. Notes by Jacob Mordecai, 1836," *Pennsylvania Magazine of History and Biography*, vol. 98 (1974), pp. 131–170.

———. "Benjamin Franklin and the German Charity Schools," ibid., vol. 99 (1955), pp. 381–387.

Blake, John B. "The Inoculation Controversy in Boston: 1721–1722," *New England Quarterly*, vol. 25 (1952), pp. 489–506.

Bloore, Stephen, "Joseph Brientnall, First Secretary of the Library Company," *Pennsylvania Magazine of History and Biography*, vol. 59 (1935), pp. 42–56.

———. "Samuel Keimer. A Footnote to the Life of Franklin," ibid., vol. 54 (1930), pp. 255–287.

Boyd, Julian P., et al., eds. *The Jefferson Papers* (20 vols., to date, 1950–).

———. *The Susquehanna Company Papers.*

Brady, Frank, and Frederick A. Pottle, eds. *Boswell in Search of a Wife, 1766–1769* (1956).

Brett-Jones, Norman G. *The Life of Peter Collinson, F.R.S., F.S.A.* (1926).

Bridenbaugh, Carl. *Cities in the Wilderness. The First Century of Urban Life in America* (2nd ed., 1955).

———. *Rebels and Gentlemen. Philadelphia in the Age of Franklin* (1942). With Jessica Bridenbaugh.

Brigham, Clarence. "James Franklin and the Beginnings of Printing in Rhode Island," Massachusetts Historical Society *Proceedings*, vol. 65, pp. 537–544.

Brooke, John. *The Chatham Administration, 1766–1768* (1956).

———. *George III* (1972).

Bruce, W. C. *Benjamin Franklin Self-Revealed* (2 vols., 1917).

Brunhouse, Robert L. "The Effect of the Townshend Acts in Pennsylvania," *Pennsylvania Magazine of History and Biography*, vol. 54 (1930), pp. 355–373.

Burnett, Edmund C. *The Continental Congress* (1941).

———. *Letters of Members of the Continental Congress* (8 vols., 1921–1936).

Butler, Ruth L. *Doctor Franklin, Postmaster General* (1928).

Butterfield, Lyman H., ed. *Letters of Benjamin Rush* (2 vols., 1951).

———, et al., eds. *The Adams Papers. Adams Family Correspondence, 1761–1778* (2 vols., 1963).

———, et al., eds. *The Adams Papers. The Diary and Autobiography of John Adams* (4 vols., 1961).

Buxbaum, Melvin H. *Benjamin Franklin and the Zealous Presbyterians* (1975).

Carey, Lewis J. *Franklin's Economic Views* (1928).

Carlson, C. Lennart. "Samuel Keimer: A Study in the Transit of English Culture to Colonial Pennsylvania," *Pennsylvania Magazine of History and Biography*, vol. 61 (1937), pp. 357–386.

Chaffin, Robert J. "The Townshend Acts of 1767," *William and Mary Quarterly*, vol. 27 (1970), pp. 90–121.

Chastellux, Marquis de. *Travels in North America in the Years 1780, 1781, and 1782* (2 vols., 1963), revised translation by Howard C. Rice, Jr.

Christensen, Merton A. "Franklin on the Hemphill Trial: Deism Versus Presbyterian Orthodoxy," *William and Mary Quarterly*, vol. 10 (1953), pp. 422–440.

Cochrane, J. A. *Dr. Johnson's Printer: The Life of William Strahan* (1964).

Cohen, I. Bernard. *Benjamin Franklin: His Contribution to the American Tradition* (1953).

––––––. *Benjamin Franklin's Experiments: A New Edition of Franklin's Experiments and Observations on Electricity* (1941).

––––––. *Franklin and Newton: An Inquiry into Speculative Newtonian Science and Franklin's Work in Electricity as an Example Thereof* (1956).

Cohen, Norman S. "Philadelphia Election Riot of 1742," *Pennsylvania Magazine of History and Biography*, vol. 92 (1968), pp. 306–319.

Colbourn, H. Trevor. "A Pennsylvania Farmer at the Court of King George. John Dickinson's London Letters, 1754–1756," ibid., vol. 86 (1962), pp. 241–286, 417–453.

––––––. "John Dickinson, Historical Revolutionary," ibid., vol. 83 (1959), pp. 271–292.

Cone, Carl B. *Torchbearer of Freedom: The Influence of Richard Price on Eighteenth-Century Thought* (1952).

Conner, Paul W. *Poor Richard's Politics: Benjamin Franklin and His New American Order* (1965).

Corner, George W. *The Autobiography of Benjamin Rush: His "Travels through Life" Together with his Commonplace Book for 1789–1813* (1948).

Crane, Verner W. *Benjamin Franklin and a Rising People* (1954).

––––––. *Benjamin Franklin, Englishman and American* (1936).

––––––. "Benjamin Franklin on Slavery and American Liberties," *Pennsylvania Magazine of History and Biography*, vol. 62 (1936), pp. 1–11.

––––––. *Benjamin Franklin's Letters to the Press, 1758–1775* (1950).

––––––. "The Club of Honest Whigs: Friends of Science and Liberty," *William and Mary Quarterly*, vol. 23 (1966), pp. 210–233.

Cremin, Lawrence A. *American Education: The Colonial Experience, 1697–1783* (1970).

Cummings, Hubertis. *Richard Peters: Provincial Secretary and Cleric, 1704–1777* (1944).

Currey, Cecil B. *Road to Revolution. Benjamin Franklin in England, 1765–1775* (1968).

––––––. *Code Number 72: Benjamin Franklin, PATRIOT or SPY?* (1972).

Cutler, William Parker, and Julia Perkins Cutler. *Life, Journals and Correspondence of Rev. Manasseh Cutler* (2 vols., 1888).

DeArmond, Anna Janney. "Andrew Bradford," *Pennsylvania Magazine of History and Biography*, vol. 62 (1938), pp. 463–487.

––––––. *Andrew Bradford, Colonial Journalist* (1949).

Dictionary of National Biography (24 vols. thus far, 1917–).

Donoughue, Bernard. *British Politics and the American Revolution: the Path to War, 1773–1775* (1964).

Dorfman, Joseph. *The Economic Mind in American Civilization, 1606–1865* (2 vols., 1947).

Duane, Roller and H. D., *The Development of the Concept of Electrical Charge* (1954).

Duer, William A. *The Life of William Alexander, Earl of Stirling* (1847).

Duniway, Clyde A. *The Development of Freedom of the Press in Massachusetts* (1906).

Eames, Wilberforce. "The Antigua Press and Benjamin Mecom," American Antiquarian Society *Proceedings*, vol. 38 (1928), pp. 303–348.

Eddy, George S. "Account Book of Benjamin Franklin kept by him during his First Mission to England as Provincial Agent, 1757–1762," *Pennsylvania Magazine of History and Biography*, vol. 55 (1931), pp. 97–133.

————. *Account Books Kept by Benjamin Franklin 1728–1729, Journal 1730–1737* (1928).

————. "A Work Book of the Printing House of Benjamin Franklin and David Hall, 1759–1766," *Bulletin of the New York Public Library*, vol. 34 (1930), pp. 575–589.

Eiselen, Malcolm R. *Franklin's Political Theories* (1928).

Eliot, Thomas D. "The Relation Between Adam Smith and Benjamin Franklin Before 1776," *Political Science Quarterly*, vol. 49 (1924), pp. 67–96.

Ellis, Kenneth. *The Post Office in the Eighteenth Century* (1958)

Ernst, Joseph A. "The Currency Act Repeal Movement: A Study in Imperial Politics and Revolutionary Crisis, 1764–1767," *William and Mary Quarterly*, vol. 25 (1968), pp. 171–211.

Evans, William B. "John Adams' Opinion of Benjamin Franklin," *Pennsylvania Magazine of History and Biography*, vol. 92 (1968), pp. 220–238

Fennelly, Catherine. "William Franklin of New Jersey," ibid., vol. 6 (1949), pp. 361–382.

Ferguson, James E. "Currency Finance: An Intepretation of Colonial Monetary Practices," ibid., vol. 10 (1953), pp. 153–180.

Fetter, Frank A. "The Early History of Political Economy in the United States," *American Philosophical Society Proceedings*, vol. 87 (1943), pp. 51–60.

Fisher, Daniel. "Extracts from the Diary of . . . 1755," *Pennsylvania Magazine of History and Biography*, vol. 17 (1893), pp. 263–278.

Fleet, Elizabeth, ed., "Madison's 'Detached Memoranda,'" *William and Mary Quarterly*, vol. 3 (1946), pp. 534–568.

Fleming, Thomas. *The Man Who Dared Lightning. A New Look at Benjamin Franklin* (1971).

Flexner, James T. *Mohawk Baronet: Sir William Johnson of New York* (1959).

Ford, Paul L. *The Writings of John Dickinson* (1895).

Ford, Worthington, C. "Franklin's *New England Courant*, " *Massachusetts Historical Society Proceedings*, vol. 57 (1924), pp. 336–353.

Fox, R. D. *Dr. John Fothergill and His Friends* (1919).

Franklin, Phyllis. *Show Thyself a Man* (1969).

Gilbert, Felix. *The Beginnings of American Foreign Policy. To the Farewell Address* (1961).

Gillingham, Harold E. "Philadelphia's First Fire Defenses," *Pennsylvania Magazine of History and Biography*, vol. 56 (1932), pp. 355–377.

Gipson, Lawrence H. "The Great Debate in the Committee of the Whole House of Commons on the Stamp Act, 1766, as Reported by Nathaniel Ryder," ibid., vol. 86 (1962), pp. 10–41.

————. "Thomas Hutchinson and the Framing of the Albany Plan of Union, 1754," ibid., vol. 74 (1950), pp. 5–35.

Gleason, J. Philip. "A Scurrilous Colonial Election and Franklin's Reputation," *William and Mary Quarterly*, vol. 18 (1961), pp. 68–83.

Granger, Bruce I. *Benjamin Franklin: An American Man of Letters* (1964).

Gray, Austin K. *Benjamin Franklin's Library* (1937).

Greene, Jack P., and R. M. Jellison. "The Currency Act of 1764 in Imperial-Colonial Relations," *William and Mary Quarterly*, vol. 18 (1961), pp. 485–518.

Greig, J. Y. T. *The Letters of David Hume* (2 vols., 1932).

Hagedorn, Ralph K. *Benjamin Franklin and Chess in Early America* (1958).

Hall, A. R. *The Scientific Revolution. The Formation of Modern Scientific Attitudes* (1962).

Hanna, William S. *Benjamin Franklin and Pennsylvania Politics* (1964).

Hare, Robert R. "Electro Vitrifico in Annapolis," *Maryland Historical Magazine*, vol. 58 (1963), pp. 62–66.

Hart, Charles H. "Letters from William Franklin to William Strahan," *Pennsylvania Magazine of History and Biography*, vol. 35 (1911), pp. 415–462.

Hawke, David. *In the Midst of a Revolution* (1961).

———. *A Transaction of Free Men* (1964).

Heathcote, Niels H. deV. "Franklin's Introduction to Electricity," *Isis*, vol. 46 (1955), pp. 29–35.

Henretta, James A. "Economic Development and the Social Structure in Colonial Boston," *William and Mary Quarterly*, vol. 22 (1965), pp. 75–92.

———. *Salutary Neglect* (1972).

Hindle, Brooke. *The Pursuit of Science in Revolutionary America, 1735–1789* (1956).

Hines, Norman E. "Benjamin Franklin on Population: A Re-examination," *Economic History*, vol. 3 (1934–1937), pp. 388–398.

Hoffman, Ross, J. S. *The Marquis: A Study of Lord Rockingham* (1973).

Horner, George F. "Franklin's *Dogood Papers* Re-examined," *Studies in Philology*, vol. 37 (1940), pp. 501–523.

Hutchinson, Peter O., ed. *Diary and Letters of Thomas Hutchinson* (2 vols., 1884).

Hutson, James H. "Benjamin Franklin and the Parliamentary Grant of 1758," *William and Mary Quarterly*, vol. 23 (1966), pp. 575–595.

———. "Benjamin Franklin and Pennsylvania Politics, 1751–1755: A Reappraisal," *Pennsylvania Magazine of History and Biography*, vol. 93 (1969), pp. 303–371.

———. "Benjamin Franklin and William Smith. More Light on an Old Philadelphia Quarrel," ibid., vol. 93 (1969), pp. 109–113.

———. "An Investigation of the Inarticulate Philadelphia's White Oaks," *William and Mary Quarterly*, vol. 28 (1971), pp. 3–25.

———. *Pennsylvania Politics 1746–1770. The Movement for Royal Government and Its Consequences* (1972).

Jacobson, David L. *John Dickinson and the Revolution in Pennsylvania 1764–1776* (1965).

James, Mrs. Thomas Potts. *Memorial of Thomas Potts, Junior* (1874).

Jeffrey, Francis. review of Franklin's *Works*, *Edinburgh Review*, vol. 8 (1806), pp. 328–341.

Jenkins, Howard M. "Fragments of a Journal Kept by Samuel Foulke, of Bucks County, While a Member of the Colonial Assembly of Pennsylvania, 1762–3–4," *Pennsylvania Magazine of History and Biography*, vol. 5 (1881), pp. 60–73.

Jensen, Merrill. *The Founding of a Nation. A History of the American Revolution 1763–1776* (1968).

Johnson, Victor L. "Fair Traders and Smugglers in Philadelphia 1754–1763," *Pennsylvania Magazine of History and Biography*, vol. 83 (1959), pp. 125–149.

Jordan, John W. "Franklin as a Genealogist," ibid., vol. 23 (1899), pp. 1–23.

Kammen, Michael G. *A Rope of Sand: The Colonial Agents, British Politics and the American Revolution* (1968).

Kaplan, Lawrence S. *Colonies into Nation: American Diplomacy, 1763–1801* (1972).

Keith, Charles P. "Sir William Keith," *Pennsylvania Magazine of History and Biography*, vol. 12 (1888), pp. 1–33.

Kenny, Robert W. "James Ralph: An Eighteenth-Century Philadelphian in Grub Street," ibid., vol. 64 (1940), pp. 218–242.

Ketcham, Ralph L. *Benjamin Franklin* (1965).

———. "Benjamin Franklin and William Smith, New Light on an Old Philadelphia Quarrel," *Pennsylvania Magazine of History and Biography*, vol. 88 (1964), pp. 142–163.

———. "Conscience, War, and Politics in Pennsylvania, 1755–1757," *William and Mary Quarterly*, vol. 20 (1963), pp. 416–439.

Kimball, David A., and Miriam Quinn. "William Allen–Benjamin Chew Correspondence, 1763–1764," *Pennsylvania Magazine of History and Biography*, vol. 90 (1966), pp. 202–226.

Kistler, Ruth M. "William Allen," Lehigh County Historical Society *Proceedings*, vol. 24 (1962), pp. 7–58.

Kite, Benjamin. "Recollections of Philadelphia Near Seventy Years Ago," *Pennsylvania Magazine of History and Biography*, vol. 19 (1895), pp. 264–266.

Knollenberg, Bernard. *Origin of the American Revolution 1759–1766* (1960).

Konkle, Burton. *Benjamin Chew* (1932).

———. *The Life of Andrew Hamilton, 1676–1741* (1941).

Korty, Margaret Barton. "Benjamin Franklin and Eighteenth-Century American Libraries," American Philosophical Society *Transactions*, vol. 55, part 9 (1965), pp. 3–82.

Labaree, Leonard W., et al., eds. *The Papers of Benjamin Franklin* (14 vols., 1959–1970), additional volumes continuing under the editorship of William B. Willcox.

———. *The Autobiography of Benjamin Franklin* (1964).

Langford, Paul. *The First Rockingham Ministry, 1765–1766* (1973).

Lawrence, D. H. "Benjamin Franklin," in *Studies in Classic American Literature* (1953 reprint), pp. 19–31.

Lemay, J. A. Leo. *Ebenezer Kinnersley* (1964).

———. "Franklin's 'Dr. Spence': the Reverend Archibald Spencer (c. 1698–1760), M.D.," *Maryland Historical Magazine*, vol. 59 (1964), pp. 199–216.

———. "Franklin's Suppressed 'Busy-Body,' " *American Literature*, vol. 38 (1965), pp. 307–311.

Leonard, Sister Joan de Lourdes, C.S.J. "Elections in Colonial Pennsylvania," *William and Mary Quarterly*, vol. 11 (1954), pp. 385–401.

Lester, Richard A. "Currency Issues to Overcome Depressions in Pennsylvania, 1723 and 1729," *Journal of Political Economy*, vol. 46 (1938), pp. 324–375.

Levin, David. "The Autobiography of Benjamin Franklin: The Puritan Experimenter in Life and Art," *Yale Review*, vol. 53 (1963), pp. 258–275.

Levy, Leonard W. *Freedom of Speech and Press in Early American History: Legacy of Suppression* (1963).

Lingelbach, William E. "Franklin's *American Instructor*. Early Americanism in the Art of Writing," American Philosophical Society *Proceedings*, vol. 96 (1952), pp. 367–387.

———. "William Trent Calls on Franklin," *Pennsylvania Magazine of History and Biography*, vol. 74 (1950), pp. 43–50.

Logan, Deborah Norris. *Memoirs of Dr. George Logan* (1899).

Lopez, Claude-Anne. *Mon Cher Papa. Franklin and the Ladies of Paris* (1966).

Lucas, F. L. "Benjamin Franklin," in *The Art of Living* (1959).
Lydon, James G. "Philadelphia's Commercial Expansion, 1720–1739," *Pennsylvania Magazine of History and Biography*, vol. 91 (1967), pp. 401–418.
Maclay, William. *Journal . . . 1789–1791* (1927).
McAnear, Beverly, ed. "Personal Accounts of the Albany Congress," *Mississippi Valley Historical Review*, vol. 39 (1952–53), pp. 727–746.
McCardell, Lee. *Ill-Starred General. Braddock of the Coldstream Guards* (1958).
MacLaurin, Margaret Lois. *Franklin's Vocabulary* (1928).
McNear, Beverly. "An American in London, 1735–1756," *Pennsylvania Magazine of History and Biography*, vol. 64 (1940), pp. 164–217.
Mariboe, William Herbert. "The Life of William Franklin 1730(1)–1813, 'Pro Rege et Patria,' " unpublished dissertation, University of Pennsylvania (1962).
Meyer, Gladys. *Free Trade in Ideas, Aspects of American Liberalism Illustrated in Franklin's Philadelphia* (1954).
Miller, John C. *Origins of the American Revolution* (1943).
Miller, C. William. *Benjamin Franklin's Philadelphia Printing 1728–1766. A Descriptive Bibliography* (1974).
Miller, Perry. *The New England Mind: From Colony to Province* (1953).
_____. *The American Puritans: Their Prose and Poetry* (1956).
Morgan, Edmund S., and Helen M. Morgan. *The Stamp Act Crisis: Prologue to Revolution* (rev. ed., 1962).
Morgan, William. *Memoirs of the Life of the Rev. Richard Price* (1815).
Morris, Richard B. *The Peacemakers* (1965).
_____. *Seven Who Shaped Our Destiny. The Founding Fathers as Revolutionaries* (1973).
Namier, Sir Lewis. *England in the Age of the American Revolution* (1961).
Namier, Sir Lewis, and John Brooke. *Charles Townshend* (1964).
_____. *The History of Parliament: The House of Commons, 1754–1790* (3 vols., 1964).
Nash, Gary B. *Quakers and Politics. Pennsylvania 1681–1726* (1968).
_____. "Slaves and Slaveowners in Colonial Philadelphia," *William and Mary Quarterly*, vol. 30 (1973), pp. 223–256.
Nash, George H., III. "From Radicalism to Revolution . . . Josiah Quincy, Jr.," *American Antiquarian Society Proceedings*, vol. 79 (1969), pp. 253–290.
Newcomb, Benjamin H. *Franklin and Galloway. A Political Partnership* (1972).
Nolan, J. Bennett. *Benjamin Franklin in Scotland and Ireland: 1759 and 1771* (1938).
_____. *General Benjamin Franklin: The Military Career of a Philosopher* (1936)
Norris, John M. *Shelburne and Reform* (1963).
Olson, Alison G. "The British Government and Colonial Union, 1754," *William and Mary Quarterly*, vol. 17 (1960), pp. 28–34.
Osgood, Herbert L. *American Colonies in the Eighteenth Century* (4 vols., 1958 printing).
Oswald, John Clyde. *Benjamin Franklin, Printer* (1917).
Pargellis, Stanley M. *Lord Loudoun in North America* (1933).
Parrington, Vernon L. *Main Currents in American Thought*, vol. 1, *The Colonial Mind* (1930).
Parton, James. *Life and Times of Benjamin Franklin* (2 vols., 1864).
Pepper, William. *The Medical Side of Benjamin Franklin* (1911).
Phillipps, Hugh. *Mid-Georgian London* (1964).
Pound, Arthur. *The Penns of Pennsylvania and England* (1932).

Quincy, Josiah, Jr. "Journal of . . . during his Voyage and Residence in England from September 28th to March 3d, 1775," *Massachusetts Historical Society Proceedings*, vol. 50 (1916–1917), pp. 433–471.

———. *Memoirs of . . .* (1850).

Quinlan, Maurice. "Dr. Franklin Meets Dr. Johnson," *Pennsylvania Magazine of History and Biography*, vol. 73 (1949), pp. 34–44.

Read, Conyers. "The English Elements in Benjamin Franklin," ibid., vol. 64 (1940), pp. 314–330.

Read, William R. *Life and Correspondence of Joseph Reed* (2 vols., 1847).

Riddel, W. R. "Benjamin Franklin and Colonial Money," *Pennsylvania Magazine of History and Biography*, vol. 54 (1930), pp. 52–64.

Ritcheson, Charles R. *British Politics and the American Revolution* (1954).

Roach, Hannah Benner. "Benjamin Franklin Slept Here," *Pennsylvania Magazine of History and Biography*, vol. 84 (1960), pp. 127–174.

Roller, Duane, and Roller Duane H.D. *The Development of the Concept of Electric Charge* (1954). Number 8 in Harvard Case Histories in Experimental Sciences.

Root, Winifred T. *The Relations of Pennsylvania with the British Government, 1696–1765* (1922).

Rossiter, Clinton. *Six Characters in Search of a Republic* (1964).

Rudé, George. *Hanoverian London, 1714–1808* (1971).

———. *Wilkes and Liberty. A Social Study of 1763 to 1774* (1962).

Rush, Benjamin. "Extracts from the Papers of," *Pennsylvania Magazine of History and Biography*, vol. 29 (1905), pp. 15–30.

Sachse, Julius F. *Benjamin Franklin as a Free Mason* (1906).

Sachse, William L. *The Colonial American in Britain* (1956).

Sanford, Charles L. "An American Pilgrim's Progress," *American Quarterly*, vol. 6 (1954), pp. 297–310.

Sayre, Robert F. *The Examined Self* (1964).

———. "The Worldly Franklin and the Provincial Critics," *Texas Studies in Literature and Language*, vol. 4 (1963), pp. 512–524.

Scholfield, Robert E. *A Scientific Autobiography of Joseph Priestley (1733–1804)*, (1966).

Schutz, John A. *Thomas Pownall, British Defender of American Liberty* (1951).

———. *William Shirley* (1961).

Seed, Geoffrey. "A British Spy in Philadelphia, 1775–1777," *Pennsylvania Magazine of History and Biography*, vol. 85 (1961), pp. 3–37.

Sellers, Charles Coleman. *Benjamin Franklin in Portraiture* (1962).

———. *Charles Willson Peale* (rev. ed., 1969).

Sharpless, Isaac. *Political Leaders of Provincial Pennsylvania* (1919).

Shepherd, William R. *History of Proprietary Government in Pennsylvania* (1896).

Shy, John. *Toward Lexington. The Role of the British Army in the Coming of the American Revolution* (1965).

Smith, Horace Wemyss. *Life and Correspondence of the Rev. William Smith* (2 vols., 1880).

Smith, William. "The Colonial Post-Office," *American Historical Review*, vol. 21 (1916), pp. 258–275.

Smyth, Albert H. *The Writings of Benjamin Franklin* (10 vols., 1905–1907).

Sosin, Jack M. *Agents and Merchants. British Colonial Policy and the Origins of the American Revolution* (1965).

————. "Imperial Regulation of Colonial Paper Money," *Pennsylvania Magazine of History and Biography*, vol. 88 (1964), pp. 174–198.

————. *Whitehall and the Wilderness. The Middle West in British Colonial Policy, 1760–1775* (1961).

Sparks, Jared. *The Works of Benjamin Franklin* (10 vols., 1856).

Stearns, Raymond Phineas. *Science in the British Colonies of America* (1970).

Stourzh, Gerald. *Benjamin Franklin and American Foreign Policy* (1954).

Strahan, William. "Correspondence between . . . and David Hall, 1763–1777," *Pennsylvania Magazine of History and Biography*, vol. 10 (1886), pp. 86–99, 217–232, 322–333, 461–473; vol. 11 (1887), pp. 98–111, 223–234, 346–357, 482–490; vol. 12 (1888), pp. 116–122, 240–251.

Tatum, Edward H., ed. *The American Journal of Ambrose Serle, Secretary to Lord Howe, 1776–1778* (1940).

Thayer, Theodore. *Israel Pemberton: King of the Quakers* (1943).

————. *Pennsylvania Politics and the Growth of Democracy: 1740–1776* (1953).

Thomas, Isaiah. *The History of Printing in America* (1970 ed., edited by Marcus A. McCorison from the second edition).

Tolles, Frederick B. *James Logan and the Culture of Provincial America* (1957).

————. *Meeting House and Counting House. The Quaker Merchants of Colonial Philadelphia 1682–1783* (1948).

Van Doren, Carl. *Benjamin Franklin* (1938).

————, ed. Benjamin Franklin's Autobiographical Writings (1945).

————. *Jane Mecom, Franklin's Favorite Sister* (1950).

Wainwright, Nicholas B. *George Croghan, Wilderness Diplomat* (1959).

————. "Governor William Denny in Pennsylvania," *Pennsylvania Magazine of History and Biography*, vol. 81 (1957), pp. 170–198.

————. "Nicholas Scull's 'Junto' Verses," ibid., vol. 73 (1949), pp. 82–84.

Walker, Lewis B., ed. *The Burd Papers: Extracts from Chief Justice William Allen's Letterbook* (1897).

Wallace, Anthony E. C. *King of the Delawares: Teedyuscung 1700–1763* (1949).

Wallace, Paul A. W. *Conrad Weiser, Friend to Colonist and Mohawk, 1696–1760* (1945).

Warner, Sam Bass. *The Private City of Philadelphia in Three Periods of Its Growth* (1968).

Warren, Charles. "A Young American's Adventures in England and France during the Revolutionary War," Massachusetts Historical Society *Proceedings*, vol. 65 (1932–1936), pp. 234–267.

Weaver, Glenn. "Benjamin Franklin and the Pennsylvania Germans," *William and Mary Quarterly*, vol. 14 (1957), pp. 536–559.

Wecter, Dixon. "Burke, Franklin and Samuel Petrie," *Huntington Library Quarterly*, vol. 3 (1940), pp. 315–338.

Wendel, Thomas. "Keith–Lloyd Alliance: Factional and Coalition Politics in Colonial Pennsylvania," *Pennsylvania Magazine of History and Biography*, vol. 92 (1968), pp. 289–304.

Wetzel, William A. *Benjamin Franklin as an Economist* (1895).

Wharton, Anne H. *Social Life in the Early Republic* (1902).

Wickwire, Franklin B. *British Subministers and Colonial America, 1763–1783* (1966).

————. "John Pownall and British Colonial Policy," *William and Mary Quarterly*, vol. 20 (1963) pp. 543–554.

Williams, David. "More Light on Franklin's Religious Ideas," *American Historical Review,* vol. 43 (1938), pp. 803–813.

Willcox, William B., et al., eds. *The Papers of Benjamin Franklin* (vols. 15– , 1972–).

Woody, Thomas. *Educational Views of Benjamin Franklin* (1931).

Wroth, Lawrence C. *The Colonial Printer* (1938).

Zimmerman, John J. "Benjamin Franklin and the *Pennsylvania Chronicle,*" *Pennsylvania Magazine of History and Biography,* vol. 81 (1957), pp. 351–364.

_____. "Benjamin Franklin and the Quaker Party, 1755–1756," *William and Mary Quarterly,* vol. 17 (1960), pp. 291–313.

_____. "Governor Denny and the Quartering Act of 1756," *Pennsylvania Magazine of History and Biography,* vol. 91 (1967), pp. 266–281.

INDEX